CULTURE

DATE DUE

CULTURE
SOCIOLOGICAL PERSPECTIVES

JOHN R. HALL
University of California at Davis

MARY JO NEITZ
University of Missouri at Columbia

PRENTICE HALL
Englewood Cliffs, New Jersey 07632

Library of Congress Cataloging-in-Publication Data

Hall, John R.
  Culture : Sociological perspectives / John R. Hall and Mary Jo
Neitz.
       p.   cm.
  Includes bibliographical references and index.
  ISBN 0-13-816471-1
  1. Culture. I. Neitz, Mary Jo, (date). II. Title.
HM101.H223 1993
306--dc20   92-26352
                                                             CIP

Production Editor: KERRY REARDON
Acquisitions Editor: NANCY ROBERTS
Cover: Painter in the Rainforest by ROY DE FOREST
Cover Designer: BRUCE KENSELAAR
Prepress Buyer: KELLY BEHR
Manufacturing Buyer: MARY ANN GLORIANDE
Photo Research: FRAN ANTMAN
Page Layout: JOH LISA
Editorial Assistant: PATRICIA NATURALE

© 1993 by Prentice-Hall, Inc.
A Simon & Schuster Company
Englewood Cliffs, New Jersey 07632

Printed in the United States of America

10 9 8 7 6 5 4 3 2 1

ISBN 0-13-816471-1

PRENTICE-HALL INTERNATIONAL (UK) LIMITED, *London*
PRENTICE-HALL OF AUSTRALIA PTY. LIMITED, *Sydney*
PRENTICE-HALL CANADA INC., *Toronto*
PRENTICE-HALL HISPANOAMERICANA, S.A., *Mexico*
PRENTICE-HALL OF INDIA PRIVATE LIMITED, *New Delhi*
PRENTICE-HALL OF JAPAN, INC., *Tokyo*
SIMON & SCHUSTER ASIA PTE. LTD., *Singapore*
EDITORA PRENTICE-HALL DO BRASIL, LTDA., *Rio de Janeiro*

CONTENTS

PART II: SOURCES OF THE CONTEMPORARY CULTURAL FORMATION

PART III: STRATIFICATION, POWER, AND CULTURAL PRODUCTION

APPENDIX

PREFACE

We believe that understanding culture—so basic to life in complex societies—depends upon developing a sociological imagination. We hope to foster such imagination by way of illuminating sociological perspectives for readers interested in cultural studies. The book may find use as a core text for undergraduate courses concerned with the sociology of culture. It may also prove relevant to undergraduate courses in particular domains of cultural studies—for example, art history, mass communication, literary criticism, popular culture, and American studies. Not only people directly concerned with culture, but also those interested in journalism, market research, clothing and textiles, hotel management, and diverse other fields stand to gain from a sociological basis for understanding their own professional worlds and their personal biographies. Finally, the book may serve as a "window" to the field for graduate students in various fields where the sociological analysis of culture is relevant.

Several features of the book deserve comment. First, we have sought to provide readers with an understanding of the basic dynamics of culture and the major contemporary controversies about culture, without claiming to offer an exhaustive or comprehensive review of all theories in relation to all forms of culture. To enhance the possibilities of liberal education, we draw on diverse topics to illustrate the sociological issues at stake. We thus hope to help readers to see the things they are most familiar with from an "outsider's" perspective and to see the "backstage" organization of culture that they previously experienced only from the outside. If this book succeeds in our terms, it will give readers tools for considering specific topics that have not been treated in the book—on the basis of approaches and issues that have been included.

Second, the book is intended to offer pathways to further study and research in the uses of sociology for cultural studies. We have included extensive citations in the text, as well as an appendix with a bibliographic essay for each chapter, which is intended to guide readers to further discussions of issues considered in the chapter. Undergraduates should be able to use the bibliographic features as a basis for starting work on research papers, while it is our hope that we have framed issues in ways that will provoke graduate students to further reading, theoretical analysis, and empirical research. To these ends, we also have included in the appendix a brief essay on methods of cultural analysis.

Third, this book is relatively short: we have sought to be concise. This approach allows for teachers to use the book as a core text in conjunction with additional readings of their choosing. There is a multitude of fascinating books and articles about diverse aspects of culture. To treat this literature within a framework of sociological discourse in a typical "comprehensive" text would crowd out the use of other materials in a course, doing a disservice to the vitality of cultural studies. It is our hope instead to contribute to that vitality by offering one vision of how the discipline of sociology can inform the understanding of culture. Too often, textbooks are written as overbearing compilations of received knowledge. The results rarely are interesting to read. Worse, they reduce the experience of education to yet another exercise in memorization. At a time of rapid cultural and intellectual change, it is our intention instead to encourage readers to recognize the controversies about culture and think critically about them in a way that will enhance the current dynamism of cultural studies.

John R. Hall

Mary Jo Neitz

ACKNOWLEDGMENTS

In writing this book over the past few years we have benefited enormously from the encouragement of our colleagues, students, and editors. It was Wayne Spohr of Prentice Hall who initially encouraged us to take time from other projects and write a comprehensive introduction to the sociology of culture. Harriett Prentiss offered early editorial guidance and support. Special thanks go to our editor at Prentice Hall, Nancy Roberts, and her editorial assistant, Pat Naturale, for maintaining that delicate editorial balance—keeping a discrete distance, but being there when we needed editorial advice and answers to myriad questions. Along the way, we have benefited enormously from our colleagues and students interested in culture. Indeed, a book like this simply would not be possible without the diverse research efforts of our colleagues and their support for our own efforts. We are particularly grateful to Howard S. Becker, Muriel Cantor, Wendy Griswold, Richard Peterson, and the anonymous reviewers who offered useful guidance based on the Prentice Hall draft manuscript. In addition, we wish to thank Susan Porter Benson, who advised us on chapter 5, Peter Mueser for his comments on chapter 8, and R. Stephen Warner for providing a very thoughtful reading of chapter 2. Judy Elam provided secretarial support. Finally, and most importantly, students, both undergraduate and graduate, at the University of Missouri–Columbia and the University of California–Davis have brought focus to the book and acted as a first audience by offering useful critiques of the manuscript as it went through various drafts. Particular thanks go to Rebecca Anne Allahyari, Marshall Anthony Battani, Molly Cate, Pamela J. Forman, David R. Hall, Lisa Hoffman, Rosemary Powers, Ksenija H. Vidmar, and Tony Waters for their comments on chapters 1, 4, 6, 7, 9 and 11, and to the culture reading group at the University of Missouri, where John Daniel, Jane Downing, Sharlene Knoerschild, Sharon Stevens, and Karen Vickers read and offered comments on the manuscript.

The authors gratefully acknowledge the permission of The University of Chicago Press for including in chapter 6 a revised version of sections from the essay by John R. Hall, "The Capital(s) of Culture," which first appeared in Michèle Lamont and Marcel Fournier, eds., *Cultivating Differences: Symbolic Boundaries and the Making of Inequality*. © 1992 by The University of Chicago. All rights reserved.

1

SOCIOLOGY AND CULTURE

At the end of the twentieth century, culture once again has become a central focus of sociological theorizing. This return to culture in sociology occurs at a time when culture is an increasingly important concept for all the disciplines of the social sciences and the humanities. For anthropologists, historians, literary critics, and philosophers, as well as for a wide range of sociologists, culture has come to be something of a missing link. Increasingly, "cultural studies" are seen as ways of linking our understandings of history, texts, and social life.

Yet how to understand culture? Is it centered on religion, art, literature, music? Or does it include TV and soccer? Our own view is that we must cast an even wider net. The broadest question of how society is organized in general requires cultural analysis, and though this book could not possibly treat culture in all its manifestations, we need an approach that is open to encompassing all kinds of culture, including, for example, political culture and—a topic that compels the attention of corporations—organizational culture. A broad approach is necessary because, for example, businesses have their own distinctive cultures of the office, the shop, and the enterprise (Harper 1987; Biggart 1989; Denison 1990; Meyer and Scott 1992). And the connection between business and culture now goes much deeper. There has been a decline in the industrial sector of manufacturing production and a corresponding increase in service-sector employment—in restaurants, the travel industry, marketing, the media, political opinion polling, finance, education and research, social services, counseling therapies, and a long list of other occupations. We have fewer factory workers and a great many more "cultural workers"—people employed in constructing experiences for other people. In addition, increased leisure for some people and the general and increasing reliance on purchasing to satisfy needs and wants have resulted in an increased "consumption" of culture. Culture has become an important product of economic activity and an important source of jobs.

If we must recognize the cultural aspects of politics and business, the politics and business of culture also seem important. In a famous book, *The Sociological Imagination,* C. Wright Mills once remarked about overarching cultural symbols: "Their social relevance lies in their use to justify or to oppose the arrangement of power and the positions within this arrangement of the powerful" (1959, p. 37). Events in the United States in the years after Mills wrote seem to have confirmed his views about the relationship between culture and power. In the 1960s the idea of a value consensus fell victim to assassinations, ghetto riots, protests against the Vietnam War, and the coming of age of the first wave of the post-World War II baby boom generation in a youth culture of "sex, drugs, and rock'n'roll." The Watergate scandal and President Richard Nixon's resignation in disgrace sorely tested the civic culture of democracy. The left-liberal countercultural social movements that were spawned in the antiwar years—feminism, ecology, and peace—became institutionalized parts of the American political scene, and conservative groups borrowed their tactics and strategies. Religious movements outside the previous mainstream—both fundamentalist and "New Age"—seem to have become a permanent fixture of cultural diversity. In the late 1970s, President Jimmy Carter worried about a cultural "malaise" and some observers described a predominant culture peopled with self-centered, "narcissistic" young urban professionals, or "yuppies." By the 1980s, President Ronald Reagan was able to sustain a popularity based on the reaffirmation of American values, yet critics noted that his accomplishment succeeded in part on the basis of skillful media consultants' construction of a public image. By the 1990s, the U.S. was undergoing a series of social conflicts about the control of public cultural expression—from federal funding for the National Endowment for the Arts to the question of satanic influence in textbooks and the issue of obscenity in the rap music of "2 Live Crew" (cf. Hunter 1991)—and economic recession, ethnic conflicts, and environmental degradation were leading some people to advocate new cultural frameworks and less consumption-based lifestyles. This list of recent episodes of cultural politics is nothing more than a sketch, but it reveals a diversity and incongruity of developments. Indeed, terms like incongruity, juxtaposition, collage—these are words that social critics bring to mind when they describe the contemporary cultural scene as "postmodern" (Gitlin 1988; Jameson 1991).

We will consider in chapter 11 whether there has been a cultural shift that can be called postmodern, somehow different from the relentless advance of "modern" culture described in chapters 4 and 5. But one thing is clear—a self-described postmodern movement has unleashed a torrent of new ways of studying culture. No longer is literature studied independently of the social circumstances that might give rise to it. No longer is "science" presumed to be free from storytelling, or narrative. No longer can sociologists and anthropologists assume a monopoly on social theories of culture. Other areas of study—American Studies, Art History, and Literature, for example—are also being infused with new methods of investigation and new questions. In some quarters, "cultural studies" is regarded as a new field that stands above the old and outmoded disciplinary boundaries (Johnson 1986/87; Grossberg, Nelson, and Treichler 1992).

Why then concern ourselves with the *sociology* of culture? The reason is simple. Precisely at the time when substantive fields of cultural studies—from popular culture and mass communications to music history, literary criticism, and cultural history—are undergoing rapid change, it is useful to take stock of how sociological thinking can contribute to the analysis of culture. To make a strong claim, culture is always a social phenomenon, subject to analysis in sociological terms. Therefore, literary critics, for example, will need to do more than simply add a sociological gloss to their work. When they ask questions outside the conventional boundaries of literary criticism, about the origin of the novel or the changing organizational conditions of theatrical performance, they will do well to consider how sociologists are thinking about these issues. Hopefully, they will at least learn not to repeat already discredited approaches. Perhaps their own studies of literature will even be enhanced by a sociological understanding of social processes.

What about the opposite possibility, of using approaches of the humanities in sociological analysis? Let us ask, "Will an adequate social analysis result simply from turning the *methods* of literary criticism, linguistics or narrative analysis to the topic of the social world?" No doubt there is a great deal to be learned by using the techniques of literary criticism or linguistics to read "war" novels, for example, or to study the shifting motifs of wartime propaganda in an era of television and computers. And it may be useful to look at things, like neon signs, using the vocabulary of the art historian or the literary critic. But culture is more than a set of artifacts, codes or signs to be catalogued by cultural archaeologists of our own era. Culture gets produced, one way or another, and at least some of it comes into our lives in ways that may change our experience and how we live. How are we to understand these processes? These are classic sociological issues in their own right, and currently, they are the subject of intense controversy. Considerations about sociology certainly do not exhaust questions about culture, but they are a necessary component of practically any discussion of culture. Yet for sociological thinking to help us understand culture, the sociological issues need to be considered as such.

This is the purpose of our writing here. In the remainder of this chapter, we show that defining "culture" is a project that immediately brings into play central sociological issues. Then, at the conclusion of this chapter, we offer an overview of the "analytic frames" that organize the sociological perspectives we bring to bear on culture in the remainder of this book.

DEFINING CULTURE SOCIOLOGICALLY

On the surface, debating definitions may seem trivial. But those who write about culture sometimes define it in very different terms, and they thereby fit "culture" into alternative theories that offer radically different ways of analyzing culture. Anthropologists at the beginning of this century defined culture as the way of life of a people, or as what an individual needed to know to survive in a society, or as what could be learned by an individual and passed down in a society. In recent years social scientists have tried to narrow the concept in various ways in order to make it more powerful. Yet the narrower definitions have led to debates about what should be included. The general ferment around the concept of culture today also makes it impossible to pin down a definition that could be considered "definitive." With a word that covers as much as "culture," we can never hope to capture reality simply through careful definition. It would be a mistake to define "culture," thereby making it into a "thing" different than all the range of cultural subtleties in the world; we should dismiss such an approach as "reifying" culture. Yet considering how to define culture may help us move beyond mere issues of definition to understand the complexities of the social world that make any definition of culture controversial.

A number of approaches define culture in part by differentiating it from other sociological concepts of analysis. Thus, some sociologists speak of the difference between culture and society. Other approaches offer *internal* differentiations of culture: "high" culture versus "mass" or "popular" culture, for example, and "material" versus "symbolic" culture. Exploring these distinctions offers a good way of finding out what is at stake in defining "culture." In these explorations, and throughout this book, we are not interested in proclaiming some point of view as the "right" answer. Instead, we wish to pursue the pragmatic idea that there may be alternative useful ways of analyzing culture. We want to explore those alternative approaches and see what limitations they might have and how they can contribute to our understanding of culture.

Culture: Material and Ideal Aspects

We can ferret out one issue—material versus ideal culture—by proposing an inclusive working definition of culture as (*1*) *ideas, knowledge* (correct, wrong, or unverifiable belief) *and recipes* for doing things, (2) humanly fabricated *tools* (such as shovels, sewing machines, and computers), and (3) the *products* of social action that may be drawn upon in the further conduct of social life (an apple pie, a television set, or an interstate highway, for example). It is worth remembering that "culture" comes from the Latin for "cultivating" or tilling the soil. Culture, in this sense, amounts to the ways of taking care of things.

With this definition we intentionally include both "material" as well as "symbolic" culture. Why might such a definition prove controversial? Some anthropologists (Harris 1979) give material culture its due, and archaeologists emphasize the importance of material culture, perhaps because some of it tends to survive the ravages of time, while a song or a gesture will easily be lost. Tools, from the plow to robotics, seem central to how we conduct life. So material culture has obvious importance. Yet sociologists and most cultural anthropologists have tended to give pride of place to symbols and ideas, not tools and material objects. Clifford Geertz, for example, defines culture as "an historically transmitted pattern of meanings embodied in symbols, a system of inherited conceptions expressed in symbolic forms by means of which men [*sic*][1] communicate, perpetuate, and develop their knowledge about and attitudes toward life" (1973, p. 89). This narrower, "idealist" (for its emphasis on ideas) delineation of culture seems to come from two directions: (1) from many cultural sociologists themselves, who see symbols and ideas as *the* theoretically important aspect of culture, and (2) from their sociological opponents—"materialists" who see the significant social forces as non-cultural processes of economics and politics. Apparently the "idealist" cultural sociologists would hope to establish their own distinctive realm of expertise, while the "materialists" may think that limiting culture to ideas and beliefs will make it easier to discount arguments about its importance.

The distinction between material and ideal culture obscures more than it reveals. This book will refer to all identifiable complexes of culture, from the very concrete (e.g., a painting) to the more nebulous (e.g., a way of life) as "cultural objects." Griswold (1986, p. 5) defines a cultural object as "shared significance embodied in form. Significance refers to the object's incorporation of one or more symbols, which suggest a set of denotations and connotations, emotions and memories." In using this term, we must not "reify" the "object" as a *physical* thing, for, as Griswold makes clear, even seemingly very concrete objects—texts or paintings for example—may exist not only (and perhaps not most importantly) as physical objects. They also surface as episodes of our shared subjective experiences. Are not obviously material cultural objects also ideal in some respects? Consider a play viewed by a theater audience. This cultural object has both material and ideal elements—speech

---

[1] In the remainder of this book, any quotation of other authors who use gender-specific language to refer to persons in general will not be noted as such. Readers are asked to understand that, for the authors' part, non-gendered language for persons in the generic sense is in all cases implied.

and gestures, costumes and sets. Yet all of these features have their rationales as material practices for the effects they create in the minds of audience members. So it is with television, or with material products that become significant symbols, like apple pie and Coca-Cola™. In a world in which "oral tradition" has come to play a less significant role in the transmission of culture, even ideal culture is passed along through use of technologies that depend on some material process—the printing that makes this book possible as a medium for ideal culture, for example. Given the interdependence and interpenetration of material and ideal culture, it would be presumptuous to rule some kinds of culture out of bounds by fiat. Instead, it is important to consider the interplay of ideas and material things in cultural objects.

High Culture and Popular Culture

Another kind of distinction—between "elite" (or high) culture and "mass" (or popular) culture—poses problems for the study of culture similar to those of the material/ideal debate. The very word "culture" is intimidating to some people because it seems to signify "refinement" and "manners." The adjective "cultured" describes someone who is "cultivated," or practiced in the "social graces." In a similar vein, some cultural analysts think that the only important culture is culture of the very highest quality. But who is to define quality? What if quality is defined by literary, art and music critics who embrace "high" or "elite" culture? In these terms, not surprisingly, Madonna doesn't count as culture, but Mozart does. Art used in advertising doesn't count as culture, but the work of Andy Warhol does, even if he started out as a commercial artist before he succeeded in displaying his "pop" art as high culture. Among the aficionados of Culture with a capital "C," the "mass" culture of the popular classes doesn't count; it does not need to be taken "seriously." Countering this view, Herbert Gans argues, "The term *mass culture* is obviously pejorative; *mass* suggests an undifferentiated collectivity, even a mob, rather than individuals or members of a group; and *mass culture,* that mob's lack of culture" (1974, p. 10). So Gans prefers the term "popular culture."

"Mass" culture may seem pejorative, but the term "mass" does capture an important aspect of contemporary culture, namely that in the late twentieth century, much (though certainly not all) culture is *mass* produced, *mass* distributed, and consumed on a *mass* basis. Indeed, the increasingly predominant transmission of culture via some medium other than face-to-face communication has given rise to concerns about the emergence of a "mass society." In the aftermath of fascism that gave rise to World War II, social theorists and critics in the 1950s (Kornhauser 1959; MacDonald 1962) worried that individuals were losing their connections to local social institutions such as church, schools, recreational groups, and civic organizations. Theories of mass society are open to debate, but whatever their merits, recognizing the increasing importance of mass production, mass distribution, mass media, and mass consumption does not necessarily imply that we all act as robots, marching lockstep to the output of the culture factories. Mass production has come a long way since the days when Henry Ford offered Americans a car of any color they wanted, as long as it was black: What is remarkable is the very diversity of culture that abounds, even when production for any given item—a soft drink, a car, a book—runs into the millions and more. Shorn of its pejorative connotations, the term "mass" reveals a fundamental aspect of contemporary culture, one that cultural studies will have to confront.

Nevertheless, the term of choice, of Gans and others, is *popular* culture, and since the 1970s the serious study of popular culture has come into its own. In part the interest in popular culture derives from a populist anti-elitism in the U.S. In part it stems from a crisis within *high* culture circles. Works of pop art like Andy Warhol's 1961 Campbell's Soup cans have brought into question the validity of elite aesthetics by which art is judged good or bad. Moreover, even elite culture often is produced by mass techniques—films, compact disks, books—and distributed like more popular culture, albeit with smaller production runs. These developments suggest that there is no easy line of demarcation between high culture and popular culture. Furthermore, it is not evident that the audiences for high culture are formed in ways that are distinct from popular culture audiences.

The potential significance of the popular culture processes of mass production and audience formation in supposedly high culture should suggest a reason for taking popular culture seriously: we can only ignore it at the peril of ignorance about a significant force that shapes our lives. There are still a few individuals who do not watch television as a matter of principle, because they are too busy with other things, or because they are homeless. Yet the influence of television is so pervasive that the *New York Times* routinely reports to its (largely elite) readers how the more popular medium of television has been covering dramatic events like the Gulf War against Iraq. In this case, the television coverage itself is news. Whatever aesthetic judgment any individual may make about popular culture, it is a pervasive aspect of contemporary society.

All the same, there remain the questions of *how* to study popular culture, and *why*. Should soap operas receive the same sort of serious critical attention that goes to novels by Jane Austen or George Orwell? If cultural analysts avoid all issues of aesthetic judgment (for example, by treating soap operas seriously), how can we hope to ask whether popular culture offers a mass road to enlightenment or is simply a non-narcotic opiate of the people? Are evaluations based on other than aesthetic standards appropriate? Should cultural analysts simply accept mass media cultural stereotypes about sex and gender, race and ethnicity, class, religion, and the like? These questions are important for deciding how we approach culture sociologically, yet they cannot be asked without bringing value judgments into sociology from outside the discipline. Advocates of a so-called "value-free" sociology will charge that evaluating culture robs sociology of its scientific status, and they will argue that all culture—soap operas *and* operas—can be studied by the same methods, posing the same questions. But some sociologists hope to draw on the capacity of the discipline to offer "critical theory" that will help us live freer lives. They will argue that contemporary society faces a crisis of its culture. Only on the basis of a critical examination of pedestrian and ideological culture, they suggest, can we hope to understand the relation of our culture to issues of personal fulfillment, political freedom, and our ability to exist within meaningful social communities. While popular culture should hardly be ignored, in this view, neither need it be accepted uncritically. Of course, the same can be said of high culture. The sociological task of understanding culture is, in the tradition of C. Wright Mills, also an act of personal liberation.

The distinction between high culture and popular culture, like the one between material and ideal culture, can only be useful if it is not overdrawn. It shows that not all culture reaches all audiences equally (see chapter 6), and it suggests that some people or groups may disproportionately control who has access to what kinds of culture (an issue considered in chapter 7). In all this, culture is a controversial issue because there is reason to suspect that the ideas people have make a difference in how they negotiate a complicated world, and what kind of society is thereby sustained. This issue, in turn, suggests that a working definition of culture cannot be developed without considering the analytic distinction between culture and other aspects of the social world.

Culture and Society

Among others, theorist Talcott Parsons (1951) distinguished between culture and society: A "social system", for Parsons, is an interacting set of individuals, while a "cultural system" makes up the shared meaningful symbols by which social actors communicate. Significantly, the cultural system defines a patterned or institutionalized set of social roles and their expectations. Parsons was particularly interested in values and norms through which, he theorized, a culture channels the behavior of individuals in a society. For example, the social role of rock musician may be thought to have a certain place in the social order, as the member of a group ("the band") and in relation to audiences interested in entertainment. The (typically unconventional) values and norms of rock musicianhood shape the performance of the role, not only on stage, but also in relation to club managers, record producers, fans, and so on. The same argument may be applied to the musicians' audience. There are many ways that people in an audience might conceivably act, but at any given performance, the range of how audience members do act is much narrower and more specific than the theoretical range of possibilities. A whole different culture of audience activity gets acted out at a Grateful Dead concert than at a Madonna one (to say nothing of a classical music performance).

For Parsons, culture is sociologically important when it offers values and norms that shape performances of social roles. According to this perspective, social order is achieved through the mostly unconscious conformity of individuals to the informal and formal cultural patterns of social life. More recently, cultural analysts have become interested in the coexistence of many different sets of patterns and rules. Some observers postulate that western societies are actually experiencing a kind of breakdown in the cultural pattern, while others argue that the Parsonian definition of culture was a "distorting lens" that led observers looking through it to see cultural consensus when it did not actually exist.

Beyond the debate over cultural consensus, there is an additional issue: Norms and values are not all there is to culture, even in contrast to society. To pursue the same example, what about music itself? Clearly it is not exhausted in its cultural content by norms and values: It may have qualities of rhythm and melody that appeal to an audience in ways that exceed any straightforward social meanings. The question of how audiences, consumers, or people in general take in culture, and with what consequences, is a controversial one; we will explore it throughout this book, especially in chapters 9 and 10. At this juncture, the point is simple: As Herbert Gans argued, some culture is a matter of "taste." Some people like poetry; others do not. One person may like folk music; that person's friends may loathe it. Without opening the can of worms about how strongly culture "carries" norms and values, Gans says that there are *taste cultures* which function to entertain, inform, and beautify life, among other things, and which express values and standards of taste and aesthetics." Gans's conception of symbolic culture is more encompassing than Parsons's emphasis on norms and values; moreover, it includes material things such as automobiles and appliances, "insofar as ordinary consumer goods also express aesthetic values or functions..." (1974, pp. 10–11, italics in orig.). His approach should make it possible to theorize about a complex of cultural tastes that forms some sort of package. We might then engage in empirical research to identify the contents of such taste cultures—local skateboard culture or country-club culture, for example. Such a usage of Gans's approach prefigures a growing tendency among sociologists to conceptualize culture in terms of situated meanings and "expressive symbols."

Like Parsons, Gans distinguishes culture from society: "Users [of a particular taste culture] who make similar choices of values and taste culture content will be described as publics of an individual taste culture, or *taste publics,* even though they are unorganized aggregates rather than organized publics" (1974, pp. 10–11, italics in orig.). It is important to note that Gans underscores the difference between culture and society (where society is composed, in his terms, of "publics"). If we did not distinguish between cultural "tastes" and societal "publics," we could never understand how culture works. This is so because there is no simple relationship between taste cultures and taste publics. The *same* culture may be used by *different* publics in ways that have little in common. Consider the country and western bar in a city of the American midwest. The distinctive rockabilly and neo-bluegrass music, the cowboy/girl style of dressing, two-step dancing, and special forms of sociability and courtship offer badges of honor and a culturally saturated arena of action for a public attracted to a "country" taste sensibility. Other people (that is, participants in another taste public)—say upper-middle class urbanites—may visit a country and western bar not to *participate* in the spectacle (they would hardly know how), but simply to *view* it as some exotic anthropological excursion.

Members of taste publics do not necessarily congregate in a single place like the country and western bar: Gans's definition of the term "public" explicitly describes a diffuse social stratum. However, the same logic about

FIGURE 1.1 The Texas two-step remains popular today, although other features of the taste culture have changed somewhat. (*Source:* Copies from the Collections in the Center for American History, The University of Texas at Austin.)

diverse publics applies for the diffuse and the face-to-face group: "Country" fashions—cowboy/girl boots, hats and belts, "duster" jackets and the like may be worn by urbanites, but the meanings they convey by doing so mostly do not connect with the core meanings of country and western culture. Conversely, the hard core of the country and western bar crowd may connect with quite different culture when they watch football games on television. People of *one* taste *public* may participate in a *variety* of taste *cultures,* perhaps always maintaining their own distinctive way of doing so.

The country and western example shows that culture is often deeply embedded in our daily lives. It is important to keep in mind that distinctions such as the one between taste cultures and taste publics are analytic ones. There is a danger in reifying such analytic distinctions. Culture includes more than discrete cultural objects like books, music, paintings and identifiable sets of tastes concerning food, fashion, music, and so on. And it can permeate people's lives in a much more pervasive way. We all live by way of habits, manners, recipes, rules, mores, ethics, rituals, procedures, and other cognitive or symbolic devices. These kinds of "ideal" cultural objects can be distinguished analytically from structural features (enduring patterns) of societies, but in the empirical world, "culture" and "structure" may in some cases amount to mirror-image ways of describing the same thing. In other words, some culture forms a seamless part of our worlds, which sociologists and other analysts may cut into with different slices, so to speak.

As an example, consider a hierarchical organization with definite positions of authority, such as a corporation that produces household appliances. It would be possible to describe the factory floor in "structural" terms, based on its role positions and their relationships, both formal and informal. Yet obedience to authority is itself a cultural trait, as are respect, camaraderie, and an ethos of equality, to say nothing of all the rules, policies, and rituals of the corporation. Thus, we must recognize, in the example of the corporation and in general, that "structure" does not always exist independently of "culture." Indeed, insofar as culture delimits a patterned basis for a group's structure, we may speak of those patterns as "cultural structures."[2]

The analytic distinction between taste culture and taste public and the problem of culture and structure have divergent implications for understanding the relation between culture and society. On the one hand, the taste culture/taste public distinction absolutely requires that we maintain a firm distinction between culture and society, so that we can begin to examine the complex ways cultures are sustained as well as how people draw on culture in their everyday lives. On the other hand, the embeddedness of culture in the structures of society suggests that maintaining a distinction may sometimes prevent us from seeing the ways that structural aspects of society are cultur-

---

[2] One of us has used the term "cultural structure" to describe institutionalized patterns in nineteenth century U.S. communal groups; see Hall 1988.

ally shaped. Rather than adopting any rigid theoretical position emphasizing a distinction between culture and society or their inherent unity, we therefore must explore the complicated relationships between aspects of things described by both terms.

Classification, Typification, and "Shading Off"

The fact that the distinction between society and culture is both problematic and important brings us to a related point, namely that cultural objects often are not clearly fixed in their boundaries and their forms. When a cultural object is entirely and unambiguously contained within a category, we may speak of "classification." There may be a question of where to draw the line that establishes the boundary of a class of cultural objects, but once that boundary is drawn, cultural classification may be straightforward. Indeed, significant social processes have to do with forcing unambiguous choices, even in sometimes ambiguous situations. The choice between "pure" and "impure" does not leave much middle ground (M. Douglas 1966; cf. Zerubavel 1991).

However, there is also a cultural logic that goes against the grain of clearcut classification. Describing a cultural object often involves some sort of "typification" (the identification of a general pattern), even though the cultural objects themselves may "shade off," or differ in varying degrees, from any typical form. Specific concrete cultural objects often seem to have discrete forms and boundaries that lend themselves to classification. Thus, we know that the Mona Lisa painting is a particular cultural object (even if what the Mona Lisa "is" differs for its producer and its millions of viewers over the centuries). Similarly, one brand of cold refreshment beverage is not to be confused with another (at least if their manufacturers have their way). Yet cultural matters are not always so straightforward. A given couch ends at the floor on which it sits. Yet the typification "couch" overlaps with other typifications of cultural objects, for example, "love seat," "day bed," "settee," and "sofa." Similarly, we may know a given famous rendition of a song (the Beatles' "Yellow Submarine"), yet songs can be performed in many different ways, by both their originators and others. Particular folk songs that have been passed down through generations often come in alternative versions, no one of which is "correct." At a more general level of typification, the categorization of music can run into trouble, for example, at the borders between calypso, reggae, and ska. Thus, we need to keep in mind that the activities of *typifying* culture do not match the diversity of culture in any consistent way. Therefore, the contents of any given category or typification (rock'n'roll music or Christian theology) may change over time, and the same cultural object (e.g., a Picasso painting) may be typified in more than one way.

One well-known example of "shading off" has to do with the cultural symbols of social interaction. As Clifford Geertz (1973, p. 6) observed,

"Contracting your eyelids on purpose when there exists a public code in which so doing counts as a conspiratorial signal *is* winking." The definition of a wink seems straightforward. But the important thing to remember, Geertz goes on, is that a person can make this objective sign take on diverse meanings. A given wink can be an act of flirtation, a high sign, a parody of another's wink, or even a fake wink to make a third person think something clandestine is afoot between the winker and someone else. Geertz's example shows that the cultural materials we deal in are often especially important for the shades of meaning and nuances they take on in concrete situations, while by the same token, the very capacity to recognize shades of meaning depends upon the cultural activity of typification. "Typification" and "shading off" together represent a counterpoint to the alternative approach of classification. In either approach we deal mentally with ranges of cultural objects which are themselves sometimes heterogeneous, but we deal with them in different ways. How culture works thus depends on both the particular culture and upon the cognitive ways we attach significance to it.

The cultural possibilities of classification and typification that are part of social life are also problems for cultural analysis. This is so because the institutional patterns of culture identified by cultural analysts—such as "the Renaissance," "the Protestant work ethic," "jazz," and "the hippie counterculture"—do not have the same empirical reality as, say, a chair, a painting, a person, the activity of singing, or a book. Such patterns are sociologists' (and literary critics' and historians', etc.) "analytic constructs"; that is, they are *themselves* classifications and typifications. Cultural analysis thus is engaged in a process found in culture more generally—drawing lines of categories and defining patterns of typifications. Such analytic constructs do not completely describe reality, but they are useful nevertheless. Classifications give us ways of identifying what may be important aspects of a phenomenon, so that they can be examined in relation to comparable phenomena or other aspects of the same phenomenon. Typifications can be used as working hypotheses about how a complex of cultural material "fits together" as a set of meanings, and perhaps how it works in social processes.

For example, we might wish to study the culture of a particular social group, say Italian-Americans. Various classifications might identify certain cultural traits of dress, diet, manners, childrearing practices, and so forth. A cluster of such classifications that describes features of Italian-American culture might be proposed as a typification. Such a sociological typification is called an "ideal type" (or sociohistorical model [Roth 1976])—"ideal" not in the sense of "perfect," but in the sense of representing a hypothesized fundamental coherence of Italian-American culture as a meaningful way of life. In turn, we could use this model (or ideal type) to ask such questions as: How has the culture changed over time? Why and how do people of Italian-American heritage invoke this culture (as opposed to other cultural possibilities)? How has Italian-American culture been diffused into usage by a wider population of Americans? How has it been modified in the process of diffusion? It is important to note that the possibility of asking such questions depends upon *not* using the ideal type as a "stereotype." That is, the ideal type is not assumed to describe any empirical reality. Instead, it is a concept hypothesizing what reality would be like under a given set of conditions (i.e., like a perfect vacuum in physics); this ideal type can then be compared with a variety of actual realities.

By contrast, the "stereotype" is based on the assumption that the conceptual type accurately describes the empirical cases related to it. Such stereotypical "pigeonholing" of individuals on the basis of cultural constructs is a social practice itself worth studying. Indeed, stereotypes may be used by social groups to maintain boundaries and power, for example, in relation to gender, ethnicity, and social class. Yet the very possibility of taking on such issues depends upon avoiding the use of sociological concepts as stereotypes. Here, as with the distinction between culture and society, the relations between categorization and typification are complex. They do not suggest any easy answer about how to use concepts to study culture, but they do suggest that cultural analysis must be sensitive to the ways that categories and typifications work, both in general and in cultural analysis.

FIGURE 1.2 Predominant public stereotypes about urban black men fail to acknowledge the diversity of individuals and their actual cultural practices and social relationships, such as those enacted in this scene of summertime street chess in Manhattan. (*Source:* David M. Grossman/Photo Researchers.)

Culture in General, Socially Significant Culture, and the Question of Structure versus Agency

In turn, the issue of categorization versus typification helps bring into focus the question of how people deal with the infinite array of culture, whether by active agency or out of unconscious immersion in a culturally shaped world. Everything humanly created or thought has its cultural aspect. But not all of that culture is "in use" at any given moment, and the culture that *is* being used may be accorded various kinds of significance by different users. A good deal of the culture ever produced or used has been destroyed, lost, or forgotten. Much of the culture that survives (folk techniques of hog slaughtering, for example) is not used very often; it remains "in storage" in the documentations of archaeologists, folklorists and cultural historians, in museums and in the memories of people who remember "how we used to do things."

Even culture that is in active use does not always have uniform significance for everyone. The automobile is an example. It is a cultural creation; a complex machine dependent on sophisticated engineering knowledge, wrapped in styling, designed for personal transportation, responsible for the emergence of other cultural features such as highway systems, motels, and shopping malls (Belasco 1979). There is so much culture implicated in automobiles that describing it would be an enormous task. However, much of the time, for most people, the automobile attains significance only in some limited aspect. And it is precisely how people attach significance to particular culture that helps to delineate the sociological relevance of culture. For many people, the car is a utilitarian vehicle of transportation and little more. Other people develop more specialized cultural stances. Mechanics take on car maintenance as a special kind of cultural knowledge, and sports and performance enthusiasts will care about certain parts—the fuel system or camshaft, for example, and give little thought to other aspects, such as water pump design. Many people attach to their cars a kind of iconographic significance as to their own social status. The culture of the automobile includes all these possibilities and more, but insofar as cultural analysts are concerned with *meanings,* we need to know what matters about cars for particular people who produce them, work on them, or use them for diverse practical and symbolic purposes. In short, in order to understand automobile culture, we would need to investigate how members of one or more particular social groups take for granted certain aspects, and pay attention in highly nuanced ways to other aspects of their own and other people's cars.

The issue of social significance is equally important to the study of more purely symbolic culture. Consider a field of knowledge like medicine. In the first place, we need to recognize that people's actual states of health and cultural knowledge about health and sickness are quite different matters. Physical problems of the body were once the province of shamans and blood-letting barbers. At a later time surgeons came to be distinguished from physicians. The category of medicine itself is a modern clustering of practices under a single institutional category (Foucault 1975). Medical knowledge today is still a form of culture, necessarily partial and probably wrong in certain respects, even as an amassed body of knowledge. Moreover, positive results of therapeutic practice seemingly can be attained from alternative and competing cultural models of health and disease, from western medicine to osteopathy and homeopathy, Chinese acupuncture, Christian Science, and faith healing. Finally, *within* any particular institutional culture of medicine, the knowledge which actually finds its way into practice can be quite different from the knowledge which exists on a shelf somewhere. Thus, a sociological study of a medical school revealed that in part students learned to be doctors by finding out how they could get by with what they *really* had to know, in the face of demands that they master overwhelming amounts of information (Becker et al. 1961). As with the automobile, the study of how people attend to and draw upon medical culture *in practice* offers a sociological strategy for learning how culture works, by the simple device of seeing how people treat aspects of that culture as significant.

Some sociologists will not agree with the emphasis given here to culture as it is rendered significant by the social actors involved. They will rightly suggest that some things happen *to* people despite their own meaningful intentions, and in ways that are beyond their control. Epidemics, crop disasters, economic catastrophes—this is a suggestive but hardly exhaustive list of *non*-cultural events that may affect what meanings we make about the world, as well as the character of our actions and our society.

Moreover, some cultural analysts place emphasis on the centrality of symbolic structures that exist *prior* to individuals and their judgments of significance. Analysts of culture need to be open to the possibility that certain *cultural* processes happen *to* us, in ways that can be described in the scientific terminology of cause and effect, rather than in the language of symbols and meaning preferred by many interpretive sociologists of culture. Certain such cultural "causes" of our individual situations seem quite direct: Consider the "accident" of our birth to particular parents with particular social locations and their own distinctive family culture. Not all cultural causation may be so obvious. The example of medicine discussed above is instructive. Medical students have to learn what is truly significant, but that learning presumes a previously established calculus of significance. French structuralists like Emile Durkheim (1964), Claude Lévi-Strauss (1966), and Michel Foucault (1965, 1980) treat cultural systems as forces external to any individual, and they point out that culture can affect our personalities and actions without our conscious appropriation of culture in a meaningful way. Language offers a useful example. Of course we may choose to alter how we speak. But in general, we use language unselfconsciously, and thus, much of the time, we are beholden to the categories and concepts of our natural language (Sapir 1956; Whorf 1956;

Bernstein 1975). What is true with language may also be true with our manners, ethics, or habits. Therefore, in the study of culture, we must remain open to the question of whether the processes by which people act in cultural ways are, on the one hand, habitual and unconscious, or on the other hand, meaningful ways of interpreting and acting in the world. Are we products of our culture or are we its users?

ANALYTIC FRAMES FOR THINKING ABOUT CULTURE SOCIOLOGICALLY

Our exploration of definitions of culture has raised difficult questions that go beyond simple definition. The problem of definition unfolds into questions about different kinds of culture (material versus ideal, high versus popular), the relation of culture to society, cultural categories and typification, and the social and structural significance of culture. Part of what has been at stake in these considerations is a basic question. This question has to do with the subject matter of the sociology of culture. Given that most of us look at the world and comprehend a multiplicity of things from our own points of view, it seems worthwhile to ask: What do cultural analysts look at when they study culture?

"Analytic frames," like frames of photographs or paintings, define the focus and boundaries—in other words, the subject matter—of sociohistorical inquiry. A given analytic frame brings into focus particular aspects of phenomena in the social world that are relatively distinct from the aspects brought into focus by other analytic frames. Some disagreements about culture come about because different analysts use alternative frames for defining the field. Based on the practices of inquiry about culture, we may identify five such frames: (1) institutional structures, (2) cultural history and legacies, (3) production and distribution, (4) audience effects, and (5) meaning and social action.

Institutional Structures of Culture. This frame focuses on the overarching "patterns" of material and ideal culture that are represented in various social institutions such as language, personal identity, family, popular culture, work, etc. In this frame—employed especially in chapter 2—culture is assumed to have the character of a "social fact," independent of individual consciousness. As an aspect of the social process, its tendencies cannot be reduced to the actions of individuals. In the U.S., for example, we might be interested in a "culture of individualism" or "the family" as an institutional pattern.

Cultural History and the Persistence of Cultural Forms. Historians, some cultural anthropologists and historical sociologists take seriously the observation that much contemporary culture has its parallels in cultural practices and processes that have also occurred at other times and in other places. Through imitation and diffusion, cultural objects can spread from place to place and over time. Moreover, all societies may share certain basic kinds of cultural processes. In chapter 3, we take these possibilities seriously by asking about the significance of folk culture for cultural studies and for contemporary society. Chapters 4 and 5 pursue similar questions about the legacy of preindustrial cultural forms and about the consolidation of mass culture associated with the rise of industrial society beginning in the nineteenth century.

Production and the Social Distribution of Culture. All culture is not equally accessible to all individuals in a society. Instead, diverse cultural objects tend to end up among different social strata and groups on the basis of socially organized production and distribution of culture. As chapter 6 argues, the stocks of culture of different social strata and groups are central conduits through which social differentiation and association occur on the basis of class, ethnic, gender, and other distinctions. Nor are the differential arrays of culture among individuals in diverse social locations natural occurrences; they are the consequences of how culture is distributed. The ownership and control of cultural distribution—as well as the content of what is distributed—raise questions of the relation between culture and power, questions which are discussed in chapter 7. The culture that is distributed does not come out of thin air either; it has to be produced by (often organized) social action. This frame thus also posits the sociological centrality of the processes, resources, actors, roles, activities, organizations, genres, conventions, and recipes by which production and distribution of culture occur—a set of issues pursued in chapter 8.

Effects of Culture. The word "effect" is, in the narrow sense, debatable if it is taken to imply that the social actor is a passive receptacle of culture, but if taken broadly it conveys concerns with the reception of cultural items by social actors, and whether (and how) any particular cultural item affects the beliefs, meaningful relation to life, and actions of an individual or social group. As discussed in chapter 9, we might want to know, for example, about the effects of television violence, pornography, or news coverage on public opinion. In more subtle ways, we would also want to know about how audiences draw meaning from culture, and with what consequences.

Meaning and Social Action. If, instead of analyzing the reception of a discrete cultural item by actors, we invert the focus—as we do in chapter 10—the frame becomes centered on actors and how they draw from among their enormous cultural inventories in actual conduct, and, in turn, how these processes reproduce or shift institutionalized culture. In a somewhat different way, the final chapter of the book, chapter 11, asks whether certain contemporary cultural developments can be described as "postmodern," what the connections of any such postmodern culture might be to earlier cultural forms and industrial social organization, and how a postulated postmodern situation might shift the relationship between people, their cultural milieux, and their resources for participation in political, civic, and social life.

The five analytic frames represent a division of labor in sociohistorical inquiry, in the sense that any particular frame seems to generate boundaries, and the cultural analyst who becomes committed to a particular frame tends to concentrate efforts within it, and to link other frames with it as the central frame of analysis. How these analytic frames help us to account for culture sociologically is a question that can be considered only by launching into the sociological study of culture proper. We begin by pursuing an issue made famous by turn-of-the-twentieth-century sociologist, Emile Durkheim (1965), who believed that culture offers an important basis of social solidarity that helps bind individuals to groups.

2

CULTURE AS MORAL DISCOURSE

What does it mean to be a "good person" or to have a "good society"? How do good people create a good society? How does a good society create good people? These questions are bound up with notions of how cultures guide behavior in such a way as to produce both the good society and the good person through established rules, with rewards for conformity and punishments for deviance. Ancient questions though they be, they acquire new meaning as the circumstances of people's lives change. Debate about the moral order was very much a part of early social science, but fell out of favor with the growth of positivism and empiricism in the twentieth century. Yet in recent years active public debate about moral issues has been revived. In the 1970s—labeled "the me decade" by the media—and the 1980s—labeled "the decade of greed"—politicians, intellectuals, religious leaders, and the media expressed concerns about the moral order.

A number of social scientists have taken up these questions about the good person and the good society, and they have addressed a broad audience in popular books. Dominating the critical discourse is a pessimistic evaluation of American culture: the critics argue that the replacement of "traditional" (often religious) values by a "therapeutic culture" has created an American culture that promotes "individual fulfillment" at the expense of community and society. An alternative discourse exists, however, with a different view of the nature of the self and the relation between the self and society. This perspective sees the self in relation to others and looks at the continuing existence of various kinds of community life in American culture. In looking at these perspectives we see how social critics use the concept of culture to explore the moral order of American society.

One strand of the sociological tradition stretching from Emile Durkheim to Talcott Parsons assumed that culture works to tie together individuals and integrate a society. It focused on the ways that shared norms and values created social order. This formulation implies that culture is a kind of system for the social control of individuals to the benefit of the society. A major movement of modern society has been toward "freeing" individuals from constraining norms and rules. Yet we can ask as Durkheim (1951) does in his discussion of anomic suicide—which occurs when normative regulations are relaxed and no longer offer sufficient guidance for human behavior—if it is possible that a culture could exist where, for some reason, the rules offer so little constraint that the society and the individuals within it both suffer.

The writers considered here are concerned about how we think about the rules, what the rules are, how they are changing, and with what consequences. These writers do not stand outside of society observing it: they are (and for the most part see themselves as) engaged in the society and its culture. Their writings have become part of a public debate on the nature of the good person and the good society. Their arguments are not only texts *about* the culture, but the texts are *part of* that culture. One can argue that this is true of all writings, but because these writings have attracted a much broader audience—a number of them have been best sellers—their impact within the culture has been much more direct.

Even in cases where the authors do not acknowledge the normative content of their statements, a normative stance is often implicitly present. John Hewitt reminds us that:

> The social types created by social scientists, which are typically intended solely as description, engender responses of normative judgment and of identification that give continuing voice to the opposing conceptions of the person that characterize American culture (1989, p. 30).[1]

Because these works are not just interpretations of culture but have become a part of the culture they comment upon, the texts themselves are central to the discussion here.

INDIVIDUALISM AND THERAPEUTIC CULTURE

The authors of *Habits of the Heart* (Bellah, Madsen, Sullivan, Swidler, and Tipton 1985) question how, and if, Americans preserve or create morally

---

[1] Furthermore, Hewitt argues that the sociologists with the broadest influence have often developed a "rhetoric in service to a more collective orientation to life and in opposition to the 'individualism' they perceive in American society" (1989, p. 55).

coherent lives. *Habits of the Heart* has generated lively debate about the nature of American culture. It is the best selling book written by a sociologist since David Riesman's *The Lonely Crowd* (1950). Drawing their framework from the nineteenth century Frenchman, Alexis de Tocqueville, the authors see a fundamental tension between the individual's desires for self-fulfillment and the needs of the social order, in their terms, between individualism and commitment.

Alexis de Tocqueville was a young French aristocrat when he visited the United States in 1831. His observations of the American political system as well as of social relations and cultural mores were published as *Democracy in America*. Even in the early nineteenth century, Tocqueville saw Americans as having broken loose from the constraining forces that bound Europeans to traditional authorities. He admired the freedom and equality of Americans, although he was concerned about the repercussions of the continuing existence of slavery in the southern states, and he noted the relative lack of freedom among married women (single women he found free in comparison to European counterparts).

Yet, he also worried about American individualism. If individualism was not balanced by other factors, and Americans lacked sufficient commitment to common goals, he feared that they would not be able to govern themselves. The American experiment with democracy would fail. However, Tocqueville found evidence of two factors which could mitigate against the destructive aspects of individualism in American culture. He suggested that Americans saw "self-interest rightly understood" as coinciding with the interests of the society (1945, p. 129–132). Second, he observed high levels of participation in voluntary associations. These, he asserted, created ties between individuals and gave people the experience of participating in something larger than themselves. For Tocqueville, democracy depended on the development and maintenance of civic culture, and he saw associations of volunteers as well as involvement in institutions such as churches (which, in America, looked a lot like voluntary associations) as providing support for the emerging civic culture.

Individualism in American Culture

One and a half centuries later, Robert Bellah and his co-authors are less sure that the negative effects of individualism have been avoided. On the contrary, they argue that modern individualism is producing a way of life not personally or socially viable. They find that individualism has deep roots in American culture, and that it exists in several variations among the middle-class Americans interviewed for *Habits of the Heart*.

When asked about the goals of a morally good life, these people spoke about success, freedom, and justice. Bellah and his associates describe these concerns as expressed in four different types of individualism, each type embodying particular strands of the American cultural heritage. The different kinds of individualism provide different rhetorics for talking about balancing the basic goals of success, freedom, and justice. First is "biblical individualism" with the Puritan John Winthrop, first governor of Massachusetts Bay Colony, as a representative figure; second, "republican individualism" represented by Thomas Jefferson; third "utilitarian individualism" represented by Benjamin Franklin; and fourth, "expressive individualism" represented by Walt Whitman.

Biblical individualism and republican individualism are the older strands. The high regard for self-reliance and independence embedded in both traditions is moderated by the tie between success and the creation of ethical community for biblical individualists, and by the commitment to political equality for republican individualists (Bellah et al. 1985, pp. 28–32).

Modern individualism encompasses "utilitarian" and "expressive" strands. As originally conceived, utilitarian individualism resembles Tocqueville's self-interest rightly understood. In its most general form utilitarianism holds that the rightness or wrongness of an action is judged by the goodness or badness of its consequences. Utilitarianism originated as a political philosophy in the eighteenth century with British reformer Jeremy Bentham. Bentham and his followers, including John Stuart Mill, believed utilitarianism provided a rational basis for developing social policy. For them the end goal which defined moral action was "the greatest good to the greatest number." Bellah and his co-authors, however, fear that, in its current manifestations, utilitarian individualism primarily provides a rationale for individuals to pursue their own wants and desires with little thought to the common good. They find a similar problem with expressive individualism, with its goal of the cultivation and expression of the self (1985, pp. 33–35). They argue that expressive individualism provides few reasons for making commitments to the community, given that self- expression is the primary good.

All four traditions include a basic emphasis on self-reliance. In the past, at least the first three types of individualism were also tied to traditions that defined the common good and provided reasons for individuals to contribute to it. However, Bellah and his colleagues argue that, over time, "a primary emphasis on self-reliance has led to the notion of pure undetermined choice, free of tradition, obligation or commitment, as the essence of the self" (1985, p. 152). In interviewing middle class Americans the authors found all four types still in evidence, existing in tension with one another. They find Americans characterized by ambivalence:

> we found all the classic polarities of American individualism still operating: the deep desire for autonomy and self-reliance combined with an equally deep conviction that life has no meaning unless shared with others in the context of community; a commitment to the equal right to dignity of every individual combined with an effort to justify inequality of reward, which, when extreme, may deprive people of dignity; an insistence that life requires practical effectiveness and "realism" combined with the feeling that compromise is ethically fatal (1985, pp. 150–151).

At the same time, however, the authors of *Habits of the Heart* express concerns about the ascendancy of the therapeutic modality. In their discussion of love and marriage they find the "therapeutic attitude" much more widely diffused than the older notions of obligation and willingness to sacrifice oneself for others. The middle class mainstream sees the authentic self as the source of one's standards, and good relationships are based on self-knowledge, self-realization, and open and honest communication (1985, pp. 98–99). The authors find that "for such expressive selves, love means the full exchange of feelings between authentic selves, not enduring commitment based on binding obligation" (1985, p. 102).

The therapeutic attitude takes one's own feelings as a starting point, and this has profound implications for moral culture. The authors describe a "view of personal relationships centered on contractual exchange, enacted in communication and negotiation and grounded in each person's ultimate responsibility to himself or herself alone" (1985, p. 129). Values, in this popular understanding, are preferences based on knowledge about one's feelings.[2] One uses a preference structure to generate possible strategies. The healthy person follows the plan to self-fulfillment. However, because one's values are held to be subjective, joint decisions can be reached only through daunting negotiations:

> In theory, each person is supposed to decide what it is 'important' to do in relation to the other and 'judge the relative merits' of acts in relation to the other's reactions. Each must do so in the light of self-set values and accept that 'you can only be responsible for your own actions' (1985, p. 129).

Bellah and his colleagues suggest that this same set of assumptions makes politics impossible, in part because the therapeutic attitude does not allow for moral consensus to exist, but also because the negotiation process involved in decision-making cannot be performed with large numbers of people. Many people interviewed by Bellah and his colleagues found interest group politics repugnant; ironically, toleration of diversity in their personal lives does not appear to lead to support for pluralism in politics.

Of the four types of individualism, Bellah and his colleagues find expressive individualism to be gaining dominance in American culture. The founder of psychoanalysis, Sigmund Freud, is a critical figure in the creation of the therapeutic culture which is at the base of this expressive individualism. Psychoanalysis advanced the destruction of traditional moral authorities and attempted to free individuals from some of the inhibitions and repressions of bourgeois morality. In the following sections we review Freud's thesis and then look at two contemporary critics who offer analyses of the

---

[2] This understanding of "values" as subjectively defined is so different from the older sense of cultural values used by Parsons and others that Bellah et al. (and Rieff, discussed below) avoid using the term at all.

consequences of the destruction of moral authority. Like the authors of *Habits of the Heart,* these critics see the individual existing in opposition to the moral order.

The Advent of Therapeutic Culture

In the late nineteenth and early twentieth centuries, many intellectuals, artists, and scientists—identifying with the modernist movements of the times—saw themselves in rebellion against "traditional culture." They saw the latter as dominated by arbitrary rules with little pay-off for individual conformity. In the lives and writings of critical theorists such as Wilhelm Reich (1960) and Herbert Marcuse (1955) or artists like Henry Miller and Anais Nin (depicted in the movie *Henry and June*), sexual experimentation was championed as a way to break down middle class morality.[3]

Psychoanalysis was both part of and contributed in important ways to this rebellion against the restrictiveness of nineteenth-century bourgeois culture. Freud, like many theorists of his day, defined culture as inherently restrictive. Freud's ideas provided a theoretical rationale for the rebellion, and his "talking cure" laid the basis for the development of "therapeutic culture." Yet, as we shall see, Freud himself was ambivalent about the restrictions imposed by moral cultures.

A member of Freud's circle of psychoanalysts and students, Gez Roheim, once commented, "In general we have no cause to deny the hostility of analysis to culture. Culture involves neurosis which we try to cure. Culture involves super-ego which we try to weaken" (quoted in Rieff 1991, p. 321). For some writers in the early part of the twentieth century, psychoanalysis was to personal life what marxism was to economic life: a revolutionary way of thinking that could free people from the repressive orders of the past. Psychoanalysis sought to replace the authoritarian moral culture with a therapeutic culture. Yet starting with Freud, some psychoanalysts and interpreters of psychoanalysis retain a certain ambivalence about the permissiveness of the therapeutic culture that has replaced the older moral order.

These psychoanalytically-based critics acknowledge that psychoanalysis participated in a (perhaps necessary) destruction of the old morality and the traditional authorities, but some worry about the "moral anarchy" that they see as the result of destroying the authority of the father. They see therapeutic culture as presenting its own dangers.

---

[3] The works were viewed by the authorities as threatening as well: Miller's *Tropic of Cancer,* originally published in Paris in 1931, was banned in the United States as pornography. In the 1950s that book along with *Lady Chatterly's Lover,* by D.H. Lawrence, became the test case in obscenity trials in Britain and the U.S. that resulted in rolling back censorship practices. Anais Nin's most famous work, her diaries, were not published until the late 1960s.

Freud saw an inherent antagonism between the demands of civilization and instinctual desires.[4] In his early writings he saw these instincts (or drives) primarily as sexual and attributed them to the id (the sub-conscious part of the psyche associated with demands for immediate satisfaction of primitive needs). In later writings, Freud added a discussion of aggressive drives, at first seeing them as related to self-preservation. Later, in *Beyond the Pleasure Principle* (1920), he described a "death instinct," a complicated human drive to self-destruction. In *Civilization and Its Discontents* Freud developed the argument that both sexuality and aggression must be curbed for the survival of human society: in Freud's view, humans trade some of their possibilities for happiness for the security that civilization offers.

As the metaphor suggests, this "trade" was not without cost. For Freud, the cost took the form of guilt, administered by a punishing superego. In Freud's system, the superego acts as the conscience, judging the actions and intentions of the ego (the partly conscious part of the psyche that tries to balance the demands of id and superego). The individual's superego is formed in the developmental process when external authority becomes internalized. This happens when the child renounces his desires for his mother and recognizes the authority of his father. Freud originally described the process for boys. Because it is based on male children giving up their mother in the process of identification with their father, Freud called it the Oedipus complex. His explanation of the process for girls was less satisfactory. It included the claim that because girls did not have to break their primary relationship with their mothers in order to achieve identification with the same sex parent, their superegos never develop as fully, therefore their capacity for justice is always less (Freud in Young-Bruehl 1990).[5]

In *Civilization and Its Discontents* Freud posited an analogous process between the development of the superego in the individual and civilization's development of cultural ideals and ethical codes. Freud argued that the two are interlocked, but that:

> the mental processes concerned are actually more familiar to us and more accessible to consciousness in the group than they can be in the individual man. In him, when tension arises, it is only the noisiness of the superego which, in the form of reproaches, lets itself noisily be heard: its actual demands often remain unconscious in the background. If we bring them to conscious knowledge we find that they coincide with the precepts of the prevailing cultural super-ego (1961 (1930), p. 89).

---

[4] Freud's understanding that civilization is costly is not unique to him. For example, in his rather different system of thought Durkheim, too, spoke of the "need for restraint" and the "limitations imposed by the discipline" of the social order. See especially his *Moral Education* (1925), excerpted in Thompson (1989).

[5] Freud's analysis of female socialization has been criticized by many, including female analysts of his own day and recent feminists, e.g., Karen Horney (1967), Melanie Klein (1984), Nancy Chodorow (1975), and Jane Flax (1989).

For Freud, then, individuals suffer conflict within themselves and with civilization. The desire for community can be achieved only through the restrictions imposed by culture.

The Triumph of Therapeutic Culture

For Philip Rieff, a major sociological interpreter of Freud, this description of ambivalence at the core of human nature is Freud's major contribution. For, unlike previous conceptions of a divided self in Greek and Christian cultures, Freud did not judge the warring factions. Freud did not believe that human nature is "fallen" nor did he see the superego as "above" the id and ego. For psychoanalysis, the "modern project" was to free the individual from guilt—punishment by the superego. For Rieff, the success of this project, in the "triumph of the therapeutic," has been "the defeat of culture," culture here meaning traditional moral authority that was the source of feelings of guilt. Used in this way, what does the concept of culture entail?

The common use of the term "culture" to describe a people's whole way of life includes a range of behaviors and norms, as well as material objects. Culture in psychoanalytic theory is narrowly construed as moral culture, the cultural proscriptions that restrict and inhibit the behavior of individuals. It distinguishes between "maximalist" cultures (those with many rules and proscriptions) and "minimalist" cultures (those that tolerate a wide array of behavior).

We see an example of a maximalist culture in Lynn Davidman's book, *Tradition in a Rootless World,* about Jewish women returning to orthodoxy. A rabbi explaining to a group of women why they might want to observe the rules of a kosher kitchen tells them: "[T]he bottom line of Judaism is the sanctity of life. Keeping kosher is a way of beginning to *limit* the life you eat" (1991, p. 138, emphasis ours). Orthodox Judaism is a maximalist culture with rules that govern many aspects of daily behavior. Keeping a kosher kitchen is one example. The rabbi uses the word "limits" in the same way that Rieff does when he talks about the essence of culture being that it puts limits on what is permitted to us for whom, as humans, all things are possible.

Critics like Rieff (and Christopher Lasch, discussed below) see the last hundred years as a period when western cultures have moved from maximalism to minimalism. Traditional moral authorities such as the churches and parents no longer have or, in many cases, want, the power to make rules and enforce them. There is a sense in which, compared to other eras, almost anything goes. Rieff and Lasch argue that this new freedom has released the contemporary middle class from the excesses of guilt that were part of the Victorian bourgeois childhood of Freud's youth, but that the current lack of restrictions has been pushed to the point that individuals and society no longer have any direction.

For Freud and Rieff culture provides the "limitations" that are necessary to give shape and direction to human activity. Yet culture is not just a set of rules; cultures also provide symbolic systems with forms for expressing the forbidden desires, e.g. rituals that invert the social order, exalting the lowly and lowering the exalted, and art which through sublimation is expressive and repressive at the same time. Culture, then, is the set of controls and releases. Both Rieff and Freud studied the tension between them.

Rieff explains that Greek and Christian philosophers had argued that individual fulfillment came through positive identification with the symbol systems and the subordination of the self to the social order: The healthy person and the good citizen were the same, and the therapeutic and the moral were connected. However, in the emerging social order of industrial society individuals were integrated into the society through economic interdependencies. The mechanisms through which the social order was bound together changed dramatically. Freud's theories worked for individuals living in the new order in societies that no longer demanded their sacrifices in the old way.

For Freud, psychoanalysis represented a departure from the past in part because the therapist did not (as the priest had) stand for the culture or reinforce the legitimacy of the traditional authorities. Instead, Freud believed, psychoanalysis provided a way for the individual to come to understand his/her own authority (Rieff 1966, p. 77). The person in analysis is supposed to learn "that particular style of detachment in which his individuality can function within a greater range of alternatives and yet do so with a more conscious set of limitations" (1966, p. 75).

Rieff argues that the modern project destroyed religious culture, *based in interdiction* (rules), and replaced it with a therapeutic culture *based in relations*. For Rieff, meaning and direction come from the ability to set limits, and the replacement of a maximalist culture by a minimalist culture destroys the possibilities of order, morality and truth. In a fascinating essay on the trial of Oscar Wilde, which Rieff portrays as a conflict between moral and aesthetic standards, Rieff argues that "repression is truth" (1991, p. 279). Modern individuals have only "the new criteria of the well and ill, interesting and uninteresting" (1991, p. 320). He explains:

> A culture in crisis favors the growth of individuality...Hypothetically, if a culture could grow to full crisis then everything could be expressed and nothing would be true. To prevent the expression of everything: that is the irreducible function of culture (1991, p. 279).

This understanding of culture is both elitist and public. It is public in its focus on the expression of norms and values in the public sphere, not on private behavior. In Rieff's view, culture is the rules, not what people actually do.

Rieff notes that one of the ways that guardians protect a culture is by maintaining a separation between public and private worlds. For example, consider the relatively "maximal" culture of fundamentalist Christians: The rule that "wives are submissive to their husbands" shapes the public culture, and it is regarded as appropriate that men hold the leadership positions.

However, in private women exercise power in many ways (Neitz 1987; Rose 1987; McNamara 1985). For the guardians of the culture to create some way of checking to make sure that women are submissive in every context (and punishing those who were not) would be self-defeating: not only would it be a lot of trouble for the guardians, but it would probably result in a loss to the community of the creative energies of the women.

In somewhat similar ways ritual and art—not only high culture but popular genres such as romance novels and horror films—provide forms that translate between the public and private, sometimes offering remissions that serve the culture. As Rieff has stated, "For the very life of every culture depends upon its powers to mask and transform private motive into something very different, even opposite, when it appears in public" (1991, p. 282).

This understanding of culture is elitist in the sense that it requires a cultural elite, which may be identical with the social elite, but may also be separate or even opposed to the social and political elites. The cultural elite expresses, even embodies, moral demands in a maximalist culture (Rieff 1966, pp. 246–249).

Ironically, as Rieff himself recognizes, therapeutic culture—a minimalist culture—itself has been carried by an elite. By the end of the twentieth century, however, therapeutic culture has undergone a remarkable diffusion. No longer is it primarily situated in intimate relationships between therapists and patients. Rather, self-awareness movements and a small industry reproduce the therapeutic culture through self-help books, workshops, seminars, tapes and videos and distribute them to a mass audience. Therapeutic culture looked liberating when it was the culture of avant-garde intellectuals and artists in rebellion against rule bounded bourgeois culture. However, some critics now wonder to what extent those old rules created feelings of responsibility for others and a work ethic, both of which are floundering in the current moral climate.

The Democratization of Therapeutic Culture

Christopher Lasch (1978, 1984) looks to psychoanalytic theory to explain not the guilt of the Victorian bourgeois, but the narcissism of twentieth-century managers, artists, academics and others. His most popular book, *The Culture of Narcissism,* can be read a sequel to Rieff's *The Triumph of the Therapeutic.* Lasch addresses the democratization of the therapeutic culture through personal growth and self-awareness movements of recent times. Unlike others who have offered a critique of the self-awareness movements, Lasch sees the movements themselves as a sign of the problem, not the problem itself. Why is it, he asks, that people have so much trouble sustaining relationships? Why is the divorce rate so high? Why do so many fathers fail to support their children? We might add, what kind of society produces a situation where children take an elderly parent to the dog track and then abandon

FIGURE 2.1 These illustrations from grade school text books demonstrate changes in American culture. In the *Dick and Jane* stories the happy middle class family has rigid gender roles. *America Will Be* shows the value of diversity.

Dick said, "Look, Mother.
See what we can make.
Guess who this is."

"Guess who this is," said Jane.

"Guess who this is," said Sally.
"And see the two little ones.
Guess who.
Guess who."

(*Source:* The New York Public Library Picture Collection.)

► Dark rye bread came from northern Europe.

▲ Greek and Syrian immigrants brought pita bread to America.

▼ American Indians baked corn bread long before Europeans arrived in America.

► French bread came with French immigrants to New Amsterdam (New York) and North Carolina in the 1600s.

You may not know that words you use every day have come from other cultures. The word *kindergarten* is German, meaning "children's garden." *Cookie* comes from Holland. *Mosquito* is Spanish. *Corral*, a place where horses are kept, comes from the African word *kraal*. Early settlers in the Western United States learned the word

UNDERSTANDING CULTURE

*I*mmigrants to the United States often begin living just like other Americans. They buy the clothing, furniture, and foods used by their native-born neighbors. In this way immigrants come to feel that they share in the culture of America.

Similar Cultures

Culture is the way of life shared by a group of people. For example, many Japanese people share similar ideas about how a person should behave. These beliefs have been handed down from generation to generation. They are cultural beliefs.

A group of people who share a culture often live in the same area. However, people who live in the same area do not always have the same culture. If the people in an area do not share the same beliefs, outlooks, and values, they do not have the same culture.

Pluralistic Cultures

Pluralistic cultures are made up of many subcultures, or cultures within a culture. For example, Japanese immigrants may practice Japanese customs while still being part of American culture.

People who are part of a culture have a sense of belonging. Even in America, with its pluralism, people share many beliefs and want many of the same things in life.

Figure 2.2 (*Source:* Photograph by Ralph J. Brunke from *America Will Be* in *Houghton Mifflin Social Studies* by Beverly J. Armento, et al. Copyright © 1991 by Houghton Mifflin Company. Reprinted by permission of Houghton Mifflin Company.)

him there?[6] Lasch sees the "devastation of personal life" as a fact of life in advanced capitalist society.

Some have explained the therapeutic modality—and especially its democratization in the rise of the self-awareness movement—by post-war affluence and leisure which provided money and time for the pursuit of the self. Lasch resists such an explanation. He suggests that the therapeutic attitude is a typical middle class attempt to apply typical middle-class problem-solving techniques (education, self help) to a significant problem (the collapse of personal life).

In order to explain the collapse of personal life, Lasch considers many factors—among them the growth of bureaucracy and technology, and the collapse of liberalism—but he analytically separates these long-term trends from the more recent growth of narcissism. Lasch suggests that this psychological condition and the link between it and recent changes in social relations hold the key to understanding the moral crisis in the U.S.

Early psychoanalysts wrote mostly about "primary" narcissism, a normal stage in the development of the infant. Modern writers—Lasch included—tend to be more concerned about "secondary" narcissism, a pathological condition occurring at a later stage in development. Infants must learn to separate themselves from the mother. Before this is accomplished, infants confuse dependence upon the mother (who satisfies their needs) with omnipotence. This is primary narcissism. As infants mature they perceive that they and their mothers are separate, that the need is within the self and that the source of satisfaction is outside of it. In secondary narcissism (due to some trauma in the separation from the mother, the theory claims) the child's disappointed love (and rage at those who do not seem to respond to his or her needs) is turned back upon the self. The child compensates by creating a grandiose self, merging images of an omnipotent parent with images of the self. Later on, in adulthood, the narcissistic person may be unable to distinguish between these self images and the objects of his or her feeling which are outside of the self. In addition, the preservation of archaic images of the parents in the self makes it impossible for the person to synthesize "good" and "bad" parental images. Therefore, "good" and "bad" images of the self (and of objects) are kept quite separate. Threatened by bad images (i.e., aggressive feelings of rage and envy) the person compensates with fantasies of omnipotence. These exaggerated good and bad images also become a part of the grandiose self. In short, the formation of the self is disrupted in the narcissistic condition.

The result, in psychoanalytic terms, is not the neurosis familiar in Freudian days (i.e., hysteria and obsessional neurosis) but rather character disorders (sometimes referred to as borderline personality disorder). Despite illusions of omnipotence, the narcissist needs others to validate his or her grandiose self. This twentieth-century condition differs from that of the nineteenth-century

---

[6] This actual story made the news in April of 1992, but it reflects more generally the serious problems facing the society regarding care for the aged.

individualist. In Lasch's view, "For the narcissist the world is a mirror, whereas the rugged individualist saw it as an empty wilderness to be shaped to his own design" (1978, p. 10).

Drawing heavily on recent theories of narcissism, Lasch (1978, pp. 37–40) has put together the following catalog of characteristics of a narcissist: Vague, diffuse dissatisfaction with life; feelings of futility and purposelessness; emptiness and depression; the experience of wild oscillations of self-esteem and a general inability to maintain meaningful human relationships; heightened self-esteem coming only through attachment to a strong admired figure from whom acceptance is craved; the tendency to act out impulses rather than to repress or sublimate them; the tendency to cultivate a protective shallowness in emotional relations, and to be sexually promiscuous, even polymorphously perverse. The narcissist finds it difficult to play, to have close involvements, or to mourn. Although the narcissist can get along in the world (and may be a charming person) his or her devaluation of others and lack of curiosity reinforce feelings of emptiness and an impoverished inner life. The narcissist lacks engagement with the world and has little capacity for sublimation (the modification of instinctual urges and expression of them in socially acceptable ways). Self-esteem is dependent upon the constant approval of others. Yet fear of emotional dependence and fear of commitment, together with a manipulative and exploitative approach to personal relations, makes these relations unsatisfying.

Lasch considers the psychoanalytic personality disorder of narcissism of such importance for two main reasons. First, he believes that changes in the prevalent form of pathology reflect changes in the society as a whole. For Lasch, narcissism is the psychological dimension of our increasing dependence on bureaucracy and on the state and corporations; just as we have grown dependent upon the society to meet our various practical and organizational needs, narcissism represents our dependence upon others for self-esteem (1978, p. 10). Second, current demands of the society actually put a premium on some narcissistic characteristics, giving narcissists a certain market value. Lasch suggests that there may be a certain fit between the narcissist and the demands of the social order:

> The narcissist rises to positions of prominence not only in awareness movements and other cults but in business corporations, political organizations, and government bureaucracies. For all his inner suffering, the narcissist has many traits that make for success in bureaucratic institutions which put a premium on the manipulation of interpersonal relations, discourage the formation of deep attachments and at the same time, provide the narcissist with the approval he needs in order to validate his self-esteem...(1978 pp. 43–44).

It is the apparent "success" of the narcissist in today's world that leads Lasch to postulate a "culture of narcissism." He moves from the discussion of individual pathology that is part of a limited discourse within the psychiatric community to the argument that American culture today supports and expresses narcissism. Just as Freud argued for a correspondence between the individual superego and the cultural superego, Lasch argues for a correspondence between the contents of individual narcissism and cultural narcissism.[7]

Lasch criticizes our "over-organized society." Depersonalizing bureaucracy and the intrusiveness of the "mechanical reproduction of culture, the proliferation of audio and visual images in the society of spectacle," along with the emergence of a therapeutic ideology reinforce the survival value of narcissism. Lasch also connects the growth of narcissism to the changing relation between workers and their work, embodied in the relocation of work from factories to offices. When people feel no personal responsibility for an end product and style is more important than what one actually does, doing good work ceases to be a source of self-esteem. What counts is recognition by others. Lasch sees the roots of contemporary narcissism in the deterioration of the work ethic which, he argues, no longer makes sense—it does not offer the key to "success"—in the contexts in which most people work. Furthermore, Lasch argues, the changing definition of success at work has had repercussions for leisure, which is now more tied to consumption. These changes in the nature of work and play have strained other institutions, particularly family life and education, which, Lasch argues, used to provide some distance between the individual and the economy.

There are many parallels in the arguments of these social critics. Bellah and his co-authors as well as Rieff and Lasch formulate social life in terms of an essential antagonism between the desires of the individual and the demands of the culture. They all describe a moral crisis in the U.S. today related to the growth of a therapeutic culture that allows the expression of individual desires to such an extent that moral culture is undermined.

The social critics analyzed here do not see the main *source* of the problems they describe in the motives and behaviors of individuals. Although they have sometimes been misread in this way, they do not believe that the problems of moral culture can be resolved by simply exhorting the American population to be better people, to be less selfish, for example. Lasch explicitly refutes this common misinterpretation of his work (e.g., 1984, p. 19). In fact, one problem they see in expressive individualism is that it espouses a degree of choice that people in fact do not have. They hold that changes in the division of labor and the development of bureaucracy are among the causes of modernity, and it is modernity itself which fails to support commitment. Like

---

[7] The psychiatric community is not unanimous in agreeing with Lasch's interpretation of the meaning of the change in the predominant form of pathology, but they do seem to agree that they are seeing fewer neurotics and more people with character disorders. Some psychoanalysts are unwilling to generalize to the degree Lasch does with this data (see Lasch 1978, p. 35). For other possible interpretations of the rise in the number of cases of narcissism and borderline personality disorders being reported by psychiatrists, see 1978, pp. 43–44.

the therapy Rieff describes, their writings foster an understanding of the problems created by modernity, but few solutions.

Part of the attraction of psychoanalysis is that it captures so well the internal tension in people's experience between immediate wants and desires and their sense of what is socially beneficial or morally good. Freud departed from earlier formulations of this tension in that he argued that the repression of desire could have harmful effects. He said that culture (the rules of society) can be overly punitive. Yet by defining culture largely in terms of its rules and negative sanctions, psychoanalysis helped to promote the imbalance that critics like Freud and Lasch now find threatening.

What does the approach of Bellah and his colleagues add to the discussion? Early on they state the main purpose of their book: "to deepen our understanding of the resources our tradition provides—and fails to provide—to enable us to think about the moral problems we are currently facing as Americans" (1985, p. 21). By choosing to use the language of individualism rather than psychoanalysis, the authors have attempted to put us in touch—*through the very language of the discussion itself*—with particular American rhetorical traditions. In the act of analyzing the American discourse on moral action they are also promoting a discourse. They deeply desire more serious discussion of moral issues. In order to discover resources for combatting the dangers of individualism they explore its roots in the biblical and republican traditions, and look to see how those traditions—as well as expressive and utilitarian individualism—are present today. They attempt to recover a connection to the past and express that connection in the substance of their critique.[8]

The understandings offered by all of these critics, however, may be based on unnecessarily limited conceptions that pose an opposition between character and culture, and between traditional communities and modern societies. There are other theoretical approaches to moral culture. One approach comes out of feminist theory and sees the person in relation to the culture and society rather than—as we find with the critique of individualism and psychoanalysis—in opposition. The other approach suggests that rather than rules and sanctions, moral culture is defined by concrete practices—stories, rituals, expressions—that create ties between people in communities of various kinds. In rejecting the assumptions of the Freudian theory of culture and the critique of individualism, these two approaches begin to recast the discussion of moral culture.

MORAL CULTURE AND NARRATIVE

Alternative sources exist for talking about the self, community, and moral culture. One such source is in social movements. Feminists, for example, are beginning to articulate an ethics based on practices of caring. One strand of

---

[8] We will assess the success of this part of their project below.

contemporary feminist theory posits a model of the self that is connected to others as opposed to the model of the self as separate and autonomous. In addition, the notion that modernity has been characterized by a linear move from community to society with increasing autonomy for the individual may reflect the experience of men more than women.[9]

Nancy Chodorow (1978) argued that this connected or relational self develops out of the early childhood experiences. Males must develop their gender identity in households where "women mother" and fathers are largely absent. Boys therefore establish their gender identity by becoming "not female." Girls identify with their mothers, who are present and with whom they remain in relation. They never separate in the extreme ways that boys must. Gilligan's (1982) work on moral development showed girls with "connected selves" working through moral choices in ways that are markedly different from the prevailing models developed with male subjects. Subsequent work has emphasized that the observed differences in behavior are not due to some essential characteristic of women (even one that is based in nearly universal early childhood experiences) but rather comes out of a particular context.

Conceptualizing the Self-in-Relation

The notion of the separate and autonomous individual is central to political theorists from Thomas Hobbes in seventeenth-century England to the contemporary philosopher John Rawls. Social contract theory is based upon a set of premises about the actions of free and autonomous men. In this tradition, morality (and justice) resides in the individuals' observance of the contract. The nurturance of women is not seen as "moral," in part because it is assumed to be "natural."

While it may seem that the therapeutic culture, based as it is in social relationships, acts against this separateness, Bellah and his colleagues suggest that in American society utilitarian individualism has become "allied with" expressive culture. In this therapeutic culture, healthy persons follow their own plans for self-fulfillment based on subjective evaluations of individual preferences, and the "coolly manipulative style of management" is brought into intimate relationships (1985, p. 48).[10]

Psychological theories of moral development glorified this separation, placing the achievement of autonomy at the top of their maturation scales. Freud is not the only one who found women less individuated, and therefore, possessing a less developed sense of justice: Carol Gilligan's work began with her puzzlement that males always seemed to come out "at a higher stage of

---

[9] See Hartsock 1983 for a critique of the dominant interpretation.

[10] The work on the culture of narcissism offers an even more ominous interpretation: By definition the narcissist is unable to establish connections, but he or she has not really succeeded in establishing an autonomous self, either.

development" in the studies of her teacher, Lawrence Kohlberg (1981). In commenting on Kohlberg's studies she notes a paradox: "the very traits that traditionally defined the 'goodness' of women: their care for and sensitivity to the needs of others, are those that mark them as deficient in moral development" (1982, p. 18). Gilligan went on to describe a different path to moral development based on what she calls an "ethic of care," as opposed to Kohlberg's "ethic of rights."

Both Kohlberg and Gilligan used a research methodology in which they presented people of various ages—most often adolescents—a set of hypothetical dilemmas and then asked them what they would do. Kohlberg formulated the problem of Heinz: Heinz's wife is dying and needs a drug that Heinz cannot afford to buy for her. Kohlberg asked the participants in the study if Heinz should steal the drug to save his wife. Males tended to weigh the rights of the pharmacist to receive money against the rights of the wife to life. Females, on the other hand, Gilligan found, were less likely to accept the terms of the problem. For example, Gilligan cites one participant who sees the problem as the druggist: If the druggist knew that Heinz's wife would die without the drug he would surely give her the drug (1982, pp. 26–29).

On the basis of tests like this one Gilligan came to argue for the "different moral voice" of the women she had studied. She saw three ways that the ethic of care differed from moral development as described by Kohlberg. First, it emphasizes responsibility and relationship instead of rights and obligations. Second, Gilligan argued that it employed a form of moral reasoning that is concrete and contextual rather than formal and abstract. Third, it is not a set of abstract principles but rather is made up of activities and daily practices.

In Gilligan's studies females moved from an early "selfish" stage to an overly altruistic stage. The developmental task for the women in Gilligan's study was to achieve a position where they could take their own interests into account as much as anyone else. A mature person, according to the ethic of care, recognizes her connection to others and theirs to her, and at the same time can articulate her own wants and needs. Gilligan writes that, "Morality is seen by these women as arising from the experience of connection and conceived as a problem of inclusion rather than one of balancing claims" (1982, p. 160).

While Gilligan's theory came out of a critique of Kohlberg's universalizing a male model, a number of writers have questioned whether it truly describes a female morality. In addition, Tronto has argued that an "ethic of care" should not be regarded as a "separate but equal" morality. She suggests that the notion that there is a "women's morality" is especially dangerous for our culture: Rather than opening up alternatives such a distinction could serve to reify differences between men and women. She claims the ethic of care should be developed as "an alternative moral theory, rather than simply as a complement to traditional moral theories based on justice reasoning" (1987, p. 663).

There is some evidence, for example, that members of other subordinate groups behave much like the females in Gilligan's study (Tronto 1987, pp. 649–651). In these contexts as well there is an emphasis on context, and on relations between people. Here we rarely find the individual portrayed as the isolated person, separate and autonomous, released from the bonds of community, not captured by society but doing his job and riding off into the sunset.

Gilligan's work and the controversies that have arisen around it have stimulated an alternative discourse about moral culture: Developmental psychologists, philosophers, sociologists and others are talking about a form of moral reasoning that is contextual rather than universalistic, and that is embedded in relationships. The different voice that Gilligan has made it possible for us to hear differs not only from the voices of Lawrence Kohlberg's subjects, but also from the "individualistic voices" Bellah and his colleagues found.

Gilligan, like Freud, develops her understanding of moral culture in the context of theory about human development. For both of them, however, the ramifications of their understandings of culture do not hinge on our acceptance of the various stages of their developmental models. Gilligan allows us to consider a model of culture in which the individual exists in relation to her community, rather than caught in a conflict between self and society. She also suggests that culture is not rules, but rather is activities, practices, and contextualized interpretations. This latter is similar to an understanding of culture that challenges the emphasis on rules characteristic of Durkheim and Parsons, as well as Bellah and Freud.

Constitutive Narratives

One of the criticisms about American culture in *Habits of the Heart* is that Americans talk individualism as our "first language." We lack resources for talking about moral issues—we have no meaningful concepts or rhetorical devices for conferring legitimacy on commitments to others. Yet people do make commitments. Bellah and his associates admit that "second languages" exist, languages of "tradition and commitment." These languages can be found in "communities of memory":

> Communities, in the sense we are using the term, have a history—in an important sense they are constituted by their past—and for this reason we can speak of a real community as a "community of memory," one that does not forget its past. In order not to forget its past, a community is involved in retelling its story, its constitutive narrative...(1985, p. 153).

This constitutive narrative includes tales of exemplary individuals, as well as stories about the community's origin, its hopes and its fears. Community rituals also commemorate the past and make it meaningful in the present. In addition, community members are "socially interdependent,...participate together in discussion and decision making, and...share certain practices which both define the community and nurture it" (1985, p. 333).

This "strong form" of community is outside the experience of the mostly urban middle class Protestant people interviewed for the book. These people, unencumbered by commitments, live in "lifestyle enclaves" with other people like themselves: upper middle class singles in upscale urban apartment buildings; married people with children in suburban "neighborhoods," segregated by class and race; retirees in their "residential communities" of trailers or condos segregated by class. If communities of memory can be found, the authors suggest it might be in ethnic and racial communities, and among some religious communities. Other people—the majority—lack a community with a constitutive memory. *Habits of the Heart* recognizes the importance of narrative as a resource for moral culture, but argues it is inaccessible for most Americans.

The philosopher Alasdair MacIntyre (1984) has argued persuasively that moral arguments only make sense to people when the claims are embedded in a narrative framework. It is narrative that links actor and community, intentions and acts. Bellah and his colleagues seem to be arguing that Americans can only find these frameworks through recovery of our roots. Yet what MacIntyre and others are arguing is that moral culture is about making sense of our lives, and that this making sense is done not by referring to abstract principles and rules but rather in contextualized interpretations that take the form of narratives.

Sara Ruddick (1989) describes how, at a very basic level, families develop their own constitutive narratives. In doing so she shows that families can exhibit some of the characteristics that Bellah and his colleagues (1985) find in communities of memory, and one way that strong families provide their members with resources for transcending the self. Knowing oneself to be connected to (even in debt to) previous generations and believing that this obligation can be met only by preserving one's heritage for future generations is another example of transcending individualism. It is not mentioned in *Habits of the Heart,* which has little to say about relations between parents and children. Yet mothers use narratives when they tell stories to their children as part of the process of "nurturing a child's developing spirit."

Ruddick suggests that mothers often tell their children stories about themselves, and that through such stories "a mother creates for herself and her children the confidence that her children have a life that is very much their own and inextricably bound up with others" (1989, p. 98). She identifies the virtues of mothers' stories: realism, compassion and delight. Ruddick posits that with realist stories children learn trust; with compassionate stories children learn sympathy; and when their mothers' stories show delighted admiration for their normal accomplishments children learn generosity (pp. 98–101). In the nurturing of children, independence is tempered by relationship. The stories that mothers tell their children show both.

Ruddick argues that learning the virtues of good story telling (and becoming adept) is itself a social process learned within communities of mothers. The stories themselves no doubt show subtle differences reflecting the experiences of mothers in different local communities. This kind of "moral teaching" is accomplished through the links that mothers have with each other and with their children.

Bellah and his colleagues (1985) put little emphasis on how parents (or teachers) transmit traditions and values from generation to generation.[11] In part this is because they yearn for an American moral culture and a "national community" (1985, p. 153). Their arguments exhibit tension between their acknowledgment of the power of local communities ("communities of memory") and their desire for a cohesive national culture. Even though the idea a "national community" contradicts their strong definition of community, cited above, it is in line with their view of a hegemonic Protestant past:

> For a long time our society was held together, even in periods of rapid change, by a largely Protestant cultural center that sought to reconcile the claims of community and individuality. Rejecting both chaotic openness and authoritarian closure, representatives of this cultural center defended tradition—some version of the civic republican and biblical traditions—but not traditionalism.... That task has become increasingly difficult...(1985, p. 155).

This hope for a coherent American culture is at odds with the general argument of the book regarding the thinness of cultural resources available to most Americans in relation to the density of the tradition offered by communities of memory. The nostalgia for a "national culture"—an elite, largely Protestant, cultural center—also neglects an important thesis of Tocqueville. For him it is participation in institutions and voluntary associations (middle range organizations that may span several communities but do not constitute a national culture) that counters the destructive tendencies of individualism.

Furthermore, in the opposition between communities of memory and lifestyle enclaves, Bellah and his colleagues underestimate the degree to which other kinds of communities—communities of choice—provide resources that support Americans in their moral commitments and ethical stands. *Communities of choice can also be communities of memory.* In the United States, religious groups—frequently chosen by the participants—offer many examples of the development and elaboration of constitutive narratives by people who certainly make up communities of memory. Neitz (1987) and Davidman (1991), for example, provide us with the extreme example of converts who form such communities. In a modern pluralist society individuals who belong to such communities frequently are there because of their own *choice.* Within such communities individuals adopt "elective parochialism." For the pastor of an evangelical Presbyterian congregation, "parochialism was, ironically, a general philosophy: Pay attention to the here and now. He called it 'working with the given'" (Warner 1988a, p. 203). In a large Charismatic Catholic prayer group people used the

---

[11] But see 1985, p. 154.

language of individualism, of self love, with the understanding that through self love they could better serve the group (Neitz 1987, p. 280).

R. Stephen Warner argues that in the United States "community" is rarely simply given:

> The freedom of Americans to choose with whom they will congregate in service of their most basic values is a freedom not to "pass" as biological kin but to partake as full legatees of the traditions which themselves add depth and richness to the associations. Literate converts to a religion of the book have immediate access to its holy writ...The religious groups I have seen working the best...are those that recognize the mobility of their memberships and bring them into contact with great cultural traditions by incessantly and elaborately recounting the founding myth (1988b, p. 38).

What makes a community is cultural, and culture seen not in terms of acceptance of a set of rules, but rather participating in the rituals, knowing the stories and passing them on to others. Commitment to others is based in particular practices in specific communities. What Bellah and his colleagues describe as a "'second language' of commitment" may well be a local dialect, one reason that it is not always apparent to sociological researchers.

Beyond Individualism versus Commitment

Sociological theory often has presented the transition to modernity as a linear one from communal to societal modes of organization. In reality, John Hewitt suggests that "the modern world is one in which community and society are locked in tenacious and perpetual tension" (1989, p. 109). In everyday usage "society" is spoken of as constraining and coercive. Unlike the more political concept of the nation, it is a social structural idea: "Society" encloses communities and provides the context in which they exist.

Hewitt claims that the imagery of "community" has changed as well. While some communities are still territorial, he sees more of a new understanding of community that removes it from local boundaries. He claims:

> As human beings come to live in society...the field of activities extends beyond the geographical horizon...the possible scope of social relationships widens which is partly why modern people have found it necessary to differentiate community from society, seeing the latter as the wider field on which they operate and the former as a sheltering home...(1989, p. 115.)

Many people want both the intimacy of community and the anonymity of society: each is constraining in its own way, but each offers us something of value. Confronted by choice we feel ambivalent—an ambivalence that may continue even after we have chosen.

A parallel sociological debate focuses on inherent tensions of modern social life between role and person. Role relations in modern society are specific rather than diffuse—roles tend to be more contractual than perhaps they were in the past. However, over time, people may take on more diffuse obligations so that co-workers may become friends. Hewitt stresses that despite the destruction of many of the organic communities of the past something endures—"the human propensity to construct and live in a world of concrete particularity, of contact with whole persons and not simply with roles…" (p. 120). He suggests that we need to conceive of modernity as involving not simple transformations but rather a contrast "between the organic communities that have sheltered (and oppressed) individuals, and a new larger world of society in which new forms of community…come into being" (p. 121). What is important in his formulation is that he sees individuals both pursuing their personal goals in society and making commitments to community. Hewitt offers "not a Freudian image of a human organism whose biological instincts are pitted against civilization, but a pragmatic conception of a symbolic creature who in gaining a self also acquires a taste for freedom" (1989, p. 126). These tensions between self-interest and commitment to others are demonstrated in a recent study of volunteers.

In an attempt to test empirically the arguments of the critics who see a resurgence of individualism as the dominant trend of the last quarter of the twentieth century, Robert Wuthnow has studied volunteer activities in America. *Acts of Compassion* (1991) uses both survey data on volunteering and extensive interviews with volunteers to address what Americans do and how they explain it to themselves and others. Among those he surveyed, Wuthnow found that most people value caring and volunteer their services in some context. He also found that most put strict limits on how much of themselves they give to those outside of their immediate circle.

As Bellah and his colleagues suggest, Wuthnow found that Americans do speak the language of individualism. However, individualism was only one of several languages that people used to explain their motives for engaging in volunteer work. When he paid close attention to the actual talk of the people interviewed he found that people tend to use the language of self-fulfillment in a formulaic way: "it is a socially acceptable way of bringing closure to a story" (1991, p. 94). Americans' use of the rhetoric of individualism does not necessarily mean the breakdown of community. Ironically, Wuthnow found that among his sample, individuals are more likely to use the language of individualism to mean non-conformity: They believe their caring activities to be deviant within American culture. The talk of themselves as non-conforming individuals should be seen as part of the narrative they use to explain their behavior in service to others.

CONCLUSION

The literature on moral culture reveals a discourse about the nature of the self. We see evidence of the language of individualism but there is also evidence of a language of connection. The discourse includes images of both community and society. However, at least some of the evidence suggest that Americans have difficulty talking about justice and equality. It is also the case that the many available languages of self and motivation do not talk about power conflicts nor about the state. Perhaps the two are connected.

People tell narratives about Mother Teresa or about Martin Luther King. People do not tell narratives about the local WIC (Women, Infants and Children) program, even though it offers important care, feeding mothers and their children. To the extent that moral culture is embedded in narrative, how is moral discourse possible in a society based in mass culture, bureaucracy, and a strong state? Languages of morality fail if they only address private concerns. Yet to say that language of moral culture is particular does not necessarily imply that it must be parochial (Warner 1988a). Furthermore, to argue that it is not a lack of rules, per se, that is the problem, is not the same as saying that there are no problems: clearly we need to look for ways to strengthen local communities and develop our moral languages.

The themes raised in this chapter demonstrate a narrowing between the ways that humanists are thinking about moral categories and the ways that some social scientists are thinking about culture (Addleson 1990). One point of convergence is the growing emphasis on narrative in both the humanities and the social sciences. Another point of convergence is a greater attention to texts of all kinds as constructions. A third point of potential convergence to be explored is the relation between symbolic acts (what is expressed) and rules about what can and cannot be expressed—Rieff's concept of remissions. The new scholarship in cultural studies (from both those in the humanities and those in the social sciences) contends that understanding how things get expressed is integral to understanding what is expressed. These themes will be explored further in the chapters to follow.

Once we begin to talk about narrative and texts as constructed, however, the critical question becomes whose story is being told, who is constructing the texts. We begin to explore this question in chapter three by looking at how the dramatic changes brought about by industrialization and urbanization led to new attempts to understand the past and the present. We discuss the development of the analytic concept of culture—as well as ideas about "community" and "society"—and show how the use of those concepts to analyze folk and traditional culture was deeply embedded in the western scholars' own contexts.

3

DECONSTRUCTING FOLK CULTURE

Our understanding of what it means to analyze culture has been shaped by attempts to analyze the cultures of smaller, more homogenous societies of other times and places. Yet our conceptions of those societies have been strongly influenced by the western experience of modernity. The nineteenth-century social scientists who introduced the term *culture* into English usage approached their subject in ways shaped by their own society and culture. Dramatic social changes wrought by industrialization and urbanization led to new attempts to understand both the past and the present. In one nineteenth-century development, the romantic movement looked backward with nostalgia for a "simpler past" and nurtured an intense interest in folk life and national traditions.[1] Social Darwinists in the nineteenth century, on the other hand, applied the idea of evolution to societies and developed an evolutionary hierarchy with western civilization at the top and primitive culture at the bottom. For both the romantics and the social Darwinists, the attempt to establish the notion of culture as an analytic construct developed out of concerns for the changes taking place within mod-

---

[1] E.B. Tyler is usually credited with being the first to introduce the word culture into English usage, in his work *Primitive Society* (1871). The idea, however was familiar to those who knew German where the celebration of the "volk" was very much a part of the romantic movement to reclaim a traditional agrarian past, "purer" spiritually because it was uncontaminated by the customs (and genes) of other ethnic groups.

FIGURE 3.1 The artist of this early woodcut, ca 1505, never visited the Americas but based his images on a description by Vespucci. He features his subjects practicing cannibalism and open sexuality, dresses them in feathers and gives them beards. (*Source:* The New York Public Library Picture Collection.)

ern societies. The notion of traditional or "folk" culture, like the *Gemeinschaft* (community) to which it was intimately related, developed as an ideal type to be paired with (and contrasted to) the modern culture of the *Gesellschaft* (society).

For anthropologists, who used the concept of culture earlier than sociologists, to speak of a "culture" implied a whole way of life. In a lecture given at the University of Chicago in 1939 Robert Redfield talked about how, returning from fieldwork among isolated primitive people, he found it odd to hear sociologists refer to different neighborhoods of Chicago as different "culture areas." The following remarks of Redfield's are telling:

> …(A)nthropologists commonly use the terms "community," "society," and "culture" interchangeably; while the distinctions among the concepts may be of significance in dealing with the modern urbanized and industrialized societies, in using them with reference to primitive societies there is often no need felt to make them, for the reason that there the group of people who live physically together are the same people who share those common understandings we call culture, and they are very nearly the same people who produce and consume their own goods…(1940, p. 739).

For the many anthropologists of Redfield's generation who studied traditional ways of life in small, often remote, societies, "culture" was how the society was organized.

In the same essay Redfield noted the methodological implications of this understanding of culture: he explained that in a stable folk society, sampling is unnecessary. Given that the anthropologists understood the culture to be ubiquitous and that roles were undifferentiated, one informant could tell all that the anthropologist needed to know: "What one adult male knows is enough like what the others know to make it possible to learn much about the whole society from no more than a single case" (1940, p. 740).

Scholars today who are aware of the biases in the original anthropological formulations of the concept of culture may still want to use some concept to talk about the ways that certain cultures of specific groups are meaningfully different from cultures of modern industrialized societies. For example, how is it that some aspects of a culture will differ from ours if the society is small enough so that social norms are enforced almost entirely through face to face interaction? What if the society is homogenous? How are cultural forms different if they are not subject to commodity exchanges in economic markets?

We need to ask if there is some way that we can legitimately continue to use the concept of "traditional" or "folk" culture as a comparative benchmark for how culture works in some generic sense. This chapter reflects a tension between two sorts of knowledge: We know about empirical shifts in daily life activities and the ways that people think about themselves and their worlds that have taken place with the emergence of the modern world economy and the advent of industrialization, yet this knowledge co-exists with our sense of the inadequacy of the concepts that scholars have most often used to talk about those shifts. This chapter offers fundamental criticisms of those concepts. We begin with a brief review of how this topic has been approached by social scientists. We then trace in detail how assumptions about religion, meaning, and community solidarity are reflected in the use of the concept of ritual, as applied to "primitive" societies and as applied to modern society. Finally, we show how some current work on rituals challenges these assumptions.

CONCEPTUALIZING THE PAST AS A MIRROR OF THE PRESENT

The concept of traditional or folk culture is one half of a dichotomy, contrasting with its opposite, modernity. The characteristics attributed to traditional culture thus varied as the inverse of particular theorists' concerns about their own societies. Ferdinand Toennies and Emile Durkheim were primarily interested in community solidarity and the problem of how, with the decline of traditional community, individuals were (or were not) integrated into a common moral order. Max Weber focused more on the development of rationality and the routinization of social life in bureaucracy, and the parallel decline of religion. While the sociologists assumed that behind the "traditional society" they theorized about was a "primitive society," the anthropologists took it as their task to investigate the primeval state. Noted anthropologists—including Henry Maine, Louis Henry Morgan, E.B. Tyler and James G. Frazer—pursued a description of the original society. What they saw was an inversion of their own society:

> For them modern society was defined above all by the territorial state, the monogamous family, and private property. Primitive society therefore must have been nomadic, ordered by blood ties, sexually promiscuous and communist.... The pioneer anthropologists believed that their own was an age of massive transition. They looked back in order to understand the nature of the present, on the assumption that modern society had evolved out of its antithesis (Kuper 1988, p. 5).

Early societies were seen as tightly bounded communities. maintaining individuals' commitments to the social order. In comparison with modern cities, earlier forms of community appeared to experience little "social disorganization," and social control appeared to be "spontaneous."[2]

When anthropology moved from the armchair to the field, it was clear that there was a lack of fit between the ideal type of the primitive society and what anthropologists were observing. Truly primitive societies were hard to come by: Fewer and fewer had not experienced some encounter with the west, and, even when they could be found, the most isolated groups did not match the theory. In the 1930s anthropologist Robert Redfield puzzled about "intermediate societies" where religion and family are strong, crime rates are low, and yet members participate in a money economy and possibly see themselves as part of larger political and economic structures. This intermediate type more closely approximated what he had observed in the Mexican village he studied (Redfield 1930). For these intermediate groups—where local culture had adjusted to the civilization of the cities—Redfield offered the term "folk" society (1940: 735).

For Redfield, the contrast between folk and modern societies accomplished a number of goals. It provided theoretical grounds for extending the scope of anthropology: "If all the 'vanishing peoples' of the earth should indeed vanish, we would still have to study the acculturated people, the folk people changing under the impact of urban growth," Redfield maintained (1940, p. 742). He pushed for more than just a change in subject. He urged anthropologists to move from refining theoretical typologies to studying actual social processes, often with tendencies that opposed one another, in concrete cases of social change.

The notion of finding a pure conceptual contrast to modern society continued to be alluring, however. In anthropology, Lévi-Strauss's two forms of

---

[2] The word "spontaneous" comes from Redfield (1940, p. 737).

knowledge, the savage and the domesticated (mythical and magical thinking versus scientific thought) parallel the dichotomy between primitive and modern culture. Lévi-Strauss postulated these as two "strategic levels at which nature is accessible to scientific enquiry: one roughly adapted to that of perception and the imagination: the other at a remove from it" (cited in Goody 1977, p. 7). Lévi-Strauss characterized modern thought as scientific, abstract, and historical—as opposed to primitive thought which he described as concrete, magical, intuitive, atemporal and mythic.

Sociologists tended to work within a shorter time frame than anthropologists, looking at the relatively recent, and in some places on-going, transition to industrial society. In the period after World War II, Talcott Parsons influenced many students of modernization with his formulation of the "pattern variables." He argued that a set of five interrelated variables, taken together, distinguished between the value orientations of modern society and their opposites in traditional cultures. Parsons's association of modernity with rationalization and bureaucracy is evident in his choice of variables: achievement versus ascription; affectivity versus neutrality; orientation to self versus orientation to collectivity; diffuseness versus specificity; and universalism versus particularity (Parsons 1951, pp. 101–112). Although based on differences between western industrial and other societies noted by western observers, such dichotomies also serve to reify the observed differences, making them explanations of development. Parsons and his followers assumed that if they could describe modernization as the west experienced it, then they could predict how it would happen in the developing countries, and explain why some societies remained "undeveloped" (Rostow 1960; McClelland 1961).

By providing an abstract model, these dichotomies contributed to the theory-building efforts of several generations of sociologists and anthropologists. But the sweeping generalizations of these dichotomies have been challenged by empirical and theoretical work since the 1960s. These challengers have asked whether standard concepts of traditional and modern accurately portray either traditional or modern cultures. The switch from talking about traditional culture to traditional cultures (in the plural) suggests the more recent concern with understanding the specific conditions of particular groups instead of trying to develop a grand theory about primordial society or about modernization in general. The challengers have discovered self-interested rational peasants living in folk cultures (Popkin 1979) and bureaucrats in modernizing countries who maintain affective and particularistic commitments (Taub 1969). They have found that particularistic and ascriptive factors are important in the bureaucracies of modern societies (Blau 1955, Granovetter 1974). Yet intuition and observation tells us that there are meaningful differences between those cultures we might describe as "modern" and those we would describe as "traditional," even if the differences are not captured by the generalizations of the theories.

One response to this puzzle is to try to identify particular determining mechanisms that might give rise to the differences which the typologies attempted to describe. An important and identifiable difference is one based on forms of communication. There is a movement among anthropologists toward using as categories "oral" (or sometimes, "unlettered") cultures and "literate" cultures. Goody (1977, pp. 146–162) provides a rationale for doing so. For Goody, this conceptualization avoids a dichotomy, as cultures can be literate to different degrees. Furthermore, this distinction is based on things that are directly observable and is less eurocentric than some of the earlier ones.

The presence (and degree) of diffusion of writing has tremendous implications for any given culture, and oral cultures differ in important and systematic ways from literate ones. Not only does writing greatly increase the possibilities for the storage of culture, but it has another function which alters the nature of language. As Goody explains, writing "shifts language from the aural to the visual domain and makes possible a different kind of inspection, the re-ordering and refining not only of sentences but of individual words" (1977, p. 78). Thus writing makes possible not only the recording of oral traditions, but the development and elaboration of other forms of writing. Lists of various kinds—inventories of persons, objects, or events, guides to future action, inventories of concepts—permit higher degrees of abstraction and ordering. Indeed, three-quarters of the cuneiform inscriptions that have come down to us from the ancient middle east are administrative and bureaucratic records covering a wide geographical area and chronological period (Goody, 1977, p. 79).

Another possible way to measure the differences between premodern and modern societies is to describe their relations to the market. In early societies it is likely that the work of artists and poets was oriented to rituals connected to religious and political institutions (themselves closely tied together in some settings). For example, Raymond Williams has traced how the functions of Celtic bards became increasingly specialized with the emergence of changes in social organization and the mode of production. After the Christianization of Ireland the priestly function and the bardic function separated, with the priests becoming associated with writing while the bards remained tied to the oral tradition for a longer period of time. For centuries bards and other artists established relations with patrons who protected and supported them. This patronage was quite different from the situation that emerged in later stages (and overlapped in time with some forms of patronage) where artists offer their works as commodities for sale to a general public on a market. As Williams points out, there are historically specific forms of patronage to be considered as well as different kinds of market relations (1982, pp. 33–54). The general point remains, however: The culture of the bard who lived in the castle of a local lord differed from that of the modern poet who sells his work to a publisher who prints and distributes it to an anonymous public.

Looking at forms of communication and at the market relations provides ways of taking into account some of the concrete differences between specific premodern and modern societies. However, the social sciences, like the popular depictions of the contrast between traditional or folk culture, and modern culture, have relied upon idealized and eurocentric dichotomies. These conceptualizations have been the basis for the development of the ideas commonly in use for understanding contemporary cultures and their predecessors.

RITUAL AND COMMUNITY SOLIDARITY

Anthropologists once used the terms "culture" and "community" interchangeably when talking about traditional societies. The early theorists saw the cultures they studied as autonomous, economically independent groups. Group members shared values and achieved social control through face to face interaction and informal mechanisms; therefore, they had no need of legal sanctions. These cultures often had names for themselves, which translated as "the people." For the theorists, this fact symbolized the sense of integrity and cultural autonomy that they tried to capture with their ideal types. For Toennies the community form achieved social integration through "organic" solidarity. For Durkheim, it was modern society that was organic, and traditional communities were "mechanical." While the two theorists evaluated the contrast in opposite ways, each believed that traditional communities were less differentiated than modern ones: They had less elaborate hierarchies, the repertory of social roles in the community was smaller, and individual personalities showed less variation. In short, traditional communities were seen as homogeneous, autonomous entities where all individuals subordinated themselves to the common good.

Classical social theorists held that kinship organization, religious beliefs, and rituals integrated traditional societies. For anthropologists, kinship categories were critical. The theoretical contrast between modernity and primitive society was based in an opposition between family organization and the modern state for the legal theorists from Maine to Morgan who founded the discipline and left their mark on it (Kuper 1988). Many sociologists had concerns about "social disorganization" in modern cities, and, more generally, the "problem of order" in society. For them, religion was believed to have been the critical integrating force in traditional societies which were seen as lacking the problems of modern society. The notion of "secularization" was built into classical sociological theories: The theorists assumed that religion had been important in integrating traditional societies and providing individuals with meaning, but that, with modernity, religion as an institution had declined.[3]

---

[3] James Beckford (1989) argues that this assumption largely incapacitated sociological theory in terms of dealing with the widespread religious activity that continues in modern society.

Religion and Ritual

Early studies of traditional and primitive cultures often emphasized ritual as a defining characteristic of the religious practice of pre-modern societies. Social scientists postulated that through ritual, defined as standardized, repetitive activities, oriented toward the sacred, individuals in these societies established and affirmed their common bond. Emile Durkheim laid the groundwork for a functionalist understanding of religion. He was concerned with how religious rituals integrated a society, rather than with tracing historic developments and causes or with the personal experience of individuals. Durkheim postulated that when pre-modern peoples worshipped their deities they were in fact worshipping society, the powerful social reality that is greater than any individual.

Durkheim argued that cultures divide the world into two categories, the sacred and the profane, and that rituals tell people how to behave in the presence of the sacred. Rituals are structured in such a way that when people gather together and perform the required acts as a group the result is an intense emotional experience. Durkheim argued that while this was defined as the power of God, in fact it was the power of the group. For Durkheim, the idea of God in a ritual is a symbol for society.

In *The Elementary Forms of the Religious Life* Durkheim argued that religious rituals served four main functions in primitive society. For Durkheim, the first function of ritual is disciplinary; ritual practices often require self-discipline—even the self-denial of asceticism can be involved in certain aspects of some rituals which reproduce the submission of the wills of individuals to the demands of the group. The second function is cohesive; the collective practice of religious rituals reaffirms the social solidarity of the group. The third is vitalizing; in ritual, sacred symbols are maintained in such a way that they can be passed on to future generations as signifying the values of the group. Finally, the fourth function is euphoric: rituals counter individuals' experiences of loss or inadequacy—such as the inevitability of death—by reasserting the plausibility and legitimacy of the moral order (Harry Alpert, cited in Coser 1971, p. 139).

Durkheim thought that ritual fulfilled these functions most effectively in primitive, traditional, or folk cultures. In his earlier work Durkheim argued that integration in modern societies is based predominantly on the division of labor, given that people are more dependent upon each other economically. However, the presence of alienation and anomie in modern society imply failures of integration, and in his later work Durkheim looked for "functional equivalents" of religion—secular organizations and rituals that could accomplish the functions of integration—in modern societies.

Ritual as Habit

A key part of the definition of ritual—across times and places—has been that they are standardized, repetitive activities. In modern secular society, removed from the cultural contexts which gave traditional rituals meaning, they have been seen not only as standardized and repetitive, but as empty. Social scientists' use of the term "ritual," as applied in modern society, has moved further and further away from the understanding of the centrality of the experience of the sacred that was part of the original formulations. Robert Merton, for example, used the term ritualist for one who performs the outer gestures of an act without any commitment to the ideas and values that might be expressed through an act (1957, p. 131).

We can trace this change in the symbolic interactionist approach as well. Early advocates of dramaturgical analysis used the word "ritual" according to the older meaning of publicly established ceremonial activities. They mainly saw rituals as ways of communicating and maintaining group traditions (e.g., Burke 1950, pp. 272–273; Duncan 1968, pp. 185–191). Erving Goffman, however, spoke of rituals (much as Sigmund Freud did) in an ironic tone: he took the term out of its customary usage in order to emphasize habitual behaviors in everyday life. In *Interaction Ritual* Goffman examined "the ultimate behavioral material"—the "glances, gestures, positionings and verbal statements that people continuously feed into the situation, whether intended or not." He asked that we use ethnography to identify the "countless patterns and natural sequences of behavior occurring whenever persons come into one another's immediate presence" (1968, pp. 1–2). Goffman assumed that individuals use these "glances, gestures, positionings and verbal statements" in ways that are recognizable (that is to say, interpretable) to others. In *Relations in Public,* Goffman goes further and argues that the older kinds of rituals ("rituals performed to stand-ins for supernatural deities" and "extensive ceremonies involving long strings of obligatory rites") have little place in modern society. "What remains are brief rituals one individual performs for and to another...what remains are interpersonal rituals" (1971, p. 63). The rituals that Goffman analyzed consisted of the presentation and reception of small units of behavior in face-to-face interaction. His brilliant work shaped the way that many sociologists following him have thought about ritual.

Perhaps because of Goffman's influence, anthropologist Mary Douglas complains of the "anti-ritualist" bias among contemporary sociologists, whom she sees as part of a "revolt against ritual". She attempts to reclaim the concept of ritual for describing meaningful activities. She also seeks to break the theoretical connection which assumes that meaningful ritual occurs in primitive societies whereas ritual in modern society will necessarily signify empty conformity. Douglas points out:

> to use the word ritual to mean empty symbols of conformity, leaving us with no word to stand for symbols of genuine conformity, is seriously disabling to the sociology of religion. For the problem of empty symbols is still a problem about the relation of symbols and social life, and one which needs an unprejudiced vocabulary (1973, p. 21).

Putting aside the usual evolutionary frame that has dominated the theorists discussed so far, Douglas goes on to specify the conditions under which ritualism will be highly developed. One condition is the belief that symbolic action is effective in accomplishing the desired results. The second condition is that the culture be sensitive to condensed symbols—rich symbols that have different meanings at different levels which become integrated in the subconscious and connect inner and outer aspects of experience (1973, pp. 26–29).

Douglas turns to the ethnographic record to argue that ritualism will be strong when a group is characterized by tight social bonds, and she finds examples of high and low ritualism among both primitive and modern cultures. She argues that "Secularization is often treated as a modern trend, attributable to the growth of cities or the prestige of science, or just to the breakdown of social forms. But…it is an age-old cosmological type, a product of a definable social experience which need have nothing to do with urban life or modern science" (1970, pp. 36).

Sociologists of culture may want to participate in reclaiming the concept of ritual as meaningful activity. In looking at contemporary religious movements one can observe that rituals help to maintain the community of believers as a group. They also help individuals in such groups to maintain a deviant belief system. Rituals are also an important mechanism for incorporating changes of various sorts into an established tradition. For example, among Catholic Charismatics, rituals such as testimonies and healings were performed in public and the established meanings were generally available to group members, yet the rituals were also the context in which changes of meaning were negotiated (Neitz 1987, pp. 30–38). The degree of negotiation that occurs may vary: a developing sect like the Catholic Charismatics may be more open to negotiation than more established groups (Hall and Spencer-Hall 1982). In any case, new members are both socialized into a tradition and must appropriate it and make it their own.

In his study of orthodox Jews in contemporary urban America, Samuel Heilman has argued that if a religious tradition is to survive it must be able to "make the new holy" and "make the holy new" (1981, pp. 144–145). New aspects of the present (some of them at least) have to be brought into the world of meaning of the tradition, and the tradition has to be understood as applying to new members and their world. It is clear that maintenance of the group is accomplished not only through preserving the tradition, but also through constantly redefining the tradition.

Any tradition which cannot incorporate the new is a dead tradition. A story illustrating this comes from Zaire (then the Belgian Congo) in the first half of the twentieth century: Young tribe members excitedly brought motorcycles to show the Kuba king, but he was unimpressed by the noisy and uncomfortable vehicles. He was fascinated, however, by the tracks that motorcycle tires made, and he had his artists incorporate the patterns into the designs that marked his reign. Modern people tend to be romantic about "tradition" and view "innovations" as corruption—especially when the source of the innovation is outside what is defined as the tradition. This, however, is to fundamentally misunderstand the nature of culture (Burke 1978, pp. 23–64).

Rituals and Innovation

Barbara Myerhoff examines this process of making the holy new and the new holy in her remarkable book, *Number Our Days*. This book is about elderly Jews, most of whom had migrated to the United States as children or young adults at the turn of the century, and were living in Venice, California. They gathered around the Aliyah Center where they tried to make sense of their being Jewish and American, old and deserted by their children. In the book they are, as yet, survivors, but without heirs to their culture and witnesses to their past. The book is organized around four crises that occurred at the Center and the resolution of each crisis in an improvised, but elaborately staged ritual. The crises (two were crises of social relations and two were crises of beliefs) each threatened the fragilely constructed collective life of the group. The rituals reasserted some aspect of the community's common Jewish heritage, yet each ritual also reflected the fact that in America they have not retained the old ways and that their lives are constrained by old age.

Myerhoff, herself a secular Jew, is inspired by the old people's continuing ability to celebrate life and honor the sacred. In the book, however, she dialogues with Schmuel, a community member, tailor and autodidact, who continually points to what is "false" in these rituals, what has been lost to them as Jews in the migration to America and their assimilation into the dominant culture.

Myerhoff attempts to tease out what allows these innovative rituals to achieve the desired effects of reintegration of the group. For example, some substitutions can be made in the ritual as long as enough standard items are included (1978, p. 104–105). The power of rituals to establish continuity, both personal and collective, inheres in the repetition of specific acts. Yet for rituals to work, the repetitive acts must be personally meaningful to the individuals, invoking the sense of belonging to a community outside oneself and of continuity with a past and future existence. For this population of elderly Jewish migrants, continuity must be constructed across diverse experiences in the United States after the dissolution of the stable family life in leaving the shtetl (the small segregated Jewish towns in Eastern Europe). As Myerhoff notes "For this personal coherence, this sense of psychological integration to take place, the individual must be capable of finding and reliving familiar parts of his/her past history" (1978, p. 108).

For Myerhoff it is the achievement of continuity in the face of discontinuity that is of interest. The discontinuity can occur when the repetitious acts no longer strike resonant chords in those who practice them. Or, as is the case for the people at the center, people may lack the cultural or material resources for performing the standard rituals in standard ways. (Shabbat candles must be lit at noon, when all are gathered for the main meal which the Center provides. Standard practice demands lighting the candles at dusk, but by then the old people are at home, as they do not feel safe on the streets of their urban neighborhood after dark.)

Continuity is not necessarily created by the repetition of standard acts, however: the new must be made holy. The old people at the Aliyah Center are thrust into creating rituals because, even though their internal conflicts threaten the dissolution of the group, they are psychologically dependent upon one another. Myerhoff, the modern anthropologist, judges that these innovative rituals succeed because they do the work of rituals. Her critic from the community, Schmuel, is not so sure. He remembers the traditions of the Yiddish community where he grew up; to him the innovations are lies that people tell themselves. At one point he tells the anthropologist the following story:

> When the great Hasid, Baal Shem Tov, the Master of the Good Name, had a problem it was his custom to go to a certain part of the forest. There he would light a fire and say a certain prayer, and find wisdom. A generation later, a son of one of his disciples was in the same position. He went to that same place in the forest and lit the fire, but he could not remember the prayer. But he asked for wisdom and it was sufficient. He found what he needed. A generation after that, his son had a problem like the others. He also went to the forest, but he could not even light the fire. "Lord of the Universe," he prayed, "I cannot remember the prayer and I cannot get the fire started. But I am in the forest. That will have to be sufficient." And it was.

> Now, Rabbi Ben Levi sits in his study in Chicago with his head in his hand. "Lord of the universe," he prays. "Look at us now. We have forgotten the prayer. The fire is out. We can't find our way back to the place in the forest. We can only remember that there was a fire, a prayer, a place in the forest. So Lord, now that must be sufficient" (1978, p. 112).

The story captures a profound sense of loss. It also suggests that the nostalgia for the past "folk society" that we saw in the conceptualizations of middle-class social theorists at the end of the nineteenth century may be echoed in ordinary people's sense that there was a time when meaning in the present and continuity with the past and future were easier to achieve. Yet it is important to recognize that Schmuel himself is not nostalgic for some organic folk culture, as such. Speaking of the others who participate in the Center's activities, he tells Myerhoff at one point that they are "trying to get back what they saw in others but themselves never really had" (1978, p. 112). He thus acknowledges the importance of a learned elite, the shamans, priests and rabbis who carry cultural traditions, oral and written. Schmuel's comment raises questions about the existence of a truly "common culture" even in folk societies: He suggests at least that people had very different degrees of access to the "common symbols" of the culture and that the symbols may have had different meanings for different people.

Some anthropologists have come to espouse the notion of ritual as process. The influential work of Victor Turner (1967) suggests that rituals create a special space and time outside of ordinary interaction within which innovation, as well as the maintenance of tradition, can occur. He calls this "liminal" after the greek word for threshold. In Myerhoff's book the folk culture of the old people's eastern European childhood is contrasted with the heterogenous and pluralistic urban world they have come to inhabit. In these two settings individuals performed different rituals, but in neither case are the rituals appropriately described as "empty." Indeed, following Turner, Myerhoff focused on the power of rituals to constitute a liminal space/time in which meanings can be reborn.

Anthropologists such as Douglas, Turner, and Myerhoff share with Goffman the notion that it is daily life which is routine. Yet they differ from Goffman in offering an appreciation of ritual as a break in the routine of daily life. The possibility of meaningful ritual is no longer associated solely with folk culture, nor with repetitious, or even overtly religious, acts. Instead, ritual is treated as a symbolic and expressive act, a structured means of creating a special time and place, in which individuals experience themselves as part of the community. This understanding of ritual is continuous with the views of the founding theorists insofar as it associates rituals with integration into the community. However, while the founding fathers assumed that such integration into a community was most characteristic of folk societies, these theorists also see effective ritual—civil and political as well as religious—occurring under certain conditions in modern society. Douglas would add that ritualism is not always present among indigenous peoples (1973, pp. 37–39).

Secular Rituals and the Nation State

Social solidarity is an issue for secular nation states as well as for religiously bonded communities. Symbols and rituals are important for maintaining and reinforcing the sense of belonging. In the U.S., secular holidays such as Thanksgiving, Memorial Day and the Fourth of July commemorate important "events" in the history of the nation and offer opportunities for re-telling stories and making connections between past and present.[4]

Jeffery Alexander (1988) argues that Durkheim's analysis of ritual in archaic religion in fact provides a model for understanding how symbolic processes work in their own terms that can be applied in modern societies. In *The Elementary Forms of Religious Life* Durkheim claims an independent

---

[4]Bellah (1970) analyzed these and other "national symbols" and suggested that a "civil religion" tying citizenship and public duty to religious behavior in a set of national symbols surfaced in the United States in the nineteenth century after disestablishment of the churches.

causal importance for symbolic classification through the elaboration of the sacred/profane distinction, and he demonstrates the close relationship between ritual processes and the formation of social solidarities. For Alexander the value of this work is that it lays out a model—"the religious form of transcendent experiences"—which is a model for "certain universal processes" (1988, p. 191).

The model suggests that even in modern societies secular power has a certain numinous or sacred quality—it cannot simply be reduced to role obligations of office. Furthermore, values are created and maintained through rituals which allow members of groups, and citizens of nations to experience this "sacred" or non-mundane power. In Alexander's view what is of use in Durkheim's sociology of religion is not the notion of rituals as standardized and repetitive acts, but rituals as institutionalized ways of achieving social solidarity by putting individuals in touch with the sacred, the non-routine. Alexander's analysis of the Watergate crisis gives an illustration of how he would apply this on a national level.

Alexander reminds us that when the events of the Watergate break-in first became known, they were treated as "politics as usual" by most Americans. He argues that in the two years of the Watergate crisis, people's evaluations changed as they came to perceive the Watergate break-in as threatening to core American values. He states:

> If we look at the two-year transformation of the context of Watergate, we see the creation and resolution of a fundamental social crisis, a resolution that involved the deepest ritualization of political life. To achieve this "religious" status, there had to be an extraordinary generalization of opinion *vis-à-vis* a political threat that was initiated by the very center of established power and a successful struggle not just against that power in its social form but against the powerful cultural rationales it mobilized...(1988, p. 195).

Alexander puts forward a five stage process for a society experiencing crisis and ritual renewal. First, a sufficient number of people have to come to agree that an event or act is deviant or polluting. Second, among those people significant groups have to decide that the event endangers the "center" of the society. Third, institutional social controls must be used against the deviants. Fourth, these social control mechanisms must be accompanied by the formation of counter-centers, by elite groups who have some distance from the structural center. Fifth, there have to be ritual purification processes "that continue the labeling process and enforce the strength of the sacred symbolic center of society at the expense of a center which is increasingly seen as merely structural, profane and impure" (1988, p. 195).

According to Alexander's analysis, the key to the process of crisis and renewal in the Watergate case was not the break-in itself, but the congressional hearings. The decision to hold the hearings represented the sense of some people that a violation had occurred, but as the hearings progressed their mandate broadened until the hearings became a modern ritual that attempted to renew America's faith in truth and justice (1988, pp. 193–216). Subsequent scandals in the post-Watergate era (Billy-gate, Korea-gate, Iran-gate) have been referred to as "little Watergates."[5]

Removed from the evolutionary (and hierarchical) frame of the founders, the concept of ritual need no longer be limited to understanding it as the defining characteristic of unchanging primitive or folk culture. The consequence, however, is an undermining of the standard contrast between modern and primitive or traditional culture. Insofar as the concept of folk culture depends on the contrast between traditional and modern, then the concept of folk culture is itself called into question. Let us turn briefly to other dimensions of a critique of the concept of folk culture.

CONTACT AND CONTINUITIES

Like Myerhoff's protagonist, Schmuel, we may wonder about the nature of the "community" that is evoked in the conceptions of folk culture. As we saw at the beginning of this chapter, the early theorists saw folk societies as autonomous, economically independent groups where members shared values. Social control was maintained through face to face interaction and informal mechanisms, especially rituals. The theorists saw folk communities as less differentiated than their own, with less elaborate hierarchies, fewer social roles, and little variation in personality types. They described folk communities in contrast to modern societies as homogeneous, autonomous entities with little contact with outsiders and preserving the "traditional" ways.

The assumption that premodern communities were autonomous and isolated can be shown to be flawed. We know that migration is a fact of human existence. Adjustments in the often fragile balance between populations and food supplies, conflicts between nomads and cultivators, and the search for trade all provided reasons for individuals and whole groups to move, thereby encountering other settled groups. The notion of undiscovered or pre-contact cultures is meaningful in relation to the experience of the west and the particular consequences of that contact, but it would be foolish to think that most groups of indigenous peoples had no contact with others outside of their own group. Yet that notion is embedded in the concept of traditional culture.

An alternative approach is offered by Eric Wolfe, who argues that we must understand human history as "bundles of relationships." In a review of the contacts and encounters experienced by "peoples without history" before 1400, Wolfe traces extensive patterns of trade, conquest, and settlement exclusive of

---

[5] The resolution of the cultural crisis of Watergate, Alexander notes, did not necessarily solve all the social and political problems that it raised.

the activities of Europeans (1982, pp. 24–72). He suggests that we look for connections between peoples rather than see each society as an "integrated and bounded system set off against equally bounded systems."

In fact, it is possible that cultures become defined not in isolation from other cultures but in interaction with them. Groups create boundaries in order to differentiate themselves from those outside, and the boundaries continue to exist despite movements of people across them. In his work defining ethnic groups Fredrick Barth has argued that, contrary to the common assumption about the importance of isolation for the maintenance of distinct cultures, "categorical ethnic distinctions do not depend on an absence of mobility, contact and information, but do entail social processes of exclusion and incorporation..." (1970, pp. 9–10). Barth further argues that ethnic groups often maintain stable relations across boundaries, and that cultural distinctions can be maintained even in the context of long term interaction and interdependence.

IMPLICATIONS

By developing concepts of primitive, traditional or folk culture as reflections of their own concerns, the social theorists produced dichotomies that distorted critical aspects of modern society and premodern cultures. There are two implications of this analysis. First, as we have argued, traditional cultures were by no means isolated and autonomous before contact with the west. It is important that they not be isolated in our analysis, either. In part that means taking account of economic and political relations within and between cultures. Second, we need to think about how the dichotomous distortion reflects the larger "crisis in representation" of concern to cultural studies today.

Folk Cultures and the World System

We have asserted that folk cultures were not as isolated as early theorists led us to think. Recent theoretical developments outside of the sociology of culture suggest that rather than seeing traditional and modern cultures as opposing types we should look at relations between them. Contact of various kinds—including trade and warfare—had cultural as well as economic and political ramifications for the people involved.

Looking at relations between folk and modern societies raises issues of power that were hidden by the earlier formulations. "Contact" has not usually been neutral, even for various social strata within the more powerful of two societies in contact. Even trade in luxury goods, for example, involved the extracting of resources from one part of the local population to pay for items to be consumed and displayed by another part in a demonstration of their status and superiority. Long before Marco Polo's journey in 1270, the demand for silk and other luxury goods in Europe spurred contact between the east and the west: traders traveled over land along the "silk road" from the Mediterranean to China. The goods themselves were purchased by elites who often paid for them with money raised by taxing their subjects or by surpluses raised through warfare. World systems theory is one theoretical approach that explicates particular relations between core capitalist countries and those on the periphery (Wallerstein 1974). The theory seeks to explain the existence of a "world economy" in which primary producers profit from an unequal labor exchange with economically and politically subordinated peoples in the countries on the periphery. Looking at relations among countries in the capitalist world economy is one way of seeing connections between peoples rather than a dichotomy which falsely separates them.

To recognize relation and power is not necessarily to privilege structural categories over subjective ones, although world systems theory often does so. Local cultures often responded to contact with dominating forces on the basis of their own meaning systems, shaping the transformations of their cultural orders that occurred with the encounter with western forces (Sahlins 1985). We are not left just with structural categories to explain how societies function. The world has been and continues to be fundamentally shaped by the cultural meanings as hooks of structures. Only with this recognition can we see and understand the diversity of responses of local cultures' contact with western societies.

Folk Culture and the Crisis of Representation

We have argued that the early theorists developed the concept of folk culture as a mirror image of their own societies. They "created" images of the past that they believed could explain the things that they were seeing in the present. To say this is to raise questions about what any of us do when we write histories or ethnographies. How is the account we give shaped by who we are and where we are located? What is the status of the texts we generate?

These are important questions. In an essay titled "Partial Truths," James Clifford speaks for the new epistemological critique of the assumption that ethnographers and historians "represent" or capture reality when they write their descriptions of people in other times and places: "Culture [is] composed of seriously contested codes and representations; ...the poetic and the political are inseparable, and...science is in, not above, historical and linguistic processes" (1986, p. 2). This claim—that social scientists invent rather than represent reality—is intentionally provocative, but the issues examined in this chapter help us to see why Clifford might make such a claim. In trying to understand the dislocations of their own time, early social theorists "invented the past." The dichotomies they developed to contrast their own times with the past were driven by particular theoretical and practical concerns. In talking about texts, the new ethnographers are making claims about "contexts of power, resistance, institutional constraint, and innovation," (Clifford, 1986. p. 2). Through their critique we can see how uncritical acceptance of the contrasts invented by the early social theorists have limited our analyses of both the past and the present.

How then could ethnography any longer be possible? George Marcus has explored the specific problems involved in the writing of anthropological texts "once the line between the local worlds of subjects and the global world of systems becomes radically blurred" (1986, p. 171). If "everyone is connected to everyone else," what reasonable boundaries can we draw in writing ethnography? Marcus discusses two possibilities: the multi-local ethnography and the strategically situated ethnography. He also suggests the possibility of mixed genre writing by social scientists, in hopes of more self consciousness and reflection about the choice of site and subject.

Our discussion of the concept of folk culture has identified two related problems. One has to do with content. If we can no longer think about cultures as isolated and autonomous, how do we write about their connectedness without moving to a level of abstraction that loses the rich description of local cultures? The other is a concern about the authority and legitimacy of the writer and the representation: How do we represent ourselves and our subjects?

A recent study of contact between an exploratory patrol of an Australian colonial administration and six Papuan New Guinea tribes demonstrates one response to such questions (Schieffelin and Crittenden 1991). In 1935 a party of explorers consisting of two Australian patrol officers and forty Papuan carriers and police set out. They encountered six different Papuan societies, still using tools made of stone, with no prior contact with Europeans. The patrol ran out of food and was unsuccessful in trading with the local inhabitants. In places the contact turned hostile, and over 50 Papuans were killed. In constructing their account of the patrol, the authors use many sources: the patrol report, diary and book written by one of the expedition's leaders, the reports of the patrol officers and police who gave depositions at an official inquiry that followed the expedition, and ethnographic reports of Papuans from the six societies—some of whom were present at the original encounter.

Schieffelin and Crittenden point out that the encounter was an *encounter between cultures*. Although exploration of the New Guinea highlands was motivated in part by the search for natural resources—gold had been discovered across the border in the Dutch Mandated territories—the meaning of the encounter was shaped by cultural factors. In this case it is clear that for both the colonialists and the indigenous people, "the other" did not fit their preconceived notions. The explorers, for example, falsely assumed that any people they met in the highlands would be similar to Papuans in coastal regions and would value the same trade goods. But at least the Europeans had a category—"natives"—which gave them an advantage:

Europeans were used to meeting new people and almost always had the upper hand over them both in armament and in the element of surprise. In addition they had a well-prepared category—"natives"—in which to place those people they met for the first time, a category of social subordination that served to dissipate their depth of otherness (1991, p. 5).

The Papuans had no easily available categories, and their responses to the exploratory party was based in part on their cosmologies and in part on their relations with neighboring Papaun groups: When those relations were hostile the response depended on the extent to which the patrol was associated with the hostile neighbor and/or the extent to which the Europeans could be used against suspect neighbors.

For some of the societies encountered by the patrol this first encounter had very little significance: recollections of indigenous people confused the first group of explorers with subsequent groups in their retelling of the event. In other cases, the arrival of whites had profound effects because it coincided with cosmological beliefs about spiritual beings living beyond their world whose return would result in "a plague of troubles." For the Huli peoples this interpretation was reinforced by the fact that the explorers came from the direction where the spirits were supposed to reside. This study shows that historical activities and cultural structures are not necessarily closely articulated: "the historical importance of an unusual event depends to a significant degree on the importance and centrality of the cultural ideas in terms of which it is grasped…" (1991, p. 286). But we know this only because of the presentation of historical and cultural materials that reflect the many voices from within and outside various social groups.

CONCLUSION

Although the concept of traditional culture—and behind that, of primitive culture—was integral to the theoretical enterprises of the founding fathers of social science, these concepts are now extremely problematic. The concept of primitive culture with its eurocentric base is no longer acceptable. In current academic work the idea of "traditional culture" has mostly lost its meaning. While we may want to talk about the radical changes that occurred with modernization and times and places in which those changes had not yet occurred, somewhat less grandiose conceptualizations seem more appropriate. Some researchers may still want to speak of "traditional cultures," but they are more likely to use a term that designates more specifically place and time, e.g. the culture of early modern Europe. For some purposes it is useful to use a term that designates specific technologies or production processes. The degree of integration into a market economy may also be important. As was noted earlier, among cultural anthropologists it has become common to talk about oral or preliterate cultures, and Eric Wolfe (1982) uses "peoples without history."

FIGURE 3.2 Because use conveys authenticity Bambera carvers have learned that these antelope headpieces will sell for higher prices when set on top of caps. (*Source:* Phoebe Hearst Museum of Anthropology, University of California at Berkeley.)

Rejecting the dichotomy between premodern and modern societies also has ramifications for our analysis of modern society. Where previous theoretical constructions pointed primarily to discontinuities, now we see the possibilities of finding continuities. In this chapter we have examined how the concept of ritual—developed in relation to primitive societies—can be used by sociologists of culture to understand fundamental human experiences and actions.

Finally, what of the concept of folk culture: where does it stand? In a pluralistic world, where every corner has been invaded by the mass media and everything has its price, folk culture acquires a narrow meaning. In Europe, folk culture refers to traditions of local peoples, including, dress, food, dialect, religious practices, and remnants of distinct local cultures—all now part of the on-going struggle between national identity and European unity.

Folk culture in the U.S. often refers to specific cultural artifacts transmitted orally from one generation to another. In its most common contemporary sense it is almost a genre of arts and crafts, defined by cultural transmission and learning outside of schools or books. Such a definition, of course, reifies "tradition" and excludes the normal processes of innovation. Is a carving of a traditional subject by a traditionally trained carver from an indigenous population using traditional methods and subjects—but using non-traditional materials—authentic folk culture? What if the innovation is partly a response to market demand? (Graburn 1967, 1976). If two identical objects—e.g., stools or masks—are produced, one for use in a traditional ritual, and one for an American dealer in primitive art, are both authentic to the same degree? Is folk culture produced for a market still folk culture? These questions speak to a set of important cultural shifts which took place, among other times and places, in early modern Europe.

4

PREINDUSTRIAL SOURCES OF CONTEMPORARY CULTURE

We might find a few pristine examples, but what are conventionally called "traditional cultures" have changed: They survive, if at all, disconnected from their origins, within an encompassing and alien social order. Most of what persists of traditional cultures has either become marginalized by the increasing predominance of other kinds of culture, or it has become incorporated into other culture by way of motifs, melodies, myths, and other elements. Much of what people call "folk" culture today are these remnants, reworked and distributed through the mass media. Thus, the "folk song" has become a genre—a conventionalized form—of music that is produced and distributed in a manner similar to other kinds of music, for example, "classical music" or "new age." Similarly, nostalgic "folk festivals" are produced using the generally available techniques of concert promotion.

If "traditional" culture has become transformed into "folk" as one of the genres of contemporary mass produced culture, actual culture contents of traditions still have diffused into contemporary culture by many different routes. Music of West Africans was carried by them when they were captured, forced into slavery, and brought to the Americas, and the motifs of this music have found their way into contemporary samba, jazz, rhythm and blues, soul, and rap music (Thompson 1959). Modern artists—for example, Paul Gaugin, Henri Matisse and Pablo Picasso—have taken inspiration, "borrowing," as Kubler

(1962) calls it, from the visual motifs of indigenous cultures (Gardner 1959). And contemporary architects have been told to appreciate buildings built "without architects" (Rudofsky 1964). But these importations of motifs and styles presume an already established modern culture. How did this come about? The question is contentious in the sociology of culture, and answers to it differ depending on how one views the relation between society and culture: Does culture have independent causal importance, or do technological and social class theories explain the significant changes of cultural form and content? An initial question concerns how much contemporary patterns of cultural content and form have changed from those of earlier, non-market societies based on simpler technologies. As an orienting hypothesis, it seems reasonable to suggest that there are parallels between culture today and earlier cultures, for example, in the ways rituals and myths work. Still, most culture today, including important rituals and myths, is profoundly different in content from earlier cultures, and we also must suspect that culture is subject to processes that make it work differently in relation to society.

It is commonplace to attribute much of the difference between earlier cultures and modern culture to two factors: (1) the Industrial Revolution that began in the late eighteenth century, powered by harnessing non-human, non-animal energy—steam, gasoline, electricity, nuclear fission and fusion, and (2) the related emergence of real-time mass media—mass-distributed newspapers during the nineteenth century and the twentieth-century developments of radio, television, and computer networks. No doubt these all are important factors, yet accepting them as a sufficient explanation of modernity would obscure other important questions. What about sources of modern culture that *preceded* the industrial revolution?

This chapter can offer only a sketch of earlier cultural developments that are particularly important sources of cultural dynamics today. We do not give a full historical account. Instead, we identify key preindustrial shifts, beyond folk cultures, toward the contemporary situation. We ask whether the ways that culture works today depend in part on processes that already were established before the advent of various modern mass media. In addition, given the importance of the modern mass media, we explore an early case—printing—that shows how technology manifested itself in cultural change. To consider these issues we look at the region of the world where an interrelated set of changes shaped the subsequent character of modern culture in key ways. In old Europe, beginning at least as early as the eleventh century, a broad sweep of changes occurred leading up to the Industrial Revolution that began in the late eighteenth century. What changed? Two linked sets of developments were of the greatest cultural significance. First, processes of "routinization" and "rationalization" changed cultures, social organizations and individuals, while a connected set of economic changes transformed the conditions of cultural production and distribution. Second, as towns became increasingly central in a growing market economy, the forms of culture, as well as support for it, became tied to new social groups. We explore each of these broad and in-terrelated complexes of developments in turn.

ROUTINIZATION, RATIONALIZATION, AND THE EMERGENT CAPITALIST ECONOMY

Perhaps the central debate in the sociology of culture concerns the question of whether cultural phenomena (often too narrowly described as "ideas") can have causal significance in their own right. In the crudest version of the "idealist" position, an idea such as "freedom" represents a "spirit" that has causal force of its own. More sophisticated arguments for the importance of culture link it with the interests and actions of individual people and social groups. In this view, reality is "socially constructed," in part through the ideas that give meaning to action and shape to social organization (Berger and Luckmann 1966). As Clifford Geertz put it in a quotation famous among social scientists: "man is an animal suspended in webs of significance he himself has spun" (1973, p. 5). In these terms the crucial question is: Can concrete culture be deduced from the personal and group situations and interests of the people who advance it? If culture can simply be "read off" from the interests of individuals and groups, culture can be treated as derivative. If this cannot be done, on the other hand, culture has to be considered causally important in its own terms. One way to address this issue is to consider the puzzle of rationalization and routinization.

When Max Weber described the changes that mark the emergence of the modern world, he identified rationalization and routinization as key processes (1978). *Rationalization* may be defined as a process in which a particular activity is increasingly overtaken by "rational" ways of doing things: Goals are met in ways that are considered to be as efficient and effective as possible.[1] When aspects of the world become reorganized according to rational dictates, we may speak of rationalization. Thus, it would be possible to consider the changes in how fast food restaurants operate as a process of rationalization, ever more efficiently producing and serving hamburgers.

Often associated with rationalization is the parallel development—*routinization*. When activity is organized in ways that systematize sequences of action so that the same activity can be repeated over and over again, we may speak of the development of routines, or routinization. For example, the old-style cafe or lunchcounter waitress (typically) may have a variety of tasks, but lacks an overall routine, and she will take it as a prerogative to stop and joke

---

[1] Weber did not think that goals themselves could be rationally determined, except in relation to other goals (in which case they are means). The use of rational *means* indicates nothing, in his definition, about the value of the *ends*. The ultimate demonstration of this came after Weber's death, in the Nazi concentration-camp organization of genocide, where the techniques used were those of "rational" bureaucracy; see Rubenstein (1978).

with delivery men and talk with customers. By comparison, the job of the contemporary McDonald's or Wendy's worker has been narrowed to a set of clearly circumscribed routines: one person takes orders, another flips hamburgers, and so on. With routinization, the predictability of social life increases, and large numbers of people become systematically organized into closely coordinated activities.

Weber thought that the processes of rationalization and routinization gradually became important in transforming the organization of social life in parts of Europe during the Middle Ages, and especially with the spread of Protestant Christianity after the Reformation beginning in the sixteenth century. Yet Weber did not advocate the idealist position that rationalization took hold as the manifestation of some "spirit" of history: His own argument and other research suggests that multiple currents of rationalization took hold in spheres as diverse as personal life, work, and the distribution of culture. These developments took place in parallel with a radical reorganization of economic life that came with the gradual emergence—beginning in earnest in the sixteenth century—of a world economy of production and trade. Diverse though the sources of rationalization were, and as complex as their connections with world-economic changes, the consequences were greater than the sum of the independent developments.

Rationalization and Personal Life

To understand that the world was not always dominated by rationalized culture, let us briefly consider the problem of social identity, as portrayed in the film, "The Return of Martin Guerre." By the sixteenth-century, developments toward rationalization were under way, but they certainly had not taken hold everywhere. The people of a village in the south of France one day in 1556 received a man who looked to be Martin Guerre, who years earlier had simply disappeared, leaving his wife of nine years, Bertrande, and a newborn child. He had gone off to war, the returned Martin Guerre told the villagers, and now was happy to be back. The townspeople welcomed him, and Martin's wife Bertrande took him into her arms. But in the aftermath of this happy reunion, rumors began to surface that the man who claimed to be Martin Guerre was an imposter. This accusation gained support among some relatives, but Bertrande defended Martin as her husband up until the point when the man she said was Martin Guerre was confronted in court with the return of the real Martin Guerre, who exposed the imposter.

The story of Martin Guerre is the topic of historians' heated debates (Davis 1983; Finlay 1988; Davis 1988). At greatest issue is whether Bertrande really could have been duped by the imposter sharing her bed, or whether she played along in order to regain her respect and a husband. Yet this question obscures a more basic question: What kind of world could sustain such a situation? In a word, a world in which personal identity had not become rationalized. Perhaps the deceit would not have worked in more cosmopolitan areas of sixteenth-century France, and perhaps even today a similar charade could be pulled off among some people. The processes of rationalization are spatially, socially, and temporally uneven, and they are always subject to reversals based, if nothing else, on the resistance of people to the regimentation of their lives (Roth 1987). Still, on balance, the imposter Martin Guerre's trick would seem much more difficult to sustain in our era of rationalized identity. Today newborn babies may become confused in a hospital, yet the confusion usually can be settled by blood and DNA tests, and these techniques also can be used on adults. People today may adopt aliases, and move to new places to start new lives, but if they try to assume someone else's identify, they have to obtain fake social security numbers, drivers' licenses, and other organizationally produced badges of identity. The imposter Martin Guerre faced no such problems of bureaucratically rationalized identity, so long as he could play the social role of Martin Guerre. What we tend to assume today as a concrete reality—public personal identity—was a more precarious thing in the sixteenth century, at least in areas like Martin Guerre's village.

Rationalization penetrates the individual more deeply than the exterior signs of identity. There is evidence that the inner being of humans—personality—is a product of rationalization as well. This is apparent in the historical emergence of the categories that distinguish madness from sanity, described by Michel Foucault (1965). Foucault's evidence may be disputed by specialists, yet his general argument is important. In his view, madness is a social construct that can exist only as the opposite of the disciplined, organized mind. Thus, he theorizes about an era in which neither madness nor the modern person yet existed. The average person lacked a self-disciplined personality subjected to the dictates of modern reason, just as communities lacked the standards, labels, and facilities of "confinement" by which to establish a separate identity of "madness." In a sense, "madness" was invented through rationalization. Rational answers had to be formulated in response to difficult questions. How was a classification system and its relation to other categories to be established? Was madness rooted in animal passions, a product of idleness and poverty, or based in a moral failing of the individual? Were the insane to be imprisoned, segregated from society-at-large, or treated for diseases? Foucault showed how rationales of classification concerned with madness and confinement changed over the centuries.

But not just the mad have become subject to rationalization. The rationalization of conduct among people deemed sane is equally important. In part, that rationalization involved the development of a "culture of civility." As social historian Norbert Elias has argued, in the twelfth century even the elite classes of territorial lords and warring knights still were "untamed." Using the language of Freudian psychology, Elias painted an image of a feudal elite who lacked "drive-control" and failed to channel their "elementary urges" into "refined pleasure"; instead they lived by the sword and acted out impulses of gratification and aggression in plunder and rape (1982, pp. 72–3). In the long, slow rebuilding from the so-called "dark ages" that followed the collapse of the Roman Empire in the fifth century, M.E., the culture of civilization and manners gradually became reestablished. By the eleventh century, courtly society could be found in some of the domains of the wealthier feudal landlords. This court life offered a locus for the display of wealth through patronage of the arts and entertainment, and it was the scene of performance by minstrels, poets, and wandering "troubadours." This setting gave greater importance to refined behavior—manners. The courtly person of early modern Europe no longer could depend solely on physical strength; instead, self-control became important. By the seventeenth century, La Bruyère could say, "A man who knows the court is master of his gestures, of his eyes and his expression; he is deep, impenetrable. He dissimulates the bad turns he does, smiles at his enemies, suppresses his ill-temper, disguises his passions, disavows his heart, acts against his feelings" (quoted in Elias 1982, p. 272). In short, courtly action became calculating; the courtly person was not unselfconscious. Instead, life became something of a performance: Acting out social roles rationalized social intercourse and created a gulf between the private self and how the self was publicly presented—a feature which sociologist Erving Goffman (1959) has shown is central to modern life.

The "inner" rationalization of personal thought and conduct can take the most diverse directions. The courtly development of manners has its historical significance in the refinement of personal relationships; its inventions of manners persist today in high-society etiquette, in some kinds of courtship, and in modern Western ideas of romantic love. Yet the self of sociability—rationalized in conduct or classified as mad—only amounts to half the equation of modern personal identity, for the question of work remains to be considered.

Rationalization of Work

The feudal estates that depended on the labor of peasant farmers were not the locus where rationalization of work initially took hold, for the lords of such manors could rarely gain direct control over peasants' activities. In the medieval monasteries, on the other hand, the Church could claim absolute obedience to religious authority, and by the eleventh century monastic authorities were using their power to rationally organize agricultural and other kinds of production (Duby 1968, pp. 175–81). This "outer" rationalization of organized activity was accompanied by demands upon the monks for "inner" rationalization of conduct, not only in relation to religious duties, but also in matters of devoted and dutiful work.

Such "asceticism" of individuals—their self-sacrifice out of devotion to God—has taken various forms historically, and those forms have had consequences beyond their religious meanings. Medieval monasticism was designed to be an "other-worldly" retreat from "this" world, a kind of heaven-on-earth. Yet its basis in religious authority achieved a rationalized organization of work that was not possible under secular agrarian social relationships of feudalism: The feudal lord could demand rent and labor from peasants, but the feudal manor was not organized as an integrated unit of production. Monastic administrators, by contrast, had to provide for the needs of the members of their communities, and they engaged in planning and strict organization of work. The monasteries' systematic organization of productive activity was a social innovation that later became important in the rationalization of work processes in the capitalist manufacturing that began to slowly emerge beginning in the sixteenth century, and with greater force in the industrial revolution of the nineteenth century (Hall 1978, pp. 40–41; Collins 1986, pp. 52–54).

With the Protestant Reformation beginning in the sixteenth century, the work asceticism enforced externally in the monasteries became psychologically internalized by Protestant believers, who treated work in "this" world as a "vocation," or calling by God. In the famous argument of Max Weber, Protestant religion had important consequences for economic life: Under a regimen of "inner-worldly asceticism," Protestants with anxieties about their own salvation were told by ministers to quell their anxieties by working hard, avoiding either indolence or the pursuit of personal pleasure. The Protestant rank-and-file ascetics engaged in self-disciplined work that reinforced a modern, rational form of capitalism, providing workers who were predictable and reliable. In short, workers themselves were rationalized in their conduct such that they became almost human machines. It was the advent of the inwardly disciplined Protestant type of worker that reinforced more rapid economic growth in Protestant regions of Europe than in Catholic ones, Weber argued (1958a). Religion also became an important basis for certifying the integrity and honesty of people engaged in business: Eventually, members of a religious group might screen potential members concerning their economic practices, and they thereby could vouch for the honesty of one another (Weber 1946, p. 302ff.). In these ways, religion contributed to the rationalization and predictability of economic life, while at the same time, religiously bounded groups became loose associations of like-minded economic actors. As a form of culture, religion thus operated not just as a basis of integration for a social order, but as a revolutionary and transforming force consequential beyond the boundaries of religion itself.

Rationalization and the Distribution of Culture: The Cases of Music and Text

Weber did not argue that religion caused capitalism, even if he showed the significance of religious rationalization of conduct and work organization for the way capitalism developed. Nor did he limit his consideration of rationalization to the economic implications of the Protestant ethic. In *The Rational and*

Social Foundations of Music, Weber showed that the development of music using complex harmony depended upon the invention of a rational system for notating music on paper based on a standardization of musical time and pitch. Traditional music is seldom reproduced exactly, and it is reproduced without notation on paper; because of the resulting slippage, or "drift" (Kubler 1962), it can be difficult to identify the definitive version of a folk song (Burke 1978, p. 114). By comparison, in Weber's view, "A somewhat complicated modern work of music…is neither producible nor transmittable nor reproducible without the use of notation" (Weber 1958b, p. 84). The modern Western system of notation originally grew out of the medieval Church establishment of a liturgy, or speci-fied form, for its services. A great systematizer of religion, the Roman Catholic Church developed an interest in imposing a uniform liturgy across Christendom. With the careful copying of liturgies by monks, what counted as the "same" mass could be performed simultaneously in all the cathedrals and churches of Europe, beginning as early as the sixth century, and attaining increasing com-plexity as monks continued to refine their systems of notation (Seay 1965, pp. 40–1; Weber 1958b, p. 86). The medieval Christian mass thus represents an early case of "mass production" that did not depend upon machines or technology, even printing.

Much earlier, writing had accomplished for the spoken word what nota-tion accomplished for music, but the notation problems of the written word were not so difficult as those of music, since pitch, tempo and timing of words usually do not require explicit notation. However, so long as notation in music and copying of writing remained the province of scribes and monks, these cultural innovations for reproducing cultural materials remained in the hands of social elites. Culture did not change the social order: It reinforced the existing one. But the letter alphabet, itself a rationalized "notating" of oral words by their combinations of sounds, ultimately made possible the inven-tion of movable-type printing of texts.

As Elizabeth Eisenstein has shown, the invention of modern printing was a technological change that altered the social equation momentously (1979). The changes are broader than can be described in any detail. But three complexes of change stand out. First, printing broke the monopoly of church authorities on religious ideas; Protestant reformers depended heavily on printing for the dissemination of their ideas, and the Bible itself became widely available to an increasingly literate population. The consequences for religious organization and authority were tremendous. Second, printing argu-ably transformed the conditions of cultural work. Intellectuals previously had their hands full with the laborious tasks of maintaining culture, and intellec-tual work was largely restricted to copying and interpreting classical and reli-gious texts, rather than producing new ideas. The labor-intensive process inhibited wide distribution even of ancient texts. Printing freed up intellectual labor, and gradually intellectuals began to pursue questions beyond the dic-tates of religious theology, through secular humanistic and scientific inquiry (cf. Wuthnow 1989). Not only philosophical books were published, but also practical ones about construction engineering, swamp drainage, and agriculture. Third, the activity of printing emerged as an important occupation in the growing towns. Printers supported and reinforced the new religious and intellectual developments that were good for the printing business. Partly on the basis of rationalization and routinization involved in printing, the medieval social order of feudal and religious authorities was weakened, and new social classes began to emerge and assert their power.

Rationalization, the World Political Economy, and the Cultures of Consumption

In concluding his study of the Protestant ethic, Max Weber wrote, "it is, of course, not my aim to substitute for a one-sided materialistic an equally one-sided spiritualistic causal interpretation of culture and of history" (1958a, p. 183). Weber did not limit his analysis of rationalization to religion and the systematization of culture. He argued that, in the economic sphere, rationalization touched the most diverse activities, from the production of iron to the organization of bureaucracies. Especially important was the gradual, long-term, and uneven emergence of "absolutist" states as organizations that claimed absolute authority and monopoly on the use of force in their territories. While any attempt to date the beginning of this process would be arbitrary, from the fourteenth and fifteenth centuries onward, and especially by the seventeenth and eighteenth centuries, absolutist states rationalized the conditions of commerce by moving toward universally applicable laws; thus, business entrepreneurs increasingly were able to anticipate their profits and losses in rational ways (Weber 1981; Collins 1986; Schluchter 1989).

Nor was the preindustrial emergence of early modern cultural forms solely a product of routinization and rationalization of social organization, technology and consciousness in Europe. These changes were coupled with an economic transformation beginning to take hold in the sixteenth century that eventually would encompass the entire world. This centuries-long process itself amounted to a rationalization and routinization of trade relationships, but the relationships that emerged were especially beneficial to the states that dominated the process—initially, states in Europe. The fundamental engines of change were capitalist agriculture and the gradual emergence of long-distance trade with colonies that brought raw materials, wealth and investment in new enterprises to Europe: By the sixteenth century there was a European-centered world economy (Wallerstein 1974). Mercantile capitalism reinforced the growth of towns, and the power struggle between the feudal lords of the countryside and the towns' craft producers and entrepreneurs was resolved by the absolutist states that established centralized governments and uniform laws. The exact interrelations among this broad array of changes are matters of scholarly debate.

As a part of the debate, the significance of culture for these changes has recently begun to receive attention. Capitalist trade involved material objects. Cultural practices shaped the nature of goods traded, and by the opposite token, new goods from afar like sugar and tobacco transformed European culture. We might ask, for example, why clothing in Europe for centuries was dominated by the use of black cloth, rather than cloth made with color dyes. According to Schneider (1978), black cloth fashions were not simply a matter of cultural tastes, for people knew the economic costs and consequences of their choices of dress, and acted accordingly. Textiles were a central economic activity of the European-centered world economy that became established in the sixteenth century. But Europe lacked the fancy dyestuffs that made polychrome cloth production possible. Such dyestuffs were part of the luxury trade from Asia, and brightly colored clothing was a sign of wealth, while from the eleventh century onward, black cloth could easily be produced from dyestuffs available in Europe. For both medieval monks and later for Calvinist Protestants, black symbolized asceticism, and for the population as a whole, black had a non-elitist, egalitarian significance. Favoring black in cloth established European strength (especially northern) in cloth production as early as the beginning of the twelfth century, and avoided siphoning off capital toward a dependent trade relationship with Asia. A continuing cultural preference for black, ever reconstituted in new circumstances, supported the sixteenth-century shift in the core of the world economy from the Mediterranean to England and the Atlantic coast of Europe. Partly because Europeans developed cultural tastes for local goods among the broad population, European entrepreneurs were able to establish themselves at the center of a growing world economy.

Cultural tastes in textiles figured in economic development in later centuries as well, but in a different way. By the seventeenth century, Britain was importing inexpensive, brightly colored calico cotton cloth from India, and the demand for these goods was becoming unshakable in the face of spreading consumerism among the popular classes. Unsuccessful in taming the cultural taste by banning calico imports, British entrepreneurs developed innovations in cloth production and dyeing that halted the unfavorable trade by creating a nationally produced alternative. The impetus to the nineteenth-century industrial revolution that was centered in English textile production thus had its origins partly in European capitalist responses to cultural tastes that shifted with the appearance of competing textiles arriving through long-distance trade (Mukerji 1983).

The studies of Schneider and of Mukerji only scratch the surface of connections between culture and trade in the early modern era, but they do show that European economic development was not a one-sided process driven by the emergence of the world economy. On the contrary, cultural tastes created demand for material goods that contributed to the routinization of markets and trade relationships, and they influenced the locations of economic growth and the character of technological innovation.

Rationalization and routinization are forms of cultural change that shape the production and distribution of symbolic and material culture, the efficiency of organization, and even the personalities of individuals. Yet they are not abstract forces, and they do not represent any inevitable process. Concrete individuals and social groups acted in rationalizing ways out of their own self-interest, and they used new technologies to their own advantage in the process. Those who rationalized their conduct and organization gained power in early modern Europe in ways that could not be anticipated simply on the basis of their initial social positions. Put differently, the cultural processes of rationalization were influential in transforming the social and economic order, changing the life chances of entire social classes of people. Nor are rationalization and routinization necessarily the consequences of technology alone. As we have seen, the development of work discipline as routinized conduct preceded industrialization, and the invention of musical notation for mass distribution of culture came before the technological invention of printing. Rationalization of social processes sometimes developed prior to, and independently of, changes in economic conditions that would make the processes so significant. Moreover, rationalization was central to the conditions of economic predictability that made expansion of the world economy possible. The origins of the multiple developments of rationalization are diverse, as are their connections to other social changes. But together, their consequences have been enormous: The technical, economic, cultural and organizational advantages of rationalization to those individuals and groups who pursue it have accumulated to the point at which rationalization is an institutionalized feature basic to society today.

THE URBAN-BASED ECONOMY AND EMERGENT FORMS OF CULTURE

In a variety of ways, culture had significance for the emergence of modern society, economy and personality. But what were the consequences of changes during the early modern era for culture itself? The cultural changes of the era did not take hold in a uniform way: Differences arose depending on how culture was connected to emergent social groups. To get at the diversity of cultures, sociologists sometimes draw on Robert Redfield (1956), who distinguished between two separate but interdependent cultures—the "great tradition" of an elite and the "little tradition" of common folk. The great tradition is taken to be one of serious music, art, and a literature that claims to capture the greatness of a civilization. The culture of the little tradition, on the other hand, is passed along without the benefit of formal academies, through the telling of tales, craft production of daily needs, and the singing of songs passed from generation to generation. This distinction suggests a basic, widespread stratification of culture that has existed since ancient times. How were these traditions affected by the changes during the early modern era?

For all the significance of the commercial revolution that started in Europe, the spread of the market was—and continues to be—uneven in its effects on people depending on their class situation, religion, gender, ethnicity, region, and whether they are city dwellers or people who live in rural areas. All the world is never equally transformed. Nor have rationalization and routinization been the only vehicles of cultural change. To the contrary, the very kinds and forms of culture have shifted. These changes can be traced as the intersection of the great and little traditions with a growing urban society. For the early modern era, it is important to trace three related developments: (1) the diffusion of the little tradition in urban space, (2) the emergence of market economy in a way that transformed elite culture and forged a distinctive basis of popular culture, and (3) innovations in genres of cultural production tied to new kinds of audiences.

Popular Culture as Traditional Culture: The Case of the Guilds

Trade, the towns, and craft production for market grew in fits and starts during the late medieval and early modern periods and, as a result, the little tradition was transformed and eventually eclipsed. To be sure, the older cultural forms of the little tradition did not entirely disappear. Peter Burke (1978) has shown that, as late as the late eighteenth century, members of the elite who became fascinated with what they called "folk" culture still could go out and collect fairy tales, folksongs, and popular poems and rhymes. The same can be done today (Randolph 1976). In the countryside, many people persist in lifestyles of peasants (and rural aristocrats), clinging to a diverse range of old ways. But even rural culture has changed dramatically. And as the towns grew during the early modern era, elements of the "little tradition" were incorporated into—and eventually overshadowed by—an emergent urban popular culture.

In part, popular culture was simply traditional culture brought to town, improvised in its forms and adapted by town dwellers to their new situations. Thus, the festival and trade fair culture—long part of the little tradition— found its way into the towns, but with a difference. The badges of folk cultures became mapped onto urban patterns of social stratification, and the popular classes among town dwellers participated in new ways of life and entertainment. The craft guilds represent an interesting example that shows this remapping of the little tradition as popular culture.

In the medieval period the guilds were relatively egalitarian associations of craftsmen who sought to monopolize a craft activity—such as weaving—within a particular region. As trade spurred production in the late middle ages, the guilds increasingly opposed the rationalized specialization of tasks within a particular craft—such as cloth production—but in the long run, they could not stop it, and from the fourteenth to the eighteenth century, they gradually lost their monopolies to more capitalistic practices of entrepreneurship. The greatest challenge came from the "putting out" system: as early as the thirteenth century, and increasingly thereafter, entrepreneurs began to subcontract with separate workers, guild members or not, to perform discrete tasks (washing, spinning, weaving of wool cloth, for example) (Weber 1981, pp. 136ff.).

How did the guilds try to maintain solidarity in the face of competition from the putting-out system? Part of the answer seems to have involved redeployment of longstanding traditional cultural practices. The solidarity so important to maintenance of an egalitarian guild was nurtured by distinctive craft guild cultures. Just as small communities often possess distinctive cultural "badges" of identity that distinguish the people of one community from those of another one, guilds too developed their distinctive cultures. As Burke observes, "Guilds had their own patron saints, their own traditions and their own rituals, and they organized the leisure as well as the working lives of their members." Religious festivals like Corpus Christi, Burke goes on, "often were organized on a guild basis," and the guilds were true fraternities, "particular about who they admitted to the craft" (1978, p. 36). Not only is a craft by definition a culture based upon a distinctive set of skills, but particular craft guilds created their own informal cultures of dances and work songs and sagas of craft life that, for example, might tell the story of a shoemaker as a hero. These are the sorts of practices that define what Max Weber called a "status group": A group of individuals who "successfully claim a special social esteem, and possibly also status monopolies" (1978, p. 306). Status groups occur in many different situations—religious, political, social. What is interesting about the guilds as status groups is this: They seem to have replicated folk kinds of culture in urban, occupationally stratified society.

In the long run, guilds could not maintain their status-group monopolization of craft activities. The guild's individual career ladder from apprentice to journeyman to craftsman amounted to an internal stratification that contradicted the egalitarian culture of the elite craftsman. More important, capitalist rationalization and the search for profit pushed against inefficient monopolizations of work activities by the guilds. Craft work thus gradually became reorganized through the "putting-out" system. Eventually, in the eighteenth and nineteenth centuries, the factory system came to dominate production (Weber 1981). In the long run, the culture of guild solidarity could not be sustained against the push toward capitalist rationalization. Yet even today, particular occupational groups seek, sometimes successfully, to monopolize their skills through enforcement of cultural boundaries (Collins 1979), and occupational groups such as computer programmers, travel agents, and restaurant workers develop their distinctive sense of social esteem and their own cultures. The example of the guilds and their occupational descendants shows that part of popular culture amounts to improvisations on tradition adapted to historically new circumstances.

Popular and Elite Culture: Money, Consumption, and Patronage

If the guilds established popular cultures of the little tradition reformulated for town life, commercial popular culture proved even more dynamic during the early modern era. Indeed, the towns witnessed a complex and interconnected flowering of high and popular cultures. The major force probably was the increasing importance of money, however obtained. Capitalist trade involved profit, and this profit placed wealth in the hands of the entrepreneurs and the state. As capitalist activity spread, more money found its way into the hands of common people. These changes altered the economic or "material" basis of support for cultural production.

With the little tradition of small communities, we have the sense of culture that grows out of the daily lives of people. By contrast, popular and elite culture both depend in part on some kind of "patronage," if patronage is defined broadly as the support for cultural workers by other individuals and groups. Sometimes patronage occurs through direct support of cultural workers (i.e., outside of market relations), sometimes through marketplace consumption. The terms and conduits of patronage have changed dramatically over time, and with them, the kinds of culture also have changed.

In the so-called dark ages after the collapse of the Roman Empire, the "great tradition" of elite culture in Europe had been maintained by patronage in the Church, and to a lesser extent, at the feudal courts. Much of what is exhibited today as medieval "art" really amounted to paintings and carvings that served as visual stimuli in religious rituals and practical items such as tapestries and knightly armor that supported the medieval elite's way of life. Such objects typically were produced communally by highly skilled artisans who combined functionality with aesthetics to create fine craft objects (cf. Becker 1982, ch. 9). As for the live cultural performances of the medieval world, insofar as they can be distinguished from folk practices, they were religious ceremonies, and, at the courts, the entertainments offered by a diverse assemblage of jugglers, troubadours, magicians, fools and jesters, poets and bards, and companies of actors. The growing money economy, commercial production and trade, and new occupational classes changed things. By the sixteenth century, both popular culture and elite culture were becoming cultural alloys subjected to ever shifting mixtures by way of market processes.

Among newly wealthy entrepreneurs, new kinds of high culture took hold. Religious themes in "art" were supplanted by new kinds of material objects, and the notion of "art for art's sake" gradually became established as a basis for criticizing and collecting art. Thus emerged the artists as individuals free to explore their aesthetic visions on canvas destined for the art markets rather than for individual patrons (Hauser 1982, pp. 280–82). To be sure, the newly wealthy wanted to affirm their own status and self-esteem. They therefore continued the institution of religious patronage, and they improvised on

FIGURE 4.1 The material culture in this seventeenth century painting by German artist Wolfgang Helmbach suggests the increasing material abundance of the period, while the postures toward the well-heeled man by the other people seem to represent deference and, perhaps, an ambivalence about the inequalities connected with such abundance. (*Source:* Alinari/Art Resource.)

patterns of court patronage by commissioning paintings of themselves and their families. But the entrepreneurs of the emerging bourgeoisie and other newly wealthy people also developed secular and urbane tastes that countered those of religious and courtly life, and by the sixteenth century, themes ranging from Greek mythology to landscape and scenes of social life began to be treated in oil paintings.

Moreover, a new culture of material consumption became established beyond the arts as well. Mukerji (1983, pp. 15, 24) argues that Weber's explanation of Protestantism's significance is "idealist" or unconcerned with consumption. It is therefore important to note that Weber's argument focused on issues of the rationalization of *all* conduct in regulated ways; methodical consumption—as opposed to the "self-indulgent" consumption of luxuries—is as central to the Protestant ethic thesis as work asceticism. Yet what of the material objects themselves? Mukerji develops a compelling and important account of how material culture figured in the expansion of capitalism. Goods, after all, were the stock in trade of capitalism, and the new economic pattern became established through the increasing significance of material goods available through commerce to broader classes of people. However sober and ascetic they may have been, the Protestants—wearing black or not—did consume goods, and other people of means reveled in material culture, buying books, clothing, furniture, and tableware.

Whether luxury or necessity, material consumption in the money economy of the towns always had extended beyond the upper classes, and this tendency increased as towns expanded, especially from the fourteenth century onward. With the consolidation of the Europe-centered world economy in the sixteenth century, production of consumer goods became more specialized by region, and supplies in regions where particular goods were no longer produced became more dependent on trade. This meant that goods were not produced, as formerly, on special order; instead they were made according to increasingly routine processes and to conventional standards. The net result was less expensive goods affordable to a wider public, so that by the late sixteenth century in England, a fairly well-off farmer could have "a fair garnish of pewter in his cupboard...three or four feather beds, so many coverlets and carpets of tapestry, a silver salt, a bowl for wine (if not a whole nest) and a dozen spoons to furnish up the suit" (q. in Burke 1978, pp. 246–7). Not everyone could afford such niceties, of course, and diffusion of consumer goods was regionally and nationally uneven. Nevertheless, the purchase of culture was not limited to an elite social stratum.

The gradually increasing availability of goods and art for purchase during the early modern period raises the question of whether the "great" and "little" traditions still can be distinguished from each other with the rise of commercial conduits of cultural distribution. Amassed wealth no doubt continued to be important for patronage of art, for only substantial assets could support the production of art. But who were the groups with such assets and how did they act as patrons? In Florence, Italy, patronage traditionally was based on support of the Church, and Florentine art remained heavily religious after other regions had shifted to more secular themes. But over the centuries, the sources of Florentine Church patronage shifted as the political economy of Italy changed. In the thirteenth and fourteenth centuries, the trade guilds controlled artistic production. But in the fifteenth century the guilds lost out to less monopolistic organization of craft production; it was the wealthy merchants, such as the famous Medici family, who then took on patronage. Finally, as the merchant class became politically powerful, merchant patronage was supplanted by the city's ruling princes, the Medici Grand Dukes, who used their powers of taxation to finance patronage that enhanced their public image (Pillsbury 1971; Goldberg 1983).

Not in Florence alone did the shift toward state patronage take place, nor was the emergent approach simply a matter of promoting the general public welfare:

> ...at the time of the Renaissance, the princely courts took over both the cities and the Church. Therewith they took over both the production and the direction of art, and made it serve their propaganda and their prestige. Art was pressed into service for evanescent outward shows, in the public spectacles, the triumphal processions, the "Joyous Entries" of princes; it was made permanent in great princely collections, the continuation, in a new age and a new form, of the medieval princely treasure-houses (Trevor-Roper 1976, p. 8).

Elite patronage was not simply a matter of collecting or of charity; it served ends of state and of self-aggrandizement.

How distinct was this elite culture from popular culture? Clearly the subject matter was sometimes worlds apart, as with paintings depicting the pomp and circumstance of the courts and others of elite family members. Yet social analysts from Redfield to Burke have emphasized longstanding continuities between the great and the little traditions. In the first place, cultural workers seeking to gain a livelihood could not always be choosy about the source of their patronage. Some artists, like Dürer at the beginning of the sixteenth century, found success in careers that combined painting, woodcuts, and engravings—works by the same hand that went to taste publics of different economic means (Mukerji 1983, p. 64). There were also the connections between great and little traditions embedded in the structure of social life: Robert Darnton shows that seventeenth- and eighteenth-century servants and wet nurses could bring popular stories like Little Red Riding Hood and Sleeping Beauty into the homes of the rich and directly into the minds of their young (1984, p. 63).

As Burke suggests, though, cultural access was not exactly a two-way street: the elite in 1500 participated along with everyone else in popular culture, for example, in the great festivals. The popular classes, on the other hand, lacked access to the princely collections in palaces and the private performances of music and plays. Nevertheless, there was substantial mutual influence of elite and popular culture: Cultural producers for the elite would often rework popular themes, and by the opposite token, the popular classes interested in mobility would imitate the culture of higher status groups. Mass-produced pictorial prints, for example, offered an affordable medium of art accessible to broad classes of people, yet capable of transmitting images similar to original works of art. On this basis, Mukerji argues that techniques of commercial production diffused a cosmopolitan artistic aesthetic: "The movement of *goods* could be such a powerful cultural force because the increased production and use of consumer commodities was helping to join rich and poor into similar market relations and gathering together buyers throughout Europe into common patterns of taste" (1983, p. 77).

In short, clear continuities have developed between high and popular culture in production techniques, marketplace relationships, and content. Despite, or perhaps because of, these continuities, elite taste publics often have been at pains to distinguish their culture from popular culture. Thus, Burke has described two significant movements: (1) the attempts to "reform" popular culture on the part of "the educated, usually the clergy," and (2) by 1800, the effective withdrawal of the elite from participating in popular culture, marked by divergences between classes in how they viewed the world (1978, pp. 207, 270). This divergence can be addressed by considering a final issue about pre-industrial culture.

Cultural Performance and Audiences

Medieval entertainers often did double duty, performing at the feudal courts, and also wandering through villages and towns, gathering audiences on the spot, traveling to the great and small markets and trade fairs and offering sideshows to the main business of buying and selling necessities and trade goods. It is this sort of practice that suggests to Burke the accessibility of popular culture to the medieval, and subsequently, the early modern social elite. Yet there are two connected developments of the early modern era that alter this equation. First, performance became conventionalized in new ways; the emergence of the modern dramatic form eventually all but eclipsed the types of medieval performance that took place at the courts and the fairs. And second, both the taste public audiences for performances and the themes of drama shifted along class lines. It does not seem too much to say that a new, modern relationship between performance, cultural meaning, and socially stratified audiences was already established before the advent of the mass media, on the stage of the theater.

Changes in the nature of performance, and more specifically, the theater, offer a fascinating topic for speculative efforts at historical reconstruction. The late nineteenth-century cataloguer of myths, Sir James Frazer, sought to connect Greek mythology with the cycle of the seasons; from this argument comes the more general thesis that theater emerged from seasonal celebrations, festivals, carnivals, and pageants. In an alternative view, performance has been thought to have origins in traditional religious rituals of healing and magic, performed by shamans (conventionally called medicine men). In this account, the performances of rituals and trance magic that shamans used were meant to intervene in the "other" world of spirit forces—sometimes codified by mythology and personified with deities (Kirby 1975; cf. Weiss 1973). Dance-drama ritual in more formalized religions such as Hinduism—and in highly conventionalized secular dramas in China and *Noh* theater in Japan—may also amount to a codified version of shamanistic ceremonies, in Kirby's view. As distant as such practices may seem from modern theater, and as speculative as the theories are, they remind us that performance is culturally conventionalized, and that the specifically modern dramatic performance of a story is an invention that has radically different precursors. What are the medieval and early modern forms?

In Europe, religious drama in the Christian Church probably represents an elaboration of the medieval Mass, which was embellished with theatric devices such as someone riding an ass to church on Palm Sunday. By 1000

FIGURE 4.2 Medieval mummers combined elements of magic tricks, drama, and, sometimes, a commercial pitch. (*Source:* Giraudon/Art Resource.)

A.D. the Mass's liturgical dramatic devices were supplanted by what amounted to ritual dramatization. Christian Church dramatization in the form of morality plays also may have been a competitive response to the emerging secular theater against which the Church railed (Kirby 1975, p. 152; Tydeman 1978; Kuritz 1988, pp. 124–7).

Whence this secular theater? There is no clear answer. The European genre of the folk mummer's play—with some origins traced as far back as the year 395 M.E.—did not necessarily give rise to the dramatized Christian mass, as Kirby argued. However, the mummer's play is still an important antecedent of modern performance. In a typical medieval staging of such a play, in the clearing of a space amidst a gathered audience, possibly at a market, two performers brag about their exploits and then fall into mock combat. One of them dies, a doctor enters and claims miraculous healing abilities, and brings the slain combatant back to life. "The performance ends with a collection of money from the audience and with a song" (Kirby 1975, p. 142). Perhaps the doctor is the functional equivalent of, and a stock theatrical type derived from, the shaman, as Kirby argues. But it is also important to recognize that much of the market life of medieval Europe revolved around seasonal celebrations. One notable source for the development of performance was the pre-Lenten celebration of Carnival.

So, if popular theater did emerge out of the fairs and marketplace, there were diverse elements of entertainment—from seasonal rituals to magicians and the mummer's plays—that could serve as sources. What is of interest overall is the commercial turn of what was becoming entertainment in a modern sense. At fairs and markets, the serious business of buying and selling the necessities of life took place amidst a jumble of diverse entertainers, jugglers, musicians, lay preachers, and a host of other figures who might try to drum up an audience and ask for donations on the basis of a performance. As a genre of performance, the mummer's play amalgamates entertainment, medicine, music and the hawking of "cures," a sort of acted-out advertisement. It represents the commercialization of shamanism, ritual and entertainment, a form of popular culture that survives today in diffuse ways—in circuses, television shows, fairs and conventions, and advertising.

The mummer's play is not modern theater. Nevertheless, the distance between the mummer's play and modern drama is not great. With Foucault and Elias, we already have explored how, in the early modern era, the self became rationalized in a way that created a gap between the private self of inward feelings and the presentation of self as public performance. "All the world's a stage," William Shakespeare had the character Jacques tell us in *As You Like It*. This statement could attain its easy acceptance because Shakespeare and his contemporaries established a new form of drama. Shakespeare was "acutely aware of the fabricated nature of conduct both on and off the stage" (Burns 1972, p. 10).

Acting in dramas on the stage became a basis for exploring the tension between self and acting in the wider world. This kind of self-conscious exploration itself was revolutionary as a cultural development, and according to Steven Mullaney (1988), the revolution was a popular one, that offered an alternative to the dramatic genres favored by the elite. Mullaney, who offers a genealogy of London theater to the dawn of the seventeenth century, argues for the social and geographic marginality of the popular stage in the city. As Darnton (1984, ch. 3) has shown for a different time and place, the city itself can be "read" as the stage for a parade, and parades reveal much about the social order. Mullaney details the way that sixteenth-century London was itself recreated as a sort of stage setting for royal pageantry and hangings at the scaffolds—forms of public spectacle promoted by the elite for popular consumption. But the popular theater of Shakespeare and his contemporaries took root elsewhere, in the zone known as the Liberties, at the suburban boundaries of London. There, the lazar-houses filled with lepers, the brothels, the bear-baiting rings, open-air marketplaces with their circus-like sideshows—all this comprised an already-established cultural template of "marginal spectacle" that set the stage for the radical and licentious popular stage. To the authorities in London, Mullaney suggests, the popular theater itself represented a plague that replaced leprosy (like leprosy, to be contained at the margins). If so, it drew into a conventionalized format of theater much of the spectacle of jugglers, musicians, fools and jesters, actors and hawkers who took part in the outdoor spectacle located precisely where the popular London theater became established.

Shakespeare's plays, of course, were popular entertainment of the times. Yet their treatment of some elite-oriented themes, political drama for example, reinforces Burke's thesis that the social elite of the early modern era itself participated in popular culture—at the least, there was much they would enjoy. Elsewhere in London, in so-called private playhouses, other variations on popular theater—"city comedies"—were beginning to serve a more specialized clientele. As a genre, city comedies hardly meet any definitional criteria that suggest the importance of enduring values of civilization in the "great" tradition. Nevertheless, these farces often gained special popularity with an elite audience, mostly younger sons of noble origin, who, lacking inheritances, sought their fortunes in London. English Puritans of the late sixteenth and early seventeenth centuries took a dim view of the London theater, and the nature of the city comedies, and their significance for their primary audience suggests the reason for the antipathy. As Griswold has described it:

> City comedy presents wily, ambitious characters pursuing fortune, status, and love. The genre celebrates the adventures of urban and urbane rascals operating in the wide-open economic milieu of Renaissance London. Its characters demonstrate skills appropriate to an age of expanding opportunities, as they unblushingly lie, scheme, take risks, ignore propriety, flout conventional morality, fleece the gullible, and enjoy themselves hugely all the while (1986, p. 14).

Hardly the sort of cultural material Puritans would sanction.

Worse, from the Puritan viewpoint, the city comedies can be read as more than just humorous entertainment. Drawn from the stock theater types such as the trickster of folklore and Vice of the medieval morality plays, the central characters of these plays—the "gallants"—offered obvious role models to the young private playhouse patrons.

> In city comedy the smart and aggressive, be they younger sons, servants, or con men, achieved wealth, forgiveness, and sometimes even respectability.... This portrait of the reconciliation of economic activism with elite social status was obviously appealing to the young gentlemen in the private theater audience, for it made a cultural virtue of their economic necessity (Griswold 1986, p. 52).

In a sense, the city comedies offered an alternative ethic to that sober model of rational industry favored by Puritans—a comic treatment of the capitalist entrepreneur as wheeler-dealer; theater that made a virtue of living by one's wits.

The emergence of concerns with status, money, and property in a market economy mark the consolidation of a modern bourgeois class of entrepreneurs prior to the Industrial Revolution of the nineteenth century (R. Williams 1982, p. 161). Today the London city comedies are rarely presented on the stage, and not to the bourgeois classes. Yet major elements of the genre live on in a host of popular movies directed to other social strata facing anxieties about social location that parallel those of the early bourgeois. "Ferris Bueller's Day Off" (1986), for example, follows the adventures of a high school student who cuts school for a day by faking an illness to his loving parents, then gets into outrageous difficulties, and somehow manages to talk, walk or drive his way out of trouble by the time his parents arrive home at 6 P.M. In the process, Ferris shows his audience that there is more to life than school. His is a "city comedy" of the young middle class moving into adulthood.

There are many other continuities between the plots of popular movies today and the plot structures of Shakespeare's time, but the continuity over time of the one plot type explored here already suggests what is obvious in general if we think about it: However dramatic entertainment works for audiences, the effectiveness of drama was established before the advent of the mass media through which it is now commonly distributed. The question of what transpires in individuals' "reception" of culture is pursued in chapter 9. For now, we may simply point to one theory drawn originally from Aristotle's account of tragedy: The audience becomes engaged in the struggles of protagonists by identifying theatrical struggles with their own fears and anxieties. For Aristotle, "catharsis" is the emotional cleansing or release the audience experiences from this process. A similar thing happens with comedy: We laugh at things about which we have hopes and anxieties. The city comedy thus connects best with an audience which shares the narrative space of its plot. The social strata that are targeted as the audience for a genre of drama may change: The "city comedies" of today most often seem directed to middle-class youth coming of age. Certainly the settings, situations, and props change, but there are aspects of how dramatic culture offers recipes and meanings of life that preexist the mass media upon which their distribution now largely depends.

CONCLUSION

Studies of the mass media today often attribute to them a tremendous power. Theories of culture often point to the industrial revolution as the significant basis for the flowering of a mass consumer culture, and, indeed, the modern way of life based on a stratified society. The next two chapters will explore the significance of these developments in some detail. Yet our all-too-brief survey of culture in the late medieval and early modern era suggests that any thesis about the significance of the industrial revolution and the mass media must be balanced by the benchmark of comparison with preindustrial culture. Rationalization and routinization—two processes reorganizing thought and activity—have their origins prior to the industrialization that reinforced their impact. Moreover, the commercialization of economic activity in the early modern era created a central tension in "popular" culture. Before commercialization, popular culture was the culture of and by the people, and the term popular culture is sometimes used (for example, by Burke) as synonymous with traditional or indigenous culture. Yet especially with the consolidation of mercantile capitalism beginning in force in the sixteenth century, another kind of popular culture took hold—culture produced for audiences and consumers by entertainers, artists, musicians and artisans for whom cultural work was a business. And just as specialization of occupation was developing in the economy, the products of cultural workers were becoming increasingly geared to different strata of consumers. Thus, by the early modern era, culture was becoming organized and distributed in routinized ways, on a mass basis, in a differentiation of styles and genres meant to appeal to increasingly differentiated audiences. On an ever widening basis, these audiences began to participate in and consume culture in self-conscious ways, rather than simply following the traditions of indigenous and elite cultures handed down from generation to generation.

These developments had only a rudimentary and tentative form, compared to today. Yet their occurrence at all suggests certain important points about the sociological explanation of culture. First, a theory of technological change is not a sufficient basis to explain cultural change. True, as Eisenstein and Mukerji show, the technology of printing had tremendous consequences. Yet the innovations of printing themselves were anticipated by procedures of mass distribution of culture that predated movable type. As Schudson (1978) has argued for a later time period, technological innovations themselves may arise out of social forces such as changing patterns of social organization. Innovations in technology are not autonomous "prime movers" of cultural change. In particular, rationalization and routinization represent transformations of social interaction and social organization that do not always depend upon technological innovation.

A second, related, point is this: There are some aspects of how culture "works" that do not depend on any particular technology or medium. We certainly will want to raise the question of whether a sound recording is "the same" as a live performance of music, or whether a film or TV drama is "the same" as live theater (see chapter 5). And we must recognize that the question of how culture affects its users and audiences is a subject of great controversy (discussed in chapter 9). Nevertheless, there does seem to be a solid "cognitive" or symbolic core aspect of culture—the meaningful communication of aesthetics and ideas—that "works" in similar ways across a variety of technological contexts, and in traditional, elite, and popular culture. Thus, in discussing culture, it is important to distinguish the effects of media of communication from consequences of people's interaction with the symbolic content of cultural objects.

Finally, culture is not simply a "natural" byproduct of societies. Instead, within a social situation, various social groups will try to control the content and character of culture, how it is distributed, and by whom. The cultures of religious groups, the elite, and the popular classes differ from one another, as we have seen especially in the example of theater. Thus, it is a basic sociological thesis that there is no "pure" culture: all cultural objects—symbolic and material—have to be understood in the contexts of their social origins and their significance for their audiences and users. To say this, however, is not to reduce culture to its material conditions. As Baxandall has demonstrated, it is possible to analyze the material conditions of artistic production, at the same time, recognizing that the artist is engaged in an intentional process of solving a variety of cultural problems (1985). Given the diversity of factors we have considered, and the role of intentional social action under specific historical and other working conditions, no reductionist sociological theory about culture—idealist, materialist, or other—can be adequate to historical explanation. Ideas and cultural tastes sometimes are important in ways that cannot be reduced to their material origins, and by the opposite token, material developments of economic structure and change often generate the distinctive cultural problems, meanings and products of various social groups.

5

INDUSTRIALISM AND MASS CULTURE

Industrialization brought widespread changes in the ways people lived their lives: There were changes in where and how people lived, as the cities grew; there were changes in the kind of work that people did, and the degree to which they had control over the work that they did; there were changes in their leisure time pursuits, and in the choices available for consumption. As chapters 3 and 4 argue, even before the processes of industrialization took full force in the nineteenth century, there was a growth of rationality and increasing routinization of daily life, and a development of "society" and of "individualism." These changes took place gradually and affected different groups of people at different times in different places. This chapter focuses on how people in Europe and the U.S. changed their patterns of consumption in the context of a cultural change that argued that consumption, not frugality, was a primary social good.

Patterns of consumption changed at different times for different people as well. Although there is considerable debate about when things changed for whom, following McCracken (1988) we posit three moments in the development of modern consumption. McCracken points first to the consumer boom in sixteenth-century England. In this period, nobles began to consume "with new enthusiasm on a new scale." Consumption came to be valued in a new way: novelty and fashion began to appear as indicators of status. Nobles in

London started following trends from European capital cities, and they used consumption in competing with each other for attention from the queen. In this period differences between the consumption patterns of nobility and other people in the society increased not only in degree but in kind (McCracken 1988, pp. 11–15).

The beginning of mass consumption in the eighteenth century marks the second moment in the history of modern consumption. Consumption spread beyond the nobility as individuals in other classes began to use consumption as a form of self-expression. While consumption increased throughout the century, the value of consumption continued to be debated: What had been considered a vice began to be seen as a virtue. Prior to 1700 the dominant mercantilist views held that demand for goods was inelastic. An early statement of the new view was Mandeville's controversial poem, "The Fable of the Bees," first published in 1705. Presenting the slogan "private vices, public benefits" Mandeville argued that the very characteristics that the moralists cautioned against—such as luxury, pride, avarice, vanity and envy—could benefit the economic system (McKendrik 1982, p. 16). His writings, encouraging the production and consumption of luxury goods, outraged his contemporaries but marked the beginnings of a revolution in consumption patterns that would continue into the twentieth century.

The third moment in the history of consumption came in the nineteenth century. Consumption continued to increase and new styles began to appear. Whereas in the eighteenth century the middle-class had primarily imitated the wealthy, by the nineteenth century different styles were emerging. Bourgeois style dominated, but young dandies developed their own taste culture in opposition to the bourgeois style, while the decorative arts movement (associated with William Morris and his craft workshop) attempted to reform it. Consumption became a way of expressing more than status—or desired status: it could also express one's *attitude* toward the dominant bourgeois culture (McCracken 1988, pp. 22–28; Rosalind Williams 1982).

Questions about the implications of these changes were very much a part of nineteenth-century social thought. After World War I, however, the public discussion of these issues was more and more frequently framed in terms of a concern about "mass society" and "mass culture" bred by mass consumption. These concerns about the nature and meaning of mass society first surfaced in connection with the issues of citizenship and universal suffrage. Governed by elites, the precapitalist European states recognized various status groups, and the status of individuals was "ascribed" on the basis of their group identity. Modernizing societies saw the growth of individualism both in the psychological sense of the development of personality and in the legal sense of the gradual extension of rights to all adult individuals in the society. Many writers hoped that industrialization would release the laboring masses from the constant toil that had characterized their existence, freeing them to pursue the higher things in life: They would become active and informed citizens; they would cultivate an interest in the arts and participate in the cultural life of the society.

Some of this hopefulness can be seen in the following description of mass society by a defender of the modern social order, the theorist Edward Shils:

> The new society is a mass society precisely in the sense that the mass of the population has become incorporated *into* society. The center of society—the central institutions and the central value systems which guide and legitimate these institutions—has extended its boundaries....
>
> Modern industrial techniques, through the creation of an elaborate network of transportation and communication, bring the various parts of mass society into frequent contact. Modern technology has liberated man from the burden of physically exhausting labor, and has given him the resources through which new experiences of sensation, conviviality and introspection have become possible....
>
> Mass society has aroused and enhanced individuality. Individuality is characterized by an openness to experience, an efflorescence of sensation and sensibility.... People make choices more freely in many spheres of life, and these choices are not necessarily made for them by tradition, authority or scarcity... (Shils 1967, pp. 1–3).

Even in the nineteenth century some thinkers (including Jacob Burckhardt and Fredrick Nietzsche) saw dangers in the growth of this mass society. On the political side they feared that the masses would be vulnerable to manipulation by demagogues. On the cultural side they feared that high culture would be overwhelmed by the imposition of the commonplace. In the words of Ortega y Gasset, "The mass crushes beneath it everything that is different, everything that is excellent, individual, qualified and select" (1932, p. 19).

In the period after World War I, however, the concern about mass society took a different turn. It was different in two ways. First, the development of new forms of mass communication raised many issues. Initially photography, then moving pictures, radio and television all allowed for the passive consumption of mass produced culture. Critics feared the homogenization of the population as well as an increased susceptibility of individuals to fascist appeals. Second, the twentieth-century critics of mass culture increasingly included radicals as well as conservatives. These critics had no nostalgia for a golden agrarian past. Rather they felt that the promise of freedom for the masses that industrialization might offer had been lost to modern society. Radicals as well as conservatives in the twentieth century have regarded mass culture as vulgar and exploitative.

This chapter will explore some of these debates about the meaning and value of mass culture. We will briefly look at how consumption patterns changed with industrialization, both in terms of what people consumed and how they came to consume it. We include new forms of distribution such as department stores and new forms of persuasion such as advertising and the availability of credit which made consumption possible for a wider stratum of people than might otherwise have been able to participate in it. We will also look briefly at how participation in the culture of consumption varied by class and gender. We thus explore how consumption changed and the concerns raised by twentieth-century intellectuals about the implications of the changes.

THE MEANING OF MASS PRODUCTION

When one thinks of industrialization it is common to think of the development of capitalism and the technological innovations that created a factory system of large machine production, with the laboring population moving from agriculture to manufacturing. That period was preceded, however, by the growth of small scale industry, increasing participation in a money economy by people of all classes through changing ways of distributing goods, and increasing consumption. In England, between 1550 and 1750—before James Watt's steam engine—daring entrepreneurs initiated a variety of projects producing goods for local and national consumption. They employed a surprising portion of the poor in part time work as "artificers"—making pins and nails, buttons, salt and starch, knives and tools, pots and ovens, ribbons and laces, knitting stockings and so on (see Thrisk 1978, pp. 6–7). To take the last example:

> By the beginning of the seventeenth century knitted stockings had become standard articles of clothing, and if we reckon that the average person wore out two pairs a year...somewhere around 10 million pairs of stockings were needed to dress the whole population. The merchants reckoned that one knitter completed two pairs of stockings per week—a reasonable estimate for knitting was commonly a by-employment—13 percent of labourers and paupers in 1695 could have supplemented their income by knitting (Thrisk 1978, pp. 5–6).

Women and children engaged in such part time work, or by-employment, and supplemented the household income.

With that income they could buy felt hats and iron cooking pots, sword blades and glass bottles, nails, gloves, and knitted woolen stockings. Thus, as sellers of their labor and buyers of goods, they engaged the growing market economy. At the beginning of this period an older set of values and economic constraints sustained an intense prejudice against the importation of such "fripperies"—such as felt hats or gloves of Spanish leather—into England. Thrisk observes:

> Such value judgments, setting a price upon goods whose raw materials were recognized as having a substantial value, while despising those whose value lay principally in the labor conferred upon them,...(were) part of a world which was passing away...in which people spared cash only for the purchase of substantial

goods that were essential to maintain life and to facilitate work. Now it was becoming possible to indulge in a few luxuries to delight the eye... (1978, p. 15).

In medieval society "the market" designated a particular place where commerce occurred, clearly bounded in time and space, and regulated by law. As production and consumption grew, this concrete market gave way to the modern sense of the market as an abstract process. In his work Jean-Christophe Agnew compares the changes in the market from the sixteenth to the eighteenth centuries to the changes in the theater (described in chapter 4). In medieval societies both the market and the theater were special arenas set apart by custom and law from daily life. As such special arenas they had many things in common, often including shared space. However, with the penetration of daily life by the market economy, a division occurred between the market and culture. Agnew argues that the rise of interest in "Civilization" in the nineteenth century is an acknowledgement of the growing dominance of the market:

> Far from contradicting the claims of political economy, the Victorian champions of Civilization merely consented to operate outside its dominion. Aestheticism and economism effectively cartelized the social world by dividing up cultural exchange and market exchange into separate disciplinary jurisdictions. As a consequence, the juncture of these two aspects of life vanished from view, and the deep and unacceptable *division* within market culture reemerged as a deep but eminently acceptable division *between* the market and culture (1986, p. 67).

Yet both what Agnew refers to in this passage as "the market" and what he refers to as "culture" would be deeply affected by the development of mass culture. Despite efforts to keep the two realms separate, the arts themselves became increasingly vulnerable to becoming commodities available to a mass public through mass production. In both the realm of goods and the realm of the arts, for most people production became displaced by consumption, the act of "making" in their daily lives became replaced by "looking."

Social critics of the early twentieth century began to ask if the average person's quality of life was enhanced by mass production, how society was served by it, and what its hidden costs might be. For critical theorists of the Frankfurt school one of the costs of mass production was a loss of "authenticity." While the analyses center on music and painting, their arguments also apply to fast food and to furniture. As we will see, the arguments also came to be applied to identity and the self.

CRITICAL THEORY

In the 1920s a group of young German intellectuals committed themselves to reexamining the foundations of Marxist theory, and for a time, worked to bring about a conjunction of Marxism and psychoanalysis. Known as the Frankfurt

School, they established the interdisciplinary Institute for Social Research dedicated to a radical examination of bourgeois society through both philosophy and empirical investigation. Among the important contributions of the first generation of Frankfurt School researchers was their analysis of the crisis of modern culture. They judged the grand enlightenment project as a failure: The attempt to control social life through the exercise of reason and science had produced only manipulation (such as taylorism in industry) and imitation (in culture). They were deeply influenced by the rise of fascism in Europe. Due to their radical political positions and to the fact that many were of Jewish descent, Institute members were physically threatened by the Nazis, and the Institute relocated in New York City from 1936 to 1949. Their critique of mass culture incorporated a psychoanalytically-based analysis of mass culture's conscious and unconscious openings for fascism.

Unlike other Marxists of the period, the critical theorists saw culture as something more than simply a superstructure reflecting the base of economic structure, yet they repudiated the notion of "art for art's sake" because it neglected the political importance of art. While they looked for "general social tendencies" reflected in particular forms of art, they did not perform reductionist analyses which would seek to tie such tendencies to particular social groups. They considered the relation between art and social structure to be mediated or dialectical: Even the most reified artifacts of affirmative culture—that is, culture which affirmed dominant bourgeois values—were interpreted to be more than derivative reflections of a more fundamental economic reality.

Like the current generation of sociologists of culture who study the production of culture, the Frankfurt theorists had little interest in seeing art as an expression of individual creativity. They did, however, argue that art had a "negative function" in relation to the "affirmative culture" of bourgeois capitalism. Theodore Adorno, who had trained with the composer Schonberg in Vienna, wrote that art "is a force of protest of the humane against the pressure of domineering institutions, religious and otherwise, no less than it reflects their objective stance" (1945, p. 678).

The possibility of the negative moment, however, was not fulfilled by modern mass culture created by capitalism. Nor did the Frankfurt theorists find much to their liking in the art of communist countries. While most of their analyses of mass culture focused on capitalist culture, members of the Frankfurt School described the socialist realism of the former Soviet Union as offering only a "sterile orthodoxy." In 1948 Adorno wrote a highly critical essay on the music of the Soviet bloc entitled "Gegangelte Musik." Martin Jay (1973, p. 196) comments that "gangeln roughly means being fettered or led around by the nose" and describes Adorno attacking "the promotion of 'healthy' art by advocates of socialist realism" in the essay.

The critical theorists described modern culture as dominated more by exchange values than by use values. Adorno argued that the precapitalist music allowed for a certain amount of autonomy and expression of an authentic subjectivity. Production, reproduction and improvisation exist along a continuum, and in precapitalist societies the composer is less separated from the performance and the performers less constrained by the text. Cultures in premodern societies existed in direct relation to their societies, but, the critical theorists argued, modern popular culture is imposed from above. As for the listeners, prefiguring later criticisms aimed at Muzak, Adorno argued that with radio, music becomes a depersonalized "ornament" of everyday life, serving to reconcile the masses to the status quo.

The issue of reproduction received special attention from another member of the Frankfurt School, Walter Benjamin. In his best known essay, "The Work of Art in an Age of Mechanical Reproduction" Benjamin argued that while something was gained with the ability to reproduce works of art, something was also lost. Uniqueness and permanence are exchanged for transitoriness and reproducibility. Reproduction allows the work of art to "meet the beholder half way" because it allows a normally inaccessible original work to be viewed, through reproduction, by a wide audience. What is lost is the uniqueness of a work of art, what Benjamin referred to as its "aura" (1969, p. 211). He argued that original works of art have qualities of "hereness and nowness" that cannot be reproduced. For Adorno, radio could reproduce the nowness but not the hereness of music: listening at home to a broadcast of a live concert one hears the music at the same time as those physically present but without sharing the sense of being at the event (see Adorno 1945).

Benjamin argues that reproduction changes the value of the original work. Part of an original work's authenticity stems from its history, its (changing) relation to a specific place over time. According to Benjamin, at one time works of art had cult value: that is, they were used for particular purposes in religious rituals. With reproduction a work instead has an exhibition value: its value can be expressed in terms of what it sells for. Viewing such a work of art is enhanced by the viewer's sense that it is an important work. With a widely reproduced work, anyone who views the original sees the original of the reproduction, i.e. "the real Mona Lisa." But, Benjamin argued, the authority of the work is gone, detached from tradition.

Given this loss of authenticity Benjamin might prefer going to the movies to visiting a museum. Photography as an art form creates a conceptual problem for Benjamin: Since reproducibility is built into the form there can be no criterion of authenticity. As Benjamin observed "to ask for an authentic print makes no sense" (1969, p. 224).[1] Benjamin argues that this inherent reproducibility alters the basis of art, "the semblance of its autonomy disappeared forever" (1969, p. 226). With photography, and especially with films, we see through the lens of the camera. Replacing the subjective "I" with the "eye" of the camera radically alters perspective in a distinctly modern way.

---

[1] As a market for art photography emerged, however, it has attempted to develop ways to define some prints as "more authentic" than others.

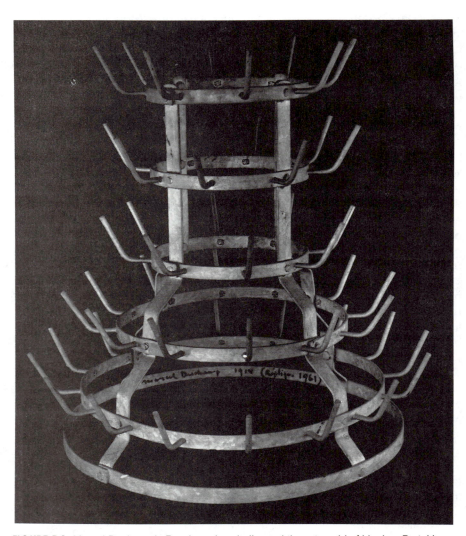

FIGURE 5.1 Marcel Duchamp's Readymades challenged the art world of his day. By taking ordinary objects and displaying them in galleries as art objects, Duchamp decontextualized
them. This "Bottlerack" from 1914 was alternately titled "Hedgehog." The Readymades show
Duchamp's sympathy with the art of the Dada movement, regarded by the Frankfurt School
as "oppositional" art. (*Source:* Philadelphia Museum of Art.)

All artistic attempts to reproduce reality produce illusions, distortions, and
manipulations. But for Benjamin there are important differences: With theater
and with painting we are aware of the illusions we witness; we are aware of the
artist's activity in the production of the work. But the camera "penetrates reality"
giving us images apparently without interpretation. When we see a photograph

(or a news documentary) we do not see the photographer, and we tend to assume we are getting an "objective view" of what is "really there."

Furthermore, Benjamin argued, the response to a film is important as well. Because it is designed to be viewed in a collective setting, "individual reactions are predetermined by the mass audience response they are about to produce" (1969, p. 234). For Benjamin, then, mass culture means the loss of authenticity, true subjectivity, and autonomy. Both the product and the audience is debased in mass culture. Dada[2] and the poetry and theater of Brecht for Benjamin, and the music of Schonberg for Adorno had displayed some of the "negative" possibility of art. Neither liked the German expressionism of their youth, and they were not defenders of classical high culture forms: Benjamin claimed that in handling high culture as "prized goods" its defenders made fetishes of it, and rendered it lifeless. Both men displayed interesting limits to their ability to understand certain cultural forms. To Adorno's amazement Benjamin once said that he did not think that music could have the negative moment—express opposition to the dominant culture—unless it was expressed in words. And Adorno had no understanding of non-western music, and revealed this bias in several articles critical of jazz.

The Frankfurt School's interest in psychoanalysis, although more fully developed elsewhere, can be glimpsed in its studies of mass media. Its members assumed cultural objects always have a multi-layered structure, and that analysis must therefore address unconscious as well as conscious effects. A later generation of social critics would continue the dialogue between Marxism and psychoanalysis that the Frankfurt School started. Writers in the late 1970s and 1980s focused on the way that a society based in mass consumption erodes authenticity not of art, but of the self (e.g., Lasch 1978, 1984; Lears 1983). Although some critics held a nostalgic vision of the past's virtues, the Frankfurt School theorists were not looking backwards toward a lost traditional community. The edge for critical theory comes from their increasing fears that industrialization failed to fulfill its promise of making possible the good society: As the twentieth century went on they saw the growing predominance of mass culture and development of a society of consumers. How did these changes come about?

MASS DISTRIBUTION

The development of shopping in the sense we think of it today is a relatively recent phenomenon. New ways of distributing goods occurred alongside of the development of mass production. The traditional market offered common people the basic necessities: food, baskets, pots, locally produced cloth and such. Itinerant peddlers brought goods as well as news from far off places. In urban

---

[2] A movement in the arts (1916–1922) characterized by fantastic and often playful expression of supposed unconscious content.

areas merchants catered to the wealthy. Their exclusive shops often had signs boasting of the noble families they supplied, but they did not display their wares to the public. Entering a shop implied the intention to buy. Making a purchase involved an elaborate negotiation process between the buyer and the seller. With the "consumption revolution" that was part of the industrial revolution the place of consumption in people's lives changed. The traditional ways of selling goods were eclipsed by a number of modern innovations. The department store was one such innovation. But department stores, along with the other new merchandising formats, such as the mail order catalog, were more than just new ways of distributing goods. They are evidence of a new ethic of consumption which they helped to create. Advertising, one of the most pervasive aspects of mass consumption, worked with department stores to spread the ethic of mass consumption. Through advertising department stores provided the financial base for the growth of newspapers: One New York reporter and editor was quoted as saying that "at the end of the nineteenth century the newspaper became 'an appendage of the department store'" (cited in Schudson 1984, p. 152). In this section we will examine the department store and advertising as two marketing innovations central to establishing the consumption culture.

The Department Store

The development of the department store is an embodiment of the attempt to routinize and rationalize selling. In the years between 1840 and 1860 a new type of store began to appear in major cities in Europe and the U.S. These stores sold a large variety of goods, which they displayed in such a way that the goods could be viewed. A major innovation was fixed prices marked on the goods. This pricing approach eliminated the time-consuming bargaining process and, together with increased sales volume, meant department stores could charge less for items and still make a profit.

Distribution is the often complex link between manufacturing processes and consumption. Department stores gained from making distribution more efficient. Department store owners and managers attempted to rationalize not only the selling process but their relationships to suppliers as well. Rapid turnover of goods and cash sales[3] provided an important part of the operating capital in the early years. Because department stores bought such large amounts, they had an advantage in their relations with suppliers. This allowed the department stores to shift some of the costs of doing business onto the suppliers: They bought goods on credit, "thereby shifting onto the manufacturer the initial financing of supplies," and they required deliveries

---

[3] This was a departure from previous merchandising practices of shops, which put department stores at an advantage in relation to their suppliers. Department stores did not offer credit until after World War II. However, the most affluent customers could charge purchases, paying their entire bills at the end of the month.

to be staggered, "so that in still another way the operating costs—this time the costs of warehousing—were largely shouldered by the supplier" (Miller 1981, pp. 54–55).

Another marketing innovation of the department stores, the reduced-price sale, was also a part of the rationalization of consumption. Obviously such "reductions" were not possible before goods were marked with set prices. At first department stores advertised special sales when they had been able to get particularly good prices on goods that the suppliers, who had trouble gaging demand, were having a difficult time selling. The sale, however, became an important promotional device in itself. Miller argues that at the Bon Marche, one of the largest and earliest Paris department stores, the week of the mid-winter white sale was "the most important sales week of the year." Miller sees the yearly white sale as symbolic of the rationalization of distribution that occurred with the development of the department store: "Begun...as a mere merchandising gimmick, the *blanc* soon came to be the most organized week at the store, a model of the sophisticated sort of planning that Bon Marche Directors and administrators were capable of producing" (Miller 1981, pp. 70–71).

The largest department stores competed in size, both in terms of physical space and the number of employees with the largest factories. In 1898 Macy's had 3000 employees; in 1900 Jordon Marsh "was the fourth largest employer in New England, surpassed only by the Amoskeag Mills, General Electric's Lynn plant, and the Pacific Mills of Lawrence" (Benson 1986, p. 34). Managers felt considerable pressure to exert control over their enterprises, and Benson documents their continuing efforts at rationalizing the selling process. New conventions for organizing goods made selling easier, from the introduction of coat hangers to the new layouts that placed bargain goods in the basement, cosmetics, jewelry and other impulse items on the first floor, and segregated men's clothing from the rest of the merchandise (Benson 1986, pp. 40–47). In the early twentieth century rationalization also brought "systematic management" in which accounting departments developed increasingly elaborate—but not entirely effective—methods of monitoring the productivity of employees from buyers to saleswomen (Benson 1986, pp. 54–67).

The owners and managers of these "palaces of consumption" attempted to cater to and define bourgeois taste. Although open to everyone, the department stores displayed not only goods but an opulent style of living. Exteriors made use of architectural innovations such as steel and glass to let in light and create display windows. Paris's new Bon Marche store, completed in 1887, was engineered by Gustave Eiffel, designer of the Eiffel tower, and became a tourist attraction itself (Miller 1981, p. 42). Interiors of the stores were luxuriously adorned with fine woods and marble. Some store owners promoted cultural events such as concerts in the stores after closing time.

The early department stores also competed with each other and with other kinds of stores in service. Store owners pledged not to misrepresent the goods, and promised refunds if customers were dissatisfied. Delivery services—often in the form of uniformed delivery boys arriving in vehicles marked with a distinctive company symbol—brought packages to the customer's door. Other services included provision of telephones, restaurants, rest rooms and meeting areas. Individual stores hoped that the provision of services would induce loyalty among customers to their particular store (Benson 1986, pp. 84–91).

With the bourgeois matron as the ideal customer, the department stores provided public spaces for women in city centers most frequently dominated by men. Consumption, described by Thorstein Veblen early in the twentieth century as the obligation of the bourgeois woman, became a respectable occupation in department stores modeled on the home and the men's downtown club. Hortense Odlum, president of Bonwit Teller, said that she "tried to have the policy of the store reflect...those standards of comfort and grace which are apparent in a lovely home" (cited in Benson 1986, p. 83). The stores provided places for women to meet as well as to shop; thus they gave women ways of participating in the urban environment.

Consumers, of course, were not the only women in the department stores; in the United States women were over-represented among salesworkers as early as 1880. In the department stores women made up from half to nine-tenths of the total employees (Benson 1986, pp. 179–180). These women felt far more ambivalent about the department store environment. For women with full-time jobs, sales work was steadier and paid more than manufacturing employment, although it did not pay as well as clerical work (which required more education). There was some chance of advancement in sales, but it was small. The long hours spent on one's feet attending to the needs of demanding customers made it a physically exhausting job. Managers offered carrots and sticks in the attempt to make saleswomen conform to their standards of bourgeois gentility. Store discounts for employees enabled saleswomen to be customers as well (although their salaries sometimes put severe limits on their ability to enjoy this benefit), and extensive penalties enforced regulations regarding dress and behavior. The manager's ideal was a saleswoman with expert knowledge about the goods to share—respectfully—with the customer. The saleswoman's position entailed class contradictions. Managers wanted the working-class women— who sold goods priced beyond their means to middle-class women—to represent the middle-class ethos of the store. Furthermore, saleswomen experienced ambiguous class status. Benson notes that they were "driven by the social relations of the workplace to see themselves as members of the working class, [and] cajoled by the rewards of mass consumption to see themselves as middle class" (Benson 1986, p. 271).

Yet the rationalization process was not entirely linear. As Michael Miller argues in his study of the Bon Marche, efforts toward rationalization were accompanied by vestiges of more traditional relationships between employers and employees. There, for example, the founders took care of loyal employees by dispensing pensions and other benefits. The tradition of the family firm appears to have been used especially effectively by the Boucicauts at the Bon Marche to promote the image of Bon Marche workers as constituting a "family." Miller cites strikes as late as 1919, many years after the death of the founding family, in which both sides claimed in their rhetoric that the other side violated the traditional practices established by the founders (1981, pp. 148–149).

In the United States various forms of paternalism co-existed with taylorism and scientific management as strategies for mitigating potential labor unrest. Workers demanded better working conditions, and they received some support from customers—some of those involved with the reform movements of the progressive era were shocked by the conditions under which saleswomen worked. To head off controversy, employers at the large department stores began in the early twentieth century to provide more for the welfare of the workers, including rest rooms, lounges, lunchrooms, recreation facilities and clinics.

Department stores not only sold goods, but they sold a vision of the middle-class way of life. Managers portrayed shopping in their luxurious stores as a pleasure in itself. They created new "needs" and suggested how they could be satisfied, e.g., how to dress when cycling, or selling new kitchen appliances with classes on how to use them. The department stores, aided by the development of mail order departments, helped to break down regionalism and create a national culture. Yet this process was not without its critics. Some observers worried about both the costs of increasing uniformity and the quality of the mass produced goods.

There was also concern about the threat to morality represented by women in public places. In both Europe and the United States in the early twentieth century sensationalist accusations circulated that the stores provided the occasion for saleswomen to turn to prostitution—because the open nature of the stores made them available to pimps and madams, because of sexual harassment by managers, or because they craved the luxuries which surrounded them and which they could not afford on their low wages (Miller 1981, p. 195; Benson 1986, pp. 135–136). A parallel concern surfaced in the reports of kleptomania among bourgeois women: The store provided an occasion of temptation that could not be resisted (Miller 1981, pp. 196–206). Both cases reflected a belief that department stores corrupted the moral order:

> Bourgeois institutions were expected to uphold the moral order, not threaten it and yet this did not seem to be the rule in the department store.... (T)he pathological frenzy to which some women were driven had become simply the seamier side of the new consumer society, where the old virtues of thrift and self-control were giving way to a culture of gratification... (Miller 1981, pp. 206–207).

Department stores were aided in their efforts to create this consumer "culture of gratification" by the expanded role of advertising.

Advertising

Industrialization vastly increased the number and variety of goods available in the market, but getting them to people who would buy them required the development of an infrastructure of marketing and distribution. Business became concerned about creating national markets for their goods as well as creating consumers among classes of people who had previously been less engaged in the market economy. This entailed changes in the ways that people thought about consumption. Advertising was instrumental in this cultural shift.

Advertising sought to replace Protestant values of Poor Richard and the Protestant Ethic—valuing saving and a certain asceticism—with the idea that consumption was a part of being a good American. In part advertising promoted this shift by helping to create a national culture in which the use of particular products carried a moral weight. For example, a good American father is told that he must buy life insurance from Prudential if he cares about protecting his family (the insurance business, rather than the family or the state, is depicted as the only source of true security).

A great deal has been written about advertising. It is a pervasive part of modern culture. Some authors celebrate advertising as part of the new availability of goods and consumer choices. Other authors excoriate it as the means by which capitalist producers manipulate and control the masses. Some defenders claim that in fact advertising is not all that powerful and can only provide information to aid consumers in making their choices. While we are concerned here primarily with arguments about if and how advertising contributed to a shift in values, we will first take a brief look at what is known about whether advertising influences people to buy things.

Ironically, price advertising,—ads that say the product is on sale or has a low price—the form of advertising that is most effective at getting people to buy things, is the least controversial (Schudson 1984, p. 64). The arguments against advertising, however, primarily target national consumer goods advertising. It is hard to assess the effects of this kind of advertising because producers use it along with other market strategies and within a larger social context where many other factors also influence the sale of a given advertised product.

In addition to advertising, producers develop a marketing mix that includes promotions—where the customer receives a material benefit for buying the product, such as premiums or sweepstakes—and direct sales. The amount of money spent on advertising does vary with consumption, but not in the way that one might expect: There is a higher correlation between sales in the previous quarter and money spent on advertising in a given quarter than between advertising in a given quarter and sales in the following quarter (Schudson 1984, p. 17). Success in sales seems to lead to greater expenditures on advertising. In addition, the quality of the product and the price of the product affect sales. Advertisers like to say that "good advertising drives out bad products" because even if advertising persuades people to buy a product once, they are not likely to buy it a second time if they do not like it.

Sales also depend on social forces such as demographic trends, the state of the economy, and on government policies. If new car sales or housing starts go down in a recession no one suggests that advertising campaigns were at fault. If fewer babies are born, the market for baby food goes down; similarly, mothers who are in the labor force have different consumption patterns than mothers who are not in the labor force. Government tax credits for energy-saving home improvements influence people's decisions about whether to make those improvements to their homes. While advertising may be the most visible persuader, it rarely acts by itself.

Furthermore, most customers are not defenseless when confronted by advertising. Benson shows department store customers in the first half of this century reading advertisements with considerable caution (1986, p. 106), and current research shows that only nine percent of television viewers can identify the brand or product category they saw advertised just before answering the phone call by the market researcher. Most people "operate in an information environment" where they have considerable resources to bring to the interpretation of any ad (Schudson 1984, pp. 3, 90–114). Consumers often have information about the product, and other products like it, that comes from their own personal experience and that of other people they know. They may have some information (other than advertising) from other sources such as the media or consumer education groups. They are likely to see advertisements from rival products as well. They may also have general skepticism about the media and about advertising in particular. Furthermore, Schudson points out that "price is a check on advertising claims" (1984, p. 114). The marked price is another piece of information about a product and may be interpreted by the customer as "too much to spend" for a given object or as too low for the product to be of sufficient quality.

Some groups of people, however, have less information and therefore are more vulnerable to the claims that advertisements make. Schudson discusses ways in which both highly mobile people and highly immobile people (including the housebound among the elderly), children, the poor, and "many of the relatively poor and poorly educated people in the Third World" can have "situational or structural ignorance" (1984, pp. 117–125). Even for such groups, however, advertising does not appear to have a direct effect of inducing customers to go out and buy a particular product.

Critics, however, charge advertising with coercive powers on another level. They claim that advertising tells people that consumption is a good thing in itself; that advertising exploits established "needs" and creates new ones. Stuart Ewen, for example, argues that business had to create a consumer culture for two reasons. First, to "feed and adhere to the demands of the production schedule," and second, to "absorb, neutralize and contain the transitional impulses of a working class" (1976, p. 52). Advertising, for Ewen, is the primary agent in a process through which individuals lost their consciousness of "class" as an identity located in their work, and instead sought identity and self expression in consumption. In Ewen's terms, "By transferring the notion of 'class' into 'mass' business hoped to create an 'individual' who could locate his needs and frustrations in terms of the consumption of goods rather than the quality of life (work)" (1978, p. 43).

Ewen's argument is too simplistic in several ways. First, working class wages were too low for them to have been involved in the consumer culture to the degree that Ewen's argument implies they were. Second, large cultural shifts such as the growth of consumer culture have many determinants:

> Twentieth century advertising and twentieth century consumer culture have roots in the changing nature of the market in the late nineteenth century which developed along with changes in modes of transportation and communication, urban growth, and a cultural climate for and social fact of social and geographic mobility. In addition, changes in the manufacturing processes in various industries and the capacity to increase output without substantial increases in product costs encouraged a new emphasis on marketing and distribution... (Schudson 1984, pp. 176–177).

Yet for many people advertising is the most visible of these processes.

What can we say about the overall effects of being bombarded with the message that through consumption we can meet all our needs and desires? Schudson suggests a provocative parallel between the official art of the former Soviet Union, Socialist Realism, and advertising, which he suggests we think of as "Capitalist Realism." Both simplify and typify life as it "should" be. The individuality of any person featured in the ad is muted; rather, people represent some larger social significance. As Schudson notes, the values that advertisements express are not usually capitalist in themselves; instead advertisers usurp values in the culture—love, friendship, youth—and use them in a capitalist way to sell goods (1984, pp. 210–221).

This leads to two concerns about the larger significance of advertising. The first reflects concerns about the effects of a kind of cognitive distancing that people exposed to the claims of socialist realism or advertising learn to do. A common response to both is disbelief. Viewers "know" those healthy, happy workers are not real people, just as viewers "know" that a new shampoo will not solve the problems of one's love life. Yet this continual suspension of belief leads to a certain detachment from reality: advertising encourages an ironic stance (Schudson 1984, pp. 224–229). The second concern is related: To the extent that advertising does constitute, if not an official art form, a pervasive public art form, it becomes the dominant mode in which thoughts and experiences get expressed. Schudson argues that advertising as pervasive art "brings some images and expressions quickly to mind and makes others relatively unavailable" (1984, p. 230). Alternative values exist in the culture, but it is harder to find representations of them. Therefore

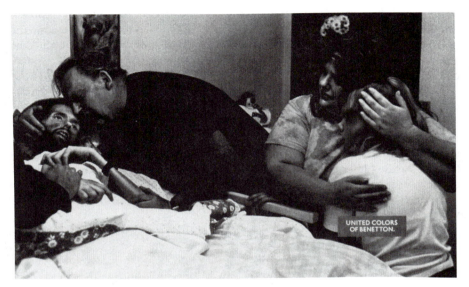

FIGURE 5.2 In modern mass media the differences between art and advertising and news and advertising are no longer clear cut. The clothing company Benetton continued the trend toward blurring these distinctions with a series of provocative advertisements showing news photos of disasters—here a young man dying of AIDS—with the company logo. (*Source:* United Colors of Benetton.)

advertising has a certain power to distort and flatten our ability to interpret complex experiences.

We can observe this happening when advertising photographs are placed in magazines with news documentary photographs. In the jumble of images people tend to respond to both kinds of images with the same distancing mechanism. Both the documentary image and the advertisement are objectified and treated as commodities. More than causing major changes in the culture, advertising reflects it. But, it does so only partially, and in ways skewed toward a capitalist idealization of our culture.

MASS CONSUMPTION

The industrial revolution was accompanied by a consumer revolution: people began to buy things in the market that previously they had produced for themselves or had done without. As goods and money became more available, the meaning of consumption changed as well. At the beginning of the consumption revolution people began to use goods to express their status (or the status they desired). Novelty and fashion began to be valued for what they indicated about the wealth of the consumer. Later, more diverse consumption

styles developed and people began to use consumption as a way of expressing other things about themselves, including their stance toward the dominant
bourgeois culture. The consumption revolution means, then, not only that
more people bought more things, but that the meaning of consumption
changed as well.

As we have seen, the point from which one dates the consumption revolution depends on what level of consumption is the focal point of one's interest:
Some analysts start in Elizabethan England with the change in meaning for the
nobility (McCracken 1988), others place it as late as the 1950s after government
loans to G.I. families created suburban communities democratizing consumption on a scale hitherto unknown (Ewen 1976). In part these different portrayals
of the consumer revolution derive from alternative understandings about class
and gender. Social position made a tremendous difference in how individuals
were incorporated into the consumption culture.

Class and Consumption

Producers have an interest in the ability of people to buy the goods they
make. In the 1920s industrialists saw they had an interest in the movement for
higher wages and shorter hours, which would increase levels of consumption.
Herbert Hoover is cited as saying "High wages [are the]...very essence of great
production" (Ewen 1976, p. 28, his editing). Shorter hours and higher wages in
the twenties affected mostly salaried workers, including the expanding middle
class; the wages of working-class people were still too low to allow for a high
level of participation in consumption. According to data about the period,
working-class wages were close to subsistence levels (see Ewen 1976, pp. 56–
57). Consumption by working-class families involved either buying on the installment plan or substituting one kind of purchase for another. The Lynds note,
for example, that in Middletown, in the 1920s, it was not uncommon for families
to mortgage their houses to buy an automobile (Lynd and Lynd 1929, p. 254).

Daniel Bell argues that mass consumption began in the 1920s. He attributes it to revolutions in technology and to three social inventions: assembly
line production, the development of marketing (including but not limited to advertising), and the spread of installment buying. Bell also links mass consumption in this period with changes in values: "The concomitant revolutions in
transportation and communications laid the basis for a national society and the
beginnings of a common culture. Taken all together mass consumption meant
the acceptance...of social change and personal transformation" (1976, p. 66).

A form of installment buying predated World War I, but it was used only
by poor people and carried the stigma of debt. People bought things from peddlers who came by every week to collect payment. Middle class morality demanded a different approach: When people want something they should save
for it. Going into debt was "wrong and dangerous." Installment buying, however, routinized the process: Businesses billed monthly charges through the

mail. It was efficient and impersonal. Businesses avoided using the word "debt," and both middle class and working class people took advantage of the opportunity to buy "on credit" (Bell 1976, p. 68). It seems likely, however, that middle-class people benefited more from this innovation than did the working class.

Boorstin (1973) and others have written about how mass consumption created a "democratization of goods." Schudson gives a slightly different account. Goods become more uniformly available, more standardized, more convenient, and more likely to be consumed in public ways. Yet while the goods displayed in a department store are available in theory to everyone, in practice, they are available only to those with the resources to make the purchase. Schudson reminds us that the displays of mass consumption create a democratization of desire and envy (1984, pp. 181, 151). To the extent that the "national culture" was based on consumption, working class and poor people were at the margins or outside of it.

Mass Consumption and Gender

The development of consumer culture also deeply affected the lives of women. Those in the paid labor force—most men and women such as the saleswomen discussed above—developed a bifurcated consciousness. On the job they had identities based on the work they did and the social relations of the workplace, but off the job they participated in consumption culture. We noted above how working-class saleswomen experienced contradictory class consciousness in their dual roles as workers and consumers. Bell describes the contradiction experienced by middle-class workers who subscribe to the norms of functional rationality at work, but to the hedonism of consumer culture in their leisure (1976, p. 15).

Women who were not employed outside the home had a different experience. Consumption became women's work. This is true in two quite different ways. First, as production moved out of the household women's work of reproducing their families came to involve primarily consumption activities. Clothing, for example, slowly went from being produced in the household to being purchased in stores. Second, among the affluent, women were also the primary vehicles for "conspicuous consumption"—the exhibition of appropriate signals of status.

The image of families before the industrial revolution as self-reliant three generational units is largely a myth of functionalist theory. Yet traditional households in western societies can generally be characterized as (1) having had greater unity between home and work, public and private, sacred and secular, instrumental and expressive, and work and play than modern households typically experience; (2) based in a patriarchal order, with jural authority residing in males and strong, often economically based, ties to paternal kin; and (3) gynocentric in the sense that activities were organized around the reproduction of the family and household, with women as significant partners in the work of the household (see Ehrenreich and English 1978). It is not until the nineteenth century that husbands and wives were likely to view each other as companions, or that males were defined as "providers" or mother-hood was seen as a woman's sacred vocation.

In the United States for most of the nineteenth century the largest effect of technological change on the household was that the husband was increas-ingly likely to have outside paid employment. Yet other changes did occur. The making of clothing was one of the first tasks to move out of the home. Al-exander Hamilton noted in 1791 that 80 percent of Americans' clothing was made in people's own households to be worn by household members. The invention and distribution of the sewing machine in the 1870s increased the likelihood that clothing would be made outside the home. By the onset of the twentieth century most of women's clothing was still made at home, but ninety percent of men's clothing was made outside of the home.

Housework itself changed very slowly: the egg beater and the cast iron stove were the only labor-saving devices widely diffused in the nineteenth century (Strasser 1982, pp. 33–49). Although gas lighting was available in most major cities by the 1820s and 1830s, only relatively wealthy people could af-ford to install gas lighting in their homes until the turn of the century. Electric-ity was not commercially available until the 1880s. Sixteen percent of households had electricity in 1912, 35 percent in 1920, and 68 percent in 1930, but, even then only 10 percent of farm homes were electrified. The majority of the latter did not have electricity until Franklin D. Roosevelt's rural electrifica-tion program in the mid-thirties (Strasser 1982, pp. 68–83).

Attempts to rationalize housework did not, however, depend solely on technological changes. By the end of the nineteenth century women such as Catherine Beecher and Ellen Swallow had developed systems of "domestic science" for running households more efficiently (Sklar 1973). Housework changed much more quickly in the twentieth century with the invention and diffusion of vacuum cleaners, electric irons, washing machines, and so on. At the same time fewer women did housework for wages: The number of women employed as domestic servants decreased between 1910 and 1920 to such an extent that World War I was seen as a kind of watershed. Paralleling these developments, fewer unpaid women—mothers and daughters of the housewife who participated in doing the work of maintaining the house-hold—were engaged in helping with domestic work. Ruth Cowan argues that the labor-saving devices increased expectations of how much housekeeping was "necessary"—clothing and linens, for example, could be washed much more frequently and ordinary people came to expect freshly prepared hot meals three times a day—so that women did not in fact end up spending less time doing housework (1976).

Weinbaum and Bridges (1978) describe women in advanced capitalist so-cieties as "consumption workers." A common stereotype has women consumers as neurotic products of modern society addicted to shopping. Disputing that,

Weinbaum and Bridges argue that women do not consume out of "psychological need" but rather because it is their job. As consumers women must make decisions about whether it is more efficient to buy things at the market or produce them at home. Rejecting the common portrayal of housewives as their own bosses, Weinbaum and Bridges point out that they must observe the schedules set by the state and economic institutions. Imagine the scheduling constraints of a woman with children to take to school, dry cleaning to pick up, groceries to buy, and perhaps a special coffee or bread to be purchased at another shop; in addition, the oil needs to be changed in the car, and her driver's license must be renewed. Assuming that she has the money to pay for these goods and services, and that she is not also working a full time job in the labor force herself, she is still dependent on the whims of the providers. In addition, the increase in "self-service" means that consumption workers are more likely to do work previously done by paid employees.

Women are consumption workers in another respect. Thorstein Veblen talked about "conspicuous consumption" through which individuals used consumption to give off information about their status. For Veblen, one of the duties of the middle-class wife is to "carry on the business of vicarious leisure, for the good name of the household and its master" (1965, p. 81). Even as more and more women enter the labor force, advertising is still aimed disproportionately at women who are expected to do consumption work and display the status of the household through their consumption activity.

When we talk about part of women's job being to display the markers of status, however, women are not only the consumers but the consumed. Women become the objects of the gaze of men. Janet Wolff has noted that women are rarely present in social scientists' discussions of the transition to modernity. This literature, written by men for men, is "essentially a literature about transformations in the public world and in its associated consciousness" (1989, p. 141). It is a world in which women are rarely present as actors in the public sphere. Women were present in the city streets, but they did not own the streets in the ways that men did: Wolff catalogues them, "the dandy, the flanneur, the hero, the stranger—all figures invoked to epitomize the experience of modern life—are invariably male figures" (1989, p. 148). Middle-class women were constrained, working and poor women disdained in the eyes of male observers and writers. Yet in the depiction of the department store presented here, we see in its customers and salesladies, the women present in the emerging culture of the modern world.

CONCLUSION

The success of the industrial revolution was to create a world of consumer goods beyond what could even be imagined by the early industrialists. In this chapter we have explored some of the cultural ramifications of that change.

Some writers, however, have also argued that mass culture has had ramifications for how individuals constitute a sense of self. Fox and Lears point to the importance of three developments at the end of the nineteenth century: (1) the emergence of a national market; (2) the development of a new layer of professionals and managers enmeshed in a complex web of business and professional organization; and (3) the rise of the therapeutic ethic (1983, p. xi). Technological and economic change resulted in a new form of material culture; it also altered the cultural constitution of self and society.

As we noted earlier, the consumption culture is based on the idea that consumption—and abundance—are positive values. The new morality was expressed in many aspects of early twentieth-century culture, including academic psychology and religious tracts. Lears (1983) argues that the new service elites (psychologists, therapists, and liberal Protestant religious leaders) offered the new ethic in response to the anxiety produced by modern existence. The therapeutic ethic promised personal fulfillment and provided authoritative answers to questions about the meaning of life, in part by getting rid of guilt and legitimating consumption.

Advertising played on both the ethic of fulfillment and the anxieties of modern individuals. Observers in the 1920s perceived a change from advertisements that essentially described the qualities of products to those that appealed to people's insecurities. In *Middletown,* for example, the Lynds described modern advertising as:

> ...concentrating increasingly upon a type of copy aiming to make the reader emotionally uneasy, to bludgeon him with the fact that decent people don't live the way he does.... This copy points an accusing finger at the stenographer as she reads her motion picture magazine and makes her acutely conscious of her unpolished finger nails...and sends the housewife peering anxiously into the mirror to see if her wrinkles look like those that made Mrs. X in the advertisement "old at thirty-five" because she did not have a leisure hour electric washer (1929, p. 82).

A host of personal grooming products came onto the market, using advertising to inform people of their needs and then offering them chances to buy products that satisfied those needs. Ewen suggests that advertisers saw their task as creating consumers' "critical self-consciousness in tune with the solutions of the marketplace" (1976, p. 38). As our earlier discussion implies, such ads probably did not create anxiety as much as they exploit anxieties that are already there. Although such ads are not generally taken at face value, the act of detaching or distancing oneself from them creates a cognitive perception of unreality that can be experienced as personally unsettling. Not only is the vision in the ad perceived as unreal but it becomes more and more difficult to maintain the feeling that the self is real (Lears 1983, p. 8–9). The crisis of authenticity identified by the critical theorists came to be experienced as a personal crisis in the therapeutic culture.

In looking at arguments such as these it is easy to create an image of "capitalists" or "advertisers" who manipulate or control the rest of us, without our being able to do anything about it or even knowing that it is happening. This chapter offers a more nuanced view. From the beginning, the consumption revolution was fueled by many different sources. Even if the consumption culture was hegemonic in its dominating, absorbing reconstruction of culture, the capitalists, advertisers and therapists who promoted themselves were "driven by unfocused anxieties as well as deliberate strategies" (Lears 1983, p. 37).

Yet it is important to ask what kind of choices this culture of consumption allows us and under what circumstances. Proponents of environmentalism have discovered how difficult it is to get people to change consumption patterns. And participation in the consumption culture is always constrained by one's income limits. These points raise the question of how social stratification is related to culture, the topic of the next chapter.

6

SOCIAL STRATIFICATION AND CULTURE IN THE AGE OF MASS PRODUCTION

Even casual observation will confirm that social stratification and cultural practices are connected. Each person has a unique life. Yet individuals often find themselves doing the culturally appropriate or the predictable thing, facing the dilemmas of youth in either conformity or rebellion, taking on roles—friend, lover, wife, mother, husband, father—and occupational positions—doctor, salesperson, mechanic, teacher—that exist independently of any individual. Each person's repertoire of cultural practices is distinct, yet a given practice sometimes is widely shared, and individual differences in repertoires are neither random nor the product of personal taste alone. True, cultural objects have no readily apparent order to them. They are everywhere, diverse, often in a jumble. But the disarray is only on the surface. Culture is constantly being subjected to organization—in collections, shows, stores, programs, series, and channels. Individuals all make choices narrower than their available possibilities.

Though each individual's cultural practices are unique, the dazzling variety of culture becomes surprisingly coherent when we view it through the lens of social stratification. People prepare and consume food in distinctive ways. Some people are quite concerned with becoming "culturally accomplished"—learning to quilt, dance, ride horses, or surf. Such orientations to culture differ systematically by social position and group. In this chapter, we are not yet concerned with the apparatus of social power or domination by which cultural objects are distributed among the population (a topic of chapter 7). The relation of culture to social stratification is a topic in its own right, and its careful consideration offers a building block upon which to consider questions about cultural domination.

What are the alternative approaches by which the relationship between stratification and culture can be understood? To simplify, we can identify three basic models of culture and stratification: (1) a model of *cultural groups,* including classes, (2) a model of *cultural markets* and *class groups,* and (3) a model of *multiple markets* and *multiple* kinds of cultural *groups.*[1] By considering in some detail studies exploring each of these alternative models, we will be in a better position at the end of this chapter to offer a general account of how social processes connect stratification and culture.

THE GROUP THEORY

The classical formulation of the thought that groups have distinctive cultural boundaries was set out by Emile Durkheim in his studies on the division of labor, and of religion (1964, 1965). Durkheim readily recognized that complex societies with highly differentiated divisions of labor have low degrees of common or "collective" consciousness. Nevertheless, for all societies, he regarded religion as establishing a distinction between the sacred and the profane, and these distinctions, he argued, really had to do not with God in some spiritual sense, but with the moral boundaries of a social group. There are always some distinctions of hierarchy and prestige within a group, but for Durkheim, a social group with strong social solidarity exists only to the

---

[1] If a cultural market operates in the same way economists understand other kinds of markets, namely as a regulative institution, then these models can be understood in terms of Mary Douglas's typology of high versus low *grid* (e.g. in this context, the degree of market regulation) and high versus low *group* allegiance (1982). The first theory is a high group/low grid theory, in which *groups* are the defining basis of cultural stratification. On the other hand, the second and third models both are based on the existence of a *market* (high grid regulation), but also treat group allegiances as important, but in different ways. Other theories would logically fill out the two other cells of Douglas's typology. Thus, a low grid/low group theory of culture and stratification would posit culture as a matter of individual self-expression, unrelated to the regulation of the market in cultural goods, and unaffected by individual membership in groups. No current theory advances this model. On the other hand, a high grid/low group theory would suggest the importance of the marketplace of cultural objects as the sole device regulating cultural stratification. While a purely micro-level economic theory might be applied to culture in this way, current thinking in both economics and sociology seems to be that if markets exist, activity is oriented to them on the basis of groups, which either preexist or emerge on the basis of individuals' market activities. Thus, neither the low grid/low group nor the high grid/low group theoretical possibilities find proponents in contemporary theories of culture and stratification.

degree that culture is fundamentally shared by all its members, and in a strong group, culture thus serves as an ingroup/outgroup marker, and as a marker of conformity or deviance. Wearing the clothing appropriate to a particular reference group is a free choice in a pluralistic society, for example, but it is one that marks the individual's relation to the group to other group members and perhaps to outsiders as well.

Durkheim was not the only classical sociologist to offer an account of the relation between culture and social groups. Georg Simmel's thesis about the "lowest common level" suggests that culture must be accessible enough in its content and form to reach virtually all members of a group (1950, p. 37). For Simmel, like Durkheim, a group can only thrive on the basis of shared culture. Max Weber wrote in a somewhat similar vein about certain kinds of groups which have an interest in distinguishing their members from society-at-large. Weber described the "status group" as a group of persons in a larger society who claim either a "special social esteem" or perhaps "status monopolies." He described "circles setting themselves apart by means of...characteristics and badges." For Weber, the sources of status are various (lifestyle, education, occupation, family), and open to the invention of status markers by actual social groups (the local skateboarding circle, for example) (1978, pp. 305–7, 932–33).

We can imagine that a group-culture model of the sort described by classical social theorists might well describe "caste" societies such as the traditional social order of India, or feudal societies like those in medieval Europe. But how can a group-culture model account for stratification and culture in contemporary societies? The most prevalent approach describes socio-economic classes as cultural groups. Thus, Karl Marx defined class positions *not* as a continuum of ranked occupations and prestige, but as memberships within opposed *groups* with conflicting economic interests (e.g., workers versus owners of capital). Although class has an objective basis (class "in itself"), a class "for itself" has members who are self-conscious about their class position; collectively, they pursue their common interests (McMurtry 1978). Marxists are interested in how culture "mediates" social participation in an economically structured world by offering people recipes for dealing with their circumstances, by providing ideologies that legitimate the existing class-structured social order and our positions within it, and by serving as a medium of reflection about the persistent problems and frustrations that people may encounter because of their class situations (R. Williams 1982, p. 24). For Marx, class is the central axis along which consciousness and ideology are shaped. The formation of culture in class groups in turn is an important element of his theory of social change through class conflict.

Marx was not alone in suggesting that there are distinct cultures of classes as social groups. Weber, for example, observed that participants in propertied classes often create status groups that affirm their prestige and monopolize their resources through marriage and inheritance. Whatever the ways they might obtain wealth, propertied classes perpetuate themselves as status groups with distinct boundaries marked by particular education and expressive behaviors (Weber 1978, p. 307). A contemporary sociologist of culture, Herbert Gans, has pursued this lead by typifying five class-based taste cultures connected to five taste publics: (1) high culture, (2) upper-middle culture, (3) lower-middle culture, (4) low culture, and (5) quasi-folk low culture. Gans was careful to note that he was describing analytic categories, not necessarily fixed cultures drawn upon by socially real groups such as the elite status groups described by Weber. Gans also pointed out that much culture gains an audience from more than one class, and that there are finer distinctions of stratified culture. Such distinctions might derive from status, ethnicity, gender, religion, region, and other bases of social differentiation. All the same, Gans did identify alternative ways that different class cultures are patterned, and his account helps us to think about how classes may form culturally bounded social groups. This can be seen by exploring three of the class cultures Gans has identified—high culture, upper-middle culture, and lower-middle culture.

Gans described "high culture" as a taste culture in which aesthetic standards are dominated by the creators of culture in the arts, theater, music, and literature, and by their primary audiences—professional critics. Though these cultural producers and critics are not necessarily of elite social status themselves, their secondary audience is dominated by a social elite and (for its less expensive forms) by an intellectual and artistic elite (Bourdieu 1984). How do the social relations among these groups work? In high culture, the usefulness of culture tends to receive less emphasis than its aesthetic properties: It is the realm of "art for art's sake." Cultural criticism thus takes an interest in the meaning of the cultural object and how it is produced: How techniques and cultural forms succeed (or fail) at producing a particular mood, effect, representation of something, or symbolic communication (Gans 1974, pp. 76–7). Thus, a painting might be appreciated for its symbolic use of color. Jazz critics similarly might remark upon a saxophonist's "quoting" of other saxophonist's "licks," as a way of identifying the musical "discourse" in which the saxophonist participates.

Because critical standards of artists, novelists, composers and their critics tend to predominate over the standards of the high-culture lay audience, the audience has to pay careful attention to high culture in order to appreciate it, and this appreciative attention often requires exceptional learning, either through privileged exposure to high culture as a child, or by formal education in art and music appreciation. Since such specialized learning is not equally open to everyone, it offers one way for elite social groups—both the wealthy and the highly educated—to monopolize high culture and exclude other people from their social world. Given limited access, the double standard of high culture demands that the popular classes defer to its greatness, even if they lack the education or aesthetic sensibilities that would be necessary to appreciate it (cf. Gans 1974, p. 78; Bourdieu 1984, p. 41).

If high culture is to reflect its elite taste public's seeming self-assurance about their social position, it cannot focus directly on status or success. By contrast, Gans's "upper-middle" taste culture is oriented to a taste public whose position in the world is less secure, and whose lives often are infused with striving and ambition. The upper-middle-class person can seek additional status by participating in upper-class culture, yet doing so involves a complex role performance that must feign self-assurance at having "arrived," when ambition—not self-assurance—gives rise to emulation. In general, compared to the upper class, the values of upper-middle culture are more pragmatic and utilitarian, and the audience is more interested in substance than in form (Gans 1974, pp. 81–2). In high culture, fictional characters like those in Henry James's short stories live "outside" the world of economic life in what Pierre Bourdieu calls a "distance from necessity." But in upper-middle culture, fictional characters are enmeshed in plots concerned with achievement, mobility, the moral dilemmas of careers, and the social conflicts that accompany the lives of people for whom the issue of "making it" is a central concern. Like these fictional protagonists, real-life upper-middle-class people on the go do not have much time for culture, yet they want to be "cultured." Thus, magazines like *Time* and *Newsweek* offer quick digests of the news and easy access to important cultural developments—both high and popular—that will establish in the most efficient way possible the "informed" and "cultured" character of their readers.

Gans suggested that the upper-middle taste public is the fastest growing, but the culture described by Gans as "lower-middle" is distinctive, and it has the largest audience (1974, p. 84). What we will call simply the middle-class[2] is less likely to be driven by career ambitions than the upper-middle class, for the prospects are not as good. What then are the compensations for acceptance of this class situation, and what social outlooks might "mediate" middle-class life situations? "Respectability" and "status consumption" frame the possibilities. In the absence of hopes for significant upward mobility, a long-standing issue is respectability. At the extreme, members of the middle class who resent people of higher classes for their privileges, nevertheless may imitate their culture (cf. Scheler 1961). Whether fueled by resentment or by a more diffuse goal of middle-class dignity and community, cultural values

---

[2] Class boundaries are historically variable and highly debated. Halle has shown that the significance of working-class culture has declined, especially outside the workplace (1984). In the broadly suburban society established since the end of World War II, people with blue-collar jobs often share income levels, lifestyles and self-concepts with people holding lower white-collar occupations (clerical, sales, secretarial and similar positions). The question of working-class culture is thus complex, as Halle shows. However, in the extensive, socially mixed, and culturally diverse suburbs where blue-collar and lower white-collar workers live, there is a predominant self-identification toward the "middle" class. In our view, the relevant distinction is between this widespread class and the upper-middle class. We therefore refer to Gans's lower-middle taste culture as "middle-class" culture.

focus on working hard to provide a good life for one's family, consuming carefully in order to stretch the resources of middle-class income, and living a lifestyle that demonstrates the moral worth of the solid middle class. The major alternative to this sober middle-class respectability treats the possibilities of status consumption and leisure as the benefits of middle-class position, and the issue of social respectability is subordinated to lifestyle consumption activities—sports, recreation, exercise, entertainment. Respectability and the pursuit of leisure through status consumption thus map the overall region of middle-class culture.

By describing class-based taste cultures, Gans shows that the stratification of culture is not simply a matter of individual whim or status gradations along a continuum of prestige. Instead, there are basic shifts in overall orientation and logic that mark a boundary between upper taste culture and the upper-middle taste culture, and between them and middle-class culture. Yet Gans's research does not argue that class-based social groups are tightly bounded by culture. Even if the taste cultures are distinctive, the boundary maintenance cannot be very strict, since classes lack sufficient organization or power to totally monopolize "their" culture. It would be difficult for a committee of the upper class to stop a lottery ticket winner from buying up high-culture paintings or becoming a patron of the opera (or, more likely, buying a Jaguar). The fact that today most cultural objects—from material objects like cars and stereos to "human capital" such as education and social skills—can be acquired in the marketplace points to the importance of an alternative theory of culture and stratification.

THE MARKET/CLASS GROUP THEORY

In his book *Distinction*, the French sociologist Pierre Bourdieu has reported on quantitative empirical research that shows for France what Gans found in the U.S., namely that there are coherent social class differences in the consumption of culture. Bourdieu states in the preface to the English edition that he wants "to rethink Max Weber's opposition between class and *Stand* [status group]" (1984, p. xii). He argues that in today's world, the ways in which people relate to making money (class position and aspiration) are closely connected to how people style their lives. Basic lifestyle—called "habitus"—is regarded by Bourdieu as constituted largely in the subtle nuances of class-located family household life, formed partly through marketplace consumption, partly on the basis of family culture (inherited both materially and through socialization) and partly on the basis of education.

What Weber described as status groups with special lifestyles, Bourdieu argues are mapped upon a class-based grid, in which the terms of the process are dictated by the dominant class, and people—individually and collectively—employ "strategies of distinction" to vie for acceptance of their own worth by others:

FIGURE 6.1 Habitus is transmitted in part through the social interaction of daily life, as with this Maine family at the dinnertable in 1944. (*Source:* Standard Oil (NJ) Co. Collection, Photographic Archives, University of Louisville.)

> Competitive struggle is the form of class struggle which the dominated classes allow to be imposed on them when they accept the stakes (of distinction) offered by the dominant classes. It is an integrative struggle and, by virtue of the initial handicaps, a reproductive struggle (i.e., approximately recreating existing distinctions), since those who enter this chase, in which they are beaten before they start, as the constancy of the gaps testifies, implicitly recognize the legitimacy of the goals pursued by those whom they pursue, by the mere fact of taking part (1984, p. 165).

In other words, whatever the origins of class situation on the basis of divergent occupational or property interests, people in stable societies come to accept their class situations by participating in a class-defined struggle for social distinction.

The stratified social space within which it is possible to map class "habitus" sociologically is defined by Bourdieu in terms of "capital," which represents the significant resources that can be drawn upon in the conduct of life. Capital, for Bourdieu, has three aspects—volume, composition, and trajectory. "Volume" is simply the amount of capital. "Composition" refers to the relative preponderance of "economic capital, cultural capital and also social capital." Bourdieu does not develop in detail his concepts of economic capital (i.e., wealth) or social capital, which presumably refers to networks—"who you know." By cultural capital, Bourdieu means the knowledge, taste and sensibilities, as well as the material possessions that together give a person the ability to lay claim to one or another kind of esteem or honor, i.e., what Weber called status. Bourdieu argues that cultural capital has two major sources—family background and education. To some extent, education can substitute for family origins in helping the individual to acquire taste and manners that mark a certain status. But, Bourdieu argues, this is truer for the more conventionally established realms of culture (such as music or art appreciation) than it is for arcane areas of freelance cultural practice (such as polo team banter or comportment in an exclusive restaurant) (1984, pp. 13, 94, 114).

Some people have so little capital—cultural or economic—that the relative composition between the two is meaningless. And at the other end of the scale, a great deal of cultural capital usually goes hand in hand with a great deal of economic capital, at least over the long run of several generations. In today's art market, wealthy buyers of famous paintings are paying such high prices ($51.3 million for a Picasso in 1989), that the difference between cultural and economic capital is all but erased. But in the middling regions, the composition of cultural and economic capital is more variable: At any given class level, one form of capital can substitute for the other, in ways that maintain distinctions between people of different occupational worlds. Thus, members of the non-wealthy but cultured intelligentsia prefer less expensive aesthetic activities such as cooking exotic foods, while wealthier individuals at the same class level of taste will tend to engage in more expensive forms of aesthetic consumption, such as going to fashionable restaurants (Bourdieu 1974). Similarly, but at a lower overall class level, in the French petit bourgeoisie, Bourdieu located junior administrative executives and small shopkeepers in a cultural realm where pop singer Petula Clark found a following, whereas primary school teachers and people in socio-medical services were more likely to hold to a range of interests that included flea markets, antique shops, and impressionist painters (1984, p. 340).

Finally, Bourdieu considers "trajectory" important. We each have status careers of mobility, from social origins to present position, to subsequent status destinations. For people of a given set of origins, say, workers in a small midwestern factory town, or large landowners in ranching states, there exists some typical pattern of individual mobility, or trajectory. For people in similar positions—bank loan officers, department store sales personnel or physical therapists—differences from other workers in trajectory (origins and aspirations) make for social distinctions among them. The recent MBA learning the banking business in a brief tour of duty as a loan officer has a different cachet than someone who has performed the job for years without hope of advancement.

In contrast to upwardly mobile individuals or groups..., individuals or groups in decline endlessly reinvent the discourse of all aristocracies: essentialist faith in the eternity of natures, celebration of tradition and the past, the cult of history and its rituals, because the best they can expect from the future is the return of the old order, from which they expect the restoration of their social being (1984, p. 111).

Connecting cultural and economic capital with trajectory and gains or losses over time, Bourdieu "sets in motion" his model of culture and social stratification. The theory thus is not based on class categories alone. Instead, cultural capital depends on a market in which individuals and families struggle for distinctions defined by the changing amount and composition of cultural and economic capital in their possession. Bourdieu's consolidation of this argument is based upon conceptualizing culture as a kind of capital—something, like money, which can be gained or lost, and used to obtain other things.

Bourdieu applies this sort of "pure" market theory to the actual social world, where things are considerably more complex. For one thing, the capital value of the culture that we invoke and consume is not fixed. To the contrary, any calculus of cultural value itself is altered by our use of it. No doubt there are simple values such as personal enjoyment that play into our cultural choices. But the purposes of our cultural usage may also include "properly" identifying ourselves for others in terms of social stratification symbols (by buying the "socially correct" car, or wearing the "right" clothes for a stockbroker, for example). The invocation of culture—from how we dress and groom to how we decorate our living spaces—offers a basis for others to "sort" our social positions and offer or refuse us their esteem (Goffman 1951). Here, money and what it can buy are not enough. For people with "old money," *how* to live is more important than what to buy in maintaining the boundary against "new money" (Aldrich 1988). For those status purposes, it is not enough to be wealthy. For the newly wealthy, however, Thorstein Veblen (1965) argued that wealth must be "conspicuous" in its consumption. Thus, in Veblen's time, wearing white clothes demonstrated that a person did not come near dirt, while a suntan was the mark of a worker who had to be outside. The meaning of a suntan has undergone shifts since Veblen's time, but then, as now, visible leisure activities offer the definitive proof that a person is not working.

In general, the cultural-capital value of objects and practices remains in flux because of two mutually reinforcing processes. First, people of a less esteemed status position may seek to alter the perception of their position by adopting the more esteemed culture, and this imitation may deflate the capital value of culture. Anyone with the money can buy a fancy car, and other people besides the rich can visit exclusive resorts. Similarly, middle-class people have increasingly adopted home furnishings with an "international" style associated with upper-class and upper-middle class tastes. This practice of borrowing and imitation is reinforced by a second practice, namely, the interest of companies in mass-marketing goods that bear the trappings of high status. *Oil of Olay™,* for example, was once a strictly high-culture beauty cream that now has been successfully mass-marketed, apparently without drastically diluting its prestige. Other name brands may go through a deflation of their cultural capital as they move through a marketing cycle. Yves Saint Laurent items for sale in K-Mart can no longer claim the prestige of availability only through exclusive department stores. Such marketing strategies culturally devalue goods, even at the same price, so that high-status users can feel their purchases have been "ruined" (to quote one shopper's response to the new product line of a high-end brand of recreational clothes—Patagonia).

Bourdieu describes a world in flux because of a status scramble, where cultural capital figures prominently in that flux, yet what counts as cultural capital shifts according to who uses it and how. Given the inflationary pressures on cultural capital, in order to maintain exclusivity, positively esteemed groups must either maintain effective monopolies on their distinctive goods, practices, and sites of sociability, or they must keep altering such cultural "badges" in order to distinguish themselves from pretenders who have appropriated their previous ones. For example, economic elites may abandon vacation spots once they are invaded by others (Belasco 1979). A similar process occurs among the self-styled avant-garde of youth culture ("punk" and "hip-hop," for example), whose participants must seek new fashion codes and cultural practices, once their old ones become the objects of imitation and mass marketing. Beauty and fashion indeed represent something of a prototypical example. Colors, fabrics, cuts of cloth, and style of garments constitute a general "language" of fashion, but the value of a particular "look" or way of dressing in part depends on the successful promotion by a class or status group of their definitions of beauty and fashion as the standards by which beauty and fashion in general may be judged (Lurie 1981; Banner 1983; Webster and Driskell 1983; Hatfield and Sprecher 1986).

Not all culture is as easy to take off and put on as clothes. People trying for social mobility can be burdened by socialization that marks their class origins (by their dinnertable manners or their lack of knowledge of Renaissance art, for example). Whereas we may attempt mobility through education (which offers cultural capital), it is difficult for us to shed the socialization of our family upbringings. Subtle cues mark us in ways that make cultural mobility an incomplete process. Significant mobility is more likely to be consolidated over several generations, rather than in an individual's biography, because over the longer time span, even arcane cultural capital can be gained by changes in neighborhood, by choices of voluntary associations, churches and schools, and by gaining entrance to exclusive clubs. Thus, if barriers of access to cultural capital constrain mobility, they need not limit it altogether.

Moreover, the occupational roles in contemporary societies are always changing, and often expanding. Cultural capital is always being defined in new ways relative to those positions. Cultural capital seems both more and less fluid than economic capital. The so-called "post-industrial" service sector expansion has established a new realm of social ranking for positions in travel agencies, tourism, restaurants, shopping mall administration, computer programming, and numerous other occupations. Yet the social mobility of people moving "up" into positions in the service sector has not necessarily required higher status groups to abandon their "currencies," for the new social strata have established their own distinctive currencies of cultural capital. Thus, despite good income, sports instructors at a resort will find a gap of distinction reinforced by their clients, and they often develop their own disdain (bordering on resentment) for the very tourists who make the livelihood of locals possible. Sensing their own exclusion, local tourist industry workers will go out of their way to distance themselves from "turkeys."

Such expansions of cultural capital suggest one reason why less privileged social classes have not tended to develop the radical political consciousness that Marx expected of them. Apparently capitalism has operated in ways that severed workers from the "inevitable" crisis predicted by Marx. One explanation may be that the economies of scale in mass production and the increasing production of symbolic culture have produced goods and services more cheaply. To the extent that inexpensively produced goods and services still represent advances in cultural capital for those who buy them, things previously beyond their reach—a television (and the connection to popular culture it offers), a vacation cruise—are acts of consumption that mark meaningful advancements in cultural capital, even if class position remains constant. Thus, the legitimacy of capitalism may be sustained if the expansion of cultural capital is greater than the cost of producing it, and if distribution of cultural capital to politically active strata is widespread. Put differently, so long as class members are able to establish their own personal cultural capital through mass consumption, they are not likely to identify with classes as self-conscious groups that can be used to pursue shared economic interests. The competitive aspects of class distinctions thus may be less critical when the sheer volume of capital increases across class groupings. Thus, the distribution of cultural capital can undermine class consciousness even though it maintains distinctions among classes as groups.

In general, the market/class group theory of cultural capital advanced by Bourdieu suggests that classes do continue to operate as groups with coherent boundaries, but the boundaries are defined partly on the basis of culture, rather than purely on the basis of collective occupational interests. How does a market theory explain the existence of groups? The issue can be considered by looking at the recent borrowing of upper-middle motifs within middle-class culture. As late as the 1950s, middle-class American culture retained an aversion to the cosmopolitan sophistication of the upper-middle class. Today, things have changed substantially. Nationwide chain stores like Penny's, Montgomery Ward's and Sears have made serious efforts to shed their dry, sober, respectable images, and they now offer an array of goods that mimics upper-middle class culture, but at affordable prices. As with these consumer goods, so also with news and entertainment; the content of culture has opened up for the middle class. News programming now includes discussion of formerly taboo topics such as child abuse and sex change operations, while movies and television dramas can depict the heterogeneity of lifestyles in the U.S. in sophisticated ways that were avoided in popular entertainment of the 1950s.

Do the changes in content and style of middle-class culture mean that a continuum has replaced any sharp boundary that previously existed between upper-middle-class and middle-class culture? The answer, for Bourdieu (1984, e.g., p. 327), like Gans (1974, p. 85), is no. Middle-class culture is oriented to an enormous audience, and there are definite limits to how far its content can challenge the dominant ideas of the public and still gain an audience. Moreover, upper-middle culture often plays on ambiguity—especially through the use of symbolism, abstraction, and analytic discourse. By contrast, middle-class culture retains its emphasis on facts, unambiguous truth (or sharply contrasted positions in controversies), clear and concrete meanings, the affirmation of central cultural values, and on the resolution of dramatic events in clearcut ways. A key to this culture is its accessibility: The audience can enter into the drama in a direct way, "identifying with the characters' joys and sufferings, worrying about their fate, espousing their hopes and ideals, living their life," without anxieties about whether they are missing "deeper" meanings (Bourdieu 1984, p. 33). Thus, film, novels, television action series, soap operas and situation comedies must have unambiguous drama, and news is reported in ways that treat resolution of events in terms of established morality and public values, packaged in a coherent story. As Gans put it, "The lower-middle public seems to be less interested in how society works than in reassurance that it continues to abide by the moral values important in lower-middle-class culture generally" (1974, p. 86).

A cultural boundary exists between the middle class and higher status classes, Bourdieu suggests, because in the middle class, what people actually know of culture falls short of what they themselves recognize as culturally important distinctions (it's important to choose a fine wine, but how do you know which one to choose?). The result of the middle-class shortfall is "pretension"—the display of culture in a way that exceeds self-assured familiarity. A parallel boundary exists for the lower class, where both distinction and pretensions of being "cultured" are disdained in favor of utilitarian adaptation to circumstance—"making do" (Bourdieu 1976). Working-class culture emphasizes suspicion of "Culture," intellectuals, manners, elitist noblesse oblige, and respectability. Rejecting these badges of civility permits working-class people to invoke a meaningful world in which people are "real," uncontrived, and straightforward in their likes and dislikes; where they may fart among friends rather than engage in presentations of self that deny the basic bodily processes (cf. Goffman 1971, ch. 2).

Like Gans, then, Bourdieu argues that people formulate distinctions (e.g., "refined" versus "common," "shallow" versus "deep") that identify class boundaries. Classes are marked by the unconscious unity of habitus (Bourdieu 1984, pp. 16, 77, 101, 327). Yet despite the parallels between Gans's and Bourdieu's approaches, there is an important difference. Gans is interested in the aesthetic rationales of social classes. By contrast, Bourdieu's theory essentially treats culture as a particular kind of capital, much like monetary capital, that can be accumulated and used in the attainment of status in a class-based marketplace of distinction. There is an important consequence of this shift to a market concept. The coherence of class aesthetics is constantly undermined by the participation of individuals in multiple markets of distinction, moving upward and downward on scales that are redefined by the very motion of individuals on them. Classes are not simply culturally stratified groups. Instead, boundary distinctions are overlaid with one another in complex arrays. Gans, of course, would not deny this; in fact, he emphasizes that his definitions of class-based taste cultures are analytical, not real. And he, more than Bourdieu, gives serious attention to other dimensions of cultural stratification—ethnicity, gender and age. The main advantage of Bourdieu's approach is that the concept of cultural capital offers a way to explain not just a static set of distinctions, but a dynamic system in which aesthetics and boundaries are placed in constant flux by the ways in which people give value to diverse cultural practices and objects.

THE MARKET/STATUS GROUP THEORY

Bourdieu's exploration of boundaries argues that markets in cultural capital are not based on purely individual participation, but upon the existence of groups. It takes groups to maintain boundaries. However, if there are groups, two questions arise. First, is class the only basis on which such groups might exist? At least theoretically, it seems that other kinds of groups—religious or ethnic groups or motorcycle gangs—could create and procure various kinds of cultural capital. Do such status groups create solidarity of people from *different* social classes? Alternatively, are they simply a further differentiation of status *within* a particular class? Second, we must ask whether the relation of non-class groups to culture might require a multi-cultural model that is more complex than a class/market theory of cultural capital. If boundaries exist between dominant and subordinated non-class groups, what is the specific character of subordinated culture? Does it help members of the subordinated group survive in the wider world, or does it encapsulate them in a limited world? In short, Bourdieu's project to "rethink Max Weber's opposition between class and *Stand* [status group]" (1984, p. xii) needs to be evaluated in terms of whether it effectively eliminates the need for a theory of, for example, gender or ethnicity. We must ask questions such as this: Do gendered cultures simply represent two sides of class culture at a given level, or do men and women, gays and straights, live in the world in ways that are fundamentally different from one another?

Bourdieu recognizes that not all culture is strictly economically determined: "As the objective distance from necessity grows, life-style increasingly becomes the product of what Weber calls a 'stylization of life,' a systematic commitment which orients and organizes the most diverse practices—the choice of a vintage or a cheese or the decoration of a holiday home in the country" (1984, pp. 55–56). This suggests that criteria other than class come into play in distinctions of pure leisure and consumption. To be sure, much leisure consumption can be located in class practices—of bowling versus handball, or horseshoes versus shuffleboard. Yet the opposite line of reasoning also warrants consideration: Class distinctions may not really subsume a variety of non-class distinctions—especially those based on what are believed to be ascribed characteristics such as gender and ethnicity.

Even if we simply look at those whose lives would seem most likely to be dictated by "necessity"—people who are poor—it is questionable whether the cultural capital model adequately explains their culture. Some scholars, notably Oscar Lewis, have advanced the thesis of a "culture of poverty"—a remarkably consistent pattern that "cuts across regional, rural-urban, and even national boundaries." This pattern, Lewis argued, could be "found in lower-class settlements in London..., in Puerto Rico..., in Mexico City slums and Mexican villages..., and among lower-class Negroes in the United States." Lewis's ethnographic accounts did not portray culture as an absolute trap; nevertheless, he argued, "One can speak of the culture of the poor, for it has its own modalities and distinctive social and psychological consequences for its members" (1959, p. 2). This line of analysis has been the subject of concerted critique from other social scientists as well as political intellectuals of the Left who take it to "blame the victims" for their own predicament (e.g., Leacock 1971, Gresham and Wilkerson 1989).

Much effort needs to be made to understand cultures of the poor and dispossessed, and the volatile political debate does not make research any easier. As Michael Harrington made clear in his famous book, *The Other America* (1962), the conditions of poverty in the U.S. are diverse, and often remote from the worlds of the more fortunate. The poor will find themselves exposed to the cheapest of petty commercial culture—"dive" restaurants and cafeterias, second-hand stores, tabloids and cheap movie theaters. And they will be the targets of culturally distinctive state- and religiously-organized welfare and charity programs. These realities would suggest that the poor partake of what Bourdieu calls a "dominated" cultural aesthetic—one defined from the outside. Yet the poor do not engage in commercial consumption to the same extent that more monied classes do, and this suggests that their culture will lie outside the realm of mass popular culture, and it likely will be considered "deviant" on this basis.

Paradoxically, the relatively greater distance of the poor from class-defined commercial mass culture will leave room for the greater importance of "quasi-folk" cultures made of the ongoing practices of the people who live socially marginal lives (Gans 1974). The interplay of such cultures with dominated culture has been described in essays like George Orwell's *Down and Out in Paris and London* (1933), autobiographies by hoboes Jack Black (1988) and Boxcar Bertha (Reitman 1988), and ethnographies of the streets such as *Tally's Corner* (Liebow 1967) and *Carnival Strippers* (Meisalas 1976). The ethnographic accounts underscore what Gans points out, that class distinctions of culture are mediated by other socially constructed boundaries, for example, those of ethnicity, gender, and geographic locale. Boxcar Bertha was a woman making it in a predominantly male world of hoboes. George Orwell described men on the road, who inhabit a different social world than those of us who have a more settled existence—in a city, suburb, town, or farm community. Tally's corner is a hangout for black men who form a status group with its own moral code about their relations with the women who live beyond their group boundary. And carnival strippers live outside conventional women's roles, at a high cost to their social status and to their interactions with men.

Multiple non-class bases of culture can articulate with the class stratification of culture in one of two ways. On the one hand, gender or ethnicity or status group culture may provide an *alternative* basis of cultural solidarity that cuts *across* class distinctions. Or, such non-class bases of culture still may operate *within* classes, and the question then becomes whether their dynamics can be explained by class. These theoretical alternatives can be explored briefly for gender and ethnicity as examples of social criteria that give rise to status groups.

Gender

If biological differences in sex determined gender roles of men and women, then we would expect similar patterns of gendered culture to exist across different social classes. The early-twentieth-century German sociologist Georg Simmel described feminine culture as tied to the specific form of "female nature," and he argued that "with the exception of a very few areas, our objective [i.e., public] culture is thoroughly male" (1984, p. 67). Feminist theorists point to the many public cultural accomplishments of women artists, novelists, musicians, and others, whose work has not been incorporated into the male-defined canon of legitimate cultural accomplishment. All the same, Simmel's point is one that feminists also advance in a theory of patriarchal society: Namely that the dominant culture—religion, art, music, legal institutions, and so on—is culture created and maintained for the most part by men as the dominant gender. Feminists also have applied this theory of patriarchy to the sexual division of labor in the household, arguing that male power defines a situation in which not only sexual reproduction, but parenting and housework are female tasks. Cultural patterns of gender relations are explained as the consequence of social differentials of power between males and females that cannot be reduced to class in a patriarchal society (O'Brien 1981; Polatnick 1983).

The overall pattern of gendered culture notwithstanding, it also must be recognized that the meanings of "female" and "male" change over time. In some periods, maleness and femaleness have been viewed as different ends on a single human-nature continuum, and at other times, males and females have been considered as entirely distinct from each other. In addition, the social construction of gender is connected to the class structure. The very concept "feminine" often is associated with delicacy and sentimentality of a leisured life, sensibilities quite different from the "matriarchal" attributes of strength, nurture and generosity. Ann Douglas argues that during the nineteenth century, the "feminization of American culture" replaced the strong mother's identity with a *less* powerful gender role for women. At the same time, the middle-class male gender identity—exemplified in the outlook of (male) novelists and Protestant ministers—was transformed from pioneer virility in a feminized direction. It is Douglas's thesis that American culture in general was feminized during the nineteenth century in ways that did not necessarily benefit women: For example, wives became families' consumers. Such changes, it would seem, are tied to the emergence of an industrial economy and society, where civility, commerce and the display of a lifestyle count more among the middle classes than physical strength, endurance, and stern moral fiber (1977).

Other analysts have pointed to the opposite tendency, still tied to class dynamics: As industrialization (and post-industrialization) have proceeded, increasing numbers of women have obtained jobs with role requirements that fly in the face of Victorian notions about "the fairer sex." Employed working-class women in New York at the dawn of the twentieth century faced the problem of how to establish a culture that would allow freer contacts between the sexes among strangers, without taking on the label of "whore" (Peiss 1986). In smaller communities, the mass diffusion of the automobile during the 1920s similarly created a new freedom for youth who could meet at "roadhouses" beyond the purview of the town square (Lynn and Lynn, cited in Bell 1976, p. 67).

If industrialization and its fruits have altered traditional gender roles and their enactment in public versus private spheres, in turn, changing gender roles and reactions to feminism as a political movement may have led some people to a sexual "nostalgia"—a longing for the supposed good old days (Doane and Hodges 1987). Changing gender roles can be unsettling for both men and women. True, since women have moved increasingly into wage and salary occupations, new male sensibilities about gender have emerged. Yet the cultural rites of passage from boyhood to manhood persist, for example in adult-organized little league baseball with its motto of "character, courage, loyalty" (Fine 1987). And one study shows that even when women and men move into traditionally opposite-gender roles—women into the Marines, men into nursing—they maintain and reinforce their own gender identities in social worlds dominated by the opposite gender (Williams 1989). In general, men and women enact changed gender roles while being exposed to a variety of cultural models, for example, the stereotyped role models displayed in advertising (Goffman 1979). The result of shifting roles and a range of role models is a set of gender contradictions—between social realities and cultural tools, and between competing cultural definitions of situation. These contradictions are the likely source of sexual nostalgia.

It also seems evident that sexual nostalgia does not claim an equal audience across social strata. Gender cultures differ from class to class so that, as Bourdieu argues, "there are as many ways of realizing femininity [sic] as there are classes and class fractions" (1984, pp. 107–8). Gans describes low culture as defining strong boundaries between men and women, such that forms of entertainment—action dramas, "confidential" gossip magazines, sports—are distinct in their gender appeals (1974, p. 90). Yet how are we to explain the distinctiveness of male versus female culture? Bourdieu's model implies that different sorts of resources and sensibilities—in the case of gender: Auto mechanics, sewing, nurturing, beauty, authority—would give the individual the cultural capital for maintaining social position within an overall class system of distinction. For a dominated cultural group—women in a patriarchal society—cultural resources would offer the basis for survival in a "man's world." On these grounds, the distinctiveness of women's culture would be explained by its function *within* a particular class fraction.

A contrasting view suggests that women's culture offers women a basis of solidarity and power that establishes an *alternative* realm to the world dominated by men. In exploring the social worlds of eighteenth- and nineteenth-century women, Smith-Rosenberg has argued, "Women who had little status or power in the larger world of male concerns, possessed status and power in the lives and worlds of other women."

> Women helped each other with domestic chores and in times of sickness, sorrow, or trouble. Entire days, even weeks, might be spent almost exclusively with other women. Urban and town women could devote virtually every day to visits, teas, or shopping trips with other women. Rural women developed a pattern of more extended visits that lasted weeks and sometimes months, at times even dislodging husbands from their beds and bedrooms so that dear friends might spend every hour of every day together (Smith-Rosenberg 1975, p. 10).

Far from concluding that women's cultural capital helped women survive in a man's world, Smith-Rosenberg suggests something different: In a time when middle-class women's activities in public were highly constrained, the existence of a separate world had its own attractions for women.

Today, most women do not live in worlds so separate from men. Yet this does not necessarily imply that women's culture solely functions to attain distinction within class cultures dominated by men. A study of contemporary women and the popular culture of romance novels by Radway suggests considerably more complexity. In *Reading the Romance,* Radway recognizes dual and somewhat contradictory practices at work (1984). Like other genres that construct realistic plots, the romance narratives about women and their love lives unfold with the twists and turns based on protagonists' dilemmas and choices. Reading romances thus suggests that women have power to shape their lives. Yet the diverse plots actually are "formulaic," in that they follow prescriptions about "the essential ingredients to be included in each new version of the form." In this respect, "each romance is, in fact a mythic account of how women *must* achieve fulfillment in patriarchal society" (1984, pp. 29, 17). Given the romances' dualism of choice and mythic prescription, they maintain an ideology of women's roles that perpetuates male dominance by focusing the exercise of power within constraints of a patriarchically organized society. All the same, the romance readers whom Radway interviewed often reported experiences of empowerment. The novels helped readers establish their own personal realms—separate from their worlds of work, of children, and of husbands (the lost world of nineteenth-century women simulated in fiction?). In addition, sorting through the issues confronted by heroines in the romances sharpened readers' skills at negotiating the trials of a patriarchal world.

The women's cultures described by Smith-Rosenberg and Radway differ radically from each other, but they both suggest that women's culture has value (capital, if you will) because it sustains either an alternative domain altogether, or a power in the world of men that cannot be reduced to the cultural values of that world. In these accounts, even if we use the language of Bourdieu's theory, some cultural capital of women is in a currency that is traded on a different market than one completely defined by class. It is a market defined by the range of different interests of women and men in their relations with each other.

Ethnicity

Like gender, ethnicity (sometimes defined culturally in terms of biological, hence "racial" characteristics) is typically assumed to be an ascribed identity, that is, one based on socially unchangeable characteristics of the individual. However, as with gender, the specific label and content of individuals' ethnic identities depend on social circumstance. Whatever their ethnic identities in Mexico, for example, immigrants become "Chicanos" or "Mexican-Americans" simply by taking up residence in the U.S.

Like gender, ethnic identity can either encompass different economic classes or an ethnic group may include predominantly members of only one class. Caste systems in general and, in the U.S., slavery and "legal" segregation of blacks before the civil rights reforms of the mid-twentieth century, provide extreme examples of predominantly class-contained ethnic groups. Under class-contained conditions, as was the case with gender, a key question concerns the uses of ethnic cultural capital within the class order.

In a classic study of a small town in the southern U.S. during the Great Depression of the 1930s, John Dollard detailed the elaborate racist ideology and strict mores of public behavior. The public culture maintained white solidarity concerning segregation by branding any white who deviated as a "nigger lover:"

> The tendency among students of culture to consider such acts as tipping the hat, shaking hands, or using "Mr." as empty formalisms is rebuked by experience in the South. When we see how severely Negroes may be punished for omitting these signs of deference, we realize that they are anything but petrified customs... (1957, pp. 178–9).

Class-contained ethnicity is rarely total, but the cultural logic of racism under such conditions has implications beyond the class-contained members of a negatively privileged ethnic group. Thus, Dollard found some class differences among blacks, with middle-class blacks often going to great lengths to avoid invoking the whites' cultural stereotypes about poor blacks—the "mammy" image, sexual promiscuity, and emotionalistic religion, for example. Here, then, was class distinction being used by middle-class blacks to counteract a stigmatized ethnicity. Among poorer blacks, Dollard painted a picture of two roles—one to conform to mores enforced ultimately by white violence, the other—roles that maintained blacks' own identities beyond the public world dominated by whites. Despite the potential of this "hidden" world of blacks as an arena for resistance, the basic posture of blacks in the town Dollard studied was to accommodate to their inferior position, as defined and maintained by the white caste (1957, p. 255).

Dollard may have missed the "inside" of Southern black culture because he was an outsider. Other researchers have argued that Southern blacks maintained a solidarity of resistance against white domination, and that the black church as a social institution was essential to this solidarity. The civil rights movement that began in the South during the 1950s seems to have had diffuse origins in a network of black churches and other social organizations (Jenkins and Eckert 1986, Lincoln and Mamiya 1990), and this suggests that Southern blacks had maintained a significant preexisting covert culture of resistance in the churches. As with the case of gender, a dominated ethnic group may use cultural capital with a currency in the wider world, while a separate kind of cultural capital establishes status within the group itself. Thus, ethnic cultural capital does not always reduce to class cultural capital by any straightforward "currency exchange."

Yet ethnic distinctions may also follow class lines. The book, *The Declining Significance of Race*, by William J. Wilson suggests that the expansion of the black middle class after the civil rights movement has resulted in a "deepening economic schism," "with the black poor falling further and further behind middle- and upper-income blacks" (1980, pp. 151–2). These changes are underscored culturally by distinctive leisure pursuits of middle-class blacks, who are likely to engage in activities economically inaccessible to the poor (Woodard 1988). The issues of cultural capital that face middle-class blacks, then, have to do with whether to completely abandon cultural distinctions that have a basis in ethnicity. This new circumstance, based on a decline in direct economic discrimination, suggests that the persistence or decline of ethnic cultural capital sometimes itself may be explained in class terms.

CULTURE AND STRATIFICATION IN SOCIAL PROCESS

It would be possible to explore other central axes along which sociologists and people in everyday life map stratification patterns—age, religion, community, social club memberships, and diffuse social collectivities such as cowboys, "punks," and "yuppies." We would find, it seems likely, that multiple kinds of cultural associations are clearly distinctive in the ways they structure inequality. Gender roles of men, women, boys and girls, for example, affect relations within the life of a family in different ways than does class. Thus, Bourdieu's theory based on class distinctions is incomplete. However, the various dimensions of stratification are also intertwined in "multi-cultural" situations of actual social life. A male corporate manager and a female secretary enact a social relationship that is simultaneously defined by inequalities of class and gender. Though class, ethnicity, gender, and so on can be analyzed separately, they come into play simultaneously in overall societal patterns of culture. Moreover, there are good reasons to suspect commonalities of the cultural processes.

Class, as well as any other criterion that social actors deem salient, can be a basis for socially constructed individual and group identity, either on the part of group members themselves, or under the auspices of outsiders who stereotype them. When we shift attention from abstract categories of stratification to the question of how people act, there may be a general set of processes that connect stratification and group culture. Bourdieu's theory of cultural capital offers a basis for understanding these processes, but his model needs to be extended beyond class to the recognition of a wider range of groups employing their own forms of cultural capital, sometimes in ways not open to direct exchange or commensurability.

The United States is a more heterogeneous country than France, the site of Bourdieu's empirical studies. Perhaps because Bourdieu has written primarily about France, he has given little attention to religious and ethnic diversity. Still, Bourdieu recognizes the importance of distinctions other than class, and he also recognizes that cultural goods are often produced and evaluated in relation to particular groups (thus, the middle class has different standards

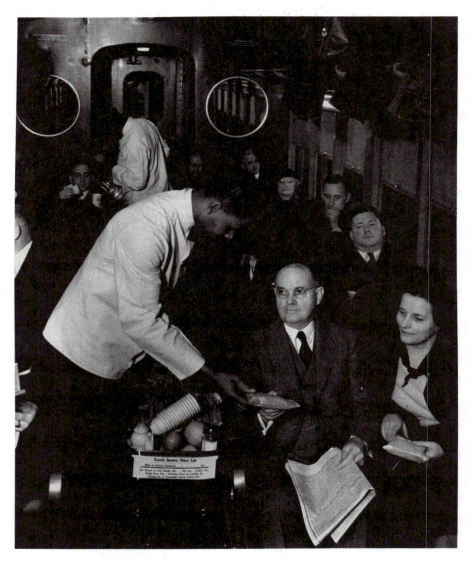

FIGURE 6.2 Ethnicity, gender and class are complexly intertwined aspects of status often enacted within situations defined by occupational stratification. Travel has changed since the days of this Pennsylvania Railroad coach around 1939, but the stratified play of distinctions has not disappeared. (*Source:* Culver Pictures.)

class). Bourdieu wanted to revise Max Weber's opposition of class and status group by showing that cultural capital operates in ways that make class distinctions into status group distinctions (1984, p. xii). Weber had wanted to restrict class analysis to market situations where people act toward each other because of their shared or opposed interests—as owners of property versus the propertyless, as buyers of labor versus sellers of labor, and so forth. Status groups, Weber recognized, might develop along class and occupational lines, but he defined them in terms of consumption of a specific lifestyle, which has attached to it a specific sense of prestige and honor. For Weber, class and status group potentially are connected, but status groups also may be established outside class situations.

Bourdieu's specific innovation, then, is to treat consumption of culture itself as a market phenomenon that parallels other market (hence, class) phenomena of contemporary societies. He thus increases the emphasis given to classes as kinds of status groups. To a lesser extent, he attempts to subsume other kinds of distinctions (avant-garde versus bourgeoisie, men versus women) within this class-as-status-group framework. Bourdieu also is prepared to apply his model of cultural capital to topics like religion, even if he has not incorporated religious capital into his overall model (1980, 1982). At its base, then, Bourdieu's approach represents an elaboration of Weber's concept of status group through his own concept of cultural capital, and the application of this status-group cultural-capital model to class-based lifestyles.

But the analysis is not yet complete, for two reasons. First, even within the framework of class-based cultural capital, there is a question about the source of value. Bourdieu recognizes that the aesthetics used to evaluate cultural choices are variable. He suggests that the working class is subjected to a "dominated 'aesthetic,'" defined from the outside, even though that aesthetic may contradict personal preferences: "Yes, it's beautiful, but you have to like it, it's not my cup of tea" (1984, p. 41). Yet the source of any external aesthetic is a key issue, and one in need of further exploration. Michelle Lamont, for example, has suggested that, in the U.S., we should look to the upper-middle class, rather than the upper class, for the source of the lower-middle class's dominated aesthetic (1992; cf. Halle 1989). Moreover, even for classes that lack dominant power, aesthetic value may not be solely defined from the outside. When Gans studied an Italian-American community, he found that workers can traffic in cultural capital that defines their class honor in a positive way, and in contradistinction to the standards of higher classes or the mass-produced consumer badges of status (1962). More generally, workers may maintain a respect for craft abilities—for being able to do things with one's hands and to work collectively in physical ways—and by these standards, many middle- and upper-class people will seem bumbling and inept. Thus, the source of aesthetic value of cultural capital is something of a struggle, as Bourdieu well recognizes. Further research of the sort conducted by Lamont, Halle, and others will help to clarify the sources of aesthetic criteria within various classes, and how these aesthetics come to be held.

A second question is equally important. Classes are not the only kinds of status groups today, and other kinds of status groups may act in ways that cannot be reduced to class-as-status-group terms. The mapping of status by use of cultural capital occurs not just in the affirmation of class sensibilities and con-sumer level. As we have seen, other forms of cultural capital can be the basis of ethnic group and gender identities. In a general way, we suspect that these anal-yses could be replicated both for abstract dimensions of stratification (e.g., age) and for concrete status groups (e.g., Mormons, or members of a sorority). In general, we may distinguish between subcultures—cultures of social groups ac-commodated to the existing social order—and countercultures—cultures of groups opposed to features of the established order. In divergent ways, both subcultures and countercultures establish "currencies" of cultural capital that do not always align in a simple and direct way with the class hierarchy of distinc-tions described by Bourdieu. Sometimes these currencies elaborate more spe-cialized distinctions within a class (Italian-American workers vs. others) and sometimes they offer a basis of solidarity and status group honor that cuts across classes (Smith-Rosenberg's women during the nineteenth century, for example). Thus, cultural distinctions that go beyond class cannot be understood simply as surviving ethnic practices from the old country or as leisure choices of people who are all seeking distinction within a single class-based status hierarchy.

Instead, as Hechter has vividly demonstrated, there is a "cultural" divi-sion of labor (1978). The patterns that Hechter found by examining data from the 1970 U.S. Census suggest that ethnic subcultures (and by extension, reli-gion, gender, and other subcultural status groups) may offer a basis for at-tempting to monopolize resources (jobs), sometimes within a class level, sometimes cutting across class levels in an economic sector (e.g., construc-tion, or banking).

In general, a status group with a distinctive culture can offer an alternative basis of individual identity from that of class, and such groups may be able to control significant economic resources. When they do, individuals will find maintenance of solidarity with the group an attractive proposition. This may be equally true no matter what the absolute value of the controlled resources. Even if the group only controls "poor" resources (lower-level government jobs, for ex-ample), these resources may be significant for group members, if they them-selves are poor. Whatever the class level or economic sector, as Reinhard Bendix argued, "In discriminating against 'outsiders,' status groups curtail the free operation of the market." Yet Bendix emphasizes that unlike classes, status groups do not need to communicate and organize to practice collective action, for "*status groups are rooted in family experience.* Before the individual reaches maturity, he has participated in his family's claim to social prestige, its occupa-tional subculture and educational level" (1974, pp. 152–53, ital. in original). In short, status groups, whatever their basis, may operate in ways that create an al-ternative to the labor market for access to occupational positions, and the individual's access may be based upon possessing and displaying the status group's specific cultural capital (cf. Bonacich 1972).

Bourdieu, of course, did not restrict his analysis to class, even if he tended to define other kinds of status group distinctions in terms of his overall class framework. There is no reason why his overall theory cannot be adjusted to incorporate the interplay of multiple forms of cultural capital and kinds of group identification (see, for example, Bentley 1987). What Bourdieu has done is to empirically establish a theory that distinguishes class-in-itself (objective class) from class-for-itself (class-conscious class). Classes in the latter sense are, in effect, special kinds of status groups, defined partly on the basis of objective class, but only through the struggles of individuals and occupational groups to establish themselves favorably within the overall social order. In short, the occupational division of labor has no inherent class divisions—janitors truly may become sanitation engineers if the management of waste becomes a complex technical problem, and conversely, stock brokers may lose distinction if their professional decision-making is taken over by computer-based "expert systems." Thus, class divisions are located through the struggles for distinction that are always in the process of redefining the boundaries of classes-as-status-groups within an overall social order.

But other possibilities exist, and they can be elaborated by filling out Bourdieu's theory. In the first place, Bourdieu's theory describes classes-as-status-groups pursuing their interests wholly within the status order. Yet Weber's famous formulation about class, status groups and power notes that status groups may pursue their interests in the political realm, and it also argues that status groups may engage in collective economic action (1978, pp. 926–39). Classes-as-status-groups would fit this formulation particularly well, since their interests often have a clearcut economic basis. Collective economic and political actions by classes-as-status-groups, we must suspect, could dramatically alter the value of various kinds of cultural capital. At the extreme, revolutionary upheavals may change class cultures altogether (cf. Hunt 1984; Swidler 1986). The strategies of distinction employed by individuals in relation to classes-as-status-groups thus may shift according to economic and political circumstances. Bourdieu is describing the status order under conditions of relative normalcy, not conflict or upheaval.

In the second place, classes are not the only kinds of status groups that may be understood in terms of Bourdieu's approach. Self-conscious ethnic groups, people of a regional or community identity, women's groups that establish a particular sense of gender honor, graduates of a particular school, members of clubs and religions, members of particular occupations, informal status groups based on leisure activities such as surfing, skateboarding, Daughters of the American Revolution—this list merely scratches the surface of the kinds of groups that may establish the value of particular cultural claims and practices. Our discussions have shown that status groups sometimes bridge class distinctions, and that the value of culture for a status group can be something other than simple distinction: it may offer a basis of survival and power in the wider world.

Bourdieu well recognizes that cultural distinctions do not represent some generalized currency of "legal tender" among all individuals and status groups.

He says of class, "one only has to see that, because capital is a social relation, i.e., an energy which only exists and only produces its effects in the field in which it is produced and reproduced, each of the properties attached to class is given its value and efficacy by the specific laws of each field" (1984, p. 113). A sociologist has explored the social meaning of money, showing that all money is not "the same" (Zelizer, 1989). This incomplete interchangeability is even more pronounced for culture than for money. A corporate executive cannot expect his or her art collection to impress a butcher, any more than a factory worker wears clothes to gain distinction with people beyond his or her social circle. Similarly, wearing diamonds will take on a different significance at a debutante's ball than in a truckstop cafe. Cultural capital, after all, is only good in the social worlds where one lives and acts, and the value that it has depends on the distinctions of currency in those particular social worlds. But if this is true, in multicultural situations, the significance of cultural capital depends upon the individual's status group of orientation. Although empirically classes-as-status-groups may predominate, the orientation of an individual is potentially fluid. Moreover, as we have seen, non-class status groups may themselves become the basis of economic action. This means that Bourdieu's approach to cultural capital needs to be understood at its base as a theory of status groups. Sometimes status groups are based on class, sometimes on other cultural criteria. Their kinds of cultural capital sometimes interpenetrate, sometimes conflict, sometimes subsume other markets of distinction. Thus, it would be important to explain the conditions under which class versus other group cultural identifications predominate, just as we would like to know the conditions under which the grounds of distinction reproduce the status social order or transform it.

CONCLUSION

In this chapter, we have found time and again that class is a significant determinant of culture. Bourdieu's theory of cultural capital shows, however, that this is not a one-way causal relationship, and it cannot be understood solely on the basis of treating classes as groups. Instead, individuals and groups are actively employing cultural capital in their competitive pursuits of distinction. Moreover, the stratification of culture and the uses of culture to affirm individual distinction go considerably beyond what an analysis of class and culture would suggest. Ethnicity, gender, and other status group distinctions can establish cultural currency. In turn, individuals can employ these cultural distinctions in ways that affect their locations in a stratified society. Culture is not just a general and widely shared set of knowledge and practices that orient people within the social world. Instead, cultural processes seem to converge with processes of social stratification and differentiation in ways that individuals draw upon in their negotiations toward multiple, overlapping and competing bases of solidarity, identity, and social position.

In our present discussion, we have sought to understand the significance of culture as a sorting device and life pathway within stratified societies. In doing so, we have suggested that the sources of aesthetics of distinction within any given social stratum may come from the outside. This possibility in turn raises two broad issues—whether culture is a vehicle of domination, and how—and by whom—the production and distribution of culture are controlled and carried out. These issues, considered in chapters 7 and 8, shift the focus of cultural studies from the relation between culture and individual and group identities to questions about cultural objects and their connections with political, economic, and organizational processes.

7

POWER AND CULTURE

If power is defined as the ability of individuals and groups to control the actions of others, how does culture figure in its exercise? One answer was offered by Karl Marx, who held religion to be the opiate of the people. Granted, Marx's view was more complex than this remark would suggest. But this strong version of class domination through cultural domination remains a useful benchmark by which to examine culture and power. This chapter explores the social and technological forces that shape the conditions under which culture might prove powerful, and then examines various theories of the relation between power and culture. These theories are diverse: In one view, the power of culture is beyond the control of any group or social stratum. Alternatively, in one way or another, the patterns of culture by which people live may be seen as shaped by the influence of powerful interests.

Any theory that explains culture by reference to considerations of power faces widespread opposition. Humanists, especially those concerned with high culture, have long resisted explaining the content and form of cultural objects by "reducing" them to the social conditions of their production. This sort of impulse also suggests that the best of culture ought to transcend the political conditions of its making. True art, literature and poetry, it has been argued, are timeless: They exist outside of history, hence, at a distance from the social conflicts of an era. In this view, for example, a great painting by Picasso cannot be reduced to economic, political or other circumstances of its having been painted, nor ought it be judged aesthetically on the basis of any political criteria (cf. Wolff 1987).

The scholarly balance shifted during the 1980s. For postmodern critics interested in the politics of culture, even seemingly apolitical culture, precisely in its claim to be apolitical, fills the media with apolitical material, thereby crowds out political discourse, and thus operates in a deeply political way. Now, postmodernists assert, all texts and all cultural objects have to be understood in terms of how they were socially produced, by whom, at what historical moment, and with what political implications.

This controversy in turn suggests a problem that derives from the social role of power. Cultural analysts of a variety of orientations sometimes want to identify an unambiguous relationship between a posited coherent shared societal culture (e.g., "British culture") and the meaningful content of particular cultural objects. If we simply assumed that objects of "high" culture, for example, the novels of Jane Austen, were produced by the force of individual genius, and if we assumed that critical acclaim accurately distinguished great work from the trivial and ephemeral ("trashy" novels), then culture—produced by individual genius—would at the same time represent the essence of a society: Its enduring accomplishments and transcendent values. A parallel argument could be made about popular culture. Rock music would be the music *of* youth, Hollywood movies a *reflection* of their predominantly middle-class audience, and fast food, the *response* to increasingly mobile lifestyles. Culture—high or popular—could be interpreted in terms of its meaningful relation to its audience as society. But this approach to the content of cultural objects can only proceed in the absence of questions of power and its relation to cultural diversity: How does culture shape action, who produces and distributes culture, which of diverse cultural possibilities gets established as a society's culture, whose interests are served by its content and what social strata are empowered by its ideas? Apolitical theories of culture typically make one or the other (or both) of two assumptions: Either that there is a relatively free market in cultural objects such that people get what they want in culture (within their financial and cognitive abilities to acquire culture), or that the culture of a society (or a social group within a society) has a consensual basis, and the culture exists for all members, equally, as the set of ideas and values and aesthetics that bind them together. Under these assumptions, cultural objects reflect the values and meaningful concerns of their audience.

The question of power gets in the way of this straightforward equation. Chapter 2 explored the question of societal culture and chapter 6 addressed issues of socially stratified patterns of culture. In both cases, culture seems implicated in power—the subordination of individuals and groups to the will of others or to the constraints of an established social order—the ongoing arrangements by which a society is organized. Culture is a basis for participating in social strata and in society at large, and it yields labels, as well as boundaries, that include and exclude. The capacity for labeling and exclu-sion/inclusion infuses culture with a kind of power—of groups and society as a whole over individuals, and of some groups and strata over other groups and strata (cf. Lamont 1989).

Power, however, is not an abstract and automatic social phenomenon. It is manifested in concrete activities. To understand power in relation to culture requires asking whether and how specific individuals and groups derive ben-efit from their disproportionate abilities to produce and distribute culture. Once we acknowledge that it takes resources to disseminate music, paint, publish or show films, and that these resources are not equally distributed in any society, then it becomes possible to investigate the political economy of culture: How the production and distribution of culture are economically sup-ported, and how these activities are connected to the structure of political in-terests and power in a society.

These questions are entangled with other pieces of the sociological puz-zle. As Wendy Griswold has observed, the audiences and patrons of culture may influence how cultural producers and distributors act, and what they pro-duce; in different ways, producers and distributors of culture shape and affect their audiences (1987a). The social organization of cultural production and the problem of the audience are addressed in detail in the following two chapters; in the present chapter we will touch on those issues insofar as they affect our understanding of the relation between power and culture. Ques-tions of power may be addressed in two broad ways: (1) by looking at power aspects of the established order of culture, and (2) by investigating the politi-cal economy of cultural production. The latter approach explores how the form and content of cultural objects may be shaped by the economic and po-litical control of cultural production. The former issue, to which we now turn, is about power implications of a society's cultural patterns.

POWER AND THE ESTABLISHED ORDER OF CULTURE

Sociologists widely recognize the importance of the ability to produce and dis-tribute culture, but there is considerable disagreement about how much, how, and which powerful interests control the content and form of culture for their own benefit. One theoretical possibility is that the overall *established order*—the ongoing arrangements—of cultural production has *functional* consequences for the power of different social groups, independently of any individual, organiza-tion, or stratum's capacity to control the shape of the established social order. It might be, for example, that the structure of the music industry is the product of multiple forces, and that it is thus "relatively autonomous" of any given com-pany or corporate sector's ability to organize the established cultural order, while at the same time, certain organizations and social strata may be able to benefit disproportionately from that established order.

The established order of culture thus may be understood in two ways. First, technology and the interplay of a variety of social forces may produce cultural patterns that allocate power. Second, independently of these processes, it is possible to understand the cultural order as a realm of ideas and symbols that are the medium by which power is organized in society.

Technology, Social Forces, and the Cultural Order

Is there a difference between a culture based largely on print and speech communication and one where people routinely watch television and use VCRs, computers, and fax machines? Do authoritarian societies have different cultural patterns than democratic ones? Posing questions in stark terms yields a ready affirmative answer. The more subtle question has to do with whether and how these differences condition the power arrangements of societies.

Technology. Marshall McLuhan's famous formulation that "the medium is the message" suggests a sort of technological determinism (1964). For McLuhan, the content of what we hear on the radio is not as important as the way that the radio organizes our world, both in the capacity to transmit information and entertainment, and in the ways we incorporate sounds from beyond our immediate lifeworld into the course of our lifeworld activities. The same goes for the automobile, television, VCR, and computer.

Joshua Meyrowitz (1985) has extended McLuhan's analysis by looking at the information we get through various media. Instead of assuming that information comes into a social world that itself is unchanged by the process, Meyrowitz asks how the medium reshapes social relationships themselves. In his view, print media—books, magazines, newspapers—offer a depth and detail of information that makes each person something of a specialist on the basis of what he or she reads, whether astrophysical theory, home hobby books, or gossip columns. With print, we each get to know a great deal about selected topics, but what we know and what others know can be quite different, because we burrow into divergent distinctive topics. Television, on the other hand, is oriented to more general audiences, and it lacks the capacity to convey detailed information, yet offers its general audiences a wide awareness of things previously known only by specialists (rituals of warfare among Pacific island natives, for example). General audiences also become familiar with knowledge previously held largely by ordinary people with distinct status positions. Special knowledge stemming from age and sex divisions is broken down when children get to see sitcoms which depict parents in ways that the children might not witness directly in their own homes. Citizens not only get to read newspaper accounts of politicians' speeches; they get to inspect very intimate details in the life of a Supreme Court nominee like Clarence Thomas or a president like Bill Clinton. For Meyrowitz, this means that the distinctions between expert and layperson, and between backstage and frontstage are blurred: The "frontstage" presentations by public figures—how they present themselves as they want to be seen—compete with images about backstage activities. As a variety of commentators have noted, public life obtains the quality of a soap opera that feeds on previously secret "scandal." In a similar way, the expertise of professionals becomes subject to second-guessing because television offers everyone a patchwork of expert knowledge in diverse fields. Television has made many of us much more sophisticated about "performances," and possibly for that reason, people sometimes are not easily impressed. We have all seen how experts and public figures work to cultivate their images portrayed on television.

Presumably, Meyrowitz's focus on television can be broadened to include other, newer technologies—the VCR, portable cassette player, compact disc, electronic computer mail, and so on. Each technology gives rise to a distinctive set of possible relations between individuals and culture, and each shapes a distinctive set of social relationships among the people who participate in it. McLuhan grandly imagined a sort of "global village" in which we all would be united into one large community by the enveloping web of communication. Yet the opposite image—of alienation—also seems relevant: People become separated from one another by their ability to select and experience culture individually, through technology like the portable cassette player. Rapidly changing technologies thus may alter both the web of communication and the degree to which people are connected.

How are these changes related to power? The answer depends on both the nature of culture under various technologies, and the relation of technologies to the established order of culture. Participants in what began as the Frankfurt School of critical theory (discussed in chapter 5) have argued since the 1930s that there can be no single theory of how power operates in societies; every change toward freedom establishes a set of conditions in which new arrangements of domination can take hold. There are dialectical shifts in the exercise of power. Thus, democracy can be subverted by propaganda. Similarly, the free choice of the marketplace can be constrained by the social conditions under which it operates, such that the range of choices cannot be assumed to match buyers' wants and needs.

In the dialectic of power identified by the critical theorists, people interested in minimizing the non-legitimate exercise of power need to identify the specific sources of power that operate in their immediate circumstances. Early on, the critical theorists wondered why the working class lacked the revolutionary fervor that Karl Marx had expected. One answer pointed to the new technological possibilities of cultural domination. Walter Benjamin identified a key divide in culture, based on the possibility of mechanically reproducing recordings, art prints, films, and so on, and distributing them on a mass basis (1969). Obviously the mass production and distribution of culture is the central arrangement by which people have access to culture in our era, and this is as true for much of high culture as it is for popular culture (Gans 1974). Both classical composers and the Rolling Stones are available on compact discs. What, then, was Benjamin's concern? As chapter 5 indicated, for Benjamin, a real cultural object has "authenticity," a special "aura," and a kind of "authority" that are diminished by mass copying. In his view, the shift to mass production—from live to recorded music, from theater to film and TV and from painting to art prints and reproductions—has dire consequences. Art loses its significance as a critical activity when mass reproduction makes it more of a commodity subject to the same forces of manufacturing and marketing as other commodities—cars or laundry detergents, for example. "To an ever greater degree the work of art reproduced becomes the work of art designed for reproducibility," Benjamin wrote (1969, p. 224).

Of course, he had not seen the half of it. Television may show clips of the world, but the technology of editing and the possibilities of acting and production mean that the world as it is depicted on television need not have any existence beyond the screen, even though the video reality paradoxically threatens to overshadow the significance of everyday life. The images brought into our homes by television create a new claim of authenticity. We are dazzled by the experiences made possible by the new technologies; they allow us to see and hear things in ways unavailable in our everyday worlds.[1] Yet for Benjamin, our individual responses to the fascinations of reproduced culture are prefigured in their design. The successful producers of popular entertainment and advertising know how to use media techniques to create certain effects in mass audiences. For Benjamin, these possibilities of manipulation are not limited to mass-produced culture, but mass production heightens their potential for promoting entertainment over critical thought and offering distraction from the circumstances of our actual lives through "the production of ritual values" (1969, p. 241).

In short, technology shapes culture in important ways: it establishes the media of cultural interchange; it may make culture more accessible to some groups, and less accessible to others; it may shift our connections to culture and change how we view the world. However, technology itself is an insufficient basis on which to explain the power effects of an established order of culture. In response to the technology argument, critical theorists Max Horkheimer and Theodor Adorno observed, "No mention is made of the fact that the basis on which technology acquires power over society is the power of those whose economic hold over society is greatest" (1982, p. 121).

Social Forces. Despite the significance of technology, empirical sociological research suggests that the established order of culture cannot be reduced to its technological basis. To the contrary, whatever the consequences of a cultural order for the distribution of power, diverse social forces help shape its emergence. We might assume, for example, that technological innovations in printing brought the modern newspaper into being. But Michael

---

[1] The relation of these possibilities to postmodern culture is discussed in chapter 11.

Schudson argues that it is just the reverse: In the United States, social forces of change came to a head in the 1830s, creating a demand for a new kind of newspaper, and this demand in turn motivated technological innovations that made printing easier (1978, pp. 31–35). What were these social forces in the nineteenth century U.S.? Schudson points to three: The emergence of a broadly-based market economy, the diffusion of political participation among wider and wider sectors of the population, and the eclipse of small-scale community by a more complex society. When increasing numbers of people became drawn into the market economy, they began to have an interest in news of commerce that previously was important solely to business. Similarly, the growing interest in politics could not be adequately served by the party-organ newspapers of the day, which primarily published views of the political parties without offering what we today think of as "news." Finally, in small communities, face-to-face conversations could serve as a medium of communication that helped bind people together. A more complex society created wider ties of interest beyond the world of people's immediate neighbors: What happened in another state or country became of interest to people whose horizons were widening. In the nineteenth century, forces were at work changing the social world and people's ties to it, and these changing conditions, Schudson argues, created circumstances in which "news" in its modern sense gained a sufficient audience to fuel the birth of the first modern newspapers.

What about other kinds of societal arrangements, for example, of material culture? Let us take the case of the motel. It would be easy to argue that technology gave rise to the motel. At the end of the nineteenth century, hotels were a form of travel accommodation appropriate to cities, and to forms of travel, such as trains, that served urban places. With the early twentieth-century advent of the automobile—a technological innovation—motels might be explained as hotels moved out to the highway. But this common-sense explanation is drawn into question by Warren Belasco, who shows that motels did originate by catering to the motoring public, but not simply as hotels at the edge of town (1979). Instead, the motel form of overnight travel accommodation emerged as a byproduct of status competition between elite vacationers and other people with whom they shared the road. When the grand elite spas and resorts began to attract a less elite clientele in the latter part of the nineteenth century, some patrons began to seek out other forms of leisure. Motivated by desires for a nostalgic return to nature and "the strenuous life" recommended by President Theodore Roosevelt at the turn of the twentieth century, some people used the first automobiles for "auto-camping," going, as they said, "a-gypsying" to escape the constraints of the increasingly industrial, bureaucratized, and urban social landscape. To cater to this trend, there gradually emerged city campgrounds, and then private ones which charged a fee, thus excluding vagrants and the migrating poor. By the 1920s entrepreneurs were offering tourist cabins and cottages on their land as more

comfortable accommodations for their paying clients. It was in these au-
tocamping facilities that the first motels were established. Thus, the motel as a
business format for lodging was born of changing tastes among automobile
tourists engaged in status competition with one another.

The importance of diverse social forces can also be seen in the
longterm developments toward contemporary culture that have taken place
over centuries. Robert Wuthnow has explored the social forces that gave rise
to three major modern ideological frameworks for the conduct of social
life—sixteenth-century Reformation religiosity, seventeenth- and especially
eighteenth-century Enlightenment knowledge, and socialist public discourse
initiated during the nineteenth century. Wuthnow argues that these world-
transforming "communities of discourse" were hardly random innovations.
The actions of the people who promoted the new discourses depended on
favorable "environmental conditions" and "institutional contexts" for their effectiveness (1989). The Reformation did not take hold equally everywhere in
the sixteenth century; the proponents of science and philosophy had to con-
tend with opposed vested economic, political and religious interests in the
seventeenth and eighteenth centuries; socialist political parties had checkered histories in various nation-states during the nineteenth century.

The emergence and patterns of culture as diverse as the newspaper, the
motel, and major forms of public discourse cannot be explained by technology alone. Established cultural forms are shaped by social forces at work in
the societies where they exist. We may suspect that similar kinds of research
would show the significance of social forces for diverse kinds of culture—
popular music, film, craft fairs, literature, motorcycle gangs, and so on. Yet to
explain the origins of an established cultural order by either the influence of
technology or social forces does not necessarily explain that order as a basis
of social power. This is true for two reasons. First, whatever the origins of a
cultural order, it may have consequences as an established set of meanings
and objects that inscribe power within society. Second, individuals and
groups which own or control key organizations in the established social order
may be able to exercise power through their ownership and management of
cultural production.

The Established Cultural Order as a Medium of Power

Do the institutionalized patterns of culture that inform our actions themselves amount to orders of power? If so, why and how? Sociologists like
Durkheim (1965) focus on culture as a force of social integration. Yet this
does not deny the power of culture. To the contrary, culture can thereby define the boundary between social integration and alienation and deviance. At
least implicitly, this means that culture is a medium of power: People who operate within the boundaries of a culture are dominated by its categories and
meanings; those who deviate from cultural expectations may be subject to

sanctions both at the hands of authority and of other people who conform to the established cultural order.

Sigmund Freud confronted the coercive power of culture much more directly than Durkheim. As we saw in chapter 2, Freud argued the existence of a fundamental conflict between the individual's subconscious desires for sexual pleasure and the demands of a civilized world for the individual to knuckle down to the responsibilities of family and work. The superego, representing normative social demands on the individual, had to be accommodated by the individual ego, or society could not persist. For Freud, the persistence of culture requires repression of individual freedom. As with Durkheim, the victory of culture over the individual is a functional necessity in any society.

In the view of critical theorists, the "necessity" of cultural domination is organized within contemporary societies by the necessity of channeling social life along lines that gear into the capitalist satisfaction of wants. As chapter 5 showed, for theorists like Benjamin, mass production of culture played into this possibility: Production, distribution, and consumption formed an organized complex that gave rise to specifically capitalist styles of life. More recently, Herbert Marcuse argued for the connection between capitalist cultural domination and the lifestyles of specific social strata—working class youth, suburban professionals, and so on—by suggesting that consumption may be an act of free choice, but the choice made is "spurious": It conceals the "universal coordination" of consumers, and it has consequences of domination for consumers, whether it reflects a wage earner's or salaried lifestyle, or even affluence:

> The high standard of living in the domain of the great corporations is *restrictive* in a concrete sociological sense: the goods and services that the individuals buy control their needs and petrify their faculties. In exchange for the commodities that enrich their life, the individuals sell not only their labor but also their free time (1962, pp. 90–1).

Like Horkheimer and Adorno, Marcuse thus emphasizes the role of corporate business interests in the structuring of a world organized to surround and envelop consumers. In this view, power is based on the ability to structure the world so that people will freely choose to define their needs and wants—their total existence—through consumption. Yet this power is hardly total: As the economic downturn of the early 1990s showed, the spending practices of consumers may radically change, with dramatic consequences for a capitalist organized consumer order.

Though critical theory offers interpretation rather than concrete research, its interpretations are not without empirical support. Sociologists who have studied commercial architecture, for example, have found that restaurants and stores may be designed to maximize sales, maintain customer turnover after purchase, and meet other corporate goals, such as appealing to multiple customer values with a strong yet inoffensive "business format." At

FIGURE 7.1 Upon entering the franchise restaurant, consumers may find themselves immersed in a world designed to maximize corporate goals, where employee action is highly orchestrated according to dictates of rationalization. (*Source:* Mike Valeri/FPG International.)

franchise restaurants, we enter worlds designed as extensions of their advertised images, on the basis of market research (Wright 1985). Similar considerations go into the design of shopping malls, which recreate the civic space of downtown, but under totally private auspices which can maximize control of the environment, excluding non-conforming business activities, the homeless and political controversy, thereby sustaining a sense of "mall gentility" in which "nothing unusual is happening" (Jacobs 1984, pp. 13–4). In the early 1840s, before Karl Marx developed his own theory of capitalism, he engaged in a philosophical critique of bourgeois society which warned against a situation in which private interests would come to structure the organization of civic space (1978, p. 33). But Marx could not anticipate the world of the mall, that so many shoppers would find so attractive.

The designs of restaurants, stores and malls are physical manifestations of a culture created by business corporations. But it is not just physical structure that is constructed according to business interests. As chapter 5 showed, the emergence of consumer society is based on core activities of market research and advertising. In this vein, Daniel Boorstin has argued that symbols produced by corporations are becoming vital links in how we experience reality (1962). A pair of jeans no longer sells for the cost of its production plus profit. Advertising for "Guess" or "Levi's" produces an image that defines the product. We are not simply "paying for" the cost of advertising when we buy clothing, high-priced toiletries or cars with high-status images; we are buying the image created by advertising, and thus the advertising is not just a cost related to distributing information about a product; it is essential to the *worth* of the objects we buy.

Of course not everyone is interested in the same images, and therefore, even for a given material need, many different products are required to satisfy a diverse population. Market research is able to identify "clusters" of consumers to "target" with goods designed specifically for them. On this basis, stereotypes are used in developing marketing strategies. Advertising and the mass culture supported by advertising—television entertainment, movies, magazines—may reinforce, modify, or create images that consumers then buy. It is possible, then, for advertising to establish images (e.g., the Marlboro man) that consumers in turn use to elaborate personal identity, even if identity depends on material circumstances that are not altered by advertising. As we suggested in chapter 5, advertising offers us an idealized image of our world which may lend it a coherence unavailable in everyday life itself.

In the final analysis, a critical theory of power does not assume the existence of a single, cohesive, powerful group, nor does it depend upon centralized control of communication. Advertising, market research, and capitalist consumer production are significant elements of a wider set of social institutions that includes politics, government bureaucracies, information processing organizations, planning agencies and scientific laboratories. The power of these institutions may lie in their diffuse yet pervasive character. In the view of the contemporary critical theorist Jürgen Habermas, the social world of everyday life—the "lifeworld"—has been overshadowed by the "system" (1987). In part this change occurs because systematic rationalization of social life invades the lifeworld: Our lives increasingly are organized via bureaucratic governmental and corporate systems of producing goods, services and information in ways that affect the environment, the character of cities and towns, what we eat, how we maintain health, how we care for the sick, and so on. The lifeworld has shifted from once having been the *location* from which action proceeded to the reverse: The realm of everyday life is now organized increasingly from the outside, by the "system."

The model of power illuminated by critical theory suggests that the social world is organized in ways that yield a de facto domination of society's members by its cultural arrangements, largely shaped in the arena of large-scale economic and political organizations. Such a theory can be put into sharper focus by asking how cultural arrangements yield such a form of power in their operations. The most insightful answer to this question has been provided by Michel Foucault, who moves in a quite different direction than critical theory.

In a fascinating array of studies on prisons, mental illness, and other aspects of social life, Foucault has added to other research that reveals a diffuse institutionalized power of culture. Labeling theorists have shown, for example, that "madness" is not simply a psychological fact; it is a shifting social construction of meaning that coordinates institutionalized arrangements designed to identify and deal with people at the fringes of society. The matter of who is at the fringes of society depends on time and place (Goffman 1961, Scheff 1966, Laing 1967, Szasz 1987). Foucault deepened this fundamental insight in his theories about a time before the emergence of the modern world in which neither "reason" nor "madness" described the average person. The emergence of reason as a category of popular personality had two implications for the social order. In the first place, it allowed reasoning *about* madness. This is a difficult project both because early categories like "delirium" give way to other labels as theories change, and because the treatment of insanity will differ depending on whether it is regarded as animalistic passion or as moral failure. For Foucault, the power of reason is limited; certainly reasoning alone does not guarantee truth. In any event, reason has not yet tamed madness.

Perhaps this failure stems from the second implication of reason's emergence: If madness was uncommon in an earlier era because reason was uncommon, then Foucault implies that the birth of reason made possible the delineation of madness. Reason established a standard of comparison by which madness could be identified. But if madness and reason are intimately connected with each other, then changes in what counts as reason will change what counts as madness too. Foucault seems to suggest that we are trapped in the boxes which are established by our own efforts to make solid categories, and make them stick. The social arrangements for processing people through treatment or incarceration or monitoring have the effect of constructing the specific conditions of madness, from back-ward schizophrenia to the "mentally ill" homelessness of the 1990s. In other words, institutionalized practices based on reasoned knowledge in the disciplines of psychiatry and psychology, social welfare and police procedure, construct both the life circumstances and the meaningful categories of "madness" (Foucault 1965, 1979). It is his critique of reason itself, and our entrapment in and through its unfolding that separates Foucault from the social constructionists.

Foucault connects "reason" to disciplines, and disciplines of knowledge become the basis of other disciplines, of power over the subjects of disciplinary knowledge. But it is not only the lives of criminals and deviants and the insane that are powerfully affected by knowledge and practices established in "disciplines." Foucault argued that the "gaze" of the disciplines is focused on the world of conventional life as well, for example, in the practice of medicine (1975). Yet his view does not necessarily cast blame on doctors, for they, like patients, are governed by the categories that discipline their thinking. What is disarming, even frightening, about Foucault is his depiction of a cultural domination that operates without conspirators yet reduces the agency of acting subjects to mere reflections of the cultural categories that frame social life. Issues of power and domination have a different twist with the eclipse of the subject: There is no privileged standpoint like that asserted for the working class by Marxists. We are all trapped within culturally constructed standpoints that imprison our reasoning.

For Foucault, even one of the most intimate aspects of personal life—sexuality—is "deployed" from outside the site of its practice. But Foucault does not follow Freud in regarding civilized power as repressing sexuality. To the contrary, there is a flood of discourse on sexuality—in movies, advertising, newspapers and magazines, therapy groups, and with doctors. These discourses are powerful not because they offer rules of conduct, but because they establish the web of meanings that embed sexuality within the framework of social life. Sexual activity, at its core an animalistic behavior, has become imbued with specifically moral attributes. Thus, we do not simply act sexually as animals. Sexual practices carry specific culture freight. Forms of heterosexual, monogamous, marital, homosexual, and other sexual conduct transpire within fields of meaning organized by professional and mass-mediated discourse (Foucault 1980). To mention but one example, the lyrics of popular music may contribute to male social dominance by distributing "overdetermined" images of gender identity, such as male aggressiveness and the nurturing female (Shepard 1987).

The accounts of the power of culture developed by critical theorists, Foucault and others differ from one another in certain respects. Some theorists emphasize the cultural patterns as products of a capitalist consumer society; others, like Habermas and Foucault, see the cultural power basis of society today as grounded in a wider set of institutions than purely economic ones. In either case, the arrangements affected by culture do not benefit everyone equally; instead, they work to the advantage of particular social classes, ethnic groups, professions, and men under certain conditions. Yet it is important to note one feature of theories about culture as an established order. Privileged groups that benefit from the cultural matrix do not necessarily achieve this benefit by the direct exercise of power, and people from disprivileged strata are not necessarily excluded from participation in the apparatus. What matters is that a diffuse but pervasive set of meanings, objects and arrangements establishes a de facto power by the incorporation of culture into our everyday lives. Insofar as the power of culture is diffuse, as Foucault suspected, political change and even a shift in economic organization would not change the powerful operation of culture in our daily lives. Indeed, for Foucault, even broad cultural change—a religious reformation, or a change in sexual mores—seems to amount to a change in the web of culture toward a new set of categories that entangle us. Thus, Foucault sometimes has been read as a conservative theorist, pessimistic about the possibilities and benefits of cultural change. Only if Foucault is wrong, and the content of culture is connected to specific economic and political interests, does the question of who controls cultural production make a difference.

THE OWNERSHIP OF CULTURAL PRODUCTION

A venerable tradition in sociology confronts power much more directly than does Foucault. If power is defined as the ability to make people do things whether they want to or not, then power to shape culture can be traced to those people and organizations that produce culture. Obviously culture is directly produced by cultural workers—artists, journalists, film producers, novelists, fashion designers, teachers, sociologists and others. The questions then become, whom do cultural workers work for, and how does the ownership of cultural production affect culture?

In the United States, the clear empirical trend over time is toward an increased concentration of mass media ownership into fewer and fewer hands. If "freedom of the press belongs to those who own one," as the old adage has it, that freedom seems increasingly narrow. A comprehensive survey by Ben Bagdikian shows that the U.S. has a huge number of media outlets. Yet, "today, despite 25,000 media outlets in the United States, twenty-nine corporations control most [i.e., more than 50%] of the business in daily newspapers, television, books, and motion pictures" (1987, p. 4). Moreover, those twenty-nine corporations represented a decrease, from forty-six controlling corporations only five years earlier. Acquisitions and mergers proceed at a dizzying pace, and they now involve concentrations across different media (such as the 1989 Time, Inc. merger with Warner Communications), as well as the ownership of media outlets by media equipment producers and by diversified corporations like Gulf + Western and G.E. (which owns the NBC television network).

Not only is there significant corporate control across different types of media, any individual mass medium is dominated by a small number of corporations. Fifteen newspaper chains controlled more than 50% of all U.S. newspaper circulation at the end of 1986, and the largest chain, Gannett Company, owned *USA Today* and 92 other newspapers, for a total daily circulation of over 6 million, or about ten per cent of all daily newspaper circulation in the U.S. In magazines, Time, Inc. controlled 40% of all revenues, even before its merger with Warner Communications. The latter corporation, together with CBS Records (since bought by Sony) controlled 65% of the market in recorded music, even by the early 1980s (Parenti 1986, p. 27–8). These statistics reveal a significant increase in the degree of media ownership concentration, a trend that led Time, Inc. executive Nicholas Nicholas, Jr., to predict in 1989 that, "there will emerge, on a worldwide basis, six, seven, eight vertically integrated media and entertainment megacompanies..." (*The Nation* 3/27/89, p. 401).

Despite the increased concentration of media ownership, it is important to recognize that ownership and control of corporations are not always equivalent, as Andrew Hacker once showed us in his analysis of control in capitalist joint-stock corporations (1965). New owners of media outlets typically emphasize that they do not intend to interfere with editorial decisions. So the question remains as to how and how much ownership yields power. There are several significant processes. The most obvious is raw political power. As Bagdikian observes, the owner of a small-town newspaper does not carry the weight with elected national politicians that is carried by the owner of a chain of newspapers. And though the presidents of large corporations *not* involved with the media (oil companies, for example) may expect a sympathetic ear in Congress and by the President, that expectation can only be increased when a corporation controls media outlets that produce and distribute news and commentary about politicians. Like other large businesses, media conglomerates have political interests in legislation that affects their operations and financial circumstances (as well as more diffuse class interests). On the other side of the fence, politicians, government officials, business spokespersons, and other news sources have interests in the "slant" or "spin" of news coverage, and they exert influence by releasing or withholding information (Boorstin 1962, Gans 1979). The meshed interests of newsmakers in media coverage and media conglomerates in politics create circumstances in which each can influence the actions of the other.

The degree to which extraneous influences affect media content varies, of course, partly depending on how high the stakes are for the subjects of news coverage. Clearly such influences can have dramatic effects in critical situations. One case study shows, for example, that newspaper conglomerates seeking exemption from an antimonopoly law received the support of President Richard Nixon for the exemption. In the months before Nixon's 1972 re-election bid, pro-Nixon newspapers "had a higher tendency to suppress damaging Watergate stories than papers making no endorsements," and papers owned by chains favorably affected by the antimonopoly exemption unanimously endorsed Nixon for re-election (Bagdikian 1987, pp. 90–101).

To elevate such incidents to a general account of the media might seem to generalize from the extreme. Yet there is little doubt about the existence of complex processes of mutual influence among news media and news sources. Moreover, there are other mechanisms by which concentration of media ownership yields power. Most significantly, it consolidates what can be called a "media-advertising-corporate complex." Essentially, the ever increasing amalgamation of media organizations is not simply a combination of financial profit centers under a smaller number of corporate umbrellas. More importantly, it actually reorganizes the structure of the mass media both in relation to each other and toward businesses in general.

In the first place, conglomerated media enhance the possibilities of "tie-ins," in which a book can be turned into a movie, then serialized on television, at each step promoted by radio stations, television talk shows, newspapers and magazines—all within a single corporate orb. High and popular cultural products do not—and probably never did—find their way to success solely on the basis of audience interest. But now, a new stage of cultural production has emerged. The critical theorists feared that culture would become a commodity of manufacture, subject to procedures similar to those for making an automobile. That, of course, has been the case for some time. Now, with media amalgamation, that process becomes more tightly controlled. Cultural objects can be moved easily from one medium to another, establishing a set of production linkages that allow for the mutual reinforcement of production and promotion in several media simultaneously, all within one corporate conglomerate.

The connection of cultural production is not exhausted by the promotion of "tie-ins" by media conglomerates. Bagdikian argues that advertising establishes a key linkage between the media corporations and the broader complex of consumer-oriented corporations. This linkage seems to have a specific consequence and a more subtle one. The specific consequence is that advertisers sometimes demand from media owners—and obtain—changes in media content and agreements concerning appropriate topics of treatment. To the degree that advertising supports the cost of media operations, advertisers represent the prime audience to which media formats and programming are "sold." That is, for media like television (and, to a lesser extent, newspapers and most magazines), advertisers are the main customers, who pay for access to audiences, while audiences pay nothing or only a small proportion of costs directly. Just as media conglomerates can have influence with politicians, advertisers have influence with the media. For example, Procter and Gamble established policies concerning the content of programs to be supported by their advertising budget, and a tobacco company during the era when cigarettes were advertised on television insisted that "no cigarette should be used as a prop to depict an undesirable character" (Bagdikian 1987, p. 158). Today, the promotion of goods through their use in movies ("Reese's Pieces" in E. T.) has become an accepted advertising expense and source of film revenue. In a variety of ways, the content of what might be innocently presumed to be something other than an advertisement can be directly affected by advertisers' initiatives.

Advertising also affects the content of mass culture in a second, more subtle way. Whereas advertising once merely purchased space or time in a medium that existed independently of advertising, that equation is undergoing change. Advertisers have used advances in market research to identify ever more specific markets for their goods. They wisely want to spend their advertising budgets in ways that deliver the most potential customers for the least cost, and this interest seems to have led to important shifts in the formats and content of mass media. Newspapers and magazines, for example, publish special sections including articles that go well with certain kinds of advertisements. The long traditions of the newspaper sections on food and real estate depend on a mutual reinforcement between news and advertising. But these represent only the first step in a progression. In some cases, such as a special section on "winterizing your car," the articles themselves can be presented as regular news articles, even though they may be written by

FIGURE 7.2 A number of contemporary magazines, like the one shown here, closely coordinate editorial and advertising content in ways that sharpen the market niche of subscribers whom advertisers are trying to reach, and provide highly relevant advertising for individuals with particular consumer interests. (*Source:* Metropolitan Home, November 1992.)

advertisers, industry associations, and their public relations representatives. A somewhat more direct approach—the "advertorial"—involves advertisers' purchase of a section in which they include "news" articles reporting on, say, investment possibilities in Brazil (Bagdikian, 1987, p. 162–5).

The interests of advertisers in reaching segmented markets can produce something of an inversion, for example, in the slick-paper magazines. Because magazines face stiff competition for advertising revenues, their publishers no longer can afford to design a format in order to reach a naturally occurring audience or establish a new one on the basis of editorial sensibilities. Instead, according to the creator of *Vanity Fair* and *Vogue*—Condé Nast—the purpose of high-status magazines is to "build the editorial pages in such a way to lift out of all the millions of Americans just the hundred thousand cultivated persons who can buy these quality goods" (q. in Bagdikian, 1987, p. 161). In the extreme, magazines such as *Glamour, Allure, Gentlemen's Quarterly* or *Metropolitan Home* are dominated by their advertisements, and the graphic format of the editorial material reduces the cognitive distance between editorial material and the ads.

As much as these developments represent a triumph of advertising in forging a transmission belt between capitalist corporations, media, and consumers, it is a triumph in which consumers actively participate. We live in a world in which consumption is important. As chapter 6 suggests, the symbolic capital of products adds status value to the products themselves. Under these conditions, the well-socialized consumer reads and watches ads carefully, shopping for images, as it were. She, or he, chooses a magazine like *Glamour* or *Metropolitan Home* less for its editorial content than for the advertisements, which display goods attractive to the sensibilities of a certain cluster of taste publics (perhaps defined statistically by their zip codes).

The ownership of mass media outlets has become increasingly concentrated into fewer and fewer hands. This process has contributed to the direct political power of owners, and to the consolidation of media under the dominance of large-scale, consumer-oriented corporate capitalism. In turn, the latter development has shaped the content and formats of mass media. This consolidation, of course, has taken place as part of a wider consolidation of corporate capitalism, in food brands, shopping mall chains, department stores, and so forth. The power entailed is not simply that of direct authority and influence. Instead, it is a power to design, produce, and distribute culture on a mass basis.

THE POLITICAL ECONOMY OF CULTURAL PRODUCTION

Culture is not produced solely by capitalists, of course, even if global capitalist enterprises have been increasingly organizing the process for a long time. The culture that gets made is the product of complex social relations among diverse people who do not necessarily share the interests of the owners or managers of the means of cultural production. A question arises, then, about the nature and degree of power *over* the work of cultural production, for it is possible that producers of culture might act in ways beyond the control of owners and managers. This question can be addressed in two different ways: first, by asking who produces culture, and second, by investigating the degree to which political and ideological considerations affect actual cultural production.

Cultural Workers

Two classical early twentieth-century sociologists—both Italians—addressed the question of power and culture in ways that considered the role of cultural workers. One, Vilfredo Pareto, was a political radical for a time, who—at the end of his life—supported Mussolini's fascist regime. The other, Antonio Gramsci, remained a committed communist, even at his death in one of Mussolini's prisons. Despite their political differences, both thought that political power is closely linked to domination of culture, and each addressed the role of cultural workers in the process.

Pareto's theory of power distinguished between elites and masses, with the elite controlling mass cultural interpretations of events. He argued that elites maintain their legitimacy and the legitimacy of their policies and actions (tax policies, controversial decisions, military actions, etc.) by appealing to popular sentiments that connect with "residues"—deep psychological orientations of the masses toward such symbols as family, community, self-sacrifice, respect for hierarchy, and fears concerning bad events, the unknown, and the non-conforming (Pareto, 1966, p. 222ff.). In Pareto's view, in-group and out-group elites "circulate"—that is, replace one another—on the basis of their relative abilities to appeal to cyclical waves of changing popular sentiments that are tied to the deeply held residues. An elite that bases its appeal on certain sentiments—for example, justice or patriotism—can only maintain power in the shifting currents of popular sentiments if it recruits new members from its elite opponents, who may try to gain power on their own by appealing to the rising tide of a new set of sentiments such as equality or security. Pareto maintained a clear distinction between what the powerful actually *do* and how they *justify* what they do; he saw justification as proceeding by appeal to sentiments rather than by appeal to reason, and he held that elites survive by successfully recruiting (elite) cultural workers who can appeal to popular sentiments.

Antonio Gramsci, like Pareto, was concerned with the role of culture in a ruling group's domination of a social order, which he termed "cultural hegemony" (meaning "cultural domination"). Though he was a Marxist, Gramsci did not describe the ruling ideas of an era as the ideas of a ruling class. Instead, he suggested that cultural hegemony is maintained by the promotion of *any* culture that accommodates people to their social fate, so long as it is not threatening to ruling class interests. Country and western music probably appeals to relatively few members of the corporate capitalist class, for example, yet its content recognizes dissatisfactions among the working people to whom it appeals, without channeling such dissatisfactions in ways that challenge the established social order.

For Gramsci, cultural hegemony is closely linked to the recruitment of workers for the staffing of positions of cultural production. He identified two polar opposite types of people doing significant cultural work: *organic intellectuals,* who are actively linked to the problems and aspirations of concrete social groups (e.g., Martin Luther King, Jr. with black Americans), and *traditional intellectuals,* who fill routine cultural roles in relatively conventional and predictable ways. If we broaden "intellectuals" to include cultural workers in general, Gramsci's theory suggests that a ruling class must insure that traditional cultural workers staff the production of culture for a wide range of taste publics, so that produced culture, whatever its specific content, will pacify the public. In this view, the elite has no interest in imposing elite culture on other people; its interests are satisfied so long as other people's culture does not threaten their power. Thus, since organic intellectuals representing other social strata pose a threat to the established order, it is in the interest of a ruling class to deflect their effectiveness. Such an interest might be fulfilled in a number of ways. "Traditional" culture itself may be modified in response to external cultural challenges. Or organic cultural workers may be recruited into traditional cultural production roles, where they tend to become cut off from the aspirations of concrete social groups, and instead represent a "diversity of opinion" within the traditionally produced culture (Gramsci, 1971).

Neither Pareto's nor Gramsci's theory is easy to test empirically, for the cultural material that might be hegemonic changes over time, as do sentiments and the significance of traditional and organic intellectuals. Yet it is instructive to explore briefly a kind of cultural production where the political stakes are particularly high—the news. When we ask who becomes a reporter, and how, the answers suggest that news personnel are drawn disproportionately from the upper-middle class, and that their secondary socialization—in college and sometimes graduate school—shapes professional orientations that may produce the "traditional" cultural worker described by Gramsci. As Michael Parenti notes, "Only one in five [journalists] comes from blue-collar or low-status white-collar families," and "most newspeople lack contact with working-class people, have a low opinion of labor unions, and know very little about people outside their own social class." To be sure, journalists are often liberals, but interestingly, their liberal views typically do not get reflected in their news accounts (Parenti, 1986, pp. 40–1). However, the horizons of their worlds do shape their outlooks, according to Herbert Gans's study of major news outlets such as the "NBC Nightly News" and *Time.* One thing that Gans found was that newspeople, like the rest of us, have outer limits to their social circles. The consequences are important:

> Journalists obtain their information about America from their customary sources; from what they themselves read in the paper; and, because they have trouble crossing the social barriers that separate them from strangers, from what they learn from peers and personal contacts, notably relatives and friends (1979, p. 126).

Based on research like that of Gans and Parenti, and the theories of Gramsci and Pareto, we have good reason to suspect that the social locations and alignments of cultural workers with the interests of particular social groups have important consequences for the culture that gets produced. What is true for journalists probably holds for other cultural workers—artists, religious personnel, novelists, and others. Comparative research on the social locations of cultural workers thus offers a rich vein for further inquiry.

Social Control and Cultural Production

There is another important issue to be drawn from the example of research on journalists: If the social origins, politics, and personal networks of cultural workers matter, they must have their effect on actual culture produced. Indeed, any political economic effect is significant only if it finds its way into the form and content of culture. We have already seen that advertisers sometimes directly influence content. But more subtle processes also seem to be at work. They have to do with how publicly legitimated worldviews get established in the first place.

Public opinion, for example, cannot be assumed to exist independently of the mass media, its practices, and its distribution of information. Benjamin Ginsberg has argued that the establishment of democratic nation-states over the past two centuries has been accompanied by a reconstruction of popular opinion, its sources, and its expression. He describes an "idea market" dominated by "the most powerful producers of ideas": "Upper- and upper-middle-class groups and the organizations and institutions they control" (1986, p.89). In Benjamin's view, this idea market is connected to processes of public opinion formation: opinion once was closely tied to social groups, but techniques of mass polling have individualized it, undermining oppositional groups within society. The ways in which people form opinions have also shifted due to the emergence of mass media polling techniques, which affect opinion both by the ways questions are framed and by the consequences for the general public of receiving reports about the opinions of a statistical sample of individuals remote from their own lives. Benjamin reports on revealing research from 1980: 66% of people in lower-income groups who watched television news "every day believed that inflation was an 'extremely' serious problem," compared to only 56 percent of lower-income people who "almost never" watched television news (1986, p. 101). Interestingly, the opinions of people in higher income brackets seem to have been much less affected by watching television news. In its broad outlines, Benjamin's argument suggests that the production of culture is shaped by the longterm emergence of a particular institutional pattern of relationships between government, the media and the most powerful social classes.

The overall institutional pattern has its parallels in the organization of more concrete practices. As Michael Schudson has shown, professional standards of factuality that emerged in the 1890s tended to exclude the insights of journalists as persons on the scene of events. In a parallel way, more recently, the emphasis on "objectivity" in news reporting has lent official news sources an aura of legitimacy which unofficial sources lack (1978, pp. 71–87, 160ff.). In the view of Daniel Boorstin, the news production process increasingly has come to depend on press releases that subordinate journalism to powerful public relations techniques of press management, conducted by corporations, governments, politicians, and celebrities (1962). It is no longer possible to draw a sharp distinction between the news that is reported and the "pseudo-events," as Boorstin calls them, that are staged by organizations and individuals in the news for the consumption of news organizations in order to achieve certain public-relations effects.

Journalists, of course, are careful to document their "facts," often by two-source corroboration. But the choice of which facts to include affects the story, and even prior to the choice of facts comes a decision of what Herbert Gans calls "story selection"—whether to cover a given set of events at all. Gans's study of newsrooms at *Time, Newsweek,* CBS and NBC shows little direct political control of news, but it does reveal a less obvious effect of "enduring values" that shape news content: "The values in the news are rarely explicit and must be found between the lines—in what actors and activities are reported or ignored, and in how they are described" (1979, pp. 39–40). Gans identified a number of central values that inform how news is reported: ethnocentrism, altruistic democracy, individualism, and moderatism, among others. Overall, he concluded that these values amount to an ideology that, though not inflexible, promotes "responsible capitalism" (as opposed to greedy, polluting, and other irresponsible kinds), while maintaining "respect for tradition" and "nostalgia for pastoralism and rugged individualism" that are "unabashedly conservative" (1979, p. 68).

It is Gans's view that values and ideology establish a contextual climate that influences news reporting on events such as oil spills, military actions, changes in communist countries, foreign trade problems, and the like. Is cultural hegemony, then, simply a matter of value influences? A study of how *The New York Times* and CBS News reported the Vietnam War suggests a more direct process. In a detailed analysis of news accounts about the war, Todd Gitlin has shown how media treatment uses "news frames" to place events within the narrative structures of news stories that are greater than the sum of their factual parts (1980). Gitlin found that early protests against U.S. involvement in the Vietnam War were reported, to be sure, but they were covered by the use of "framing devices" such as trivialization and disparagement of protesters' effectiveness. News coverage portrayed the antiwar movement as marginal, radical, poorly organized, and polarized by internal dissension. In the long run, the grass-roots character of the movement was undermined by the "spotlight" effect of news coverage and the identification of radical "celebrities."

To some extent, Gitlin's research elaborates the phenomenon of *reflexivity,* in which the course of events is affected by the ways in which they are

reported. But he offers strong evidence that, in coverage of the antiwar movement, the reflexive effect of reporting supported interests of hegemonic control.
On the other hand, the eventual partial success of the antiwar movement shows
that cultural hegemony does not always completely shape popular opinion on
controversial issues. Gitlin's study shows the hegemonic process as real, nevertheless limited, yet still ultimately powerful in shaping public ideology, values,
and attitudes. It is an analysis that has been broadened by a recent comparative
study: Herman and Chomsky (1988) describe a pattern of U.S. media "self-cen-
sorship" that results in a double standard. They find one kind of coverage for issues that advance U.S. propaganda interests, for example, antigovernment
protests in eastern Europe and the then Soviet Union. There is a much different
treatment of news about delicate foreign affairs matters that might reflect negatively on the American public's image of their own country and its government—Vietnam, El Salvador, and the Iran/Contra affair (and, after Herman and
Chomsky completed their book, the Gulf War against Iraq's Saddam Hussein).

It is not solely the news that is subjected to processes of social control. Analysts from the British Birmingham School of cultural studies and related practi-
tioners of cultural studies have drawn on theoretical perspectives of Gramsci,
Foucault and others to study television, movies, advertising, magazines and
other mass or popular culture forms. Such research shows pervasive, albeit complexly coded, ideological subtexts in everyday culture. The content of popular
culture can create a general ideological climate that seems invisible and natural
when we are immersed within it, but which contains powerful—because implicit and therefore unchallenged—assumptions about how the world is and
ought to be. A variety of studies have shown "ideological work" in popular culture media that promote public stereotypes about gender, race, class, and other
problematic issues in the U.S., the developed nation-states more generally, and
the entire post-colonial world (Goldman 1984; Angus and Jhally 1989; Miller
1990; Grossberg, Nelson and Treichler 1992).

Even high-brow art is created, distributed and appreciated within established arrangements that affect its content. Thus, Judith Adler (1979) has documented a cautionary tale about the utopian and radical origins of an art
school—California Institute of the Arts—and the ways in which the patronage
of the Disney Foundation colored the art scene there. During a period when
the Disneys were offering seed money, Adler observed:

> In the absence of a substantial endowment, any activities or "manners" which
> could be construed as making fund raising difficult were likely to become the
> subject of major controversy, until eventually the imperatives of institutional
> survival defined "reality" for the artists who came to the school.

In theory, the *least* external influence or control would operate in free
markets, where the only influence on artists depends upon their willingness
to respond to the tastes of buyers. However, research shows that even art
markets are subject to social controls.

In a study of art photographers, for example, Barbara Rosenblum showed that access to the market itself was highly controlled by gatekeepers who staffed the fine-arts photography schools and operated the galleries where photography was shown (1978b). And the buyers' side of the market is not a random "public": Today, a significant proportion of dollars spent on art purchases are spent by museums and corporations interested in defining public art. Indeed, the acquisitions by corporations recently have attained a level that establishes a separate "corporate art" market, and in this market, the subjects of art tend toward non-controversial topics such as pastoral scenes of beauty and abstract experiments with form (cf. Martorella 1990). Even aside from the social control of who gets to produce for a given art market, "money talks" in the market itself, and art thus tends to be shaped by those individuals and groups wealthy enough to buy it. At the extreme, art is subsidized by wealthy organizations such as churches or the state (Williams, 1982, pp. 36–56). Though some state organizations avoid direct artistic control, they may establish the limits and boundaries of good taste. Steven Dubin's study of a government-supported artist-in-residence program shows an "implicit control" at work, one in which "other people" tend to be invoked as the source of regulation. As one program official put it in a conversation with an artist:

> I'm not suggesting that (you change your style), what I'm saying is that *me as a person says* "just keep working," me as a person. But it can present a real major serious problem for the (arts) council, because in effect we're sanctioning you (1987, p. 140).

Social control can be of a very direct sort, but the examples of journalism, popular culture and art show that it can also involve quite subtle processes from the ideology of "objectivity" and implicit ideological subtexts of popular song lyrics to the "chilling" effect of cultural workers responding to implicit controls of organizations and the marketplace. These issues are the subjects of continuing research, for they are central to the question of whether, and how, freedom of speech and artistic expression are meaningfully exercised within societies in which flows of information and ideas are increasingly channeled through large organizations and mass media.

CONCLUSION

Research and theories that suggest the shaping of culture by political and economic forces in the U.S. can be countered by arguments that point to constitutional guarantees of freedom of the press and religion. It is also easy to show that diverse opinions are represented in journalism, and that consumers face a dazzling array of choices in music, art, entertainment, clothing, home furnishings, and the like. Yet three things must be recognized. First, the diversity is greater in theory than it is in actuality. Second, the existence

8

THE PRODUCTION OF CULTURE

The common-sense idea of how culture is produced emphasizes the inspired or creative individual. One myth has the artist, like a shaman in a premodern society, as partaking in the sacred: The artist and the artwork are divinely inspired. Another myth, which gained credence with the growth of individualism in the nineteenth century, is the image of the artist as the romantic hero: In this image the artist is a person of genius, alienated from society, working alone in a garret on some great work. Both these images of the artist emphasize the unique qualities of the creator's vision and work. These stereotypes lift out the artist of great talent and neglect the activities of multitudes of less distinguished individuals who make their living doing art work. Neither view of the artist is sociologically informed. Part of the growth in the sociology of culture since the 1970s can be credited to the application of quite different perspectives, derived from the study of organizations and work. They put aside the content of the work—its meaning to the artist or to the public—in favor of looking at art as a "product" that requires for its accomplishment the cooperation of many actors in a collective process.

During the period when sociologists of organizations began to look at culture production, many of the conventional assumptions in the study of organizations were being challenged. One challenge concerned the question of how social theorists should think about the "boundaries" of an organization.

The challengers suggested that the line between what might be considered the "organization" and its "environment" can be drawn in different places depending on one's perspective. Culture industries—made up of profit oriented firms that produce cultural products for national and international distribution—were particularly interesting in the light of such a question because the problematic aspects of any given process tended to be at the boundaries—having to do with what to produce and how to market it. This provided a theoretically interesting contrast with other industries where the technological aspects of production were most problematic. Studying cultural production, therefore, presented problems of theoretical interest for organizational theory, and the organizational sociologists, in taking cultural production as their subject matter, helped change the way sociologists think about culture. The growing academic interest in the study of popular culture further enhanced the interest in studying culture from the perspective of organizational theory because the culture industry model is obviously relevant to mass production. Once its usefulness was proven, it was applied to other areas.

In response to similar questions about how to draw the boundaries of social organizations, symbolic interactionists developed the concept of the "social world." While organizational theory has been primarily concerned with economic business organizations (Padgett 1992), symbolic interactionists have conceived of social organization more broadly. If we put the degree of social organization on a continuum, social worlds are somewhat more organized than social movements and less organized than formal organizations. It is possible to participate in various ways in a social world, but all participants share a commitment to ongoing collective activity. When accomplishing a task requires a more specialized division of labor, social worlds come to share more properties of formal organizations (Strauss 1978). The concept of social world describes a diffuse network of people who have a variety of relations with each other. Social worlds lack clear boundaries either with regard to space or to membership. To choose to study cultural production within social worlds underlines the importance of studying work activities and the organization of work rather than studying individual artists or art works. In studies of art production as collective action the unit of analysis becomes specific sets of relations between people and groups, or even the social world itself.

Thinking about "art worlds" is a good starting point for looking at the production of culture because it illustrates ways that works of art—even when credited to a single individual—are not possible without the coordinated activities of many people. We will also explore how paying attention to organizational aspects of culture production can inform our understandings of culture in modern society. These perspectives concentrate on how what is necessary to get the work done actually shapes the content of the cultural object; they are applied in this chapter primarily to the arts and to popular culture industries. Much work has been done in these areas in part because this perspective counters popular mythology about the importance of the creative individual in these endeavors. Yet the perspective is generalizable to other cultural arenas; to illustrate this we end the chapter by looking at the production of the news.

ART WORLDS

Working out of the symbolic interaction tradition Howard Becker uses the term art world "to denote the network of people whose cooperative activity, organized via their joint knowledge of conventional means of doing things produces the kind of artwork that the art world is noted for" (1982, p. x). Recall the stereotype of the struggling young artist. An inspired singer-songwriter still needs a way of making enough money to live on, instruments to play, a way of communicating to back-up musicians about what they have to do, a place to rehearse, places to perform, perhaps a manager or an agent, a recording company, distribution of records in the right stores, favorable reviews in the right places, and an appreciative audience. Artists are integrated into art worlds to varying degrees, of course. It is possible for our singer-songwriter to sing her songs to herself as she drives to work in the morning, accompanied only by her own drumming on the steering wheel. Someone can sing at weddings of friends, but rely upon other means of financial support. Less integrated artists may experience few constraints of the art world, but they are not likely to reap rewards of fame and fortune.

Focusing on cooperative activity raises questions about the division of labor in the art world. In some cases the division of labor is easy to see. People who go to see a movie may be enticed by an ad that announces stars, producers, and directors; if they stay to the end they will view the "credits", an often lengthy list of people involved in the making of the film down to the hairdressers and baggage handlers. Yet collective activity is part of the process even when it is not so directly observable. A painter may work alone but usually has a supplier from whom he can buy paints and other materials. If he wants others to acknowledge his work, he will probably choose to work in an established tradition that has commonly understood "rules" to help critics and buyers to judge work that is "good." He also needs an audience: People who will show his work to others, and who will buy it for themselves or for display in public places.

Becker points out that while some activities are usually regarded as "core activities," others are thought of as supplementary (1982, pp. 16–18). People tend to assume that the person who does the core activity is the artist. However, there can be ambiguity about who is doing the core activity. For a conductor of a symphony orchestra the performers are her "instrument." Who is "the artist" in this case? Furthermore, what is defined as "core" can change as the technology changes. In a 1990 Grammy award controversy regarding recording artists who lip-synched over the vocals of others, the question of "who is really the artist" was raised in a particularly public way. Yet in some contexts it is now standard for performers to use taped music and lip-synching to reproduce the sound the audience is used to hearing—sound created by a producer in a recording studio and impossible to replicate in an auditorium or stadium.

This raises the related question of membership: Who belongs to an art world? Membership in an art world is more fluid than membership in a formal organization. There is the core activity of those people who are defined as the artists, along with their "suppliers"—broadly understood as those who help artists to accomplish the core activity. Then there are those who are involved in distribution—the agents, and impresarios, concert hall managers and museum curators, the disc jockeys and reviewers. Finally there are the consumers, but even here we do not find an undifferentiated mass. The most knowledgeable consumers often have some training or experience in the art form themselves. These "students" make up an important segment of the art audience. One study found that between 40 and 60 percent of those who visit art galleries are either artists or art students (Haacke 1976, cited in Becker 1982, p. 53). Patrons and "serious" members of the audience can be distinguished from the occasional attender. Like other cultural systems such as science or religion, art worlds are organized around specialized knowledge. Participants are distinguished from other well-socialized members of the society by their familiarity with this knowledge, with those closest to the core activity having the greatest amount of knowledge and the occasional attender perhaps having only a little knowledge. Specialized knowledge about the practices of the art world is referred to as the "conventions" of the art world.

Conventions

Conventions are solutions to the problem of coordinating activities. A basic definition of a convention is "a common practice constructed through a tacit agreement process" (Lewis 1969, cited in Gilmore 1990). Conventions become especially important in forms of social organization, such as art worlds, which lack clear membership and authority relations. Knowledge of the conventions is also important for consumers: Just as it is more fun to watch a football game if one knows the rules, knowing the conventions of other cultural forms enhances a person's enjoyment of them.

People learn conventions of the art world in part through consumption of cultural products. For example, cultures differentiate music from noise on the basis of music's adherence to recognizable conventions. Most western music uses a familiar eight-note scale that people in western cultures learn very early. Songs of childhood such as "Twinkle, Twinkle Little Star" train children to "hear," that is, to recognize and expect, common musical progressions. Musical notation constitutes another set of conventions. Writing music for particular sets of instruments which will all be tuned in a particular way helps to coordinate the activities of people who play music. Yet artists and their supporters also have specialized knowledge that even serious members of the audience are unlikely to need. Some of that knowledge is technical: Musicians and their supporters need to know how to tune the instruments. It is also the case that people at the core of an art world often experiment with sets of conventions quite different from those familiar to people based on their general experience in the culture.

Artists group themselves into different schools of thought on the basis of adherence to certain conventions (and rejection of others). In fact, the very standardization that the existence of conventions promotes can become the basis for innovation. Appreciation of many modern art forms requires some knowledge of the conventions that are being challenged or violated. When composer John Cage plays a recording of street noise on a concert stage, appreciation of his experiment depends both on being able to tell how the staged performance departs from daily life, and on how it departs from classical western music conventions. Of sociological interest here are the relations between conventions, coordination and innovation.[1]

Gilmore (1987) explores these relations in the concert music world of composers, performers and support personnel in New York City. He finds three different groups there. *Midtown*—where classical music is played—incorporates the major symphony orchestras and touring groups that perform in the Lincoln Center and Carnegie Hall. *Uptown*—where serious academic contemporary music is played—includes the composers and performers affiliated with universities who use campus rehearsal and performance spaces. *Downtown*—where avant-garde music and performance art is found—includes musical non-specialists and composer- performers who use lofts and alternative performance spaces in Greenwich Village, SoHo and Tribeca.

The Midtown concert music world is the largest of the three. It employs the most specialized division of labor and has the largest financial investment. According to Gilmore:

> As a consequence, Midtown participants have a strong organizational interest in musical conventions with which to coordinate concert activities. Concert collaborators have rationalized the production process through the use of a performance "repertory" that standardizes musical notation, instrumentation, and performance techniques. These strong conventions create efficiency, but limit musical innovation. Midtown concerts thus emphasize virtuosity as an aesthetic focus (1990, p. 157).

The Downtown concert music world is the least formally organized. The division of labor is collapsed, with composers often performing their own works

---

[1] Similarly, conventions operate in other cultural production. Rosenblum (1978a, 1978b) documents the different conventions that separate the work of news photographers, advertising photographers and art photographers. Dianne Hagaman (1993) describes the difficulty of "unlearning" the conventions of photojournalism.

and support personnel and collaboration arranged through exchanges within informal networks. There, Gilmore observes:

> Musical notation is varied, where it exists at all, and is often open to interpretation. New instruments and radically new performance techniques are constantly being introduced.... The lack of strong conventions means concert collaboration is often laborious and inefficient, but such organization supports radical musical innovation and avant-garde aesthetic interests (1990, p. 157).

The Uptown concert music world is more organized and dependent on conventions than Downtown but less organized and less dependent on conventions than Midtown. There, "new performance practices are introduced but on traditional instruments. Notation remains predominantly conventionalized, but new symbols are introduced to represent new sounds" (Gilmore 1990, p. 157). The development of conventions, then, enhances cooperation between artists and supporters of the core activity, but reduces innovation. In general, cultural forms that require the cooperation of large numbers of people are likely to adhere more strictly to a set of recognized conventions. Gilmore sees the various musical conventions acting as a "form of musical social control" limiting and directing the behavior of the participants in the musical social worlds.

The example of concert music emphasizes the value of conventions for coordinating the activity producing the art itself. Conventions are equally important in shaping how the cultural activity is received by its audience. British critic John Berger argues that by packaging cultural content in recognizable forms, conventions serve to condition how the audience perceives and responds to the objects depicted in the art works when they appear in our environment. In his study of the visual arts Berger claims that established conventions exist for portraying various subjects in visual media—the wealthy, the poor, men, women—and that seeing representations of these subjects establishes a context for how people see them. The conventions surrounding the nude in western art, for example, treat women as objects to be observed by men; portrayal of women and non-Europeans as "other" help the dominant men feel more powerful (1977, pp. 45–64). Berger further argues that in the early modern era specific techniques of oil painting developed ways to depict objects in the paintings emphasizing their materiality—in effect painting them as objects to be possessed by early capitalists. By using of these techniques—in other words staying within the conventions—artists produced works that were recognized as "good" and exchanged through the art market (1977, pp. 83–112). Berger extends Gilmore's notion of conventions as social control in suggesting that art world conventions control both audiences (with regard to how they perceive content) and artists (with regard to how they depict forms).

The analysis of convention in the art world helps us to see that cultural workers make choices between relying on conventions that maximize possibilities for distribution and doing something more innovative that will be "riskier."[2] In the arts innovative projects are risky in part because they are outside of the standard sets of conventions and will probably appeal to a much smaller audience. Mass culture production is risky in a slightly different way, but one that similarly reduces innovation:

> The audience is unpredictable, and the people who produce and distribute the work have no real contact with it. They market the work in large quantities, as with books and records, or through a mechanical system, as with radio and television, so that they could not, if they tried, know audience members personally... (Becker 1982, p. 125).

When there is so much distance between artists, producers and audience, it is impossible to know what tastes and conventions might be shared.

Artists and Art Worlds

The relation between conventions, innovation and coordination offers an analytic tool for thinking about the various sorts of people who engage in creative activities. While psychologists and aestheticians tend to look at talented individuals—although in different ways (Zolberg 1990, pp. 115–124)—the art world's perspective classifies artists in terms of their relation to the art world and its conventions. On this basis Becker has suggested four types of artists: Integrated professionals, mavericks, folk artists and naive artists.

The integrated professional knows and uses the conventions of the art world and engages in cooperative activities in a routine way. Becker notes that integrated professionals

> define the problems of their art similarly and agree on criteria for an acceptable solution. They know the history of what previous attempts to solve those problems generated.... They, their support personnel, and their audiences can understand what they have attempted to do and to what degree it works.... Integrated professionals can produce work that is recognizable and understandable to others without being so recognizable and understandable as to be uninteresting (1982, p. 230).

Because they are integrated into the cooperative arrangements which have the goal of producing art, it is not surprising that integrated professionals produce most of what is recognized as art by art worlds.

---

[2] The relations described here between convention and innovation coordination hold for other cultural endeavors as well. In science, for example, to be regarded as a "contribution" new work must offer some knowledge or insight, but the theories and methods used must be recognizable to other scientists. New work that departs too greatly from the conventions of the discipline is unlikely to be accepted by others in the field. One way that the arts differ from the sciences is that there innovation can include the revivals of ideas that had passed out of use (Zolberg 1990, p. 130).

Maverick artists also have had experience in the art world and know the conventions, but unlike integrated professionals, they have found the conventions too constraining. In their work mavericks sacrifice cooperation to innovation, and their innovations are often not recognized as art by other members of the art world. Because mavericks ignore conventions that make cooperation easy, they often find it difficult to get their work produced. If they can produce their work by themselves then they have difficulty with distribution—getting it seen by critics and accepted by the public. If the work is something to be performed, they may find themselves recruiting and training support personnel—including the audience—from outside of the art world (Becker 1982, pp. 234–35).

Mavericks are interesting because their deliberate choice to be outside of the art world highlights the tension that exists in art worlds between convention and innovation. Becker notes that the work of mavericks suggests either ignorance or "blatant disregard for conventional practice" of other artists (1982, p. 233). The mavericks' disregard can be disturbing to others in the art world when they call attention to the constraining nature of the conventions. Sometimes the challenge of the innovator is successful and the work of the maverick is taken into the art world. The composer Charles Ives is one such case. Ives wrote music that performers would not play. But instead of forcing Ives to conform to the conventions to a greater degree, their refusal had the opposite effect: Ives felt free to write music without paying attention to the practical issue of whether or not it was possible to play the music as he imagined it. While eventually, some of Ives's work was taken into the concert repertory, the work of most mavericks is probably lost (Becker 1982, pp. 233–242).

Becker uses the concept of folk art to talk about "work done by ordinary people in the course of their ordinary lives, work seldom thought of by those who make or use it as art at all," (1982, p. 245). Singing in a group, dancing at a social event, cooking and sewing are all activities that socially competent people may learn to do as part of learning what it is to belong to particular communities. These are all activities which could be judged in aesthetic terms, but aesthetic criteria are not usually the primary way that the activities are evaluated in the contexts where they usually occur: The point of singing "Happy Birthday" to someone is not to have a virtuoso performance. Yet the possibility for using aesthetic evaluation means that folk art objects can become "art" if they are lifted into another context where aesthetic judgments are central, for example, when quilts are no longer used on the beds of friends and family members to keep people warm but are purchased for display by museums or art collectors.

Becker's analysis of folk arts points to the role that aesthetic *theory* plays in creating art worlds. For Becker "artness" does not inhere in the object, but rather in the relation of the object to the art world. Ordinary people in their daily lives make aesthetic judgments: They occasionally comment when someone at church sings off-key, or they note that someone is an especially

FIGURE 8.1 Jean-Michel Basquiat began his career as an artist writing angry poems in chalk on the walls of buildings in Manhattan. Basquiat was self-taught—a "naive artist" according to Becker's categories, although he was "discovered" by the New York art world. Commenting on a retrospective show, organized after his death from a drug overdose at 27, a *New York Times* art critic wrote, "Basquiat's art also pulls together many cultural strands—graffiti art, African art, the automatic drawing of Abstract Expressionism .... Yet, amazingly, the basis of his art is a graphic style extrapolated primarily from his own handwriting. His boxy, upright capital letters spell out poems, dangle phrases before the eyes, provide endless lists of words". Commenting on "red Joy," pictured above, a critic states, "large single figures seem to emerge out of choppy surfaces of writing and diagrams, like ghosts from the past bearing messages from the future..." (Roberta Smith, *New York Times*, Arts and Leisure, p. 41, Nov. 19, 1989) (*Source:* Photo courtesy of Robert Miller Gallery, New York.)

good cook or that a cake is beautifully decorated. But fulfilling social roles competently does not require artistic abilities or performances. In fact, one could argue that in some circumstances it is considered impolite to judge things by aesthetic standards, or to "show off" one's own abilities. Furthermore, in those cases where aesthetic judgments are made, they are usually not articulated in terms of a well-developed aesthetic theory that specifies in detail how an object can be evaluated in aesthetic terms.

Becker's last category is naive art. The people who create naive art usually view it as art, but they lack knowledge of the conventions of the art world and are usually not recognized by it. This work is idiosyncratic. Becker notes, "The artists' reasons for doing the work are personal and not always intelligible.... The works, not belonging to any tradition of artistically defined problems or solutions, seem to spring out of nowhere. No one knows how to respond to it..." (1982, p. 264). Since the naive artists are outside of the art world, the works often use nonstandard materials and nonstandard methods of construction—for example, a beer can house in Houston made out of 39,000 tin cans or a "garden" in Utah composed of 12,000 painted and arranged deer antlers (Brown, 1991). Such objects, if they receive any recognition, are more likely to end up in *Ripley's Believe It or Not* than in an art museum. They demonstrate a creative impulse, but they do not fit our ideas of art.

The boundaries of art worlds, however, are not fixed, and the work of mavericks, folk artists and naive artists sometimes (but not usually) is incorporated into art worlds when the art worlds change their boundaries. These categories stress differences not in the quality of the product but in the relation to the art world. The work of integrated professionals receives the most support, and it is the most likely to be recognized and preserved as art. It is the integrated professionals who receive most of the rewards that art worlds offer.

Editing

Becker's approach does not distinguish between the naive artist and the integrated professional in terms of talent of the artist or innate qualities of the work. Indeed, he uses the label "art" to describe those works that adhere to the conventions of some part of the art world. This shifts the focus away from the artist as creator to the labeling process of the art world. Becker states this explicitly in his discussion of editing: "...it is not unreasonable to say that it is the art world and not the artist who makes the work" (1982, p. 194).

In many art worlds there are people who carry the official title of "editor," but the editing process can be generalized to encompass much more than the duties of such people. Becker uses the idea of editing to talk about a stream of "choices" made by artists themselves (who are aware of the standards and choices of others involved in the art world) as well as choices made by all of the various support personnel that effect the character of the work. Artists revise their own work to bring the execution closer into line with their vision. There are also ample examples of editors who work with artists to hone their works to better reveal their essential greatness. Becker's understanding of editing is much broader than this.

Becker argues that much of the editing of their own work that artists do occurs with reference to what they imagine others will think and feel about their work. Using the social psychology of George Herbert Mead, Becker asserts that artists, like the rest of us, "take the role of the other" as they make choices about their work (1982, p. 200). Imagining what others might think does not mean that one is necessarily correct in predicting the responses of others. Nor does it mean that one always conforms to what one imagines others might want. It suggests that artists take into consideration the expectations, opportunities and constraints of the worlds they work in. Much of the editing, then, happens in the head of the artist; because artists internalize the conventions of the art world, making art is a fundamentally social process.

All the members of the art world also have a part in the editing process insofar as they influence the choices that the artist makes. Manufacturers and distributors make some materials available and fail to make others available (Becker 1982, p. 210). Directors, conductors, musicians and others interpret the intentions and desires of composers and writers. Artists, editors, and curators make decisions about what pieces of a body of work will be distributed in public forums. Technical considerations may limit the size or shape of a work: As an extreme case, Norman Mailer's novel, *Harlot's Ghost,* released in the fall of 1991, was declared finished when it reached the limits of the number of pages that the binding equipment could handle. Responses of patrons and audiences may also be taken into account.

Boundaries

While much of this chapter focuses on cooperation in art worlds, artists compete with each other, as do different art worlds. Because for most art worlds there are more artists than resources—including financial support for developing projects, performance space, gallery space, promotion and recognition—people will compete with each other for the rewards. Observance of conventions not only alerts a possible collaborator as to how much effort it will be to work with someone, but the conventions also help to define who is inside an art world and who is not and who is eligible for rewards and who is not.

The boundaries of art worlds, however, are not static. Especially where innovation is valued, conventions are always under some pressure to change. The work of mavericks, and even naive artists, is occasionally incorporated into the art world. Activities which had been considered crafts or folk arts may be incorporated into art worlds. In his example of the incorporation of clay as medium for art work, Becker (1982) shows how artists with little concern for the traditional craft virtuoso standards began to experiment with using clay as

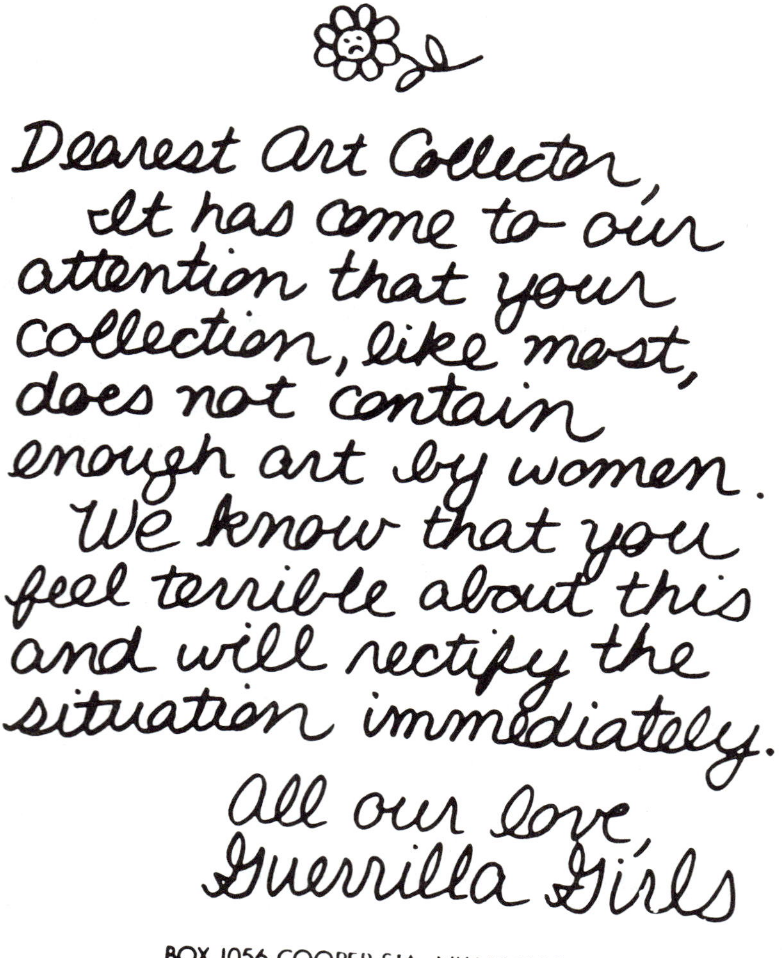

Dearest Art Collector,
It has come to our
attention that your
collection, like most,
does not contain
enough art by women.
We know that you
feel terrible about this
and will rectify the
situation immediately.
all our love,
Guerrilla Girls

BOX 1056 COOPER SIA , NY NY 10276

FIGURE 8.2 This poster, originally printed on pink paper, was distributed in New York City in April 1985 by the "Guerilla Girls." With posters and street theater, sometimes dressed in gorilla suits, this group of women artists calling themselves "the conscience of the art world" have drawn attention to discrimination against women artists by art critics, gallery owners, museums, and even collectors. (*Source:* Courtesy of the Guerilla Girls.)

a medium (making deliberately non-functional objects).In a related development, very skilled craftspeople began to compete with the artists for gallery and museum space. Such transitions have an impact on both the conventions of the craft and the conventions of the art world.

Boundaries are not always based solely on knowing and following the conventions of how to do things. Different sorts of boundaries have excluded women and minorities from many art worlds. In some cases these exclusions take the form of preventing members of the excluded group from ever learning the conventions. Women, for example, were not allowed in life-drawing classes in the nineteenth century. Sometimes it is control over the gatekeeping institutions that is critical for maintaining the boundaries. When novel writing became a prestigious occupation in Britain in the second half of the nineteenth century women were "edged out" of the profession (Tuchman 1989). Tuchman argues that men used their control of the major literary institutions to take over what they perceived as "the empty field" occupied by women novelists.

DiMaggio (1987b) suggests that different groups located at different places in the culture industry make classifications about art on the basis of different principles. Artists, such as the Victorian novelist who wanted to mark off the high culture novel as an art form distinguished from the popular novel written by women, attempt to control the development of their own and others' reputations through the use of "professional classifications." Cultural producers who sell art for profit develop "commercial classifications." Those who deal with government regulation develop "administrative classifications" (1987b, pp. 449–451). In each case they are drawing the boundaries in a different way. The emphasis on art world conventions treats the artists' classifications as important, even while it places relatively little emphasis on the artists themselves.

CULTURE INDUSTRIES

A somewhat different approach to understanding cultural production comes out of the sociology of organizations. Sociologists studying formal organizations in the twentieth century used Weber's ideal type to conceptualize modern bureaucratic organizations as "rational." In the 1960s, however, social scientists began to explore how the rationality of organizations might be limited. Some began to speak of the organizations as rational insofar as their actions were directed toward the goal of survival but an organization's ability to act rationally was limited by the extent of its knowledge. Thompson (1967) argued that an organization's ability to act rationally and efficiently is "bounded" by "uncertainties," and that uncertainty can come either from the environment or from the technical core. Culture producing organizations—for example, book publishers or record producers—came to the attention of organizational theorists in part because these industries provided cases where the uncertainties came from the environment rather than the technology.

Although the technology for recording music or producing books has changed over the years, Paul Hirsch (1972) has argued that what is more problematic for such culture producers is choosing which performing artists to record, or which books to publish. This is the "input boundary." Even more problematic is the "output boundary"—where judgments must be made as to how to distribute one product over another one, including how to promote the ones with the greatest chances of being "hits." We will talk about the activities at the input boundary as organizing *resources* for the production of cultural objects and the activities at the output boundary as organizing the *distribution* of cultural products.

Resources

This model assumes that artists are in excess supply (there are more individuals with work for producers to choose from than could ever be produced) and that choosing among them is a difficult process for culture industries. Hirsch (1972) argues that organizations deal with this kind of uncertainty by sharing the risks. Organizations make use of the judgments of agents or talent scouts who are based outside of the organization. Another way of sharing the risks is to pay artists through royalties instead of either buying the products outright or putting artists on salary. Organizations also minimize their risks by making a practice of producing far more objects than they intend to distribute and promote.

In a survey of editors employed by trade, scholarly and textbook publishers, one-third of the editors reported that they personally received from one thousand to five thousand unsolicited manuscripts per year. (This count excludes manuscripts received by other editors at the same house.) Very few of these books receive contracts: A third of the editors said they had signed no unsolicited books; a little over a third said they had signed more than two such books (Coser, Kadushin, and Powell 1982, pp. 129–131). One-third of the editors surveyed reported signing contracts for a dozen or fewer books a year, one-third signed between a dozen and twenty-five, and another third signed more than twenty-five book contracts (1982, p. 125). The statistics for children's book publishing tell a similar story: For example, HarperCollins (formerly Harper and Row) gets as many as 15,000 unsolicited manuscripts for children's books per year and may publish three of them (Cox 1991). Despite such figures, it is still the case that it is easier for an author to get a book published than to get good distribution and promotion (Hirsch 1972, p. 646).

Distribution

Once a culture industry organization has decided to produce an artist's work, the organization faces the issue of distribution, made more complex because their products are marginally differentiated from one another. This is uncertainty at the "output boundary." Several studies point to relations with "cultural gatekeepers" as a source of added uncertainty here. Gatekeepers do not work directly for the culture industries, and yet their work is necessary to the culture industry. The gatekeepers—including reviewers, talk show hosts, disc jockeys, and the like—present cultural products to a wider audience, and they promote only a small portion of the items that are produced. For example, Coser, Kadushin, and Powell estimate that out of over 40,000 book titles published every year only six thousand get reviewed (1982, p. 308).

Relations between producers and gatekeepers are complex because the gatekeepers like to make independent judgments about the worth of a product, and yet the producers and the gatekeepers have some goals that overlap. While one hears of occasional scandals where important gatekeepers were coopted by the culture producers, Hirsch points out that this is less likely to happen insofar as the goals of the mass media gatekeepers and the goals of the culture industry are in conflict with one another. He notes two kinds of conflict: First, there exists a "norm of independent judgment" among gatekeepers, which conflicts with the idea of simply endorsing a product. Second, Hirsch suggests that because the primary goal of the mass media is to deliver its audience to its advertisers, media outlets do not see promoting specific cultural items as a goal (1972, pp. 654–655). An example of this can be seen in the case of country music (discussed below) where the traditional country music audience (working class males) differed from the radio advertisers' ideal market (female consumers), with repercussions for country music style.

However, Hirsch also describes the symbiosis that exists between the mass media and the culture industries. The most striking example is perhaps the relation between record companies and radio stations: Record companies rely on radio stations for free advertising in the form of air play of new releases, and radio stations rely on record companies for programming materials. Bribery of radio stations by record companies—known as "payola"—was widespread in the 1950s, and continues despite laws passed against it in 1960. One estimate claims that in 1985 American record companies paid the equivalent of thirty percent of their pre-tax profits to independent record promoters for the promotion of new releases (Dannen 1990).

Distribution channels also affect production decisions. The record industry uses the charts to see what is selling, and bases decisions about what new records to produce on that information. But there are many ways of monitoring what is selling. Until 1991 *Billboard* gathered information by calling stores for reports on what was selling. Record companies were known to bribe store employees with clock radios, microwave ovens, refrigerators, and the like in order to influence the system. In 1991 a new computerized system was installed using the bar codes on the records to produce actual sales figures. The picture of "what is selling" changed dramatically showing both country and rap as more popular than the old charts had indicated—clerks in stores often failed to report when these sold because they did not perceive either as "popular music." Still, the new system has its critics, some of whom feel that the northeast is under-represented in the sampling of stores (Woletz 1992). The charts matter in part because acts high in the charts get more airplay and more attention. Record companies also use the new information to market their products more effectively.

There is evidence that changes in distribution can set in motion other changes that result in changing the cultural content itself. Richard Peterson (1978) attributes the significant changes in country music in the 1970s primarily to changes in the country music industry. In 1959 a group of country music industry executives formed the Country Music Association to promote country music. They were successful at convincing a number of radio station managers to adopt a full-time country music format. The number of country music stations tripled by 1965 (Peterson 1978, p. 299).

The success, however, created a problem. Before 1960, not only did country music have a distinctive sound (with many regional variations) but country music programmers—disc jockeys, music directors, and station managers—also had a distinctive style. They presented material in a conversational "folksy" manner, knew about the music, and played a variety of performers and country styles. With the expanding number of stations, however, the demand for country programmers outran the supply. Many stations found themselves shifting formats but keeping the same personnel: Staff who had formerly played rock or easy listening music now were required to play country. Because the new DJs knew little about country music, the "modern" country radio stations adopted a "Top 40" format with much more emphasis on new releases to the neglect of the older music.

Under the new system a few new performers became "stars" to a degree previously not possible for country performers, but many of the older performers got little air play. Cross-over artists were favored by the new DJs: Waylon Jennings and Dolly Parton crossed over *from* country but John Denver and Olivia Newton-John crossed from the pop charts *to* the country charts. Top 40 country music stations began to sound much more like other top 40 stations. The record industry changed as well. Country music went from being the most stable market sector, with known recording artists having predictable but not spectacular sales, to being a very unstable market. A million-selling record was rare in 1965, but expected by 1977: To be "successful" a record had to sell more because promotion became more expensive. Before, with a smaller but known audience, promotion was less necessary and a record with modest sales could still make money (Peterson 1978, pp. 307–8). Peterson's analysis shows how changes in the cultural styles cannot simply be assumed to reflect changes in the tastes of consumers in a society or innovations from the artists: The changes in the style of country music were caused by industry changes that resulted in the creation of new audiences for a new kind of country music.

Innovation in Culture Industries

This research on culture industries shows the usefulness of bringing an organizational perspective to the study of cultural organizations. Insofar as cultural production resembles other kinds of commercial productive activities in this society, sociologists of culture profit from being able to apply perspectives developed for other industries. However, the initial assumptions may not hold for all culture production. Hirsch, for example, assumes that cultural organizations are rational and efficient in the sense of being profit maximizing. Much cultural production, however, does not pay for itself but rather relies on other means of support and other justifications for its existence.

Public television, for example, is non-rational in this sense. It is supported by government grants and by gifts from individuals, corporations and foundations. One fundraising campaign from the mid-eighties played on this by touting their exclusivity: The station contrasted itself with commercial networks claiming "five percent of the audience is fine with us." Artists who are outside of the system of production and distribution also appear "non-rational" by the criteria of organizational sociology.

How do culture industries respond to risk? In part by getting other people to take some of the risk—especially the artist who often bears the costs of developing the project. They also make use of a network of "contact persons" to reduce uncertainty at both the input and output boundaries, including agents and editors who help choose which projects to produce and media gatekeepers who promote products once they have been produced.

Another possibility for both culture industries and artists is what organizational sociologists call "vertical integration" when they attempt to develop ideas and produce and distribute their own work. Vertical integration is one solution for culture industries to the problem of uncertainty (Hirsch 1972). There are some legal limits on the extent to which this is possible, however. For example, movie companies once produced, distributed and exhibited films. A 1950 U.S. Supreme court decision forced film companies to divest one of the three. Artists are less bound by such legal constraints. In producing their own work they take on more of the risk, but they may gain a great deal of control over the product. The writer Virginia Woolf with her husband Leonard, for example, founded Hogarth Press in 1917. At first, publishing their own writings and the writings of friends, they ran the press out of their house, doing the actual printing of the books themselves (Morgan 1982). Distribution is often the problem for such ventures, although it is possible for artists to form cooperatives that take on the business of distribution. This method tends to be easier for artists who do not seek a mass audience. A potter working with a cooperative crafts gallery may find it an effective way to distribute her work. Recording artists have more difficulty.

Still, some forms of "vertical integration" seem to be growing, assisted by the development of computer techniques of reproducing sounds and images. Self-publishing is considerably less labor intense today than it was in Virginia and Leonard Woolf's day, and computerized mailing lists open up possibilities for distribution. The post-sixties alternative press of the 'zine movement—hundreds of irregularly published newsletters aiming at finding networks of people with interests in common—demonstrates the viability of one kind of self- publishing (Mickey Z. 1992).

REWARDS

Art worlds, like other social worlds, offer material and symbolic rewards. Diana Crane (1976) has suggested that an important dimension of reward systems in cultural worlds—including art, science and religion—is who controls the evaluation process upon which the rewards are based. Crane argues that the more that insiders control the rewards the more innovation will occur. She distinguishes four kinds of reward systems. First are independent reward systems where the producers themselves define the problems and the appropriate types of solutions and allocate symbolic and material rewards. Second, there are semi-independent reward systems where the producers define the problems and allocate symbolic rewards, but the material rewards are allocated by consumers.

What distinguishes Crane's third type, the sub-cultural reward system, is that the work is produced for a small, relatively homogeneous audience that allocates the rewards. She calls her fourth type "hetero-cultural," which she sees as the least likely to produce innovations. New ideas begin in one of the other three systems and then are reproduced for the heterogeneous mass audience by the fourth system. Here, according to Crane, bureaucrats define the problems, consumers allocate symbolic rewards, and entrepreneurs allocate the material rewards. Within the hetero-cultural system material rewards are more important than symbolic rewards.

Crane suggests that innovation within an art world is less likely when rewards are scarce. Mavericks, folk artists, and naive artists may be wildly innovative, of course, but their relation to the art world is such that they tend to be outside of its reward system. In order for a system to produce both variety and continuity, Crane argues that (1) there has to be a balance between the availability of resources and the number of innovators, and (2) that symbolic rewards must be as important as material rewards.

Empirical studies of material rewards for artists are few. Work on the topic is complicated by the difficulty in drawing a sample of artists—do we count everyone who has ever sold something they made in a crafts fair—as well as the difficulty of assessing artists' earnings.[3] One study of the earnings

---

[3] With regard to the latter some of the difficulties include (1) many artists are self-employed and may deduct "expenses" from income, in a way that reduces their income, while their lifestyle is comparable to someone with a larger income who is not self-employed; (2) artists have considerable opportunity to participate in the "underground economy"—not only are such earnings less likely to be subject to withholding, but artists may even be willing to accept lower earnings if they are "tax-free"; and, (3) if part of artists' monetary rewards come in the form of royalties, they may be excluded from calculations of income (Filer 1986, pp. 60–61).

of artists used labor income collected by the census in 1979 to compare a sample of artists with nonartists. (The census used work done during a particular reference week to classify people into nine different categories to avoid relying on self-identification.) In marked contrast with the stereotype of the struggling artist, artists on average earned only six percent less than nonartists, although there were differences among artists with actors being the best paid and musicians and dancers the worst paid (Filer 1986, p. 61).

The study compared artists and nonartists over their lifecycles. Filer found that artists above the age of forty earned more than nonartists in the control group, and that as a group the artists are younger than workers in general. While the myth of the artist suggests that they may enter the field, struggle for a while and then transfer to a more practical occupation, Filer did not find people dropping out of the arts as they got older. When he compared the 1970 with the 1980 census he found the numbers of people in the categories actually grew over the decade (1986, p. 63). Filer argues that there is more stability among artists—fewer of them change occupations—than among the general population of workers (1986, p. 66).

The six percent difference in the average earnings of artists and nonartists can probably be attributed to the relative youth of the artists compared to the nonartists. This is likely to be a cohort phenomenon, rather than a lifecycle phenomenon. As will be discussed below, the period from 1960 to 1980 was a period of enormous growth in the arts: In that time period total employment grew 43.1 percent whereas among writers, artists and entertainers growth was 144.1 percent (Filer 1986, p. 67). More consistent with the stereotype are the findings that education relates less directly to earnings for artists, and that there is more variability in artists' earnings—both within any given field and across fields—than for workers in general. Labor market analyses do not tell us why some people choose a career in the arts, but Filer's study contradicts notions that artists are "irrational" in choosing "voluntary exploitation" in a career that leaves them at a severe financial disadvantage. While this study leaves much to be filled in about the career patterns of artists in specific fields, it is consistent with other work reviewed in this chapter in debunking the myth of the artist, in part by giving us a picture of the average person who makes his or her living in the arts.

Certain aspects of the stereotype may be partially attributed to the fact that the arts attract many students who do not end up becoming artists. In one longitudinal study of fine art students, twenty years out of school, slightly more than eight percent supported themselves primarily with their art work, and talent as students did not seem to predict later success as artists (Csikszentmihalyi, Getzels, and Kahn 1984, cited in Zolberg 1990, p. 123). The study also found that fewer women than men remained in the arts, and those who did earned 50 to 85 percent of what the men earned. For men, external rewards, access to gatekeepers and supportive personal relationships seemed more predictive of success than personal qualities of individuals.

One might think that if we turn from looking at material rewards to looking at symbolic rewards, we would find more evidence of the "extraordinary" nature of artistic work. But here too, the production of culture perspective shows us how reputation is "socially constructed." Some writers carry this perspective so far—in arguing that by doing their part in interpreting a work of art readers/receivers become participants in creating the meaning of the work—that they are referred to as "death of the author" theorists (e.g., Bakhtin 1968; see also Becker 1982, and Zolberg 1990). We find that the reputation of specific works of art, artists and even art forms is not an established fact, based on universally recognizable qualities of excellence, but rather is something that is always being re-evaluated. A study of the rise of the modern auction for art works found that "only in the past hundred years has the market ennobled paintings to a rank above objects whose major virtue was the lavish materials, skill and ingenuity that went into them" (Faith 1987, p. 95). Before 1890 works of Renaissance silversmiths could be worth more than paintings by old masters such as Raphael. A study of etching between 1880 and 1940 examined what factors made it more likely that an individual with a reputation in etching when the art form was at its height would be remembered today. In this study, qualities inherent in the work are less important than other factors.

Those artists with a reputation as etchers who also achieved fame in other mediums, for example James Whistler or Mary Cassatt, were more likely to be remembered. Among those who worked primarily in etching the likelihood that they are still remembered is increased if (1) during their lifetimes they made efforts to preserve their work, for example, by producing more objects and keeping good records of their working process and sales transactions; (2) others, during their lifetimes and after, undertook a conservator's role, preserving the reputations of the artist; (3) the artist has links to circles of people of historical interest where the reputation of others in the circle may facilitate interest in the artist; and (4) "retroactive interest" in the artist's works surface where the artist's work can be viewed as an indicator of "emerging cultural or political identities" (Lang and Lang 1988). Lang and Lang find that these very mundane factors worked against the women etchers in their study: The women often produced fewer objects and were less likely to have a spouse outlive them and take on the conservator role. Lang and Lang conclude:

> What obviously matters most in the long run is the proximity of the deceased to institutions with organized arrangements for the archiving and restoration of the historical evidence. Particularly those who have enjoyed power and influence in their lifetimes are also more likely to have friends with influence and connections to archives (1988, pp. 101–102).

These studies from various production of culture approaches highlight institutional and structural factors, including the labor market, in the reward structure. Another important factor in the larger institutional context is the government.

THE STATE AND CULTURE PRODUCTION

National and local governments have an impact on the arts in a number of ways. State funding provides significant financial support for art works and art institutions. More unusual perhaps, governments have directly influenced the content of art through censorship of individual arts and works of art, as well as by promoting certain styles (such as socialist realism in the People's Republic of China) or condemning others. Legal restrictions of various kinds can also have an impact on the environment in which cultural production takes place.

Legal Restrictions

Mass culture industries with public avenues of distribution work in an environment shaped in part by government regulations. Broadcast industries, for example, must be licensed by the FCC (Federal Communications Commission) and many restrictions apply, including how many stations a single corporate body can own and how much power a station can use in broadcasting. Before deregulation in the 1980s there were more restrictions concerning content: Broadcasters were required to subscribe to norms about "fairness" and "equal time" when presenting controversial issues, as well as to use their medium for the benefit of the public with a certain number of "public service announcements." There are also restrictions about what can be sent through the mails which have affected culture industries which use the mail as an avenue for distribution.

Restraint of trade rules have restricted vertical integration in the movie industry, and network broadcasting companies are limited in the number of television stations they may own and operate. These regulations prevent stable contracts; presumably this separation of production and distribution functions in culture industries promotes competition and enhances opportunities for artists and choices for consumers.

Copyright law regulates legal ownership of art works, and this influences who can use an art work, under what circumstances it can be sold, and who profits. Wendy Griswold's study of the American novel provides a striking example of how copyright law has influenced cultural content. Literary critics have long commented on the uniqueness of the American novel, explaining it as a reflection of particularly American character traits. One version of this argument is that while European novelists wrote about love and marriage, "classic American fiction is about men removing themselves from society, especially from women who seem to represent the constraints of social and domestic life" (Griswold 1981, p. 743). Griswold chose a random sample of 130 novels, written by American and European authors and published in America. She chose four time periods, beginning in 1876 and ending in 1910. She found that while most authors, American and European, did write about love and marriage, significant differences appeared in the content of American and European novels in the earlier periods, but styles converged after 1890. Griswold argues that the differences are explained not by differences in national character, but rather by differences in the market positions of European and American writers. Before a change in copyright laws in 1891, American companies published works that had been previously published elsewhere without paying for any rights. With that kind of competition from outsiders, American writers were pushed "to deviate from the norm, to write on nontraditional themes that the European authors had not effectively monopolized" (Griswold 1981, p. 760).

Censorship

Artistic freedom and freedom of expression are highly valued in most art worlds today, and censorship of any kind is anathema. While we can cite explicit cases of censorship, such as the Nazis' condemnation of expressionism, and even their destruction of expressionist works, as decadent, censorship is rarely so direct or blatant. Public media, such as television, radio, and film, do confront regulations designed to restrict the availability of certain content (sex, violence and profanity) to underage audiences. While occasionally the application of such restrictions causes controversy, the failure to apply them also causes controversy. As a mechanism for censorship such restrictions are probably most important in the ways that artists (and their suppliers and distributors) include them in their calculations and use them to censor themselves in order to avoid possible problems.

Governments usually are not terribly interested in the culture consumption of small elite groups. Becker makes the point that "The state is primarily interested in the way art affects mass mobilization—it supports art so that the population can be mobilized for the right things and suppresses art because it fears people will be mobilized for the wrong things" (1982, p. 187). Although individual works can be prohibited or destroyed, governments are more likely to regulate distribution networks. Literary works, for example, have been, in effect, "censored" through application of the Comstock law, an 1873 statute prohibiting sending lewd or obscene works through the postal system. As recently as 1957 Samuel Roth, the publisher of the literary magazine *American Aphrodite,* was convicted of violating the Comstock law in printing an excerpt from an unpublished manuscript *Venus and Tannhauser*—written in the 1890s by Aubrey Beardsley—and sending the magazine through the mail. Although Roth's case went all the way to the Supreme Court, he lost his appeal and served five years in prison. Justice William Brennan wrote the majority opinion in the case, establishing criteria that still exist for judging a work obscene. Brennan stated that obscene materials did not have first amendment protection, but to be judged obscene they had to "violate community standards" and be "utterly without social importance." While the community standards provision is ambiguous, in the 1950s and 1960s a number of test cases effectively fought against censorship by arguing that various works had redeeming social value (deGrazia 1991).

The Supreme Court rulings have left an opening for states or regions to apply censorship. At the local level, works are sometimes prohibited: Certain books may not be allowed in a local library or a local board made set standards for screening motion pictures in public theaters. While judgments about sex and violence have most frequently resulted in censorship, works believed to incite hatred against minority groups have also been censored. For example, D.W. Griffith's film "The Birth of a Nation" (made in 1915) which portrayed the Ku Klux Klan in a positive light was banned by the governor of Ohio, partly because of the campaigns of the National Association for the Advancement of Colored People (NAACP). More recently, in 1990 a painting ridiculing now deceased Chicago Mayor Harold Washington was removed from a student show at Chicago's Art Institute by members of the city council who viewed the painting as racist. In most cases censorship at the local level arouses less concern because copies of the work are available elsewhere.

When censorship occurs, the popular arts are more likely to be censored by regulating distribution whereas the elite arts are more likely to be effected by withdrawal of federal funds. Censorship—the degree to which the state interferes with the creative activities of artists—is only one side of artists' dependence on the state. The other side is the degree to which the state supports the creative activities of artists. In the current arguments of the art world, for the state to withdraw financial support because of objections to the content of the art work is often not distinguished from censorship. Organizational analyses of arts funding help to understand the dependence of the arts on the government.

Funding

The period following World War II has been a period of growth for the arts in the United States: More artists made more art. American art and artists gained international stature. The art market expanded and prices of art broke records. Corporate and government funding increased. Controversy over the nature of that funding also increased, culminating at the end of the 1980s in the debates surrounding the Mapplethorpe exhibition (which included photographs of men engaged in homoerotic behaviors) and the continuing attempts to restrict National Endowment for the Arts (NEA) funding in the future. One result of Senator Jesse Helms's objections to funding work he considers obscene has been an increase in the price of Mapplethorpe's photographs. The effects have been less benign for other artists. In the aftermath of the Mapplethorpe controversy, the NEA's chairman commented that "political realities" would result in some works recommended to the Endowment for funding by peer review panels being vetoed by the NEA. Shortly thereafter, a $10,000 grant for a show at a New York Gallery on Aids was revoked. In discussions about this show and about artists whose proposals were supported by the peer reviews but who did not receive aid, comments about the political content are intermingled with comments about form. At one point the director of the endowment said that if someone painted a Guernica—a reference to Picasso's famous painting protesting the Spanish civil war—the NEA would support it (Glueck 1989). The controversy is possible, however, because of a major change in the art world since Picasso's time: The growth of public funding.

The National Endowment for the Arts was created in 1965 with an annual budget of $1.8 million. It reached its highest appropriation with $155 million in 1980, then declined slightly in the 1980s. State governments increased their funding from a total of $2.7 million in 1966 to $125 million in 1983. Foundation support grew from $38 million in 1966 to $349 million in 1982 (Crane 1987, p. 6). Most of this money, however, does not go directly to artists. Less than three percent of NEA money goes to artists. Crane suggests that more than half goes to museums (1987, pp. 6, 160). Artists may benefit from money that goes to museums if museums buy their works, or if being featured in a show in a museum contributes to their reputation so that someone else is more likely to buy their work or to pay a higher price for it. Yet most of the people who call themselves artists in the U.S. census (who are integrated professionals and work regularly in an art world) do not support themselves by their art alone.[4]

Crane's 1987 study, *The Transformation of the Avant-Garde: The New York Art World, 1940–1985,* documented the growth of the arts and funding for them; her study invites questions about the impact of such growth on the arts. It also raises a number of questions for sociologists of culture oriented to the sociology of organizations: Why did the funding increase? Who benefits from public funding? Which arts get funded? What art endeavors are "nonprofit," and what does it mean to say that an organization is nonprofit? Why don't certain kinds of art world activities make a profit? As it turns out, even though art worlds are organized enough to get things done, they are not organized in such a way as to provide easy answers to these kinds of questions. Along with trying to figure out how to apply organization perspectives to culture industries, sociologists working on these issues are largely still in the process of developing data bases that will allow for systematic study of these issues (see DiMaggio 1987a).

One recent study shows that arts organizations that are labor intensive, such as museums and orchestras, are somewhat more likely to be nonprofit than those that are capital intensive (such as record companies). Yet for large organizations the profit/nonprofit distinction may matter less than it once did. DiMaggio and Useem (1978) point to the growing presence of art world bureaucrats and administrators who defend organizations' interests, themselves, and their sector of the art world. Peterson's work on administrators of

---

[4] One study reported that eighty percent of artists' income comes from their primary arts activity (cited in Filer 1986, p. 60).

arts organizations finds them modeling their organizational structures after profit-making organizations, with hierarchy, routinized procedures, and accountability: Competition for funds promotes rationalization in the nonprofit sector as well as in the profit sector (1986).

Implicit in arguments that the arts should be supported with public funds is the assumption that the arts constitute a public good. Employing the cultural capital argument (discussed in chapter 6) DiMaggio and Useem (1978) argue that historically the arts have been used primarily by the elites for their enjoyment and the enhancement of their status. There is tension between the notion that the support of the arts is a public good and elite domination of the arts. They suggest that the public and policy makers in the contemporary United States need to think about incentives and barriers to the democratization of the arts.[5]

PRODUCING THE NEWS

The production of culture perspective has been illustrated throughout this chapter primarily with studies from a variety of the arts and popular culture industries. Yet the essential insight—the emphasis on looking at how the requirements of doing the work and the structure of the organizational setting shape the cultural objects produced—can be used to explain the production of other cultural forms as well. In this final section we use a production of culture approach to examine ways that the organization of work affects the creation of the news in modern mass media. When the production of culture perspective is applied to the arts it shows that what we consider "art" is constructed in an on-going interpretive process; when applied to the news, a production of culture perspective suggests that "the news" is likewise a constructed category. As Harvey Molotch and Marilyn Lester put it: "We suspend, for strategic analytic purposes, the assumption that there is any objective reality 'out there' to be reported and instead see news as the very processes through which are created—for news professionals and their audiences—the 'things' which are important" (1975, p. 236).

What are the important things? Herbert Gans (1979) begins his study of news organizations by surveying what is covered in the national news. He finds that news is largely about individuals. Indeed, in his study of national television news, 71 percent of the stories were about individuals—often public officials—with a reputation or position that makes them already known to television audiences. Another 21 percent were about individuals who had no previous exposure in the news. Less than 10 percent of the stories were about objects or abstract ideas. The incumbent president dominates the national

---

[5] Judith Blau's controversial study argues that while the arts were once concentrated in cities with the greatest amount of inequality, that is no longer the case (Blau 1989).

news media. Gans reports that in 1975 the president took up 23 percent of all magazine space about well-known people and 20 percent of all domestic news (1979, p. 9).

In American journalism one of the conventions of news reporting is that it must be objective.[6] Ideology in news reporting in the United States is implicit, not explicit. Gans divides news stories into those about order and those about disorder (including moral disorder, such as exposés of public figures) suggesting that in these stories we find "two additional values: the desirability of social order...and the need for national leadership in maintaining that order" (1979, p. 52). The news ends up supporting the order of "public, business and professional, upper-middle-class, middle-aged and white male sectors of society" (1979, p. 61). As was asserted in chapter 7, there is little evidence that these individuals exert direct control over the news, but their values and ideologies do establish a context within which news reporting takes place. A production of culture perspective shows how the factors examined earlier in this chapter—resources and distribution—shape the construction of the news. The most important resource for journalists are their sources. Gans states: "The economically and politically powerful can obtain easy access to, and are sought out by, journalists; those who lack power are harder to reach by journalists and are generally not sought out until their activities produce social or moral disorder news. In short, access reflects social structure outside the newsroom..." (1979, p. 81). There is evidence that people in positions of power exert considerable influence on the news-gathering process. Powerful sources rarely attempt to coerce the news media into covering issues the way they want; they do not need to, since they can create "suitable news." Press conferences and congressional hearings, for example, are scheduled in such a way as to facilitate press coverage. Public officials create "media events" to get into the news (Molotch and Lester 1974).

Efficiency requirements also come into play. A finite number of journalists have to be able to produce the news, and there has to be enough news—but not too much—to fit a given amount of news space or time. The issue of efficiency means that journalists are selective in cultivating relationships with sources. A number of considerations come into play when reporters judge the suitability of a source including past suitability, productivity, reliability, trustworthiness, authoritativeness, and articulateness (Gans 1979, pp. 129–131). Again, a structural bias toward the more powerful is apparent: Powerful people are more likely to be easily available to journalists, as well as reliable and productive sources of news. Reporters who are assigned to a particular beat often develop symbiotic relationships with their usual sources: Maintaining them as sources of information requires that the journalists provide their

---

[6] Objectivity is a convention in several senses: first it is a working rule in American journalism, and second it has not always governed American journalistic practice nor is it interpreted in quite the same way by the press in other countries today.

sources with desired publicity while not reporting stories in such a way as to alienate the source. A kind of co-optation occurs almost subconsciously because a reporter's ability to get the job done coincides with the interests of the source when the source is a regular.

In a different way, reporters and editors need to be able to routinely move the flux of potentially newsworthy events through an "assembly line" of news production that will predictably produce enough news to fill the available pages or time. When dramatic local or national events take place, a story about a typhoon in a foreign country may get little more than a brief mention, whereas on "slow" news days such as holiday weekends, the typhoon may make banner headlines. Because the supply of newsworthy events is somewhat unpredictable (even despite the growth in staging of newsworthy media events), editors will want to have ready supplies of "'timeless features,' which are not 'pegged' or connected to a specific event and thus can be run at any time; these are also called pegless wonders, or evergreens" (Gans 1979, p. 109).

News organizations also have concerns about their audience—distribution concerns—although Gans argues that journalists' image of their audience is largely invented (1979, pp. 229–248). Nonetheless, journalists talk about their audience and make an effort to present stories that will attract the audience. The imagined audience is not inconsequential, however: Journalists engage in an editing process, similar to that described earlier for artists, in which they calculate whom a story is likely to attract or offend and the possible consequences. Journalists' work is also edited, in the formal sense, by others above them in the news hierarchy who decide whether the stories will make the nightly news or be published. Given that, as in other culture industries, there are always more possible stories than can be covered and more stories prepared for publication or for television viewing than there is space or time for, we find similar processes of competition—as well as cooperation—in the production of the news.

Finally, news production also has encountered censorship. The press as an institution has been a strong defender of the First Amendment of the Bill of Rights, protecting the freedom of speech. Yet, occasionally access to information has been denied or the state has forbidden the publication of materials. In the 1991 Gulf War the United States military exercised unprecedented restrictions over the press. Members of the press were denied access to information—reporters had to be accompanied by military escorts, but there were not enough escorts to go around. Photographers were told what they could and could not shoot: In at least one instance the commanding general said that no pictures of troopers could be taken unless they were wearing their helmets and had their chin-straps buckled. If reporters had a story, it could not get out except through army couriers who were "hopelessly undermanned, underequipped, poorly trained and motivated" to do the job. It took days for accounts to get from the battlefield to Dharan; in some cases it was weeks

(Fialka 1992). Clearly, the army decided that it had an interest in carefully managing the ability of the press to produce this news: yet the result was not a blackout on news about the war, rather the "news" Americans received was a constructed account.

CONCLUSION

The production of culture perspective changed the focus of the sociological study of art from emphasizing the uniqueness of artists and art works to observing how the production of art is a social process and how it is like (and unlike) other kinds of social organization. This shift away from looking at the content of art meant that distinctions between high arts and popular culture became less central for the study of culture. Within a production of culture perspective, that distinction itself becomes a matter to be explored as an arbitrary assignment based on art world conventions rather than on inherent values. The distinction between profit and nonprofit cultural organizations, however, continues to provide a basis for useful (if not easy) comparisons within this perspective.

Studies coming out of the sociology of organizations tend to focus on formally organized parts of art worlds. They depict arts organizations as "rational." Those coming out of a symbolic interaction perspective focus on emergent processes, and help us to see layers of coordination among activities. Together the interactionist and organizational approaches to the production of culture have altered the ways that we think about the relations between society and culture.

Yet explanations in terms of production factors do not tell the whole story. Wolff (1981, 1983) argues that the sociology of culture cannot wholly put aside "the specificity of art," that is, internal aesthetic issues. In its most extreme applications the production of culture perspective suggests there is no difference between the arts and other human organizations and activities. While that is often useful, as sociologists we also need to be able to take the meaning of cultural objects' content, style and aesthetics seriously. Examining the cultural object itself and its audience—the subject of chapter 9—raises issues that are largely outside of the production of culture perspective.

9

CULTURAL OBJECT, AUDIENCE, AND MEANING

How does distributed culture figure in our lives? The differences between urbane cosmopolitan individuals and people of "country and western" sensibilities show that personality and lifestyle have cultural aspects. If this is so, it follows that somehow individuals "take on" some elements of the cultural objects that they experience. That people are influenced by culture is an obvious truth. People often *live* the culture. We need think only of the rock music fan whose life revolves around concerts and new releases of music. And what about all those romance novels available at the drugstores? Someone is buying them. Nor is it uncommon to hear people repeating the jokes from last night's "Tonight Show," or regaling other people with a rendition of a skit from "Saturday Night Live."

At the extreme, the boundary between one's own personal world and the world of distributed culture is blurred. As one researcher reported, she bought a copy of *Soap Opera Digest* at the supermarket checkout stand with the magazine's cover featuring two stars from the television soap, "General Hospital." Seeing the magazine cover, the cashier commented, "I think Grant and Cecilia will work it out, don't you?" and then proceeded to offer her own views on how the soap couple might deal with their problems (Rosen 1986, p. 43). When a soap opera fan enters into a fictional world and treats the characters as acquaintances, it may seem to destroy the line between reality and fantasy. Yet such a practice hardly is unusual. To the contrary, what critics sometimes call "the suspension of disbelief" is a minimal requirement for entering into the "reality" established by a cultural object such as a soap opera. We refuse to be distracted from the show's "reality" when we have to do something as mundane as waiting for the end of a commercial break. Perhaps not as fully as the cashier caught up in the soap opera world, we all suspend our everyday assumptions about reality (e.g., that the characters are just acting) whenever we go to a play, watch a television commercial, or read a novel or a poem.

We do the same thing even when we shift from our everyday world to cultural objects that are supposed to *represent* events in the real world (as opposed to fictional creations). Thus, watching television news requires that we "enter into" a world that is organized in different ways from the world of our direct, everyday experience. The exact nature of the shift may be different, depending on the cultural object. We probably look at most news photographs differently than photographs we see in advertisements. Some sort of shift also occurs even when we take in cultural objects that are not necessarily directly representational. Thus, listening to music or looking at an abstract painting or sculpture doesn't depend on a belief that the object *represents* anything, even a fictional world. Nevertheless, to appreciate the music or the painting or the sculpture requires paying attention in a way that differs from other everyday activities such as talking or shopping. The very activity of viewing or listening itself changes our way of being in the world at the moment when it is occurring, and perhaps, later on. The salience of culture is even more pronounced when we actively engage in cultural practices such as dancing, playing music, bowling, or riding horseback.

Culture is central to our lives. What, then, are the processes by which specific culture becomes part of our personal repertoires of appreciation, knowledge, motives and actions? Somehow, the classical music aficionado finds one composer, composition or performance much more compelling than another. Similarly, a person with particular tastes in clothes will take on one new fashion trend much more readily than another.

For the sociological understanding of culture, explaining such processes of interaction between people and culture is important because the significance of other theories about culture depends upon whether and how culture becomes incorporated into our personal repertoires. One way or another, normative theories of culture, cultural theories about social stratification, and theories of the political economy of culture all assume the existence of cultural influences. Thus, research on class, ethnicity and gender (chapter 6) yields explanations about how culture functions for various social strata and their interrelations. But left largely unanswered is the question of how people become "enculturated" in the first place. In a parallel way, if culture is a basis of normative integration, as some theories discussed in chapter 2 suggest, society obtains cohesion to the extent that its members share central values. There may even be mechanisms, such as ritual, that are held to transmit values. Yet, despite the research inspired by normative theories of culture, the actual relationship between ritual and people's solidarity remains in dispute. Finally, the theories of political economy considered in chapter 7 suggest that powerful interest groups may try to affect the production of culture for their own purposes. But cultural domination in turn depends on the processes by which culture figures in social life, and accounting for such processes remains outside the domain of political economy. In short, these key approaches to the sociology of culture require that we pose—but they fail to answer—the central question of how individuals' thought and conduct is influenced by their exposure to culture.

Nor is the question simply academic. In public debates, people often want to argue that culture has (or doesn't have) direct, strong, and clear "effects"—making immediate and observable differences. The widespread assumption seems to be that in the absence of such "effects," culture would not be worth so much public concern. In the polarized public debate about the mass media, either comic books "rot the brain" or they are "harmless."

For their parts, the producers of cultural objects often assume that culture does have some sort of influence. Thus, novelists and artists sometimes have wanted to change their audiences' understandings of the world. And corporations must think that they are getting something for their money, or else they would not be spending billions of dollars on advertising. Their assumption is often shared by critics of the mass media. It is implicit in concerns expressed by the U.S. surgeon general and civic groups in 1990 about cigarette company advertising campaigns for new brands that were to "target" young, "virile" women with low levels of educational attainment ("Dakota") and blacks ("Uptown"). Some parents and religious groups have worked to control violence on television; others have sought to regulate "explicit" popular music lyrics or the formats and contents of television programs for young children. And for years, a debate has raged about the effects of pornography.

For certain groups, there are very high stakes in how the question of cultural consequences is answered. Advertisers of alcoholic beverages and cigarettes sometimes find themselves in congressional hearings where they carefully argue that advertising doesn't create *new* consumers of a product; it influences the market share of *existing* consumers for one product over its competitors. This claim notwithstanding, however, advertisers often target the young and presumably new consumers of their product category. Advertising agencies and mass media organizations that depend on advertising revenues are caught in something of a double bind: They must convince product sellers that advertising *works,* and yet they must not let the popular view of advertising accord it such power that they can be accused of *manipulating* people against their own best interests (Schudson 1984, pp. 9, 15).

Controversies over the potential negative consequences of culture—from advertising to pornography—create a highly charged civic context for the sociological debate over the relationship people have to distributed culture. It is therefore all the more important to consider the question carefully, and independently of the public pressures. But research efforts are often garbled, for one thing, because the effects/no effects formulation does not offer an adequate conceptual framework. It is one thing if someone enjoys a song by the Beatles or Madonna, something else again if song lyrics drive us to criminal acts that we would not otherwise carry out. Each is an "effect."

The so-called "effects" controversy, then, should be abandoned in favor of an alternative approach which poses three related questions. First, there is the question of whether cultural objects have unambiguous meanings and messages, and how these meanings and messages might be related to the intentions of those who produce the cultural objects. Whatever the answer to this question, a good deal of research has been devoted to a second question—how culture affects its audiences. Here, the research findings are often in conflict with one another, partly because the methodologies for studying "effects" are poorly conceived. Nevertheless, it is instructive to see the variety and types of "effects" that researchers have identified. But both the first issue of intentional meaning of cultural producers and the second issue of effects need to be understood in relation to a third: What is the role of *reception* of culture by audiences in shaping meaning? Clearly, not all individuals in an audience pay attention to culture in the same way; theories and research on audiences alter our theory of the meaning of cultural objects and the processes by which culture influences individuals. Considering each of these questions offers a basis for better understanding how cultural meanings become part of our lives.

THE QUESTION OF MEANINGFUL CONTENT

To look at a painting, watch a film or listen to music is to experience a cultural object that has been brought into being through an interactive process of ideas and, as chapter 8 showed, organized social activity under concrete social and historical conditions. These cultural objects often are distinctive and easy to identify. Some people can name a popular song just from hearing the first few notes, and many people who have studied paintings sometimes can identify a Cézanne or a Rubens at a glance, even when they have never seen the specific painting before. Yet assessing the meaning of a cultural object is a much more difficult matter. In the first place, it is always possible that a particular painting or sculpture is a forgery or a copy, and its significance as a cultural object is thereby very different from an original work (cf. Jones, Craddock and Barker 1990). But this issue, intriguing as it may be, is not nearly so problematic as the question of whether a cultural object possesses any clear and unambiguous meaning.

The cultural object—a photograph, a film, a dance—often stands on its own, sometimes rich in content, yet difficult to "read." As chapter 8 implied, the distinctiveness of any cultural object is somewhat arbitrary, in the sense that it could have been produced in a different way. The "Mona Lisa" could have a different expression on her face. As pop culture impresario David Byrne asked, what made her smile? A television situation comedy could have a different cast of characters, say, workers and customers at a fast-food restaurant, rather than neighbors on a suburban street. That choices are made in the production of cultural objects raises the question of the significance or meaning of those choices. Even if the choices are made "unconsciously"—that is, without deliberation—they still may tell us something. And if the choices are conscious ones, then it is possible to inquire about the idea or intention that gave rise to a particular choice. Thus, just focusing on the cultural object, two possible approaches to understanding arise. One approach, hermeneutics, points to the problem of uncovering the ideas and intentions by which the object was produced.[1] The other broad approach, structuralist semiotics, examines the relation of symbols in the cultural object itself, without considering the intention of its creators.

Hermeneutics and the Problem of Intended Meaning

"Hermeneutics"—the Greek word for interpretation—has its origins as a word in the idea of translating, and traditionally the term was used to describe Biblical exegesis. This original hermeneutic focus easily conjures up images of scribes guarding the faith by protecting sacred text and excavating its "real" meaning through comparison of different ancient scrolls and intratextual evidence. Yet the idea of "translating"—whether from one language to another or simply from a preexisting version to a new rendition in the same language—raises a thorny problem. How can any particular translation be validated as "correct" or "true"? If there is no single valid translation, then the special claims by "experts" lose their force. Everyone who reads, translates. That is, we each interpret cultural texts. And in turn, our texts—things we say and do, our cultural creations—are interpreted by others.

The hermeneutic attempt to understand the intended meanings of cultural objects is plagued with obstacles. One problem is that the cultural creators are not always clear about the intentions behind what is being created. And these ambiguous intentions can change over time. The author of a novel may think she has one purpose while she is writing, yet after having completed the novel, come to see its meaning quite differently. This problem can only be compounded by a second one: When more than one cultural worker is involved in production, their intentions may come into conflict with one another. There are, for example, the legendary battles between film directors and the stars doing the acting. A third problem is especially daunting: Whatever the intentions of culture

---

[1] This approach can also be used to study production of culture per se, but here it is focused on the question of the object's intended meaning.

creators, how can other people learn what those intentions were? Sometimes all we have to go on is the cultural object itself, and even when it is possible to interview cultural producers, we cannot be sure how well they remember their intentions, or whether they are willing to reveal them. Many artists just will want to let the art "speak for itself."

These difficulties suggest that it is impossible to arrive at the definitive intended meaning of a cultural object. Does this mean that we should not ask? Sociologist Robert Wuthnow (1987, ch. 2) has argued, following a longstanding debate in sociology, that the subjective meanings of action are very difficult to learn, that purely subjective meaning is not necessarily important to sociological analysis, and that alternative approaches might be more fruitful. Wuthnow's critique notwithstanding, only empirically, and for particular cases, can we answer the question of whether the study of situated meaningful social action and interaction is important. In some cases, people rework cultural meanings in their personal lives in ways that yield culturally based but unanticipated outcomes.[2] Wuthnow's position is that sociologists ought to be primarily concerned with shared meanings—meanings as they are communicated through "discourse and behavior." Despite Wuthnow's efforts to differentiate subjective meaning and shared meaning, however, the analysis of shared meanings, of course, is as much a matter of interpretation as is the interpretation of subjective meaning. Neither can be privileged as the site of sociological interpretation.

The choice of looking for meaning in intentions versus object is not without its consequences for how people make sense of culture. As John Berger points out, art critics whose theories stress formal properties of art may point to the difficulties of interpreting artistic intentions in order to try to maintain the purity of art as art, divorced from its historical circumstances of creation and its social significance (1972). Such art critics would seem to raise procedural difficulties of historical and social contextualization, but their real bone of contention concerns what will count as legitimate standards and criteria of cultural criticism. No doubt hermeneutics is something less than an exact science (but no less exact than cultural criticism in general), yet the difficulty of interpreting intended meanings does not diminish its importance. Moreover, things are not so hopeless. The cultural object itself may yield a good deal of information, and there may be other clues that help to clarify the intentions behind a painting, musical composition or play.

One method is effectively represented by Michael Baxandall's approach to constructing a "Brief" for a cultural object (1985). The Brief identifies the various problems and issues toward which the act of producing the cultural

---

[2] For example, a study of Jim Jones's People's Temple by one of the present authors (Hall 1987) shows that the group's demise in murder and mass suicide was in part a product of the ways in which Jones and his followers reworked culturally available ideas about "the promised land."

object is directed as a solution. In Baxandall's model, a cultural producer follows through on such a brief under practical constraints and opportunities related to a medium and its techniques, relevant economic conditions, personal circumstances, and other conditions affecting the production of a cultural object. Thus, a film is done either in black-and-white or in color; it is based either on a previous story or on an original screenplay; it is shot in some combination of studio sets and locations outside the studio; particular actors are used; and so forth. As chapter 8 shows, a good deal of cultural production is handled through conventions—previously established routine ways of doing things. Moreover, other conventions mediate between the cultural object and the people who experience it (Becker 1982). Thus, if the film producer uses a particular kind of musical score, say "triumphant music," at a dramatic juncture in the film, the effectiveness of that choice of music depends on the audience's shared knowledge of the music's conventional meaning. Cultural workers may "play" with conventions. For example, the use of triumphant music in a comedy typically has a different meaning than its conventional one, but the comic use depends upon the audience's knowledge of the conventional serious meaning in order to produce an ironic effect. Beyond use of conventions, the producer operates in the context of other cultural workers, distributors and the audience, all of whose interests and demands may shape the production of culture (Griswold, 1987a). By constructing a Brief for a cultural object, it is possible to identify features of the object that give clues about the intentions behind the creation of the object, and the relation of these intentions to various factors and circumstances.

As an example, Baxandall reconstructs a Brief for a 1910 painting by Picasso, *Portrait of Daniel-Henry Kahnweiler*. Part of the Brief offers a description of issues painters faced at the beginning of the twentieth century. One question concerned how to represent the depth of three dimensions, while honestly acknowledging the two-dimensionality of the canvas surface. Another issue was what importance to give to form versus color. Third, there was the problem of time: How could the artist avoid the fiction that a painting—like a photograph—captures an instant just as it is, when the painting itself is created over a much longer period of time? The intentional project resulting in Picasso's painting can be grasped by identifying his novel solutions to these enduring problems of the painter. Other considerations came into play in how this Brief was realized: The particular social circumstances and personal idiosyncrasies of Picasso as a painter, the market for paintings which Picasso had to confront if he was to be economically successful, and so forth. In making his own choices, Picasso implicitly constructed his own unfolding Brief, and he acted in terms of it, but he did so in a concrete cultural, social and economic situation that affected the character of the cultural object produced on the basis of the Brief. In turn, Baxandall argues, Picasso's painting itself became one basis upon which his own and other artists' subsequent Briefs became defined (1985, pp. 41–73).

Despite all the difficulties of hermeneutic analysis, Baxandall shows that it is possible to formulate an account of the intentions of cultural workers and their effects on cultural objects. To come to such an account requires a good deal of research and speculation, yet some critical interpretations of intended meaning, on the basis of evidence and argument, may seem more plausible than others. Such questions are difficult to resolve in any definitive way, and the intentions of the person making the interpretation can themselves be subjected to interpretation. So it is with "the hermeneutic circle."

However, the effort to interpret the *intended* meanings of a cultural producer hardly exhausts the problem of meaning. Indeed, even if puzzling over the intentions of cultural producers may help us reach a better understanding of their work, analyzing the meaning of a cultural object in any *accessible* sense does not necessarily depend on knowing the most private intentions of its producers (cf. Wuthnow 1987, p. 65). Especially when there is widespread appreciation of a painting, a piece of music or a play, we must suspect that it has some *public* meanings. That is, it must deal with issues of some cultural significance by use of symbols, conventions and aesthetics that are socially understood and appreciated. Only in this way does a cultural object seem likely to capture the interest of some general public.

Semiotics and the Structure of Public Meaning

The fact that producers of culture can draw on conventions about the meaning of various motifs in an object offers a bridge from considering the meaningful intentions of producers to "decoding" the conventional meanings of a cultural object. Words, for example, have some general range of meanings, or else it would not be possible for you to make any sense out of this sentence. In much the same way, the ability of viewers to "read" a painting or photograph depends upon conventions concerning color, texture of paint, the character of brush stokes, the representation of dimensionality, and sometimes, the symbolic content of the elements of the painting as a composition. The same is true for music, where pitch, timber, harmony, rhythm, melody and other devices can be employed in conventional ways to convey certain modes and sensibilities. In the theater, certain gestures may be used by actors to convey surprise, anger, joy or sinister motives in ways that will be readily understood by an audience, even though the same gestures in everyday life probably would seem contrived or overdone.

Because cultural objects are "read" on the basis of conventions, it is possible to describe them in terms of their use of (and play upon) conventions. In semiotics, then, the meaning of a cultural object is embodied in the structured relations of its conventional elements—the characters, costumes, setting, genre, plot, acting and camera angles in a film. That is, the meaning of the cultural object as a total object can be analyzed independently of questions about how and why it was produced. Yet there is a problem here that parallels the problem of knowing the cultural producer's intentions: To understand a cultural object's structured meaning assumes a good knowledge of the conventions, symbols, signs, motifs, aesthetics and other elements that make the object hang together (e.g., as a painting or a piece of music). As Eagleton points out, "For the structuralists, the 'ideal reader' of a work was someone who would have at his or her disposal all the codes which would render it exhaustively intelligible. The reader was thus just a kind of mirror-reflection of the work itself—someone who would understand it 'as it was'" (1983, p. 121). Such an "ideal reader" cannot exist, of course. Nevertheless, as with the problem of hermeneutics and the intentions of the cultural producer, the semiotic analyst of structure may make the attempt at a reading, and whatever the flaws of such a reading, it may reveal a good deal about the meaningful character of a cultural object in its own terms.

Whether valid or not, the assumptions about coherent meaning and the possibility of more-or-less objective reading have offered a foundation for a great deal of research on the effects of culture. They offer the possibility of decoding the meanings of the cultural material to which people are exposed. Advertising offers a ready subject for such studies because, after all, advertisers have a high degree of self-interest in affecting people's actions. Their communication therefore presumably is designed to have accessible significance for the public, whether that accessibility depends upon conscious or less than conscious understandings by the public. What, then, are the codes and conventions of advertising? The sociologist Erving Goffman asked this question specifically for the issue of gender by examining still photographs in advertisements. Exploring the photographs in Goffman's study offers the opportunity to see how gendered relations were communicated by advertisers at the time Goffman analyzed them. He was able to show how gender ranking between men and women can be accomplished through framing and perspective on the size and positioning of the models. Details are also important. With the device of "head cant," "the level of the head is lowered relative to that of others, including, indirectly, the viewer of the picture. The resulting configurations can be read as an acceptance of subordination, an expression of ingratiation, submissiveness, and appeasement" (1979, p. 46).

The structuralist analysis of cultural meaning can also focus on societal "structures"—enduring patterns—of culture, to see if they share a common code. Following the structuralist tradition of Emile Durkheim, anthropologist Claude Lévi-Strauss (1966), for example, suggested that cultural systems of classification exist prior to the individual. Activities of social life are mapped onto already existing classifications. In a similar vein, Dayan and Katz have explored the commonalities of media events such as the wedding of Prince Charles and Lady Diana, the first landing on the moon, state funerals, and political hearings such as Watergate or Iran-Contra (1988). The range of such events is diverse, yet Dayan and Katz argue, they share the character of "televised ceremonies" that ritually reaffirm the social order by staging a collective witnessing of the social order's moments of transformation. With live television coverage, ceremonies serve a "religious" function for a society as a whole. Such events, usually carefully staged, nevertheless come to represent history-in-the-making. Each one offers an idealized dramatization which reworks the meaning of the social order in a particular time of social change. Dayan and Katz state, "Without using this phrase in a pejorative sense, media events are 'symbolic manipulations.' They describe a striking affinity to the techniques used in therapeutic contexts by traditional 'shamans' [healers]. Through ceremony, a problematic situation is redefined, transcribed to another language..." (1988, p. 167).

Perhaps most striking in Durkheim's approach to sociology is his idea that cultural objects (his focus was religious ceremonies) offer an *idealized* version of the social world. According to this view, we should not expect culture to *represent* or *mirror* the world as it really is. To the contrary, culture may be expected to present the world in some normative version of how it "ought" (and sometimes, ought not) to be. In this perspective, critics of the mass media are often correct when they point to television and the movies as offering fantastic distortions of the subjects they treat. Yet from the Durkheimian point of view, this is to be expected. The important question concerns the specific meaning of the idealized version of reality.

Cultural critics have decoded everything from advertisements (Goffman 1979; Leiss, Kline and Jhally 1988), news (Manoff and Schudson 1986), television (Gitlin 1986), Hollywood movies (Miller 1990) and clothes (Lurie 1981) to popular song lyrics and high-culture paintings and plays. Sometimes such studies address particular themes—gender, ethnicity, popular ethics, and so forth; other studies offer interpretations of a cultural object as a whole.

What is at stake in the latter efforts to get at the meaning of a whole cultural object can be seen by examining different critical interpretations of the same film—*Mildred Pierce,* starring Joan Crawford as Mildred, released in 1945. One critic, Peter Biskind, portrays the film's plot as a "conservative" exercise. For Biskind, the film affirms traditional sex roles by showing the fate that confronts a woman like Mildred when she deviates from the then-normative housewife role by trying to make a go of it on her own. The trouble begins for Mildred when she kicks out her husband, Bert, for consorting with a mistress. On her own, Mildred starts a series of successful restaurants, becomes wealthy, and takes on a loafer named Monty as her lover. Things could work out, but they don't. One of Mildred's daughters dies, symbolically from her mother's inattention. Then Monty proceeds to ditch Mildred in favor of her daughter, Veda. But Veda finds that Monty considers her a "tramp," and she does him in with her mother's gun. Mildred has the opportunity to marry another guy named Wally—a representative of "the new male sensitivity," but in the end she returns to her husband. "If Mildred, in her behavior, defied patriarchy, she must, in the end, acquiesce. It is Bert, not

FIGURE 9.1 The film *Mildred Pierce* is open to multiple critical interpretations. (*Source:* Dominant Pictures Corp.)

Mildred, who rules the roost." Biskind concludes, "Ultimately the film opts for rigid gender distinctions, the traditional family, and rejects the therapeutic" (1983, pp. 296–304).

If Biskind really were the "ideal reader" described by Terry Eagleton (1983), Biskind's decoding of *Mildred Pierce* would have accomplished two things. First, it would have provided a reliable account of the film's symbolic structure, and second, the reliable account would affirm the potential of structuralist readings of cultural objects. But in fact, we know that Biskind is *not* the ideal reader (or can't be assumed to be), because *Mildred Pierce* remains a subject of critical controversy. Linda Williams shows us a considerably different film (1988). In the first place, Biskind has failed to tell us that the film does not unfold in the plot sequence that he narrates. Instead, the earlier parts of Mildred's life—her fallout with her husband and her enterprise in the restaurant business—are depicted through flashbacks. As other critics have noted, these evenly and well lit flashback scenes of positive women's discourse contrast sharply with the central plot framework of the film's "present"—more shadowy lit *film noire* scenes that reveal Mildred as something of a fallen woman, who tries to explain how she had been driven to deceit by seeking to mend lives gone wrong. The alternation of filmic styles is crucial to divergent feminist readings of the film, Williams (1988, p. 15) shows. One previous critic, Andrea Walsh, "reads the film's middle [flashback] segment from a feminist perspective as an instance of an emergent group's struggle with patriarchal hegemony." But this reading has problems, Williams suggests, because it suppresses the *film noire* context in which the film's present is set, and because it assumes the continuity of a static 1930s film genre "about the nobility of maternal courage and sacrifice." A quite different reading is offered by Pam Cook, who shows that the *film noire* narrative of criminal interrogation that holds the film together casts doubt on the truth of Mildred's narrative offered in the flashbacks. Cook argues, then, that the film should be read psychoanalytically as the "repression of female sexuality." In turn, Williams suggests that *both* these feminist readings are partial in that they fail to take into account the specific timing of the film's plot, and its release just as soldiers were coming home from World War II to a country where many woman had experienced careers outside the household made possible by a shortage of male labor. Though *Mildred Pierce* is not *about* the war, it is about the gender issues faced by men and women *because* of the war. The war is the "absent referent" of the film. In opposition to both Biskind and Cook, Williams argues that what matters are the specific workings out of gender relations as the soldiers come home, rather than any eternal ideology of patriarchy.

The existence of multiple readings of *Mildred Pierce* suggests that any particular structuralist reading of a text depends upon its specific method of criticism and thematic concerns. Any reading thus necessarily *excludes* meanings that are available in a different approach to reading the text. Yet the same thing can be said about the text itself: Any narrative or account depends on a wide range of choices concerning plot, characterization, exposition, and so forth. The meanings available in the narrative depend on the particular choices made; other meanings are excluded by those choices. For example, any film about the Vietnam War offers a particular depiction that cannot possibly capture the war's diverse meanings. In part the range of meanings depends upon the ideological controversies that surround the war. Any particular narrative about the Vietnam War will be viewed in part for how it portrays government objectives in the war, the situations that the military faced, how soldiers conducted themselves, the character of antiwar protesters, and so on. No film on the Vietnam War could be all things to all people.

To oversimplify, the recent critical method of reading a text known as "deconstruction" involves, in part, searching for the *exclusion* of meanings from the text: What is *not* in the text offers a revealing mirror image of what *is* in the text; they are, in effect, a paired opposition. Thus, in discussing *Mildred Pierce*, Linda Williams considers the significance of World War II: Even though the war is not a theme of the film, the hidden war is nevertheless present in the film. Terry Eagleton has pointed to the rationale for this interpretive approach of deconstruction: "Since the meaning of a sign is a matter of what the sign is *not*, its meaning is always in some sense absent from it too" (1983, p. 128).

The acknowledgment of multiple readings based on complex meanings that exist both in the text and in its suppression of other meanings has moved critical textual analysis past structuralism to what is called "post-structuralism." Critics no longer can aspire to the definitive decoding of a text, for other critics are waiting in the wings to decode the critical interpretations themselves! Post-structuralist interpretation continues the structuralist focus on public issues of meaning in the structure of the text, rather than the hermeneutic search for the producer's intentions. But the controversies of interpretation show that post-structuralist interpretation is faced with the same problem as hermeneutic interpretation, namely, the difficulty of getting at "the real" meaning. Nevertheless, controversies of interpretation sometimes reflect overall agreement about a text. Not one of the critics doubts that *Mildred Pierce* is about gender relations. They dispute particular points about the meaning of the gender relations depicted in the film that may go well beyond the critical analysis of the general audience. But these differences depend on "high brow" analyses of popular culture that don't necessarily have anything to do with how an audience experiences a film or other cultural object. All critical readings—hermeneutic, structuralist, or post- structuralist—leave fundamental questions unanswered: Whatever the sources and "real" meaning of the cultural object, what relation does it have to its readers, and by what processes? It is to these questions that we now turn.

USES, EFFECTS AND AGENDAS: THE INTERPLAY OF CULTURAL OBJECTS AND AUDIENCES

Trying to determine the relations between cultural texts and their audiences is not an easy task. After all, using a cultural object such as a lawn mower or a television has obvious effects, in the sense that using the object alters behavior from what it would be otherwise. But the relations people have with symbolic culture are necessarily more elusive. People experience culture through the senses—by reading a book, watching a play or going to a concert. No doubt people go through cognitive changes from the experience. But under what circumstances might such changes actually alter habitual ways of thinking or acting? Three broad approaches to the relationship between cultural objects and audiences have fueled the debate: (1) the "uses and gratifications" approach that emphasizes the audience's role in choosing culture, (2) the approach that explores the more-or-less direct effects of exposure to particular cultural objects, and (3) the approach that points to the audience's formation of general worldviews and frameworks of interpretation on the basis of "agenda-setting" in the mass media.

The obvious problem encountered by any strong theory of cultural effects is that people may—to a greater or lesser degree—select from among alternative experiences of culture those that somehow "speak to" them. If this is true, then people choose what may, in turn, affect them. In the same vein, since culture depends on an audience, to gain that audience, producers of culture may try to shape the cultural object to please the audience. Producers, to take an extreme but not uncommon example, sometimes have test screened films like *Fatal Attraction,* and changed the plot to accommodate a trial audience's reactions. In a less obvious way, writers take into account their readers; painters, their gallery dealers and patrons. Moreover, when culture is marketed in an economy, patrons contribute to the success and failure of cultural producers by their decisions to buy or not buy, watch or not watch. In short, the audience may have influence on the culture, as well as the other way around. What diversity there is in television genres may be partly explained by the absence of a monolithic mass audience, and the existence of a wider range of "taste segments" (Cantor and Cantor 1986).

As Wendy Griswold has shown, the production of culture is influenced by other factors besides the cultural composition of the audience (1981). But under the assumption that an audience's cultural choices in part reflect its interests, content analysis can be used as a methodology to identify the thematic dimensions of specific cultural objects such as novels, comic strips, and films. The themes identified through content analysis in turn can serve as an approximate gauge to assess the concerns and interests of the audience who chooses to consume them—as a taste public, social group, community, or society. Thus, Elizabeth Long premises her study of what bestselling novels during the period 1945 to 1975 reveal about the American dream on the assertion that these particular novels "are primarily a social rather than a literary phenomenon." This implies that their literary merit is not at issue for Long: What counts is popularity, which "suggests that they are finding resonance with broad segments of the reading public, rather than appealing only to certain subsections of the audience." For the task of exploring general features of cultural continuity and change, "bestsellers are a particularly useful source of information because they represent a sort of common denominator of our literary culture" (1985, pp. 5–6). Such an approach, focused on overall popularity, tends to explore culture as a reflection or barometer of society, without answering the question of whether such culture influences people, and if so, in what ways.

If the focus on popularity of cultural objects is shifted from social interpretation to the issue of individual choices, a slightly different theory of culture and audience emerges. Specifically, the idea that cultural artifacts tell us something about the people who use them can be turned into a theory. In the "uses and gratification" model, it is argued that people choose culture that confirms, extends and enriches their own perspectives. Thus it would seem that if culture has an effect, the effect is merely one of reinforcing previous ideas. Such an approach can find favor with media executives, advertisers, the general public and with sociologists like Gans (1974, p. 32) who defend popular culture: The model would seem neatly to sidestep the menace of media manipulation, reassuring us that we exercise choice, rather than making Pavlovian responses to media stimuli.[3] Even so, the simple reinforcement of previous views would hardly be politically insignificant. To the contrary, such an effect, catering to a freely choosing public, would tend to maintain the stability of the status quo.

If culture·is to some extent both a reflection of its audience, and shaped by it, a more direct causal hypothesis about effects of culture also has received a great deal of attention. People whom sociologist Howard Becker (1963) has termed "moral entrepreneurs" have always been on the lookout for the pernicious effects of decadent culture on innocent people. Just as rock lyrics are singled out today, at the turn of the twentieth century, dire warnings surfaced about the role of player-piano roll music in corruption of youth (Berlin 1980). Similar concerns target violence on television, pornography, children's television, comic books, "obscene" art, indeed, any cultural material that denigrates or challenges the values and worldview of the moral entrepreneurs. Nor does the opposition come from any single social sector: Religious fundamentalists, political liberals and conservatives, intellectuals, radicals and feminists all at one time or another have bemoaned the effects of popular culture.

Yet actually developing an empirically robust theoretical explanation of effects has proved a difficult task. "Copy-cat" crimes, in which the individual imitates an act seen in the media, are sometimes taken as proof of media effects, but they show quite the reverse: Copy-cat crimes offer evidence that a combination of factors, rather than television violence alone, must be at work, or else a much larger number of people exposed to particular media content would imitate it. Advocates of the effects thesis are thus careful to acknowledge that violence and crime "result from several forces at once" (Liebert and Sprafkin 1988, p. 161). However, given the huge sizes of mass media audiences, even a very low percentage of imitative behaviors could result in a significant increase in violent crimes such as murder, and though the findings are controversial, some researchers have found evidence supporting this thesis (Phillips and Bollen 1985; Stack 1987).

Still, skepticism persists. Based on a review of effects research on children, news, violence, and a variety of other subjects, Herbert Gans concluded:

> So far, it is difficult to attribute any large-scale permanent effects of specific items or types of media content, although it seems likely that the media may have negative effects on "media addicts," people whose entire emotional and cognitive life is centered almost entirely on the media, and others predisposed to pathology who find their behavior publicized by media content (1974, p. 39).

---

[3]From the perspective of critical theory, the uses and gratification model still does not foreclose the possibility of manipulation: If market researchers can tap into the views and desires of consumers, they may be able to market culture by seemingly reinforcing such views and desires, while actually channeling mass behavior based on those views and desires into specific product choices.

For Gans, the critics's stereotype of a society of zombies plugged into mass media does not hold up under the scrutiny of research: The gap between critical claims and findings is "sizable."

A decade later, Joshua Meyrowitz reviewed effects research. He found that quantitative researchers over the years added more and more variables controlling for personality, social class, peer influence, and other factors. On this basis they hoped to increase their ability to show a relationship between the media stimulus as cause and a research subject response as effect. But like Gans, Meyrowitz asserted "the general failure of researchers to demonstrate clear and direct effects of media content on social behavior..." (1985, p. 13). Gans readily admitted that mass media have more fundamental effects—changing the mix of culture available, reorganizing the information access of individuals, and so on. As we saw in chapter 7, Meyrowitz extended this line of thought by arguing that mass media reorganize the social life of people who participate in them. Important as such transformations may be, however, they do not resolve the issue that is of such concern to media critics—whether there are direct effects of media content.

As Gans recognized, further research might refine knowledge about media effects. Indeed, media researchers and critics have come up with some intriguing findings. Even the findings of research not directly concerned with effects can be stunning. Based on a nationwide multistage probability sample survey, one researcher found that, of the time people aged 18 years or older are at home during the hours of 7 and 11 PM and not eating or sleeping or receiving visitors, only 18% is spent *not* watching television (Bower 1985, p. 86). Under such circumstances, the effect of television is hardly measurable, simply because it amounts to a basic avenue of experience. Still, the question of what is happening when people "watch" television is tricky. One study of long-term effects found a negative statistical correlation between children's amount of television viewing and their scores on reading comprehension and language usage achievement tests: The more television, the lower the achievement scores. But, as Hodge and Tripp commented, it isn't clear whether television actually dampens achievement, or instead, whether children of low achievement watch more television. To Hodge and Tripp, it seems plausible that some children, in intellectually impoverished environments, are affected positively by television. These researchers note that television overall has a statistically negative effect, but they also point out that other factors must be much more important, since television accounted for less than five percent of the total variation in the children's scores (1986, p. 163–65).

Other research further underscores the complexity of media effects. One study argues that some people become socialized toward media "dependency" for useful information about the world and their own interests. Such viewers of television watch carefully, and on this basis they are more likely to respond to media content than are viewers who get distracted by one thing or another (Ball-Rokeach, Rokeach, and Grube 1984, p. 136). Similarly, Gerbner and his colleagues (1980) have advanced a "cultivation theory," which suggests that the "mainstream" worldview offered on television tends to provide specific television embellishment of ideas to people already holding mainstream values, while when less socialized individuals engage in heavy viewing, it results in their cultivation of mainstream viewpoints. In short, people look for role models and ways of being, and they select from the images that appear, and imitate those which appeal to them.

By these accounts of viewing behavior, television can be a powerful tool of socialization, or possibly, manipulation. If this is so, then a crucial issue concerns the particular political or other value significance of the medium's *content*. Let us return to the question of violence on television. It might be assumed that programming depicting violence would offer role models for viewers, who would, in turn, live more violently. But the reverse seems to be true. One study concerned about children suggests that children do not necessarily understand media violence in the same way as real violence; media violence may be a cultural metaphor which signifies conflict, with the result that children will recognize conflict as an important part of social life (Hodge and Tripp 1986, p. 217). Similarly, a study of television crime programs has found that heavy viewers indeed cultivate the worldview of the programs, but they do so in specific ways. Given that they learn about the legal system predominantly from television and that television provides an unrealistic portrayal of the criminal justice system, heavy adolescent viewers have less knowledge of criminal justice processes than light viewers. Moreover, the heavy viewers reflect the television police viewpoint that places more emphasis on "crime control" than on considerations of "due process" based on the Constitution's Bill of Rights. "In fact, crime shows appear to promote antiheterodoxy—the desire to punish those who deviate from accepted norms." Quite the opposite from promoting violence, the depiction of violence in crime television shows that "crime doesn't pay": Heavy viewers are more likely to view the world as a "threatening" place, and they come down in favor of "law and order" (Carlson 1985, pp. 189–90).

If the effects of violence on television crime shows are not what would be predicted by a "copy-cat" theory, it is because people pay attention to culture in ways that are more complex than a copy-cat theory suggests. It is becoming evident that audiences don't just absorb cultural material "whole hog." Instead, they actively participate in selecting and making sense of cultural objects. For example, a study of how people take in the news suggests that people are quite selective in what they will bother to pay attention to in the first place. When they do watch, they sort through information received, discarding much of it. The flood of journalistic information available thus is filtered by people who don't go past the headlines of many stories, read only the lead paragraphs of others, choose only a few stories to peruse, and absorb even fewer. "On an average, out of 15 to 18 stories in a television newscast, no more than one is retained sufficiently well so that it can be recalled in any fashion shortly afterwards" (Graber 1984, pp. 201–2). Even for a news story that can be recalled, people don't absorb the entire story; instead, they compare what they find out with one or more "schemas" that organize existing knowledge, and add information under certain conditions.

Such selective recall of media content does not suggest the absence of media influence, of course. To the contrary, if only certain cultural material receives "play," then the media can be powerful in focusing collective attention of the audience by giving particular emphasis to certain topics. This argument is at the core of the "agenda-setting" model of effects. If the agenda-setting hypothesis is true, the media do not affect the opinions of individuals so much as they help to establish the circumstances in which the public and politicians pay attention to certain issues in the first place. Civil rights abuses of racial minorities have a long history in the U.S., for example. One study shows the strong role played by the *New York Times* in the period from 1954 to 1976 in setting the public agenda on the issue (Winter and Eyal 1981). But in earlier decades, and in the period of the 1980s up until the Los Angeles riot of 1992, the media did not focus on the issue in a way that placed it on the national agenda.

The research on agenda-setting implies that the amount of media news coverage does not always derive from any intrinsic importance of a topic. That is, changes in the coverage of civil rights issues don't necessarily reflect a sudden shift in abuses of civil rights. Yet there is a methodological problem: How can researchers know about the *real* incidence of events if the news can't be argued to be a reliable reflection of actual events? It would be useful to have some standard with which to measure the "objective" importance of topics, that is, their significance independent of the amount of media coverage they receive. For example, one such standard might concern the risks measured in deaths per thousand from various potential hazards. If media coverage reflected objective risk, alcohol-related deaths would receive a certain amount of coverage, drug-related deaths a certain amount of coverage, job hazard deaths their "fair share," and so forth. The difference between the "fair share" and actual coverage would reflect the media's disproportionate attention (and, equally important, inattention) to selected issues, and thus, demonstrate its capacity for agenda-setting. In such terms, Bernard Cohen has argued that the media gave far more attention to the hazards of nuclear energy than to other hazards that cause more death, and he suggests that the overcoverage is not simply disproportionate objective coverage; rather, the excess coverage is distorted through use of inflammatory language and exaggeration (1983). Other studies of local communities have shown cases in which media coverage has set the public agenda concerning rape, and influenced the way key justice system officials deal with particular criminal cases—by plea bargaining or going to trial (Pritchard 1986; Protess et al. 1985).

These studies of agenda-setting in turn raise the question of who sets the agenda of the agenda-setters. It is at least theoretically possible that journalists reflect and respond to concerns of the public or some segment of the public (to say nothing of interest groups's public relations initiatives). The public and interest-group concerns, however, don't always calibrate with object risks (cf. Gans 1979, ch. 3). In fact, some recent research shows that certain mobilized groups, with sophisticated knowledge about media story coverage decisions, can in fact set the agenda of the media by their own activities. Thus, the "missing children" issue that received extensive coverage in the 1970s and 1980s was something of a media-created "urban legend" (cf. Brunvand 1981). The legend was propagated through the interplay of certain journalistic and mass entertainment predispositions toward sensationalism (e.g., Geraldo Rivera's programs) and the activities of moral entrepreneurs who had a vested interest in exaggerating the problem in order to legitimize their own organizations as dealing with a social problem of epic proportions. Success of this agenda-setting depended, in turn, on playing to deepseated public anxieties about children (Fritz and Altheide 1987). More recent public concerns about satanism reflect much the same process (Bromley 1991).

In sum, the "effects" of culture depend to some extent on "uses and gratification"—the ways that people choose to experience culture, and how they interpret what they experience based in part on their interests, previous knowledge and experiences. While it is clear that certain kinds of culture do affect their audiences in measurable ways, the uses-and- gratification focus on the predispositions of people to take in culture begins to turn the question around. Rather than assuming an objective content of culture and asking how this content affects people, analysts are beginning to ask about audiences, without assuming that a given cultural object has any single meaning, correct interpretation, or unambiguous effect.

THEORIES OF THE AUDIENCE

Concern with the audience has its origins in a number of theories that have converged on the problem from different directions. And because these diverse theories all have their own distinctive explanatory concerns and approaches, the audience question often replicates larger theoretical debates. Nevertheless, the debate crystallizes the theoretical issues, and all sides have recognized the importance of developing their understandings of the audience. Too often the debates have been undertaken by "armchair theorists" and literary critics with little taste for research on actual audiences and their relations to cultural objects. More recently, however, sociologists have begun to take seriously the new theories of the audience, and they have conducted some sophisticated research that offers an important counterbalance to the abstract theories.

Certain theories—hermeneutics and phenomenology—by their very nature assume a significant role of the audience in relation to cultural objects.

Other theories and perspectives—Marxism, post-structuralist semiotics, and various postmodern theories of literary criticism—have become elaborated and transformed in significant ways through their confrontation with the problem of the audience. In contrast to a structuralist theory that assumes the possibility of reading a text objectively, just as we have already pointed out for interpretations of artistic intention, hermeneutics describes the audience as actively making new meanings out of whatever cultural objects they witness. So long as objective interpretation is taken to be impossible, hermeneutics can offer no general sociological theory or explanation of what happens when people read texts. It must be content with interpreting specific instances of how people read particular cultural objects, without making any claims of offering a "correct" interpretation. Put differently, hermeneutics cannot escape its own assertion that all interpretations are partial, by offering a general theory of interpretation.

A parallel theoretical stream—phenomenology—is specifically concerned with the nature of ideas as thoughts or mental events, that is, with how the world "appears" to us in our minds. The early twentieth-century phenomenologist Edmund Husserl sought to establish a basis for achieving true knowledge without resorting to presuppositions or assumptions. Phenomenology never has succeeded in this quest. Nevertheless, Alfred Schutz's *social* phenomenology of thought processes is a useful tool for thinking about the audience problem. Most significantly, Schutz (1970) called the puzzles that we *might* think about (e.g., whether to go to a party) "topical relevances." When someone actually *does* think about a topical relevance, Schutz would say that it has become "thematic." But a thematic topic does not present itself as meaningful "as is." Instead, how an individual resolves a thematic topic is based upon two additional kinds of relevance. First, there is interpretational relevance, that is, the kinds of information that come to mind when someone thinks about a theme. This information might come from the individual's "stock of knowledge" and from observations and interactions with other people (e.g., what kind of party is it, how is it going to fit into the larger social scheme of things?). A second kind of relevance is motivational relevance, that is, the specific goals and objectives of the individual (why go to the party?). These two types of relevance, in relation to a topic which has "come up," affect what we "make of" the thematic topic.

Even this brief sketch of one phenomenological approach suggests some important things about culture and the audience. First, the cultural object "out there"—the film or musical performance—cannot be meaningful in its own right, for different people may pay attention to different aspects of it. In this view, people make meaning *out of* culture, rather than apprehending the meaning *in* culture. Taken to the extreme, this perspective leads to the viewpoint of literary critic Harold Bloom, who regards every critical reaction to a poem as necessarily founded in *mis*interpretation; reading, then, is an activity of "creative misunderstanding," and criticism is no more an objective

FIGURE 9.2 The same cultural object can mean different things to different people, depending on their social and historical locations. (*Source:* Paul Fortin/Stock Boston.)

activity than is the writing of novels or poetry. In this approach, it would seem that everyone who reads, also "writes" through the activity of reading.

Second, how people make meaning out of culture very much depends upon their own reservoirs of knowledge, and on their own immediate situations. For example, a worshiper in a church will attach a different significance to the art displayed there than will a tourist or a visiting art historian, just as a politician likely will attach significance to television news programs that differs from the "reading" of the news by someone else. Reading a cultural object, then, is not just a passive process of "taking it in." Instead, the reader is actively engaged in making new meanings, based on the conjuncture of various relevant considerations. Through this recognition of the *situated* character of individuals' knowledge, phenomenology can be aligned with historical and Marxist theories of meaning, which suggest that the meaning of a text depends upon the political and social circumstances in which it is read (Nelson and Grossberg 1988). By this logic, the meaning of Jane Austen's *Pride and Prejudice* will depend on both the personal situation and the historical and social location of the reader.

Third, and perhaps most important, phenomenology helps to overcome the analytic distinctions that separate the cultural producer, the cultural object, and the audience. Rather than seeing each as a separate entity that somehow "affects" the other, phenomenology offers a way of recognizing the cultural object as a medium that connects the producer and audience in a special kind of intersubjective relationship. The activity of "reading a book" offers a generic example. When we read, we pay attention (more or less) to a stream of words on paper. The stream of consciousness (as opposed to the stream of words on paper) is constituted through the activity of the reader who is paying attention to thematic topics, raising interpretive points of relevance, partly orchestrated by the writer's goals and motivational relevances. To the extent that readers "give themselves over" to the writer's stream of words, they can follow and explore the writer's own train of thought (filtered, of course, by the readers's own diverse ways of making meaning). But "giving oneself over" to reading amounts to "taking on" the writer's stream of words as though they were one's own. The cultural activity of reading, then, makes the cultural object a part of one's own stream of consciousness. To take extreme examples, when we watch a television commercial enough times or listen to a popular song over and over again, we absorb the cultural material: It becomes part of our own memories, ready to come to conscious awareness again if, somehow, it becomes "relevant" to some topic that comes up. For health food activists, "you are what you eat." For cultural phenomenologists, "you are what you read," but *what* you read depends on *how* you read.

Phenomenology has been imported into literary criticism most directly by the "reception theory" of German critics like Wolfgang Iser. Instead of looking at the text as structured by its own symbols, Iser is interested in examining the text to uncover the ways in which the reader might be drawn into the text. The text does not stand on its own; rather, it has to make room for the reader, offering windows by which the reader can "wander" through the world made present by the text (Holub 1984, p. 82ff.). Such an approach places special emphasis on the structure of narrative: It is not just the "facts" of the described world that have meaning for the reader; to the contrary, the possibility of a meaningful relationship between the reader and "what happens" in the text arises through devices of narration—the voice through which the story is told— and the shifts in viewpoint ("flashbacks," stories told by characters *within* the text, and so on). The reader who reads a story about adventures at sea, not just by the author of a text (Joseph Conrad), but by a *character* speaking from within the text, gains much the same experience as if the reader was listening to a friend tell the story firsthand. The author of the book (Conrad) "disappears" and the character becomes the storyteller. Thus, the "vicarious" experience that makes culture meaningful depends upon narrative devices of "performance" that make the reader a part of the events of the text (Maclean 1988).

But who is to say that the reader will cooperate? Reception theory as originally developed by Iser addresses the problem of the audience by searching for the audience's place in the text. But perhaps readers have the power to reject their assigned positions. Perhaps, indeed, readers learn how to read in ways that are independent of any given text, and in turn, shape the ways in which they "take on" the various narrators they encounter in a text. As

Maclean observes, there are a number of possible metaphors for the writer/reader relationship: Lover and mistress, master and slave, donor and beggar, host and parasite. But there is also the possibility of the presumably passive reader rebelling, rising up, and "fighting back" (1988, pp. 175–76). Carried to its logical conclusion, the rebellion of the reader establishes the reader as the one who "makes" the text what it is. Thus, for literary critic Stanley Fish, the text melts away as a real object; it is only made meaningful by the people who read it. In a way that parallels the view of Harold Bloom, reading is an active construction of a new text.

These theories of the audience range widely in their emphases and nuances. One approach includes the audience within the text. In others, the text disappears through the work of the audience. Such "armchair" theorizing stands in sore need of empirical research. Until recently, however, empirical studies addressing the theoretical controversy about the audience were poorly conceived: Rather than studying the natural audiences of texts, researchers often tried to create "laboratory" experiments. For example, an audience of college freshman—available for research because they happened to enroll in some introductory social science course—were exposed to texts, and attempts were then made to measure their changes in attitudes and values. Fortunately, recent research has used more sophisticated methods to get at the ways actual historically constituted audiences make sense of cultural objects. For example, as we saw in chapter 6, Radway (1984) has studied the ways in which romance novels play into the worldviews and lifestyles of historically situated women readers.

In a similar vein, Wendy Griswold has examined how book reviewers based in the West Indies, Great Britain, and the U.S. reacted to the same novels of a Barbadian novelist. West Indian reviewers tended to focus on issues of individual and national identity in the novels. By contrast, "Americans revealed their obsession with race by talking about it so much, while the British indicated their preoccupation with colonialism by avoiding the subject so persistently and by concentrating on style rather than content" (1987b, p. 1102). For Griswold, it would be a mistake either to assume a fixed content to a cultural object or to suggest that every reading is idiosyncratic and unrelated to the object's content. Instead, there is a dynamic relation between object and audience: Texts with "cultural power" are those coherent enough to yield a general consensus about the subject matter, and ambiguous enough to engender multiple, controversial interpretations.

How, in turn, do divergent interpretations arise? Marjorie DeVault (1990) addresses this question by studying historically situated readers, as does Griswold. DeVault focuses closely on how particular readers follow divergent textual cues in interpreting a single novel by South African writer Nadine Gordimer—*The Late Bourgeois World,* published in 1966. Liberal readers who wrote reviews immediately after the novel was first published were concerned about the "human tragedy" of South African society; they found the novel's narrator, "Liz," to get in the way of their capacity to appreciate the book. Later, literary scholars in the 1970s and 1980s expressed interest in the contradictory feelings of white Europeans about black activism; these critics could more easily accept Liz's narration. Finally, a feminist reader not only accepts Liz's narration, but considers Liz's life as an important aspect of the story, in and of itself. For DeVault, different readers make their own arguments about novels and their meaning, based partly on information available in the text. The diversity of arguments is possible because, "the conventions of literary realism mean that the fictional situation is portrayed in a way that includes much more than is necessary for any single argument" (1990, p. 915). Like Griswold, DeVault finds readers playing active roles in making meaning out of texts, partly on the basis of their own social circumstances of reading. In ways that complement the broadly phenomenological theories we have already considered, Griswold and DeVault bring to light distinctive empirical processes of audience engagement with texts.

Semiotics might seem less conducive to understanding the position of the audience than the range of reception and reader response theories tied to phenomenology. In particular, the structuralist version of semiotics assumes an ordered pattern of signs and symbols "out there," with an existence independent of any individual or audience. In the extreme version of this approach, individuals do not make meaning. Instead, the structured meanings make individuals, that is, they circumscribe the ways in which we apprehend our worlds and make choices. As George Kubler once suggested, culture is a train moving down the tracks, and we are its passengers (1962). In this view, none of us gets to decide, for example, whether fraternities and sororities exist, or what their subcultures are like; we only get to decide how to act in relation to previously established meanings about "greeks" and "dormies." Such a theory does not seem to allot much of a role to the individual. However, once it was acknowledged that no one individual can give a definitive "decoding" of the structured symbols, structuralist semiotics gave way to post-structuralist theories: Necessarily, if no one can give a definitive reading, the act of reading, and hence the role of the audience, become important. Yet the reader is not assumed to be a subjective being with a fixed identity and a consciousness that acts *upon* knowledge and perceptions (as is more or less the case with phenomenological approaches). Instead, the general theory of signs originally developed in the study of objective cultural objects is carried over to the individual. That is, the individual is not seen as a "self," but as an amalgamation of cultural material. Thus, for Roland Barthes, "This 'I' which approaches the text is already itself a plurality of other texts, of codes which are infinite, or, more precisely, lost (whose origin is lost)" (q. in Holub 1984, p. 154).

Seemingly, there could not be a greater contrast between phenomenological reception theory and post-structuralist semiotic approaches to the reader. As Holub comments, "while reception theorists have displaced their interpretive focus from the text to the reader, post-structuralists have displaced all focus by textualizing the reader" (1984, p. 154). This result is hardly satisfactory to many theorists, for.it deemphasizes the individual's active and creative engagement with culture under concrete historical circumstances. Yet it is possible to reach other conclusions about audiences and culture by drawing on the insights of semiotics in a different—but still post-structuralist—way. One person who has done so is Mark Gottdiener.

Gottdiener described his views in an article called "Hegemony and mass culture: a semiotic approach" (1985). Dissatisfied with the neo-Marxist appropriation of Gramsci's theory of cultural hegemony, Gottdiener sought to offer a schema of interpretation which takes into account the dialectical struggle over symbols between various parties to a cultural phenomenon. It is necessary to consider both the hegemonic interest of mass culture producers in imposing meanings (e.g., jeans manufacturers' product images promoted through advertising) as well as the possibility that users may impute their own special meanings, independently of the producers' purposes. The user who simply takes on the value of the cultural object imputed to it through advertising in some sense buys not only the object, but also the "producer sign value" of the object. However, if the user places *new* meaning on the cultural object, the "producer sign value" is undermined in favor of a "user sign value." Yet producers themselves are careful to monitor such user sign values, and they often respond to such transvaluations of their own products by incorporating the new *user* sign values as the basis for creating new *producer* sign values. For example, once jeans manufacturers noted the advent of certain stylistic usages of their product lines (punks tearing jeans in distinct ways), they could both modify the product (offering "pre-torn" jeans) and modify the producer sign values in advertising to resonate with the (appropriated) users's special sign values (by promoting the punk look in jeans fashion). Similarly, the car manufacturers who find their products used in unanticipated ways within a particular subculture (e.g., import pickup trucks by California automotive boom-box lowriders), may increasingly modify both the truck as a product and the advertising as sign value, in order to nurture and appropriate to their own benefit the emergent audience meaning.

If Gottdiener's model offers some hope that audiences are not totally subordinated by the signage of cultural producers, it is a fragile hope, for the producers are always on the prowl, looking for user signs to appropriate for their own purposes. This responsiveness of the mass culture producers is sometimes taken as proof that "the system works." After all, when producers take over the signs of users, the users' values are being incorporated into mass culture. Users are getting what they want. An example is the wide availability of "organic" and "natural" foods in the wake of the hippie counterculture of the 60s and 70s. Yet the responsiveness of cultural producers can be understood in another way. If every non-conforming use of cultural objects and every critical response to producers' sign values can be plowed back into a mass cultural form like television, then, argues Mark Crispin Miller, there is little capacity for people to establish their own critical awareness of social existence, outside of television, as it were. Miller argues that it is no longer sufficient for audiences to engage in a tongue-in-cheek mockery of the impoverished content of television programs and advertisements: The producers *anticipate* such mockery by the audience and incorporate a narrative viewpoint within television that assumes self-mockery. Irony isn't enough any more. "TV has all but boxed us in" (1988, p. 17). Even with a considered analysis of the role of the audience, it can be shown that cultural objects produced on a mass basis wield a tremendous power.

CONCLUSION

Despite the distinctive starting point of semiotics in the objective structure of signs, with the post-structuralist turn, it begins to converge with phenomenological approaches to understanding cultural meaning and the audience. It is no longer possible to support an argument that cultural meanings reside totally in the objectivity of the cultural object or in the subjectivity of the isolated consciousness of an individual cultural user. Likewise, any simple cause-effect relationship between cultural content and audience effect has to be abandoned. Both semiotic and phenomenological approaches, as well as the new work on audience effects, converge, but in different ways, on the social mediation between producer, object, and audience. It remains for future theorizing and research to further clarify this complex relationship. Whatever directions such research may take, one point already is firmly established: Audiences no longer can be considered simply as the passive recipients of culture. Instead, audiences themselves are engaged in cultural work. Yet that work is not restricted to the social role of "audience."

The whole range of culture-audience approaches focus on cultural users in relation to *particular* cultural objects. But people do not just "consume" culture as "audiences." In fact, cultural users partake of a broad range of cultural objects, and any single cultural object is just one of many that a cultural user takes in. People need to be considered holistically, not just as the recipients of culture. It is thus important to invert the culture-audience question, as it were, and explore the ways in which people engage in the active cultural work of daily social life.

10

CULTURE, ACTION, AND CHANGE

To understand human action it is essential to pay attention to the content of cultures. In this chapter we explore how people (often unconsciously) use culture in the enactment of traditions and everyday, taken-for-granted, practices. People also use culture in a more active, self-conscious and even contentious way. When daughters argue with their mothers about appropriate dress, this argument about tastes also implies assertions about the daughter's independence from her mother and her participation (and identification with) the culture of her peers. To think about the use of culture requires us to consider culture more fully as symbolic expression.

Looking at how people use culture thus requires a reorientation from the dominant ways of talking about culture. Here what is important about culture is not how culture reflects the structure of the social order (broadly speaking, topics of chapters 6 and 7) nor is it how cultural values and other cultural elements do or do not shape patterns of behavior (the topic of chapters 2 and 9). It shares with chapter 8 an emphasis on cultural objects. However, the production of culture approach offers little insight about the meaning of the objects produced. By the same token, the literature on the effects of culture has placed little emphasis on the active engagement of users with cultural objects, even though the role of audiences in making meaning implies such engagement.

In another sense, however, much of this book has been concerned with the use of culture. We have been interested in the distinctive ways that associations based on class, age, ethnicity, or gender structure people's everyday lives. In looking more directly at how people use culture, this chapter considers how (and under what conditions) people make choices about culture. This raises issues of interpretation, consensus and lack of consensus, subcultures and how cultural complexes change.

The broad definitions of culture circulating in the social sciences in the first half of the twentieth century—such as that culture was the whole way of life of a people—served the task of distinguishing what was biologically based from what was "superorganic." By the middle of the century Alfred Kroeber and Talcott Parsons argued that this task had been accomplished, and it was time to refine the definitions in order to distinguish better between the "social" and "cultural." What they found interesting about a culture was not everything in it, but the things that helped to distinguish one culture from another. To this end, Kroeber and Parsons offered the following definitions:

> We suggest that it is useful to define the concept *culture* for most usages more narrowly than has been generally the case in the American Anthropological tradition, restricting its reference to transmitted and created content and patterns of values, ideas and other symbolic-meaningful systems as factors in the shaping of human behavior. On the other hand, we suggest that the term *society*—or more generally, *social system*—be used to designate the specifically relational system of interaction among individuals and collectivities (1958, pp. 582–583, emphasis in the original).

Kroeber and Parsons separated the concepts of culture and society, and offered a more precise definition of culture. In his own work Parsons devoted his efforts to developing the concept of the social system. Within the social system, Parsons thought of cultures as values: Essential but abstract and relatively unexamined essences that motivate human action. In Ann Swidler's interpretation of Parson's theory: "Social systems exist to realize their core values, and values explain why different actors make different choices even in similar situations" yet values themselves are "the unmoved mover in the theory of action" (1986, p. 274).

In recent years the movement has been away from the focus on values, toward culture as expressive symbols. This change in the orientation of the field is central to the shift, described in chapter 2, in discourse on moral culture from its being primarily about rules to recent explorations conceptualizing moral culture as practices and constitutive narratives. We have seen this in works as different from one another as the organizationally based culture of production work (discussed in chapter 8) to appreciation of the late Durkheim by scholars such as Jeffrey Alexander (1982, 1988; see chapter 3).

In the work of Parsons' student, Clifford Geertz, for example, culture is viewed as the publicly available symbolic forms through which people experience and express meaning. Geertz's wonderfully evocative analyses helped advance the new definition of culture. His portrayal of the Balinese cockfight with its layers upon layers of meaning did much to legitimate the study of popular culture (1973). In the essay on the cockfight Geertz showed how the cockfight itself revealed solidarities and divisions in Balinese society and offered men the opportunity to work through those relationships in a sporting situation. It also depicted Balinese social character and the ways that character was revealed in the relationships between Balinese men and their "cocks." Geertz's portrayal of the cockfight exemplifies his notion that expressive symbols do not simply reflect relations in a society, but are both "models of" and "models for" behavior. The richness of Geertz's analysis of this popular form opened the way for sociologists and anthropologists to turn their attention to popular culture in their own societies.

This new focus on culture as expressive symbols has consequences for how we think about the ways people use culture. First, we examine how individuals use culture to express both their individuality and their identification with a group. We then explore a number of ways of thinking about the relations between (1) a dominant culture and relatively autonomous subcultures and (2) a dominant culture and oppositional cultures. The idea of oppositional culture leads to the topic of cultural change. Throughout the chapter we are concerned with how reconceptualizing culture as expressive symbols affects our understanding of action and agency.

MATERIAL CULTURE

Material goods can be an aspect of culture, but only when they are assigned some meaning. In chapter 5 we discussed the development of consumption both in terms of a change in attitude, where consuming became defined as a social good, and a change in people's consumption habits. During this "consumption revolution" ordinary individuals and members of groups began to use consumption to express themselves to a far greater degree than had been possible before. In that chapter we looked at how producers, advertisers, and merchants fostered the changes. At this point we turn to the consumers to ask what consumption means to them. We briefly consider research on individual attribution of meaning to things, and then move to examine how groups—sometimes unselfconsciously but sometimes with explicit intention—express themselves through consumption patterns and styles, thereby turning "things" into "culture."

The Meaning of Things

Goods that have cultural or subcultural meaning can be used to express meanings by individuals. Csikszentmihalyi and Rochberg-Halton (1981) have studied how people talk about what things mean to them. One finding documented by their study concerns the process of interpretation at the individual level. Unlikely associations are sometimes established between meaning and objects. A couple may cherish a specific television, for example, because it reminds them of someone. Some patterns emerge in how meanings become attached to objects. The responses elicited in this study show the extent to which the "things" discussed by the respondents had such individualized meanings.

Mary Douglas and Baron Isherwood (1979) have also considered how individuals use material objects, and much of their discussion focuses on how people use objects to convey meanings to others. They note, for example that upper-class people develop exclusive patterns of consumption which express and maintain members' status. In their view, ritual conventions such as these set up visible public definitions.

Consumption Patterns and Communities

As chapter 6 suggested, distinctive patterns of consumption, especially when they are recognized by the groups themselves as symbolically constitutive of communities, provide important examples of the ways that consumption patterns are structured in modern societies. Social communities are not always circumscribed in fixed spatial terms (consider a community of motorcycle riders). Still, proximity in physical space enhances the possibility of social community, and to some extent, culture is stratified by geographic location. For all the influence of the mass media, the relatively open cultures of the country and of small towns still differ from the cosmopolitan culture of urban life, where sheer density of social interaction encourages certain cultural solutions—aloofness, reserve, and a blasé attitude (classically described by Simmel, 1950). Moreover, there is substantial variation in culture from region to region: Even if some broad socio-economic strata and lifestyles have their counterparts in each region, there are still regional differences observable in New England, the urban Northeast, the South, the Midwest, the West, and the West coast (cf. Lamont 1992). Whether in Minnesota or Brooklyn, local denizens will be able to acquaint the outsider with the subtle but locally important cultural differences in "who we are," and "who they are."

A number of community studies have documented the distinctive cultures of urban neighborhoods, small towns and suburbs. Herbert Gans (1962) has shown how second-generation Italian-Americans in the West End of Boston carried forward certain traditional ways of doing things. The relatively poor Italian-Americans in the neighborhood Gans studied form a "peer group society" where the privacy and consumption, so valued in the middle classes, are not so important, while great emphasis is placed on visiting among family and friends, maintaining relationships of reciprocity in gifts and favors, and rejecting the upward social mobility that would undermine the solidarity of the community. These enduring qualities of Italian-American community life have been immortalized in films such as Cher's "Moon-struck." Yet for all the specifically ethnic symbols and customs, Gans asks whether the community is fundamentally an ethnic or a class phenomenon, and he concludes that class is the fundamental determinant of the culture: Even if it is elaborated in ethnically specific terms, the culture is structurally equivalent in its worldview and practices to those of other working class ethnic communities. This finding suggests that we should be wary of trends "in the suburbs," as a monolithic phenomenon, when in fact numerous categories of people are relocating to the suburbs, bringing diverse lifestyles from cities, small towns, and other countries.

At least since suburbs began to be manufactured en mass by developers at the end of World War II, they have been the source of great controversy. Both members of the urban working class and cosmopolitan sophisticates often have disdained the suburbs of the middle classes for their supposed homogeneity, alienation, and boredom. Yet Gans argues that this is in some respects an outsider's stereotype: It is true that most suburbs tend to be more homogeneous than cities or towns, where a greater variety of people can be found within a similar geographic space, and that the suburbs lack the vitality of culture and the density of social interaction found in the cities. But Gans points out that many people choose to live in the suburbs precisely to escape these features of the city. Further, his research on the early suburb of Levittown suggests that even in a nearly "instant" community, public space is more friendly than that of the city, and a new pattern of sociability quickly emerges centered around people's homes—outside of public space. Perhaps because of the relative homogeneity, combined with the fact that inhabitants choose to move to the suburb, interpersonal relations may obtain a depth and vitality that is not always easy to sustain in the more tradition-bound world of the working-class city neighborhood or the often fleeting contacts of professional upper-middle-class urban life; moreover, Levittowners were quickly immersed in a complex web of formal and informal organizations, from the Cub Scouts to babysitting exchange associations (Gans 1967).

Suburban culture may also have encouraged the development of whole new subcultures. The social observer Tom Wolfe coined the term "status spheres" to describe the nouveau creation of status on terms that fall outside traditional hierarchies (1968). Distinction does not often depend on the old symbols of wealth—playing polo or having a "coming out" party. New status orders can be established on the basis of virtually any activity or object of consumption, from hunting and all-terrain vehicle recreation to waterskiing, a music scene around jazz or rock or rap, surfing, skateboarding, folk dancing, flea markets, and craft fairs. Such status spheres may themselves be graded by class distinctions, but they may also establish a realm "beyond" class, where status is judged on other grounds, such as athletic ability or artistic talent. With the proliferation of status spheres, it is no longer easy to sustain the classical view of Marxists (and Weber as well) that class position fundamentally shapes consciousness. Workers are less and less embedded in strictly working-class communities (Halle 1984), and they participate in mass culture in ways that decrease identification with working-class culture.

The heterogeneity among suburbs also raises the issue of autonomy. What kinds of choices are available in the suburban choice: How is making the choice to move to the suburban environment a "commitment" to a constraining set of practices? On the other hand, how do people make varied use of the materiel objects they acquire? Early critics of the sameness of Levittown were surprised to find that within a decade owners had altered the appearance of their houses—changing the siding, building additions, doing landscaping, and so on, to create more personal and distinctive houses. In a move that Gottdiener could have predicted, later suburban tract housing contractors attempted to take this "taste" into effect and offer minor variations in the housing they built.

On Style

This kind of gentle resistance to homogeneity (in the context of a choice that limits difference) can be compared with the more self-conscious expressions of some groups that position themselves more explicitly at variance with the dominant culture. At the other end of the continuum are the "in-your-face" confrontational styles of some counter cultural groups. Willis (1977, 1990) examines youth subcultures in Britain, and documents the push for autonomy through the creation of various subcultural expressions: Music, dress, and styles of banter being important ones. These sorts of expressions—clothing, for example—are often taken as trivial, but Willis maintains that they are vital for the sustenance of individual and group identities. The body itself carries meaning and is manipulated in various ways by participants in particular subcultures to express various sorts of meaning (c.f. Sanders 1988).

Symbols of course, are multi-vocal—they can carry more than one meaning. In an evocative essay, Andrea Benton Rushing (1988) writes of her history, and that of her daughters and her mother, by talking about her hair. As the piece begins she has landed in Ghana, accompanying her engineer husband to a job. She and her three daughters all had their hair styled in Afros, but found they were hot: "One-third of your body's heat escapes through the scalp's pores. While it struggles to fight its way through six inches of hair, you just plain suffer" (1988, pp. 325–326). So they did the practical thing: They changed their hair style to the local closely braided cornrows. Actions are rarely only practical, however. Six years later, still in cornrows, she states, that now "wherever my three daughters and I go...people stare at us" (1988, p. 326). The cornrows have different meanings for Rushing and for her observers.

In the essay we learn of her "conversion" from the straightened hair that was the standard in her childhood. She recounts the embarrassment that

FIGURE 10.1 This table is set for the karamu feast on the last day of *kwanzaa*, an African American holiday at the end of December. Although Kwanzaa was created by Maulana Karenga, a black studies professor in California 25 years ago, it draws on a number of African festivals celebrating the first fruits of the harvest. (*Source:* Amos Chan.)

she felt when as a child she once let her straightened bangs get wet—snow melted on them—and they were suddenly curly. In the early 1960s when she saw the singer Odetta at a nightclub: "I was mesmerized by her stunning face framed in its short kinky halo..." (1988, p. 334), but it was ten years before she adopted "natural hair." She told her disapproving teachers that "the personal is political" and tried to convert others to the natural style. Furthermore, "long before they were born, back in the glory days of black being beautiful, I'd vowed that no daughter of mine would have her hair straightened as long as she lived with me" (p. 328). First the Afro and then the cornrows provided a way of instantly communicating her identification with Afro-american culture.

Yet the essay also contains a confession: Speaking of one of her daughters pleading for "just a little Vigoral or Lustrasilk in her hair to make it easier to comb," she says, "I have kept faith with the nappy pride of black is beautiful. And, yet I've betrayed my heritage after all. I am, you see, a beautician's daughter" (1988, p. 328). While telling tales of a line of female beauticians she ponders how to make that connection for her daughters:

And I've heard (my daughter) telling her web of friends about how neatly braided hairdos are one Yoruba way of reflecting order and balance in the cosmos. I've kept her from Jeri curls, blow dryers, and styling rods.... She knows about Oshun rituals, but she would give me her most bored look if I claimed all those hairdressers in our family were priestesses who could conjure.... Like the styles the Yoruba women create and wear, the ones my family did spoke, too: though what they said was about transformation, not about cosmic order... (1988, p. 331).

Using the symbol of hair, Rushing locates herself within several traditions; in the essay she speaks of the brothers of black is beautiful as well as of her hairdresser mother. In the narrative she performs a "transformation" herself: For her daughters she reinterprets the work of her mother, aunts, and grandmothers as ritual priestesses, symbols that her daughters recognize (but perhaps the women whose stories she tells would not).

Levittowners who altered the appearance of their houses were expressing their individuality in asserting their own taste preferences within the confines of the suburb. Rushing's cornrows, or a decision to celebrate Kwanzaa, signify identification with an oppositional culture, as well as her individual preferences. The examples suggest that our understandings of expressive culture need to be informed by theories not only about what things mean to people but the conditions under which they choose one expressive symbol over another. Important conditions for choice are rooted in the relation of an individual to the dominant culture, relations which are structured by race and gender as well as class and region.

CULTURE AND ACTION

To begin to reformulate culture in terms of expressive symbols has implications for how culture fits into some of the debates that have shaped the discipline of sociology. Two of those debates are relevant here. One is the debate about whether material interests or normative (ideal) concerns motivate individual behavior. If, in studying culture, we turn our focus from values and norms to practices and narratives, what are the consequences for our theory of action? The other debate is about the relation between the individual and the society, variously conceived as a debate about "order" or "agency," depending on whether the theorist wanted to put the emphasis on choices individuals make or on the ways that choices are constrained by society. While these two debates have surfaced throughout the present book, here we look directly at the consequences of the redefinition of culture for three approaches which have attempted to address one or both of these questions. First we examine a reconstruction of a Parsonian action framework by Ann Swidler and others, then a symbolic interactionist reformulation of the concept of subculture by Gary Alan Fine, and finally a semiotic approach by Mark Gottdiener that reconfigures Marxist analyses of cultural hegemony.

Culture as a Tool Kit

Swidler sees as the traditional view expressed in action theory "that culture shapes action by supplying ultimate ends or values toward which action is directed" (1986, p. 273) as flawed. Like other recent theorists, she recognizes the importance of examining expressive symbols rather than values in the sociology of culture, but she worries that the interpretive approach "skirts the issue of explanation." In discarding the older explanations of how cultural values motivate action, the interpretive theorists have—unnecessarily in Swidler's view—abandoned any kind of causal analysis. Swidler's alternative is to propose that culture should be seen as a "tool kit." Analysis then should focus on "strategies of action." In Swidler's model, culture acts as a causal agent not in defining ends (i.e., values), but "in providing cultural components that are used to construct strategies of action" (1986, p. 273).

When Weber spoke of ideas as motivating action, he was concerned with specific historical instances in which ideas and actions were shaped by complex sets of material and ideal interests. Swidler argues that for Parsons, concrete historical ideas become "global, ahistorical values" (1986, p. 274). Swidler suggests that the theory of culture as values persists because the claim that "culture shapes action by defining what people want" is intuitively plausible. But she counters that "what people want" is "of little help in explaining their action." It needs to be recognized that this notion of values as "what people want" equates values with preferences, hardly what Parsons had in mind. Yet this confusion—born out of economic and psychological models of human behavior—is so pervasive in American ways of thinking that even sociologists like Bellah (discussed in chapter 2), who continue to be interested in how ideals shape behavior, do not use the term "values" anymore, not even when describing "justice" or "success" as ideas that form people's definitions of the good society.

For Swidler, a Weberian formulation argues for ideas shaping action. By contrast, for Swidler, it is "continuities of style" or "the way action is organized" that endure. She points to Weber's own example of the Protestant ethic and argues that "reliance on moral 'work' on the self has been a more enduring feature of Protestantism than the particular ends to which this work has been directed" (1986, p. 276). From Calvin to Benjamin Franklin to modern sex manuals there have been changes in the "ends" with which the Protestant work ethic has been aligned, yet there is something of the ethos that continues to be culturally recognizable.

To think about "the way action is organized" means trying to understand how individual actions are linked. Many social theories (both idealist and materialist) present action as though people choose one action at a time. Swidler, on the other hand, believes people choose one or another "strategy" (which means not a plan, but rather a "way of organizing action"). This strategy model is similar to the notion of commitment in symbolic interaction: Taking one action may "commit" an individual to other actions in the future or make other actions easier or more likely as a consequence of the first action (Becker 1960). Swidler assumes that people "do not build lines of action from scratch" but rather that they use at least some "pre-fabricated links." When Becker wrote about commitment he was most interested in links that were organizational and institutional.[1] Swidler states that "All real cultures contain diverse, often conflicting symbols, rituals, stories and guides to action" (1986, p. 277). People choose among the "tools" available within a culture—and there are always more such tools than can be used in any given situation.

However, patterns of use will be different under different social conditions. Swidler distinguishes how culture works in situations of continuity (when people have settled lives) from how culture works in times of change (when people have unsettled lives). In stable times cultural experiences and socially structured situations reinforce each other, but when times are unsettled, ideologies which develop can establish new styles or strategies for action.

Swidler suggests that cultural strategies vary in the degree to which they can be taken-for-granted. Ideologies—sets of self-consciously articulated and deliberately linked propositions—are least taken-for-granted. But ideologies are at one end of a continuum with "tradition" at a mid-point (it can be articulated but need not be) and common sense (nearly always taken for granted) at the other end. Ideologies compete with each other for members; the competition in itself forces their promoters to make the ideologies more coherent in order to distinguish them from each other. Swidler asserts, "[Ideologies] are thus causally powerful, but in a restricted sense. Rather than providing the underlying assumptions of an entire way of life, they make explicit demands in a contested cultural arena" (1986, p. 282). However, ideologies have narrower scope than the less consistent but more encapsulating cultures of settled times. It is an empirical question to ask when and under what circumstances ideologies become traditions.

Conflicts such as the one over abortion illustrate Swidler's model of ideology. Two ideologies—each coherent, each prescribing strong control over action—compete with one another. However, each ideology continues to depend on "tradition" and "common sense" for resolution of various issues not explicitly covered by the ideology. This is particularly apparent in Faye Ginsberg's (1990) study of prochoice and prolife movements in Fargo, North Dakota. Despite finding themselves on opposing sides in one of the most bitter controversies of our time, the women on each side in this small midwestern city seemed to have a difficult time casting those on the other side as "the enemy." Individuals who have lived their lives in this small city continue to be enmeshed in relationships that are not determined by the ideology of the abortion movements, and there is always the possibility of face-to-face contact with individuals who may live on the same block or have kids in the same schools.

---

[1] Although in his work on art worlds (discussed in chapter 8), Becker develops a formulation of culture-as-practice based on the idea of conventions.

In order to understand why one ideology wins out, however, the analysts must move beyond the cultural tool-kits model. Ideologies must be placed in context, identifying particular structural constraints and historical circumstances in which they operate. Swidler's understanding of settled and unsettled times is partially an attempt to do just that. But it leaves many issues to be addressed. In Swidler's model there is little exploration of how individuals actually choose from among the tools in the tool kit. Strategies carry costs to individuals and to groups, but Swidler offers little discussion of this. Furthermore, as the abortion example exemplifies, it is not clear that it is necessarily the *times* that are settled or unsettled. It may in fact be the circumstances. In the United States with many "single issue" social movements, individuals can find themselves in settings that are highly ideological. Yet others may be able to avoid such contexts.

In contrast to the unsettled times/circumstances of the abortion controversy, in settled times/circumstances cultures are "more encompassing," but they exercise less direct control over action. Under such conditions the tool metaphor is most accurate: People select cultural elements and invest them with meaning. A family's holiday celebration may combine selected "traditions" from both the husband's and wife's pasts, as well as elements picked up from the newspaper. Swidler argues that "the influence of culture in settled lives is especially strong in structuring those uninstitutionalized, but recurrent situations in which people act in concert" (1986, p. 281).

In this model, values are less important in determining choices in unsettled times than during settled times. In unsettled times contingencies in the structures of opportunities may be more determining of what people choose. In general Swidler suggests that values do not shape actions; rather, people use values to make small adjustments in action within established patterns of living.

An important aspect of this approach is its identification of strategies of action—actions linked together into "chunks of culture." For Swidler the problem with assuming that either values or interests motivate human behavior is that both sorts of explanations seem to focus too narrowly on individual acts, while action typically is integrated into larger clusters that she calls strategies of action. It is this clustered or "package" aspect of social life that both individuals and groups play upon in order to increase commitment to a particular line of action.

This formulation illuminates how people use styles and traditional "ways of doing things," especially in settled times or places, to construct meaningful lives. There are always choices to be made insofar as there are more "tools" available than any one person can use at any one time.

Contested Meaning

Swidler's discussion of the development of ideology suggests that in unsettled times societies contain competing cultures. Also, the notions of the tool kit and of "chunks of culture" imply that cultural expressions will not be the same for everybody. Still, Swidler seems to be talking about a "dominant culture" that exists with varying degrees of taken-for-grantedness, its very existence sometimes challenged by contesting ideologies and sometimes placidly accepted. Other writers in the sociology of culture question to what extent a taken-for-granted dominant culture exists anymore. Many modern societies are characterized by high degrees of heterogeneity, in which different groups have different degrees of commitment to any supposedly dominant culture. Social theories need to be able to talk about how groups actually come into conflict over cultural expression. Swidler's settled times/unsettled times does this incompletely since at any given time some subgroups are likely to have a relation to the dominant culture which makes it advantageous for them to take it for granted: Their positions of relative privilege protect them. For others in different social locations, challenging the dominant culture may be a much more obvious strategy.

In a recent study of the Vietnam Veteran's Memorial, Wagner- Pacifici and Schwartz (1991) analyze a case where consensus was lacking: The content and the symbols themselves were contested by the parties in the negotiations. Although the memorial was to be a public symbol that would recognize those who had died in the Vietnam War, the sponsors of the monument faced the difficult task of commemorating a defeat, about which there was no public consensus, and they became caught up in a series of negotiations regarding the unconventional style chosen for the memorial itself. Wagner-Pacifici and Schwartz argue that the construction of the Vietnam memorial embodied conflicting views about the meaning of the war and about what fits within the genre of the war memorial. They argue that the break with the conventional genre corresponds to the break with previous interpretation of memorialized wars.

In addition, however, they state that after the memorial was in place these conflicts were overlaid with new meanings that arose in the use of the memorial by the large numbers of people who visit it. To make sense of these new meanings, they draw on Durkheim's influential analysis of the social functions of ritual (see chapter 3), which sought to explain how various kinds of expressive rites and commemorations—religious and other—produce individuals's feelings of identification with the group and with one another (1964). For Durkheim what produces the effect is not abstract values but the symbolic acts and expressions. It is the collective use of the Vietnam memorial in symbolic acts that makes it, in Durkheimian terms, a sacred space. Wagner-Pacifici and Schwartz argue that the wall evokes a particular response, a kind of ambivalence, that is not typical of war memorials:

> In the Veterans Memorial, then we see none of the hegemonic influence that forms the basis for..."manipulative theories" of secular symbolism.... If the Memorial were in fact a tool of state power, if it were adopted by the state in order to maintain allegiance to an elite and to promote authoritative ways of seeing society...then that tool has not been used very effectively (1991, pp. 406–407).

Wagner-Pacifici and Schwartz argue that people may need ritual to deal with the Vietnam War as a painful and controversial part of the past, even though the rituals "are not rituals that Durkheim would have recognized" since they do not reinforce common sentiments (1991, p. 417).

This ambivalence regarding a painful past can also be seen in the debates in Germany following the destruction of the Berlin Wall and the unification (of the two Germanies, East and West) or the reunification (of one Germany, temporarily separated in the aftermath of World War II), depending on whose interpretation you follow. Germans faced the question of whether Berlin or Bonn would be the capital of the new Germany; and if Berlin, whether the capital of Germany would be the Berlin of Hitler or the Berlin of Kaiser Wilhelm.

As we begin to recognize the multi-cultural base of modern societies it becomes more important to have theories that speak about the sorts of claims made for the dominant culture as well as where and when challenges are likely to occur. Wagner-Pacifici and Schwartz significantly expand Durkheim's formulation in this regard when they suggest that the rituals do not reinforce common sentiments. Yet their analysis presents the Vietnam War Memorial as a national symbol and the ritual as promoting a unifying healing. Some critics of this approach have questioned whether the groups in American society who found themselves on opposing side over the Vietnam conflict have been reunited (e.g., Zolberg 1990, p. 103).

Subcultures and Expressive Symbols

Within symbolic interactionism there is also a critique of the older emphasis on values and a movement toward examining culture as expressive behaviors and symbols. Recent interactionist work on subcultures focuses on symbolic culture in a way that is consistent with a well established line of work in symbolic interactionism that sees action as contingent and emergent, while also exploring how certain choices in fact commit a person to a line of action (Becker 1960; Becker et al. 1961).

The concept of subculture was first used in sociology to talk about ethnic groups. Later it was applied to youth culture, where, it was used extensively to talk about deviant groups. Early Chicago school sociologists such as Fredrick Thrasher and Edwin Sutherland argued against the idea that certain ethnic groups were inherently more likely to commit crimes. They had observed that the ethnic composition of neighborhoods in the city changed, but that the neighborhoods' crime rates continued at the same levels. They argued that deviant behaviors were learned through a process of cultural transmission through primary groups—friends in the neighborhood—by what they called differential association. They believed that members of delinquent gangs learned both to engage in deviant behaviors and to value deviant activities and came to prefer them to a conventional life.

The concept of subculture emerged in the context of an argument about whether differences in values could explain whether people would engage in delinquent and criminal behavior as well as behavior that simply violated norms (such as women having children without being married). An alternative explanation was posed: Deviant behavior occurred because the individuals involved were denied access to legitimate opportunities and/or had access to deviant opportunities. The theories of subculture developed by sociologists studying delinquents emphasized socialization into encapsulating subcultures with value systems at odds with conventional values (e.g., Cohen 1955; Miller 1958).

This conceptualization of deviant subcultures was challenged not only by theorists who explained deviance primarily on the basis of structural factors, but also by some who had different conceptions of how to think about subcultures. In an argument that prefigures the current emphasis on expressive symbols, David Matza suggested that there existed a "subculture of delinquency," but it was not a "delinquent subculture" (1964, p. 33). Matza argued that, while individuals participate in a social group that engages in deviant acts, it does not follow that the members of the group have repudiated the values of the dominant culture. He argued that "norms may be violated without surrendering allegiance to them" (1964, p. 60).

Matza's delinquents hung around in the company of other delinquents. They occasionally engaged in illegal activities, but more frequently did not, and most of them grew up to have conventional jobs and lives. Matza suggested that much of the subculture of delinquency consisted of forms of interaction among and between gang members. Gangs today engage in more violent acts than did those Matza studied (and are much more likely to have guns), and they are probably more involved with illegal drug-related activities. Yet Matza's point still seems to hold: Much of gang culture consists of expressive acts designed to send messages to other gang members. The "Bloods" and the "Crips" are oriented to each other: Although outsiders sometimes witness gang behavior—and may even get caught in the cross-fire between rival gangs—they are a secondary concern for gang members. Assigning colors and symbols and dividing up territory do not in themselves constitute violations of conventional behavior. Such activities do not differ in kind from the team spirit and rivalries encouraged by every high school, although gangs often pursue them in ways that are more lethal.[2] Matza argued that the sociological understandings of subculture then current placed too much emphasis on norms. However, although the two cannot be completely separated, Matza's interests were in how individuals come to identify themselves as deviants rather than in how their identification was expressed in their daily practice (see also Matza 1969).

---

[2] In Los Angeles county in 1991, 771 people are reported to have died in gang violence. The violence was not primarily drug-related: Out of 207 deaths investigated by the sheriff's department only five were directly linked to drugs (*New York Times,* May 24, 1992, p. 8).

Gary Alan Fine and Sherryl Kleinman offer a fuller and more systematic critique of how sociologists have used the concept of subculture. Their attempt at reformulating the concept departs from the tendency to associate the concept with deviant or lower-class groups in society, and the attendant pejorative connotations. Fine and Kleinman (1979) make four points in their critique. First, they argue that most analyses have confused "subcultures" and "subsocieties." Membership in a group often is lumped together with sharing values, knowing behaviors, and conscious identification with the group. Fine and Kleinman argue (as we have in chapter 1) for an analytical distinction between the group (or subsociety) and the subculture. Second, they suggest that it is important to know who the population is that shares the subculture. They find the usual demographic markers misleading: Not all people of a certain age will share in the youth culture; not all members of established social groups will share specialized knowledge that is explicitly unavailable to outsiders; and, some outsiders will have some knowledge of the culture. Third, Fine and Kleinman argue that subcultures tend to be perceived as "homogenous, static and closed" whereas in reality information "flows across the boundaries" of the subculture. Their fourth point is that the work on subculture has focused on values, to the neglect of behaviors, norms and material culture and artifacts.

Fine is less interested in the differences between dominant cultural values and subcultural values than in understanding changes in subcultural content. He wants to be able to explain both how cultural elements can be diffused widely in a population and how local variations in cultural content come to exist. Fine (1979) describes the process of culture creation in small groups; Fine and Kleinman (1979) suggest how subcultural elements diffuse across groups. While the mass media is instrumental in this process, Fine and Kleinman resist the notion that individuals or groups simply take in whatever is transmitted by the mass media. They refer to the rapid spread of cultural contents such as jokes, stories, and urban legends which travel outside the mass media, as well as to cultural forms available through the mass media that do not get picked up.

Fine speaks of the particular "ideo-cultures" created within groups such as the little league baseball teams that he studied (1987). Groups develop culture when cultural forms are already known to some individuals, when the cultural forms are usable to members of the group, and when they are congruent with the goals and needs of the group (when the new forms solve problems or entertain or contribute to group solidarity). Cultural forms are more likely to be adopted when they are appropriate to the group, especially when they support the power structure of the group. Finally, particular cultural innovations of adoptions may be triggered by an event in the life of the group (Fine 1979, pp. 738–44).

Members of any particular group also belong to other groups and carry knowledge about cultural forms between groups. The ideo-culture of a group is a product of negotiations among members situated in a particular social context: For Fine, "Culture is a construction based on the consensual meaning system of members; it comprises the interactional products that result from verbal and behavioral representation of that meaning system" (1979, p. 744). Thus, for team members, ideo-culture includes the giving of nicknames to group members, as well as rules about whether gum chewing is appropriate.

Earlier theories described subcultures as exclusive, but Fine and Kleinman make the essential point that participants in any one subculture are likely to belong to multiple groups. Even though cultural content is defined in a process of negotiation in small groups, it is through networks of participants that cultural forms diffuse to other individuals and groups. Here, as in other aspects of social life, weak ties between people promote the spread of subcultural forms (1979, pp. 10–12). Change occurs through contact between people who are members of subcultures and people who are not.

The kinds of subcultural participation and group membership described by Fine and Kleinman raise issues about the degree to which individuals identify with any given subculture and how broader communities respond to subcultures. Fine and Kleinman distinguish between *knowledge* of a cultural form and *use* of a cultural form: "culture usage consists of chosen behaviors" (1979, p. 12). Enacting the behaviors, they suggest, depends upon identification with the subculture, and it is possible for the identification to be latent much of the time. Identification with the subculture may vary in centrality—the degree of "commitment to the population segment"—and in salience—the frequency of identification (1979, p. 13). In the first instance, the same young person can identify with the category "urban youth" or with a particular local gang with different consequences for action. In the second instance being a gang member may be more or less salient, that is, it takes up more or less of an adolescent's life.

Negative responses by outsiders can have the effect of increasing the salience of identification with the subculture (Fine and Kleinman 1979, p. 15). For example, the distinctive robes and shaved heads of Hari Krishna devotees clearly mark them to outsiders, making identification with that subculture more costly and more exclusive. Subcultures that face negative labeling by outsiders may develop subtle ways of signalling participation to one another. Judy Grahn has written about gay culture in high schools in the 1950s where wearing purple on Thursdays or rings on particular fingers signified one's identity to other gay students (Grahn 1984, pp. 1–20).

Such analyses of subcultures open up ways of thinking about groups with their own cultural forms and symbolic expressions. According to Fine (1987) each little league baseball team had its own particular cultural forms and expressions with particular cultural content. Little league baseball teams across the country also had symbolic forms in common. Without having the explicit character that Swidler attributes to ideologies, subcultures cannot be entirely taken-for-granted either: They offer alternative cultural "tools" to participants.

Cultural Conflict and Countercultures

The relation between the dominant culture and subcultures is emphasized in other formulations which focus on "oppositional cultures" or "countercultures"—subcultures which define themselves in opposition to a dominant culture. Ironically, one criticism of Marxist formulations about cultural hegemony (e.g., Tuchman 1974 or Gitlin 1980) is that they fail to adequately appreciate the possibilities for cultural conflict because their framework tends to assume that the dominant culture effectively precludes alternatives.

Mark Gottdiener points out that even in cases where elites control the production of culture they cannot control the interpretations that individuals give to cultural products: "ideological domination of mass culture industries is...not guaranteed to control or even affect an audience's behavior" (1985, p. 989). Not only are individual interpretations of mass culture variable, but—more important to Gottdiener—interpretations vary with subcultural involvement.

Understanding the relation between subcultures and the dominant society is crucial to Gottdiener's analysis of mass culture. He states that "before there is 'mass culture' there must be 'culture,' that is, the conceptual forms and accumulated knowledge by which social groups organize everyday experience within social and material contexts" (1985, p. 991). In modern societies, individuals are involved in social groups and networks with their own cultural forms. British working class youth cultures, for example, developed resisting both the cultures of their working class parents and the dominant culture (Hebdige 1979; Willis 1977). American Buddhism has developed in contrast to both the dominant American culture and the Asian parent cultures of Buddhism (Boucher 1988). Gottdiener grounds such interpretive processes of culture-forming in the group life of individuals. Gottdiener is particularly interested in those cases where a cultural form that comes out of such contexts is taken over by mass culture industries.

Gottdiener outlines three stages in his analysis of the production and control of ideological meanings. The first stage occurs between mass producer and user. Producers use marketing and distribution processes to convince potential buyers that the distributed products are worth buying and will meet the customer's needs. The second stage involves the user/object relation, a point at which the users are involved in the production of meaning. Gottdiener states that "users modify objects of mass consumption in order to express certain cultural symbols or in conjunction with specific group practices or for use in subcultural activities" (1985, p. 955). But producers, as was noted in chapter 9, have incentives to reproduce the users's adaptations of their products by modifying the original products, so long as they judge that there is a market for the modified goods. This is essentially Gottdiener's third stage, the borrowing of user meanings by producers themselves. This reproduction of user meanings, however, is not identical to the meanings created

FIGURE 10.2 The collections of fashion designers reflect the ability of mass culture industries to pick up ideas that began in oppositional subcultures. These styles exhibit elements originating among rock and gay and lesbian subcultures, and now are the products of designers and reported in this 1991 *Vogue* magazine. (*Source:* Courtesy of Donna Karan, N.Y.)

within a given subculture: Producers make the personalized objects of the subculture into more marketable, less radical objects.

In this process the producers take what is meaningful within the context of the subculture and mass produce it for a larger market. Airports in major cities, for example, frequently feature little shops with mass produced items that vaguely resemble regional "material folk culture" such as jams and jellies and stuffed dolls: Busy travelers can buy regionally distinctive gifts to give to their families when they return home. At one time (and still in some subcultural pockets) such items would have been produced at home as gifts. More recently they might have been locally produced for local markets, and for the tourists driving through the countryside. The "country crafts" sold in the airport boutique have little resemblance to the objects produced and exchanged within the subculture. As Gottdiener notes, "mass culture producers have the ability to manipulate, if not dominate, the process of cultural production" (1985, p. 997).

At the same time, however, Gottdiener maintains that consciousness cannot be controlled. While he provides a basis for rejecting as too simple the idea of cultural control or hegemony, his analysis also describes a process where subcultures struggle to maintain autonomy in the face of mass culture. The threats to autonomy can be seen not only when subcultural forms are reproduced in a sanitized version by the mass media, but in a more extreme way when the subcultural producers themselves end up producing for the market, as we have seen in chapter 3 with indigenous artists who learn to produce "tourist art" to the exclusion of subcultural production. This model has implications both for talking about autonomous subcultures— those that see themselves in important ways as separate from the dominant culture—as well as cultures that define themselves in opposition to the dominate culture.

In a study that combines interactionist and Marxist elements, Richard Lachman (1988) offers insight into both a youth subculture (that of New York City graffiti writers) and the issue of autonomous culture production among oppositional cultures. Lachman studies both the "careers" and "ideology" of New York City graffiti writers. Largely through contact with "mentors," would-be graffiti writers develop a sense that they could achieve fame through graffiti writing. Once they learn the basic skills, "taggers" attempt to write their names (tags) on as many subway cars as possible in order to become "king of the line." There is an element of danger involved since the graffiti writing is illegal, and must be done covertly to avoid getting caught and arrested or beaten up by the police. Taggers have relatively short careers of intense activity during which they establish their fame, and then, according to school counselors Lachman interviewed, they rest on their laurels and go back to school. The school counselors reported that taggers actually had a better chance of finishing than other students, in part because they were people who were capable of focused efforts in different realms, but also because they had "proven themselves" through tagging and therefore did not have to get involved in more violent aspects of street gangs. Tagging is a cultural form appreciated by a local audience—other taggers and high school students—and occasionally adopted by gang patrons: One gang will recruit and hire a tagger with "style" to establish the gang's "tag" in territories where the gang is involved in a dispute with another gang.

Yet for two brief periods, in 1973–74 and 1982–83, muralists—graffiti artists who went beyond writing their tags and painted entire murals on subways cars—were adopted by art dealers in the New York art world. Lachman argues that the dealers were not really interested in coopting the particular alternative aesthetic and social form of the graffiti writers, but rather their interest was a product of the continual demand in the art market for stylistic innovation. However, because the works "violated so many of the post-modernist canons," art world interest in them did not last long. In the 1970s muralists formed their own art world, gathering in "writers' corners" in subway stations to view and judge the work of other graffiti artists. In the early period the "writers at all career levels agreed that a writer's standing was determined by his subway work...and that gallery shows and sales were the rewards not the arbiters of writers' graffiti reputation" (1988, p. 427). Lachman argues that the destruction of these meeting places by the police also destroyed the collective base of graffiti writers' art world and opened the way for the possibility of cooptation.

Following the work of the Birmingham school (Hall 1976; Hebdige 1979) Lachman makes the assumption that the dominant culture is likely to respond to the subculture's challenge either by repressive or cooptational responses. Partly on the basis of this study, he suggests that commodification as cooptational response is limited to the extent that the subculture can be maintained as a movement of resistance to the dominant culture. When people can be bought off by the rewards of the dominant culture, something else must have happened to undermine the members' beliefs in the alternative subculture: "Only by undermining the organizational bases for sustaining belief in the subculture's alternative view of reality could graffiti writers, or anyone else, be attracted to a conception of reality they had previously rejected" (1988, p. 249).

In Lachman's study of graffiti writers we see the particular culture of the graffiti writers themselves and their opposition to the dominant culture and accommodation to gang culture. Graffiti writers' style was also adopted by mass culture industries as a decorative motif, an act so distant from the graffiti writers themselves that they could not be coopted by it, in part perhaps because, as Lachman suggests, it does not undermine members' beliefs in the oppositional culture. This suggests that although mass culture industries do coopt products from autonomous and oppositional cultures and produce a sanitized version for mass consumption, the culture that first produced the item sometimes is touched by it.

CULTURE AND CHANGE

Swidler's discussion of the workings of culture in unsettled times begins to address issues of culture and social change. Her decision to locate her discussion of ideology in the context of a theory that focuses on expressive symbols has interesting consequences. It forces us to think of ideology as a set of cultural practices rather than as values or ends. Ideology becomes a tool, or perhaps a set of tools in the tool box. Swidler's attempt to sidestep the sociological debate between idealist and materialist explanations is especially noteworthy in the context of ideology. It is in keeping with several writers who conceptualize ideology in terms of "practice" rather than ideals or values.

Ideological Work

For example, one study of the counterculture during the 1960s and 70s (Hall 1978) argues that many young people formed or joined communal living groups in attempts to fulfill certain values—values such as community or spiritual growth—that they did not believe to be easily attained in society-at-large. But the comparative study shows that the diverse cultures of countercultural communal groups cannot be reduced to values, norms or ideologies in any narrow sense. Although value pursuits often inspired communal endeavors, as they became established, groups enacted fundamentally different types of collective life, based on alternative forms of time consciousness and orientations toward symbols. In some groups, the "here and now" was the locus of social life. A group consciousness was enhanced by the process of "going through changes" together: People worked together and conflicts tended to be brought into the arena of public life. Other groups were established in ways that allowed great personal freedom, but at the expense of a shared collective life: Work tended to be coordinated outside the "here and now" by use of bureaucratic planning methods, and conflict tended to remain outside the public realm or become focused in special meetings and occasions. Even in the unsettled times and circumstances of a youth culture flourishing partly through numerous efforts at communal living, only some groups—usually larger and more visible ones—tried to enact highly elaborated ideological visions of utopia. In short, it was not just values and norms that made for the diversity among groups. Communal groups enacted fundamentally different realities by cultivating ways of being in the world that transcend ideology.

Another communal study, by Bennett Berger, analyzes ideological conflict at the level of concrete practices. Berger's book about a California commune, *The Survival of the Counterculture* (1981), takes issue with the "debunking" argument—common to many social scientists' analyses of ideology—that even when people claim to be motivated by values, they are really acting out of self interest. The debunker's account of the politician who claims that he desires only to serve the people (and knows what to do because of his enlightened perspective), but is revealed to be driven by his own ambition and greed has been absorbed into American mythology.[3] But, in fact, in many aspects of life the interests of the individual are aligned with the interests of the institution or group.

Berger suggests that "values" and "interests" do not have to be in conflict and in fact people do "ideological work" to reduce the conflict that they feel between values and interests and between one value and another.

> Ideological work enables those engaged in intellectual combat to attempt to persuade their critics and their own constituencies—that apparent discrepancies between preaching and practice are in fact illusory and can be successfully resolved. However clearly "false consciousness" may be abstractly defined, it is usually a contested matter in the concrete case (1981, p. 181).

For Berger, as for Swidler, the terrain of ideology is a contested terrain. Ideological work maintains and strengthens the ideology by addressing concerns about its legitimacy.

The accusation that an ideology operates in the interests of the group has been used by sociologists and others to show how material interests and not humanistic values drive human behavior. Berger suggests that under some circumstances, groups rightly judge it legitimate for ideology to coincide with interests. (They also have ways of judging when such coincidence is self-serving or crazy.) The group's survival depends on developing ways of doing things—ways of dividing up the labor, ways of making decisions—that work for the group both in terms of making sense to members and getting the job done.[4]

Social Movements and Cultural Change

Swidler's discussion of "unsettled times" suggests that changes in practices occur during periods of social transformation. While this is no doubt true, our earlier discussion of ritual and tradition suggested that changes in practices are an ongoing kind of cultural activity: As we said in chapter 2, "the new must be made holy and the holy must be made new." We suggest that cultural change does not necessarily occur at the same time as social revolutions, nor by the same processes.

---

[3] Even volunteers in Wuthnow's study (1991), described in chapter 2, added a formulaic acknowledgment of their own self-interest to their answers to a question about why they volunteered their time to do good works.

[4] Bourdieu (1977) and Sahlins (1976) also have developed conceptualizations of "practice" that define cultural resources that people draw on in constructing patterns of action. Like Swidler and Berger they see these as neither norms and values nor as strictly material determined: There is always more than one possible way to accomplish a task, and "practices" represent the ones generally available in a culture.

Some recent work by European sociologists on what are being designated the "new social movements" suggests that in postindustrial societies we need to shift our analysis from political movements to one that encompasses cultural movements (Touraine 1985; Offe 1985; Melucci 1985; Beckford 1989). Part of the reason is that "contemporary social conflicts are not just political, since they affect the system's cultural production" (Melucci 1985, p. 798). Melucci suggests that the new social movements or movement areas are "increasingly autonomous" from political systems. Their form is quite distinct from that of older political organizations, and, Melucci argues, the form is the message. Militant activity occasionally occurs, but it is the on-going personal involvement in an alternative culture that is central to participation. Melucci argues:

> But beyond modernization, beyond cultural innovation, movements question society on something "else": who decides on codes, who establishes rules of normality, what is the space for difference, how can one be recognized not for being included but for being accepted as different, not for increasing the amount of exchanges, but for affirming another kind of exchange? (1985, p. 810).

The "structurelessness" of such movements offers a challenge both to the dominant culture and to hierarchy within traditional social movements. Certainly countercultural issues of everyday life can surface in concentrated form in communal groups. Yet the communal groups themselves were part of a wider counterculture, and practices such as vegetarianism are now likely to be found among individuals in many different social locations.[5] We are likely to miss the more diffuse and widespread processes of cultural change if we concentrate solely on more organized groups. Cultural transmission and cultural change is facilitated by the movement of transformed individuals not only through groups, but through social networks. Indeed, to the extent that groups are tightly bounded, any broader culture change—going beyond the borders of the group—may be less likely (Neitz 1990).

Rather than looking primarily at organized groups, cultural movements can be approached on two additional levels. First, we need to study the individuals who are carriers of the culture; second, we need to study the ideas and practices that make up the culture. One model suggests that each individual has a somewhat different package of cultural objects, and different parts of the package are put into use in encounters between particular sets of people. Through interaction with others, individuals may find parts of the package becoming newly salient. The emergence of new interests can lead an individual to challenge the collective understanding that is the basis for

---

[5] And many countercultural conflicts with a society at large can only partially be resolved by the adoption of alternative lifestyles because they are concerned with more pervasive cultural practices, laws, or social processes.

collective activity. It is in this spirit that we can trace the history of cultural ideas and motifs as they become reworked by individuals facing new circumstances, sometimes coaxing new meanings out of longstanding cultural themes. The idea of a "promised land," for example, is a central cultural element of both Judaism and Christianity, and one that serves as a touchstone of ever new meanings, from Puritan settlers of North America to black liberation movements of the twentieth century. Even within a given movement that has used the motif of the promised land, the ideological significance of the motif can become reworked as the movement's circumstances change (Hall 1987). Revising Swidler's thesis about the constraining nature of ideologies during times of transition, a more interactionist approach to cultural movements suggests that the choices about which tools from the tool kit to use, and how they work, will often be emergent.

CONCLUSION

In looking at the cultures of symbolic expressions we see the users of cultural objects take on the characteristics of agents. Although constrained in a number of ways—by material resources, the degree of integration into mass culture, or the limits on their knowledge—"users" emerge as something more than consumers.

Both ethnographers and students of popular culture and cultural studies have interests in the question of how people create and interpret cultural objects. At one time ethnographic accounts tended to focus on social networks and social relations, sometimes neglecting analysis of cultural content in favor of uncovering generic social processes. People in cultural studies, on the other hand, focused on cultural content, sometimes without any reference to the interpretations of people who used the culture. The perspectives outlined in this chapter show the necessity of analyzing cultural objects by connecting them to an understanding of users. Conversely, an understanding of users must include knowledge of the cultural objects and expressive symbols themselves.

11

THE FUTURE OF POSTMODERNISM

We have explored diverse ways in which sociological perspectives enrich our understanding of culture. Yet no purely sociological analysis of culture can be a complete analysis: Understanding culture is an interdisciplinary undertaking. Thus the recent interest in culture has created opportunities for drawing the humanities into closer relation to the social sciences and the social science disciplines themselves into closer relation with one another. In the latter disciplines, culture now is central to a variety of social theories—focused on political, economic and social structural analysis, organizations, issues of social solidarity, social movements and action. In the relations between the humanities and sociohistorical inquiry, the growing commitment to examine culture—even "popular" culture—in relation to society, has roots in the emergence of "cultural studies"—interdisciplinary efforts to transcend the boundaries of academic disciplines through a bridging metaphor of culture. Consolidation of cultural studies as an approach can be traced in significant respects to the work of social researchers at the University of Birmingham in Great Britain (Centre for Contemporary Cultural Studies 1980; Johnson 1986–87). Yet there is an irony in how cultural studies have developed since the 1960s: Much of the momentum has come from the humanities, yet the sources of interdisciplinary enrichment in the humanities often have their origins in social philosophy, linguistics, history, structuralist anthropology, symbolic interactionism, social phenomenology, and ethnomethodology. "Cultural studies" displaces the conventional disciplines of social inquiry. But it does so by borrowing from them.

One central thrust of cultural studies depends on taking a "textual turn," by exploring the ways in which the social world is textually represented, categorized and imbued with meaning. Texts, once limited to printed materials, are now to be found in the "cultural scripts" by which people operate in the social world. Even social space—an urban area, suburb, mall, highway, or farming region—can be treated as a "text."[1] To do so, it is only necessary to recognize that people orient actions on the basis of the "signs" we see as intelligible patterns in those worlds. *How* those "texts" are read and whether they have any stable meanings—are questions of reception (considered in chapter 9). Some theorists take a poststructuralist approach, arguing that texts and symbols order the worlds of actors; other theorists take hermeneutic or interpretive positions, pointing out how people make meaning in relation to the texts and symbols around them.

Given that poststructuralists now recognize both the instabilities of texts and the potential for audiences' divergent readings of them, the differences between poststructuralist and hermeneutic theories no longer loom so large as what unites them: They share an emphasis on the symbolic and textual construction of social reality that is marked by a lived and incessantly reworked tension between public symbols and meaningful individual conduct. Despite the nuanced differences between these theories, they share the potential of linking the *contents* of culture—its symbolic and meaningful dimensions—with the more material aspects of social life—concerned with stratification, power, economic patterns, and organizational features of cultural production. In such a move, Pierre Bourdieu, for example, argued not just that a correlation exists between social status and cultural preferences; he suggested that cultural distinctions are formative in the maintenance of social class boundaries (1984). In a different way, members of the Birmingham school of cultural sociology have gone beyond showing a consolidation of class power in control of mass media; they have used Gramsci's theory of cultural hegemony to argue that the content of culture distributed through mass media is often infused with subtle ideological meanings that reinforce the status quo (Barrett et al. 1980; Bennett et al. 1981). In diverse ways, the textual turn is important in both cultural studies and sociology because it brings to light the relationship between social organization and symbolic processes. The result is a better recognition of the powerful ways in which culture mediates social life.

To take culture seriously in this way is to revisit a longstanding debate about the relative sociological importance of "material" versus "ideal" (or cul-

---

[1] Mike Davis (1990, ch. 4) analyzes "fortress L.A.," showing how the districts of Los Angeles can be understood in terms of their orientations to "security." Though Davis's analysis can be broadly construed as textual, he sidesteps the sometimes arcane debates about poststructuralism, deconstruction, and the like.

tural) forces. At the turn of the twentieth century, Max Weber argued that the Protestant ethic of self-sacrificing asceticism reinforced the emergence of modern rationally organized capitalism (1958a). He made it clear that he did not intend to substitute a "one-sided" cultural analysis for a one-sided economic one. "Not ideas, but material and ideal interests, directly govern men's conduct," he wrote. Still, Weber reflected, "very frequently the 'world images' that have been created by 'ideas' have, like switchmen, determined the tracks along which action has been pushed by the dynamic of interest" (1946, p. 280). Not long ago, Theda Skocpol (1979) could take the opposite view, arguing that culture—in the form of political ideology—was not relevant to the outcome of major social revolutions. More recently, however, the textual turn has provoked a renewed interest in the relation of culture to change. Lynn Hunt (1984), for example, thinks that the French revolution of 1789 depended on "the invention of a new political culture" which facilitated the formation of a new French political class, and consequently established a particularly modern kind of politics based on new forms of participation in public affairs by citizens. To take up again the idea of Ann Swidler (discussed in chapter 10), culture can be construed as a "toolkit" that has particular flexibility and salience in times of rapid change (1986). If this view is correct, cultural reorderings can radically alter the "textual" meanings so central to social life. Such fundamental transformations of culture—what might be called "cultural revolutions"—may occur quickly, and in conjunction with political upheaval, as Hunt suggests for the French revolution, or, like the consolidation of the Protestant ethic in the modern personality, they may transpire as broad, glacial changes that take place over decades or even generations. Why do such cultural revolutions occur, and what is their significance for social life?

These questions could be addressed by reference to historical examples like the French Revolution or the Reformation. However, an equally relevant context for such questions is the current social situation. It is possible to consider what we have called the "textual turn" as a cultural shift itself, part of a proclaimed emergence of "postmodern" culture. In this book, we already have considered certain ideas of postmodern writers, but we have kept the focus on their sociological contributions to cultural analysis. Here, we address the connections of culture to social change via a sociological exploration of postmodernism. In this exploration, it is important to consider the postmodern shift as a cultural phenomenon in its own right, and to ask about the relation of postmodern culture to industrial and postindustrial society, and to the sociological issue of actors' degree of agency. But what is postmodern?

THE POSTMODERN TURN: NO DEFINITION

Despite a lot of talk about postmodern culture, no one seems to know what it is. There are good reasons for this paradox. The term "postmodern" has been used in different contexts—in architecture, film, art, politics, philosophy, and so on.

And it has attracted both passionate advocates and pitched opposition. The significance of the postmodern thus depends very much on who is using the term, and where. Moreover, in each context separately, and in all of them together, the syllable "post" causes problems. Post-anything implies a coming after: It is defined not so much in its own terms, but by what has come before. Thus, on purely logical grounds, we would have no reason to expect a "post" situation to have any definable characteristics; we would expect a jumble. And indeed, this jumble often is celebrated by postmodern thinkers as *itself* a defining characteristic of the postmodern. Postmodernism, Todd Gitlin has observed,

> is indifferent to consistency and continuity altogether. It self-consciously splices genres, attitudes, styles. It relishes the blurring or juxtaposition of forms (fiction-nonfiction), stances (straight-ironic), moods (violent-comic), cultural levels (high-low). It disdains originality and fancies copies, repetition, the recombination of hand-me-down scraps. It neither embraces nor criticizes, but beholds the world blankly, with a knowingness that dissolves feeling and commitment into irony (1988, p. 35).

There is also the question of time frame. The emergence of a distinctly modern world can be traced to the global expansion of Europe and the Protestant Reformation beginning in the sixteenth century, and to the Enlightenment as a philosophical movement of reason, beginning in the seventeenth century. Whatever visibly might be called "postmodern," however, has been with us in a significant way only since the countercultural and political challenges to the established social order beginning in the 1960s.

But the timing is tricky. Postmodernism clearly has antecedents in certain late-nineteenth and early-to mid-twentieth-century modernist and avant-garde philosophies and cultural movements focused on relativism, perspectivism, subjectivity, and language. Modernism may have one side that emphasizes rationality, coherence, analytic science and holistic theory, but the humanities and the arts reveal another modernism—of discordant and disjointed experience, contradictions, celebrations of the irrational, attempts to reintegrate the human animal within the total human experience. These movements were "modernist" in their day in their breaks with a monolithic Victorian bourgeois public worldview (Singal 1987). But they typically remained elitist, rejecting mass culture and advocating pursuit of "art for art's sake." This form of cultural modernism typically remained separated from the masses and from history. Under these circumstances, avant-garde movements emerged in the efforts of surrealists, Dadaists and others to offer a critique of elitist modernism by forcing art and culture into a confrontation with politics and history (Huyssen 1986; Cantor 1988, pp. 35–41).

Yet the potency of both the modernists and the avant-garde was undermined by their own successes. Impressionist, surrealist and abstract expressionist painters, for example, found their work displayed in major galleries and museums, collected by wealthy bourgeois patrons of the arts. Artists' support depended on an established gallery system, and the content of their avant-garde work seemingly could be absorbed within established modern culture so long as their careers did not threaten the institutional frameworks which orchestrated the aesthetic definition and reception of artistic work (cf. Bürger 1984). Elements of these "rebellious" cultural movements were incorporated first into elite and then into popular culture. Mondrian's abstract blocks of color, for example, were incorporated into high fashion designer dresses in the 1960s, then into inexpensive "knock-off" imitations.

Because seemingly antimodern movements are deeply implicated in modernism itself, some theorists, for example Lyotard (1984), have suggested that the postmodern—however construed—is a "moment" of modernism, not simply the time at the end of modernism. In this sense, flare-ups of the postmodern have a checkered presence in the modern era: They are marked, in Lyotard's view, by rejections of the two prevailing "master narratives" of modernity—the expansions of citizenship rights and scientific knowledge as progressive history. Yet in an ironic sense, it is the culture of modernity itself that facilitates the rejection of modernity within cultural movements— whether they be nostalgic and even reactionary, or alternatively, avant-garde (cf. Lechner 1990).

Postmodernism may ultimately prevail as a break with modernism, but only if there is a fundamental shift. Earlier avant-garde movements did not effectively resist the institutional frameworks of the modern era by which legitimacy is ascribed to art and social critique. Advocates of postmodern culture have learned from these difficulties that, to succeed, they need to challenge the very sources of cultural equations and institutional arrangements of modernism. We may chart these changes in the future by looking for something other than simply shifts in the *content* of art and culture. If postmodern culture takes hold, we would expect to find (1) changes in the *forms* by which "art" and "culture" obtain currency and legitimacy among various social strata, and (2) alterations of the institutions by which culture is produced, distributed and assimilated, and incorporated into daily life. How do contemporary changes measure up to such standards?

Artists' reactions to the exhaustion of the modernist avant-garde make up only one strand among a diverse array of often contradictory "postmodern" developments in film, photography, music, fashion and other cultural media. Some of what has been called postmodern in the past quarter-century doubtless will be viewed as ephemeral, passing fads. What of it might be significant or enduring? Architecture has been an important avenue of postmodernist culture, and it offers a useful example by which to explore the question. In self-consciously postmodern architecture, beginning in the 1960s and 1970s, certain classical forms (Roman or Egyptian columns, for example) were reintroduced, juxtaposed with modernistic elements in a way that seemed to break with the coherence aimed at in modernist architecture. By now, these postmodern design motifs have been copied so widely (in neo-classical shopping malls, for

example) as to become clichés. Yet for all the passing fads of postmodern architecture, there may also be some more fundamental change at work.

For modern architecture, Charles Jencks has suggested that the factory and
the machine offered the dominant metaphors; thus, Le Corbusier's famous
"home as a machine for living in" (1981, p. 31). By contrast, Jencks describes
postmodern architecture as the product of treating design as a matter of "language." But the language is not the result of experts defining a single, elitist vocabulary to be imposed upon the public. In place of monumental, abstract and
formal rationalism associated with modern architecture, postmodern architecture is, as it were, *conversation* between materials, motifs, people, and places.
This conversation is situated among many dialects, "quoting" many sources: The
vernacular vocabulary of popular culture, diverse revivals of earlier design motifs, the contexts of buildings, and their uses. Modern architecture was to be
judged on technical merits in terms of its ability to rationalize a single, coherent
aesthetic. Postmodern architecture—with its divergent sources—could hardly be
evaluated by such standards. In their place, Jencks proposes "plausibility" (1981,
p. 8). Postmodern architecture can be deemed successful if its aesthetic elements—however diverse—make sense of space (and in space) for the people
who inhabit it.

In Jencks' account, postmodernism does not depend on any specific
content, at least in architecture. Instead, it establishes a new *relationship* between the designer and the designed world. As a consequence, postmodern
architecture does not aim toward construction of a single, coherent, objective,
rationally ordered environment. It celebrates playfulness and even contradiction. These characteristics are not tied in any necessary way to how buildings
look (even if the juxtaposition of elements in current postmodern buildings is
immediately recognizable); they derive from a more fundamental shift in the
relation of architecture to society that is distinctly postmodern.

Whether the overall movement of postmodernism will become an enduring world-historical development on a par with the birth of the modern era remains to be seen by future generations. But clearly it would amount to a
coming-after modernism that places root cultural orderings into question: At
stake is nothing less than an assault on positivistic science, formal reason, the
imperatives of bureaucratic organization—in short, the whole fabric of modern
culture. If Jencks's standard is any index, for all the difficulties of definition, the
postmodern turn would involve a fundamental reordering of how we experience and act in the world. The very power and authority of formal, objective
knowledge would be challenged by situated knowledge. Yet by Jencks's standard, much of what is now labelled as "postmodern" architecture simply places
a new "look" onto ongoing social practices of architecture. By Jencks's standard,
much that looks and feels postmodern may not be so. If we keep to the idea of
the rise of the postmodern as a fundamental shift, then the claims for the triumph of a new culture seem premature. Even so, the affirmations of the
postmodern, however unwieldy and overstated, offer new sensibilities, a new

mood and some points of discourse that fly in the face of conventional under-standings. The sheer bulk of "discourse on the postmodern" ambiguously signi-fies (or signifies by its ambiguity) the postmodern turn which cannot be defined. Because the postmodern turn involves a rejection of objectivity, the proponents of the postmodern often make a badge of honor out of their refusal to define postmodernism: It cannot be defined, for to define it is to subordinate it to the logic of modernism, exactly what the postmodernists want to avoid. Thus, to un-derstand the postmodern requires adopting one or another postmodernist per-spective, in which the search for a definition no longer seems necessary.

THE POSTMODERN TURN AS A TEXTUAL TURN?

Even if definitions might seem worthless to postmodernists, the absence of defi-nition creates its own difficulties. Since no one need agree about the features of postmodernism, doubt arises about its boundaries. Anything goes, it would seem. For this reason, it is not possible to consider any specific viewpoint as representative of postmodernism and thus it is difficult to discuss postmodern-ism in general. However, one version of postmodern thinking—the "textual" turn—offers a vivid contrast to modernist assumptions about social processes. Considering it briefly thus helps to show the sociological issues at stake.

The textual turn, in its strongest version, asserts that society *is* a text. Thus, for Richard Harvey Brown, "selves and societies are constructed and deconstructed through rhetorical practices" (Brown 1990, p. 191). This view has a long heritage in social theory—in linguistic and cultural anthropology, in studies by symbolic interactionists, in Erving Goffman's work, in the social constructionism of Peter Berger, and in the ethnomethodology of Harold Gar-finkle. It suggests that the world is not accessible to us in its "natural" state. Rather, we mediate our connection to the world symbolically. To take a clas-sic example in anthropological linguistics, "snow" is not comprehended by us as an intrinsically natural phenomenon devoid of its cultural packaging; in-stead, it becomes part of our experience in *different* ways according to the symbols we use to represent snow and the meanings we attach to them (white Christmas?, skiing weekend?, caring for cattle in a blizzard?). If this ar-gument has at least some truth to it even for the "natural" world, it seems even more compelling for the social world, where we live our lives in terms of cate-gories (such as marital status: single, married, divorced, and more detailed nu-ances) that themselves structure our own and other people's reciprocal social actions. Diverse strands of sociological thought—from Durkheim's symbolic structuralism to symbolic interactionism and Weberian interpretive sociol-ogy—acknowledge the centrality of symbols and meaning to social life. What, we must ask, is so distinctive about the textual turn of postmodernism?

The answer is that the textual turn is not new to sociology. Instead, two things have happened. First, among social researchers in the 1970s and 1980s, it became increasingly evident that cultural analyses and macro-structural perspectives have much to offer each other, and that research excluding either dimension is incomplete. The currents within, and interchanges among, such perspectives are diverse. It is not so important to trace them as it is to recognize the rich interplay that results, once analyses of culture and structure are undertaken in relation to one another. The study of the Balinese cockfight by Clifford Geertz is an icon of the possibility: Geertz does not simply assert that the lived activity of carrying out cockfights is a ritualized representation of Balinese social structure. Instead, he maintains that the cockfight "provides a metasocial commentary upon the whole matter of assorting human beings into fixed hierarchical ranks and then organizing the major part of collective existence around that assortment.... it is a Balinese reading of Balinese experience, a story they tell themselves about themselves" (1973, p. 448). For Geertz, the Balinese cockfight story is acted out by members of society in formulaic ways that comment on the world even while the tellers are enmeshed within it. Since Geertz, for social researchers, the story and the society have increasingly come to be viewed in a hall with facing mirrors where it is difficult to tell which is which.

There is a second recent change in the relation of textual analysis to sociological thought: Outside of the once more neatly bounded "social sciences," literary critics and other humanists started borrowing from linguistics, psychoanalysis, and the more interpretive, hermeneutic, phenomenological and interactionist strands of social theory to create something of a revolution in the humanities, by awakening critics to the recognition that there are other texts than those, like Goethe's and Jane Austen's, studied in the classic canons of literature courses. Thus, the line between "high" culture and "popular" culture tends to be erased by postmodernists (Jameson 1991, ch. 1). On this basis, literary critics sometimes have turned their gaze to popular novels—mysteries, spy novels, romances or science fiction—both for their merits as significant literature, and as a way to get closer to the "social texts" of popular life.

With these broadening definitions of texts, it is only a small step toward what Richard Harvey Brown (1990) advocates—treating the social world itself as a text to be "read" rather than as an objective reality to be apprehended. Such a move blurs (even erases) the difference between fiction and reality (between entertainment and news, for example), and it always was avoided by symbolic interactionists in sociology, for they struggled to establish their legitimacy in a field in which "idealism" was scorned. Literary critics, by contrast, suffered from no such censure: Treating the world as a text actually *enhanced* the authority of literary criticism (Collins 1989, p. 131). Ironically, the textual turn has its origins in part in social theory, yet the particular kinds of social theory that served as inspiration often have been treated as marginal to the discipline of sociology, creating the odd contemporary spectacle: Literary theorists have adopted what amount to (sometimes ersatz) sociological perspectives and techniques of analysis, and they have met with great success by doing so, but those same perspectives and techniques sometimes have been (and continue to be) resisted by "mainstream" sociologists!

In short, when the textual turn is brought full circle, *back* into sociohistorical inquiry, the implications are substantial and controversial. In one aspect, the literary shift is concerned with rhetorical critique and the "deconstruction" of texts, showing how texts create a sense of reality, even in the absence of the capacity of any text to represent or correspond to reality. In the modernist scheme of things, these critical tools were applied almost exclusively to fiction, but now they have been brought to bear to show the "fictional" aspects of non-fiction narratives and stories—about news, politics, gender and race—and within academic disciplines such as history, anthropology, sociology and economics, and even the physical and biological sciences. Taken to their logical conclusion, they suggest that all knowledge is metaphoric, offering images by which we understand the world. Those images no longer are securely moored to reality; rather, they "float," that is, they lack any direct and unambiguous relation to the world they are intended to describe.

Such a view is particularly devastating for objectivist sociological theories—such as economistic marxism, structural functionalism, rational choice theory, and structuralist theories of social organization—which are supposed to use analytic concepts to get at "real" social processes that are invisible to everyday appearance (cf. Bogard 1990, and the symposium in *Sociological Theory* 9: #2 [1991]). As Hebdige framed the problem:

> It is no longer possible for us to see through the appearance of, for instance, a "free market" to the structuring "real relations" beneath (e.g., class conflict and the expropriation by capital of surplus value). Instead, signs begin increasingly to take on a life of their own referring not to a real world outside themselves but to their own "reality"—the system that produces the signs (quoted in Norris 1990, p. 141).

If formal knowledge is based on metaphor, both public discourse and everyday knowledge would bear similar fates. The world as concrete reality becomes obscured behind imagery.

The textual turn, as we have described it so far, really is a philosophical argument. It is not so much an argument *about* reality; it is an argument which critiques the modernist assumptions about how (or indeed whether) we *know* about reality. If the philosophical argument is given credence, then what the symbolic interactionists and others have been saying for decades has merit: The symbolic construction of reality occurs within modern societies and indeed societies in general, even if the claims of objectivist modernism were quite different. But there is another dimension to the textual turn, one which argues that the rise of the postmodern is nothing less than a shift in the nature of reality itself. Contradictions pose difficulties for this argument: It seems odd to describe texts as non-representational and then use texts to talk about real changes (even real changes in the arrangements of texts). In spite of this difficulty, some postmodernists want to say that the world/texts now are organized in new ways.

In part their arguments mirror sociological theories that were emerging independently of the textual turn. Thus, Herbert Gans (1974) disputed the special character of "high" culture both on the basis of content and form: He could not help but note a relentless borrowing by high culture from popular culture, for example, the use of popular tunes in "serious" music. Moreover, Gans noted that much so-called high culture depends upon the same general mechanisms of mass production and distribution—the recording industry, television, film—that are associated with popular culture. Other sociologists also pointed to social changes toward what we now call postmodernization without resorting to a textual turn. Daniel Bell, for example, argued in *The Cultural Contradictions of Capitalism* (1976) that the spheres of work and leisure were becoming disconnected from one another, such that people were something like Jekyll-and-Hyde figures playing contradictory roles on the job and off. And sociologists also have shown that with the rise of a service economy, culture has been recreated as work. Thus, Arlie Russell Hochschild examined how service workers—airline flight attendants—have been subjected to "the commercialization of human feeling" in their jobs (1983). In the opposite venue, Ann Swidler (1980, p. 135) observed that emotional relationships now require "work," and Barry Glassner (1990) has explored the leisure-time pursuit of "fitness" through exercise and diet. In an ironic and quintessentially postmodern way, the pursuit of selfhood becomes work—the therapeutic meeting by people sharing a common personal problem, the visit to the health club for regimented exercise and socializing—carefully distanced from any hint of productive labor such as mowing the lawn. In short, studies of work and leisure by sociologists suggest a shift in cultural practices.[2] But what makes the cultural changes specifically postmodern?

Architecture again provides a clue. In 1968 a group from the Yale Architecture School conducted a studio exercise, "learning from Las Vegas." They wondered whether the American commercial strip could teach architects something about the new type of urban form then emerging next to the strip highways, expressways, and interstate highway system. What they found in their field trip to Las Vegas was that commercial architecture of the strip was redefining the relationship of building forms to space and to signs. In the nineteenth century, the sign had simply *identified* the building—a hotel, store or office. To be sure, building style communicated something about its use and status. But in the early twentieth century, small-scale entrepreneurs began to experiment in radical ways with vernacular commercial

---

[2] These changes probably were connected in part with structural economic changes in the U.S. and other relatively developed societies—namely, the emergence of a postindustrial economy oriented to provision of services rather than manufacturing. This connection is considered in detail below.

FIGURE 11.1 The building-as-icon of the 1930s established an important precedent for subsequent strip and consumer-oriented building development. (*Source:* Library of Congress.)

buildings. Sometimes they made the shape itself represent a building's function. Thus, in the 1930s some coffee shops were built to look like coffee pots, and there were hotdog stands in the shape of hotdogs, gasoline stations that loomed up as giant gasoline pumps, and so on. In Las Vegas, the Yale architects made note of a related development: The signs in front of buildings were overwhelming the buildings, to the point where the buildings themselves were becoming caricatures of their signs. Ultimately, buildings were enclosed signs, decorated on the interior as continuations of the signs. The visitor to a casino enters a fantasy experience theme park like "Caesar's Palace" or goes on a "safari" into Saharan Africa. Residential space begins to follow the same tendency toward adornment. These developments have deep connections to the emergence of modern commercial space beginning in the nineteenth century, such as the department stores described in chapter 5. Overall, a fundamental inversion had occurred—"the victory of symbols-in-space over forms-in-space" (Venturi, Brown and Izenour 1977, p. 119). The architectural critics thus trace a fundamental shift: As the new structures of the suburbs and malls and vacation meccas rise up around us, we live no longer in space. Instead, we wend our way through symbols.

Jean Baudrillard has championed this view more generally, by consolidating an argument made by Daniel Boorstin, that the relation of images to reality has undergone a series of transformations. Images might once more or less accurately have reflected reality. However, as Boorstin pointed out in his book *The Image, or What Happened to the American Dream?*, "a new kind of synthetic novelty...has flooded our experience" (1962, p. 9). For example, authentic heroes are getting more and more difficult to find in the midst of celebrities (like Madonna) who, Boorstin suggests, are "well known for their wellknown-ness." By now these developments have proceeded to the point where, as Boorstin put it,

> everybody's reliance on dealers in pseudo-events and images cannot—contrary to highbrow clichés—accurately be described as a growing superficiality. Rather these things express a world where the image, more interesting than its original, has itself become the original (1962, p. 204).

In Boorstin's account, this development was foreshadowed by the rise of public relations early in the twentieth century, which amounted to a self-conscious exercise in the manipulation of images (1962).

For Jean Baudrillard, there are two alternatives here: It is possible that an image "masks and perverts a basic reality," or, more radically, that it "masks the *absence* of a basic reality." Even in the latter case, the reality assumption can be maintained, by a fictive attempt to simulate a reality that doesn't exist, as in the case of advertising that depicts a utopian world: We would be hard put to find such a world in reality but nevertheless can imagine it as real. But for Baudrillard, there is a final step, in which the image "bears no relation to any reality whatever: it is its own pure simulacrum" (1988b, p. 170). Baudrillard uses the term "simulacra" to describe as artificial, realms like national political dramas and television "virtual reality" commercials that lack any necessary and direct connection to the everyday world: "Simulation is no longer that of a territory, a referential being or a substance. It is the generation of models of a real without origin or reality: a hyperreal" (1988b, p. 166). For both Boorstin and Baudrillard, the everyday world of our lives has become overshadowed by images that give the appearance of reality, but without having to have any necessary correspondence to the world beyond their realms.

These ideas can be given concrete form through the example of tourism (Boorstin 1962). It is still possible to travel without being a tourist. But tourism has grown to the point where it often overshadows travel. It has become an enormous industry: Certain places—the Caribbean, Hawaii, and so on—are now essentially "tourist destinations." Organizers of tourism thus have worked to create images (in travel brochures and posters) of the tourist destinations in order to peak tourists' interest in an experience of novelty that does not require great personal risk. Yet the effective marketing of such images requires a reorganization of the tourist destination experience itself as a pseudoevent. The tourist has to be able to return from a trip and proclaim satisfaction that everything was as the travel brochure portrayed it. In the ongoing real world, this is not always easy to achieve, of course. Kenya is a great tourist destination, but if tourists look behind the facade of the tour, they may see social and political conditions that will be, at the least, unsettling to the idea of "vacation." Vacationing can be something like visiting a Potemkin village, a socially constructed corridor to be experienced as the real world, which nevertheless masks the real world.

In the tourist industry, the danger of offensive reality intruding can be controlled by an altogether different solution: Rather than establishing a tourist destination within a real place like Kenya or New York City, it is possible to create tourist destinations that are, to use Baudrillard's term, simulacra. Thus, Disneyland and Las Vegas are not real worlds that tourists come to visit; they are places where the controlling reality is the reality of tourism. But for Baudrillard, Disneyland—tremendous achievement of controlled imagery that it is—only begins to unveil the possibilities. Disneyland has boundaries: We know when we are going to visit it. But what if the world at large has become a Disneyland, a simulacrum? For Baudrillard, this is the current condition: "It is not the least of America's charms that even outside the movie theatres the whole country is cinematic. The desert you pass through is like the set of a Western, the city a screen of signs and formulas." To unravel the mysteries of the city, he adds, "you should not, then, begin with the city and move inwards to the screen; you should begin with the screen and move outwards to the city" (1988a, p. 56).

The possibilities of a postmodernized world are difficult for us as individuals to absorb, for they take away the foundations and the lines of connection by which we might establish our bearings. Images become the world, yet they bear no necessary logical relation to one another: Rather, they can be juxtaposed with one another in ways that don't depend on the principles—such as gravity—that operate in the real world. It no longer matters if these images cannot be claimed to represent the real world. The simulacrum is the world. Ralph Lauren manufactures images of the past—"from Scottish manor houses to African safaris, from Caribbean beach houses to clapboard cottages" (*New York Times,* 2/2/92). These images are simulacra in which we can immerse ourselves, detached from the present moment of history by their nostalgia, even as they detach themselves from the unevenness of the real world of the past by their utopian perfection. At a personal level, the implication of Baudrillard's vision thus is as disconcerting as the cultural claim: Individual people too must be simulacra—simulations of the images which construct identities that yield a sense of reality. The same would hold for the events of public life. Undoubtedly "real" events like the Gulf War against Saddam Hussein invert the old sense of reality and image: such events of historical significance increasingly are swallowed up by the simulacra which present them to us. If Baudrillard's postmodern account of postmodernization has any plausibility, the surface image has behind it not reality, but only the backstage. We all know that surfaces are produced by backstage work, but this knowledge no longer discounts the surface, and so the surface is what counts. Yet the surface no longer is the surface that represents or obscures reality; the surface as self-consciously constructed *is* reality. To be sure, people had diverse reactions (which they continued to work out) concerning the Gulf War. What is important, in the Baudrillardian vision, is that people became transfixed by orchestrated media events (thus, the complaint by journalists that they were not allowed to cover the Gulf War in a way independent of its orchestration).

The upshot of Baudrillard's form of postmodern analysis is to suggest that a dramatic cultural shift has taken place. It holds that we can no longer understand the world by using the modern tools of analytic knowledge. Moreover, the world we would understand no longer works in the ways it once did. Such claims are striking. Paradoxically, they evoke the idea of a totalistic change, and the plausibility of this idea depends upon an essentialist view of the world—the very viewpoint that postmodernists criticize when they find it in certain modernist theories. Only if the social world has a prime cause—one or another basic animating force—can a change in one aspect reshape the world in general. Some versions of postmodernism simply shift the prime mover from economics to symbols. Yet a more relativistic postmodern view would raise doubt about any such essentialist and holistic theory. Therefore, it is important to consider two issues about culture in the contemporary situations that lie outside the "strong" version of postmodernism. First, there is the question of the relation between postmodernism and the persistence of the industrial and bureaucratically organized world. Second, we must inquire about the possibility of agency—the capacities of individuals and groups in society today for conscious use of culture as self-empowerment.

PERSISTENCES OF THE OLD REGIMENS: MODERNITY AND INDUSTRIALISM

A theory of contemporary society proposed in the 1970s suggested that changes in the economies of so-called "developed" or "advanced" nation-states represented the emergence of a "postindustrial" order based on production of services and knowledge at the expense of manufacturing (Touraine 1981; Bell 1973). The working class was declining in the industrialized countries, the argument went, and a "new middle class," living in the suburbs, was forming on the basis of expanded employment in a wide range of service occupations in sectors such as social welfare, financial services, travel and tourism, computer software, restaurants, and a host of other non-industrial (at least not heavy industry) sectors of the economy. The details and significance of these changes have been hotly debated. But by now, there can be little doubt that a fundamental and long-term shift has occurred. This shift can be described as a change in the occupational structure: from 1940 to 1970, for example, agricultural employment declined from 17.4% of the labor force to a mere 3.1% of the labor force and employment of manual workers slightly decreased—from 39.8% to 36.6%. By contrast, in the same time period, there were solid increases in employment in middle-class jobs (many of them, relatively new occupations); for example, professionals went from 7.5% to 14.5% of the labor force, and clerical workers rose from 9.6% to 17.8%. These basic trends have continued more recently (U.S. Census Bureau 1975, series D182–232; U.S. Census Bureau 1983, table 89). For better or worse, the United States is no longer simply an industrial nation-state; its economy increasingly is based on middle-class, non-manual and service work.

Yet there are criticisms of the theory of post-industrial society relevant to any account of postmodernization as a cultural development. As theorists interested in the global world economy are quick to point out, the changes in advanced societies at the core of the world economy cannot be separated from changes elsewhere in the world. In this view, postindustrialization is only part of a global redistribution of economic activity in which industrial and manufacturing activities are being relocated to poorer countries, where wages and other costs are lower and environmental regulations may be less strict. So far as culture is concerned, the reordering of the world economy over the past thirty years has led to a decided "globalization" of culture (Mahoney 1989, Smith 1991). Nigerian pop music groups are achieving distribution and popularity in the U.S., and Arabs are watching television "Westerns" produced in Italy. In the news business, some observers see the information network becoming consolidated into a world information order dominated by multinational corporations and the most powerful nation-states (Stevenson and Shaw 1984).

There is also the theoretical question of whether postindustrial society really represents a fundamental change in the social order. The work of two sociologists suggests that we should at least recognize the continuities between the industrial and the postindustrial. The most direct assault on the postindustrial theory was made by Krishnan Kumar (1978). He argued that any close examination of claims about the emergence of a postindustrial society showed changes, yes, but changes that were of the same character as the changes in industrial society. For Kumar,

The "agenda of questions" for postindustrial society seems remarkably like that for the industrial society. Beneath the postindustrial gloss, old, scarred problems rear their heads: alienation and control in the workplaces of the service economy; scrutiny and supervision of the operations of private and public bureaucracies, especially as they come to be meshed in with technical and scientific expertise. Framing all these is the problem of the dominant constraining and shaping force of contemporary industrial societies: competitive struggles for profit and power between private corporations and between nation states, in an environment in which such rivalries have a tendency to become expansionist and global (1978, pp. 230–31).

Kumar's attack builds upon a wide sociological literature tracing back to the works of Weber and Durkheim, which describes the processes of functional differentiation and specialization (see Luhmann 1982; Alexander and Colomy 1990).

The analysis of Peter Berger, Brigitte Berger and Hansfried Kellner in *The Homeless Mind* (1973) offers a challenge similar to Kumar's, but one more directly concerned with culture, specifically, the culture of modernization.[3] Most telling, many of the qualities that more recent writings identify with postmodernism, Berger and his colleagues found embedded in processes of modernization. Specifically, they noted the cultural consequences of two longterm, secular trends of modernization—the rise of technologically based production and the ever advancing bureaucratization of organized activity. These trends, they argued, have had specific implications for the character of consciousness: Our ways of experiencing the world are mediated by technology and by bureaucratic organization.

Two points are important here. First, although Berger, Berger and Kellner offered their account in reference to the rise of modern societies, the trends they describe as modernization continue to operate today, in the supposedly postindustrial and postmodern situation. If anything, the implications of technology for consciousness have spilled outside of production, for we all participate much more intimately with technology in our everyday lives—by use of ever more complex home entertainment systems and communication devices such as computers. Similarly, bureaucracy mediates not only our consciousness in the workplace; increasingly, it orders our experiences of leisure, through the bureaucratized service economy's penetration of everyday life in tourism, entertainment, market research, recreation, and the like. We come to internalize the ability to play the roles of "bureaucrat" and "client." In these ways the social forces of modernization continue to structure postmodernization.

Second, long before the debate about postmodernism heated up, Berger and his colleagues identified certain cultural consequences of modernity that more recently have been proclaimed as signifiers of postmodernity. Modern identity, they argued, does not depend on a coherent self, but on the playing of roles in situations segmented from one another. Identity thus depends on an open-ended project of self-definition in a pluralistic world

---

[3]The term "modernization" is controversial because it often carries the ideological freight of "progress" as a social value and narrative of modern history. This is a point that these authors well understood. For their purposes they defined modernization as "the *institutional* concomitants of technologically induced economic growth" (1973, p. 9).

where any attempt to consolidate ultimate meaning of one's life requires the establishment of a "home world"—an enterprise that is both "hazardous and precarious." In response to these unsettling circumstances, the Bergers and Kellner suspect that we personally adopt the technological and bureaucratic sensibilities by becoming career counselors for our own lives, in both their occupational and leisure aspects: "The family unit thus operates as a life planning workshop" (1973, p. 72).

The Homeless Mind may overstate the roles of technology and bureaucracy in accounting for innovation and eclecticism in popular culture. Moreover, the authors' argument did not anticipate how the boundaries between once segmented arenas (such as the public and private) would become blurred when "meanings" or symbols became increasingly freefloating in relation to "things." But their analysis establishes a framework in which such "postmodern" changes may be understood. Indeed, the very qualities often associated with postmodernism—the quality of pastiche, the juxtaposition of cultural elements that lack coherence, the disjuncture between culture and any moorings in concrete situations—are all qualities that *The Homeless Mind* identifies as characteristic consequences of modernization, not postmodernization. In various ways, they have been with us for centuries—on a massive scale al least since the cultural confrontation between Europeans like Christopher Columbus and the inhabitants of the "new world" he "discovered" in 1492.

The analyses by Kumar and by the Bergers and Kellner suggest that postmodernism cannot be viewed simply as a total and qualitative shift in the cultural patternings of contemporary societies. Their views are echoed in the recent critical review of postmodern theory by Steven Best and Douglas Kellner: "Frequently, what is identified as a postmodern development can be seen to be a prototypical modern trait" (1991, p. 278). These observers reinforce points that we have made at various junctures in this book: Changes in how culture is produced do not necessarily change the content of culture or the processes of its reception and usage by people. Conversely, changes in content of culture do not necessarily reorder the world so drastically that the old processes are no longer significant. We already have seen in chapters 4 and 9 that the emergence of new technologies of distribution—television and film—did not destroy the basic dramatic devices by which audiences become cathartically engaged in drama. By the opposite token, the spread of postmodern sensibilities and culture does not happen by magic: The political economy and social production of culture described in chapters 7 and 8 still operate in the structuring of the simulacra.

To be sure, the power of culture may be altered by postmodernism, and the production and distribution of culture may take new forms. But that simply reinforces the point: The "textual turn" does not happen in a semiotic vacuum, somehow detached from the material and social circumstances of its production. If this is so, we should be suspicious of any "essentialist" argument that the advent of the postmodern transforms everything. Such an argument, decidedly idealist, can only be advanced by averting the gaze from the concrete, sensuous activities of people at work, attempting to control the production and "spin" of culture. Because the postmodernist possibilities themselves are based on certain features of modernization—bureaucratic and technological rationalization, pluralism, and so forth—it is best not to see postmodernism as a fundamental shift and passage beyond modernity. Rather, the insight of Jean-François Lyotard is reaffirmed: The postmodern should be understood as a "moment" of modernity (1984). Even if, in the long run, the postmodern turn may become irreversible, it will be established alongside, and in relation to, earlier social developments.

UP FROM POSTMODERNITY?

Even if we acknowledge that postmodernity is a facet of modernity, and even if we wonder about its staying power, the new sensibilities can hardly be ignored—on the street, in the media, and in the academy. With increasing self-assurance, proponents of postmodernization are laying a claim to the high ground in intellectual discourse. They go so far as to argue that the postmodern turn amounts to a cultural revolution, an important development with political consequences. For the postmodernists, the cultural transformation—which they advocate as well as document—has a liberative potential because it moves beyond modernity's controlled system of knowledge and power dominated by expertise and wealth. But this view has formidable opponents. They suggest that postmodernism is a desperate effort to validate certain lifestyles and career patterns which are deeply embedded in the established order of things. For all the hype, the critics maintain, postmodernism is either the latest ideological and cultural glorification of life in postindustrial society, or it is a false utopian impulse which masks the exhaustion of certain groups' political ideals in the late twentieth century (cf. Mascialees, Sharpe and Cohen 1989; Callinicos 1990).

Some modernist intellectuals of a variety of political persuasions—liberals, conservatives, marxists, feminists, critical theorists—therefore resist the postmodernist turn. For them, the postmodern assault on knowledge and rational discourse represents a turning away from the Enlightenment. With the loss of the Enlightenment's promotion of rational discourse, with the loss of the quest to critically understand the human condition, there is a loss of hope as well. In this view, the postmodern turn is nothing less than an abdication of citizenship, a turning away from the effort to work collectively to understand problems and to resolve differences that face societies today. In postmodernist terms, this modernist reaction itself ignores a significant feature of the Enlightenment project, one that Foucault identified, namely, the refinement of modern technologies of social control. Furthermore, the defense of modernism seems to postmodernists elitist, suspicious of mass culture, and "nostalgic": It reacts against the changes that have occurred, like

MUSIC TELEVISION®

FIGURE 11.2 The blurred genre that is MTV easily can be labelled as quintessentially postmodern, but the political implications of MTV remain an open question. (*Source:* Courtesy MTV.)

them or not. In the face of the new conditions, it laments the passing of an era in which the ideas of a knowledgeable elite really counted (Stauth and Turner 1988; cf. Brantlinger 1983).

The debate over postmodernist culture is often muddled, for two related reasons: (1) the politics of postmodernism is ambiguous, and (2) postmodernist thought does not transcend the longstanding debate about culture and agency. To take up the first point, since postmodernism avoids any coherent definition, it is a moving target, hard for modernists to hit. Postmodern culture has multiple facets. There are aspects that grow out of powerful changes of technology, the mass media, and the reorganization of popular culture genres in the mass media. Thus, we have the blurring of news, social control, and lived soap opera in programs like "America's Most Wanted,"[4] and the merger of multiple levels of advertisement and promotion with news and entertainment in the MTV music television cable channel (Kaplan 1987). These sorts of changes hardly mark an adversary culture, yet they are very much parts of the postmodern mix. On the other hand, a critical strand of postmodern thought—exemplified by the work of Foucault discussed in chapter 7—is concerned with showing the power of the existing social order to organize everyday life through the production of culture. The puzzle for people who adopt the critical perspectives of postmodernism concerns how to respond to the conditions they identify. Henry Kariel offers a poignant description of the predicament:

> Grateful for shelters ranging from preschools to maximum intensity care units, comforted by the products of industry, we nonetheless feel uneasy within the

_____
[4]A point made by Marshall Battani, Department of Sociology, University of California-Davis (personal communication).

> all-absorbing culture of modernity. Yet we are so thoroughly implicated in it that we trust no alternative culture to quiet our malaise. Even as we organize to bring the forces that trouble us under control, we sense that our very resistance is neutralized by the prevailing technique-centered momentum.
>
> For postmodernists, it is simply too late to oppose the momentum of industrial society. They merely resolve to stay alert and cool in its midst. Consciously complying and yet far from docile, they chronicle, amplify, augment it. They judge it as little as it judges itself. Determined to assail nothing, they are passionately impassive (1989, p. ix).

Other postmodernists share Kariel's embrace of postmodernism as a radical cultural politics. Yet to do so, they have to take one side of a long-standing debate that has crossed over the modernist/postmodernist divide—the debate over culture and agency (for a recent formulation, see Archer 1988).

As we have already noted, certain versions of postmodern theory have their roots in poststructuralism. On that basis, their accounts leave little room for autonomous social action: They hold that we are the products of the symbolic matrix in which we act; we are revisions of texts that already have been written. In viewpoints that dismiss the significance of individual and collective agency (for example, in the most structuralist readings of Foucault), all action is orchestrated and recouped into the circuits of social order, even when it opposes them. This postmodern despair can justify inaction.

Similar problems emerge with the postmodern view of "representation": If conceptual representation of the world always has a fictive component, that is, if any text is part story, objective sociological analysis is impossible. Instead of intellectual efforts to understand and change society we get discourse about the impossibility of discourse about social forces that might shape our lives. In the views of critics, this version of postmodernism mystifies its own mystification of the world in which we live. Thus, in a broadside against the new intellectual/celebrity culture, Otto Werckmeister lamented, "Today, cultural critique is being carried on in a self-contained microcosm of abstract political discourse disconnected from the institutional and administrative operations of actual politics" (1991, p. 186). In a similar vein, Jeffrey Goldfarb sees the emergence of a "cynical society." People, he argues, have recognized the socially constructed character of ideas and culture, and they thereby dismiss all culture and ideas as equally tainted by the interests that produce them. Hence, cynicism. Yet there is a problem, Goldfarb notes: "Cynicism makes mass society a self-fulfilling prophecy" (1991, p. 152).

What are the reasons for cynicism and what are the alternatives to it? Postmodernists, with some justification, may think that they are messengers being shot for bringing bad news. If cynicism abounds, it is not just because some postmodern intellectuals fill the literary journals and the lecture circuits with arcane *fin de siècle* abstract café debates. Rather, the cynicism would seem to have a wider following in the general population, and not without reason: A series of crises and controversies (savings and loan, drugs, the economy, AIDS,

abortion, the Thomas/Hill hearings, the L.A. riots) may produce a sense of pow-
erlessness and vulnerability among diverse segments of the population. Besides,
postmodernism does not really embrace cynicism even in its pessimistic side.

Moreover, there is a strand of postmodernism that is less pessimistic, and
it converges with modernist ideas about pragmatism and the importance of individual agency. Sociologists sometimes have conceptualized culture as an
objective phenomenon, distinct from "society." Yet in this book we have
shown that our everyday lives and actions are permeated with cultural formu-
lae that we employ, cultural meanings that we absorb and rework and cultural
actions that we take. One way of taking the postmodern turn is to extract a
political conclusion from the operations that Foucault performed to erase the
distance between culture and the world. In this view, formulated for instance
by Steven Conner, "culture could no longer be considered simply as the
sphere of representations, hovering immaterially at a distance from the brute
facts of 'real' life, since discourse theory sees the forms and occasions of representations as in themselves power (rather than merely the reflection of
power-relations that exist elsewhere)." For Conner, then, "power is best understood not in the macropolitical terms of large groupings or monolithic
blocs, of class or State, but in the micro-political terms of the networks of
power-relations subsisting at every point in a society" (1989, pp. 224–25).
Power relationships are negotiated and challenged in everyday life and personal concerns. Issues no longer necessarily turn on the central axes of industrial society: A whole new set of struggles come to the fore—over ethnic
relations, health care, gender, environment, educational access and content,
consumer issues such as credit card interest rates and affordable housing, and
a host of other issues.

To put this formulation in the more conventional (modernist) terms of
Max Weber, class interests are no longer tied to the workplace: There are
class interests of consumers and others who share common economic interests outside the workplace. The rise in awareness of multiple class situations
may well reinforce the widely acknowledged decreasing capacity of working-class consciousness to offer an organizing basis for social change (described by Michael Mann [1973]). However, the politics of class has not
disappeared; it has simply become more complexly mapped onto diverse
class situations—some of them outside the workplace. Moreover, "status
groups"—defined on the basis of some shared sense of status—advance their
own political agendas. Sometimes they do this by active politics. Following
Alain Touraine (1981) it may be argued that in industrial society, political
parties typically were aligned with labor unions or business interests—both
of them class interests tied to production; in postindustrial society, politics
may be altered within conventional party politics, and beyond it, by the
emergence of a diverse array of class- and status-based (e.g., gender, ethnic,
environmental) social movements no longer confined to the sphere of the
workplace and production.

These possibilities may not really mark significant changes from the modern era. After all, ethnicity and religion have been the spoilers of modernist class politics in the past. And whether they are changes or not, status group political activism does not necessarily mean the end of cynicism. Many people, no matter which side they take, will find themselves profoundly troubled by the status group politics of ethnic group pitted against ethnic group, men versus women, citizens versus immigrants, straights versus gays, civil religion versus multi-cultural pluralism. It is in these terms that the critical theory of Jürgen Habermas (1987) offers a formula for hope. We all share, Habermas thinks, a capacity to communicate. If we can build on communication, we have the hope of retrieving social life from its subordination to abstract systems of rationalized organization. For other observers, Habermas's embrace of communication is naive, for it overlooks the formidable conflicts that might not be so easily resolved simply by communication.

A sociology of culture, or indeed any theory, cannot resolve this debate with some general answer. Rather, the debate is resolved, one way or another, in the concrete practices of people living in the social world. Sociological perspectives on culture, however, do contribute to changing the conditions of life. If there is any fundamental conclusion to the present inquiry into culture, it is this: Societies are not organized simply in material terms, and their characteristics are not simply the products of material social forces. Rather, in a variety of ways, culture is a mediating and even ordering force. Yet in comparison to material forces, cultural processes can be unstable, mercurial and shifting in their significance. Meanings and symbols, often enduring, sometimes can become reorganized quickly and dramatically. This means that the tasks of understanding society are more complex than the modernist social scientists ever admitted. But it also means that the cultural practices of individuals and groups are potentially much more consequential than was once admitted. As Bennett Berger (1991) has observed in a wise essay worth reading, the freedom and constraint of culture exist in an uneasy tension forged by the choices people make about what culture to embrace, and how. We cannot say whether this power of culture can, will, or should be taken up or left inert, or whether, once taken up, it will work for good or ill. The possibilities of Jonestown are always with us, and not just at the margins of society: They are implicit in the economic life, social control, politics and public relations of the society as a whole (Hall 1987). But we do suspect, whatever the channels in which the cultural currents run, whichever ones predominate, they will change the world as we now know it. New people will enter the stage, acting in ways foreign to the present, using new symbols and technologies, affecting new styles, enacting new ethics. Yet even as all this transpires, it will not transform everything. The old regimens will persist amidst the new.

Moreover, broad changes in culture will not take place independently of other aspects of society. The explanations of social change by Marx and

Weber differed, but they both saw that the Protestant culture of self-disciplined individualism and the economic and organizational features of capitalism developed in tandem. And they each saw that the persistence of any given institutionalized set of social arrangements—or social order—partly depends on the ways people might culturally make sense of their situations.

Questions of culture and change thus depend for their answers on a set of more specific and situational issues. How do people act—individually and collectively—on the basis of their consciousness of social circumstance? Are people satisfied with their lot? What is their way of life, and what is its significance to them? Do they adopt rhetoric and ideologies that justify acceptance of their social fate? Do they try to impress others with their status? Do individuals seek social mobility that will change their individual life chances? Or do they pursue collective action to change the life chances of their group? How change in the future will be channeled by the cultural meanings people attach to their social situations remains an open question. But it is not a question that will be resolved in the abstract realm of culture as a sphere unto itself; it will be resolved in the concrete socially organized world. Because of the intimate connection between culture and social life, sociological perspectives on culture offer important leverage for both personal and public understanding and action. In a world at the modern/postmodern pass, cultural studies are necessarily sociological studies.

SOURCES ON METHODS

Just as many theoretical perspectives can be fruitfully used in the sociology of culture, various methods can be—and have been—used to study the different substantive questions about culture. Much important work on culture has been accomplished applying conventional methods such as surveys or interviewing. It is also the case however, that recent studies of cultural phenomenon have spurred methodological and epistemological debates. Our purpose here is to suggest some further sources for reflecting on these debates as well as references for those interested in seeing how particular methodological approaches have grappled with the issues presented by studying various aspects of culture. (A few of the sources listed here are also discussed in the text. Full references for them may be found in the general bibliography.)

THE INTERPRETIVE TURN

Starting with the assumption that as humans we exist in culture, to paraphrase Geertz, "suspended in webs of significance we ourselves have spun," places the subject of culture at the heart of our concerns and has important implications for how it can be studied. It suggests that interpretation is at the core of what we study and is also central to the process by which we study it. This point of view, sometimes called the interpretive turn, marks a departure from positivist and structuralist approaches to the social sciences. The intrepretivists hold that there is no place from which one can stand and perform neutral observations. In addition, many also argue that explanations can only be "local" and the attempts to generate grand theory are fundamentally misguided. An important collection of writings from philosophers and social scientists introducing the interpretive approach is Paul Rabinow and William Sullivan, eds., *Interpretive Social Science Reader* (Berkeley: University of California Press, 1979).

Some, however, find that these approaches give up too much of what social science traditionally sought to accomplish. Wuthnow (1987) has attacked the hermeneutic and phenomenological approaches to culture as radically subjectivist. He argues that rather than trying to describe in detail the meaning of cultural objects of various kinds that the task is to identify the rules that make a symbol meaningful. Wuthnow's ambitious attempts at developing a new way of theorizing about structure and culture attack the subjectivity of the interpretive process. In her important article, "A Methodological Framework for the Study of Culture," *Sociological Methodology* 17 (1987):1–35, Wendy Griswold has argued that one need not trade away richly detailed accounts of cultural objects in order to achieve reliability, validity, and predictability.

These questions about observation, interpretation and validity, the place of theory, and text and context have also been raised with regard to the use of particular methods. Below we suggest some sources discussing these issues with reference to specific research methodologies.

ETHNOGRAPHY AND ORAL HISTORIES

Ethnography and oral history have long been concerned with discovering and documenting culture in the sense of meanings of interactions, events, and lives. The understanding of how to do this has changed markedly in recent years as scholars have become more reflexive about their own processes in creating the meanings they ascribe to those they study, and as scholars have attempted more fully to give voice to the subjects of their studies. An important source for ethnographers has been the critiques of feminist scholars, see Dorothy Smith's "Sociology For Women," in *The Everyday World as Problematic* (Boston: Northeastern University Press, 1987). Much of the feminist work is reviewed in Michal McCall and Judith Wittner's "The Good News about Life History," in Becker and McCall, eds., *Symbolic Interaction and Cultural Studies* (Chicago: University of Chicago Press, 1990).

The discussion of "the new ethnography" (see Clifford and Marcus 1986) has occurred primarily in anthropology and has centered on the writing of texts. Articles in a special issue of the *Journal of Contemporary Ethnography,* Vol. 19, No. 1 (April 1990) share the concern about texts, but a number of them also help us to reconnect the discussion of texts to the discussion of method, here fieldwork itself. In "Beyond Subjectivity: The Use of the Self in Social Science," *Qualitative Sociology* 8 (1985):309–324, Susan Krieger suggests an analytic strategy for using the self to understand both the data and the story. Carolyn Ellis proposes a very different use of the self in her article, "Sociological Introspection and Emotional Experience" in *Symbolic Interaction* 14 (1991):23–50.

Among sociologists, Norman Denzin has been a powerful voice articulating the interpretive view position. In his rereading of C. Wright Mills in his essay, "The Sociological Imagination Revisited," *The Sociological Quarterly* 31 (1990):1–22, he castigates Mills for his modernism and calls for a "theoretically minimalist text" that is characterized by a multiplicity of voices, and thick description, where experience and its meanings are indeterminate. The aim is to tell the stories of ordinary people, recognizing that what is captured are narratives built out of particular cultural understandings. His research strategy is spelled out in more detail in *Interpretive Interactionism* (Newbury Park, CA: Sage, 1989). Denzin has also promoted interpretive ethnography through his editorship of the research annual, *Studies in Symbolic Interaction* (see especially Volumes 11 and 12, 1990 and 1991).

Finally, methodologies of ethnography and life history are beginning to incorporate the possibilities of visual media for both studying and portraying aspects of culture. Douglas Harper describes the method of "photo elicitation" in his article "Portraying Bricolage," in *Knowledge and Society: Studies in the Sociology of Culture Past and Present* 6 (1986):209–231. In this process he asked his subject to reflect on the images, what was in them and what was left out, so the photographs are not merely a method of documenting a subject, but rather become a process that reinforces a reflexivity, in contrast to the usual "fly on the wall" approach of documentary photographers.

HISTORICAL AND COMPARATIVE ANALYSIS

Many examples of the rich possibilities for tracing cultural patterns in historical contexts are cited throughout this text. Yet the questions about what it means to study culture historically are not yet resolved. Old debates about narrative versus explanation have received new attention in the context of the interpretive turn.

John R. Hall has suggested that on one level the study of cultural history involves tracing new cultural patterns (seen as cultural problems with solutions that become institutionalized), the persistence of particular solutions, and the changes they go through. In his essay, "Social Interaction, Culture and Historical Studies," in Becker and McCall, eds., *Symbolic Interaction and Cultural Studies* (Chicago: University of Chicago Press, 1990) Hall borrows the concepts of "series" and "sequence" from historian George Kubler (see his *The Shape of*

Time: Remarks on the History of Things, New Haven: Yale University Press, 1962) to describe different kinds of cultural patterns: A series is a "closed class of equivalent items directed to the solution of a cultural problem" whereas a sequence is "opened-ended" (1990, p. 24). Once patterns have been identified, the possibility for explanation or interpretations by the analyst exists, possibilities which have been approached differently by historians and sociologists. In "Where History and Sociology Meet: Forms of Discourse and Sociohistorical Inquiry" (*Sociological Theory* 11, 1992) Hall continues to deconstruct the strategies of historical sociologists and sociological historians. He describes four forms of discourse—in values, narrative discourse, social theoretical discourse, and the discourse of explanation—and asserts that for historical sociology methodology is directed toward theorizing about particular cases, while for sociological history methodology is directed toward comprehensive analysis of a single phenomenon. Sociologists who study culture historically maintain analytically different strategies than historians who study cultural phenomena.

The interest in the case has increased recently with the development of new ways to think about case studies as part of a strategy of comparison. See Charles Ragin's *The Comparative Method: Moving Beyond Qualitative and Quantitative Strategies* (Berkeley: University of California Press, 1987) and Charles Ragin and Howard Becker, eds., *What is a Case?* (New York: Cambridge University Press, 1992, forthcoming).

CONTENT ANALYSIS

The best review of content analysis is Thelma McCormack's "Content Analysis: The Social History of the Method," in *Studies in Communications Vol. II: Culture Code and Content Analysis* (Greenwich,Conn., JAI Press, 1982). McCormack traces the evolution of the method since its inception in the analysis of propaganda following World War I, and its various uses by political scientists, sociologists and social psychologists. McCormack's understanding of content analysis is broad: "content analysis has traditionally been used in studies of the relationship between symbolic systems, between a recorded test of some type and forms of consciousness—attitudes, opinions, states of mind." She adds that "...all that content analysis has assumed in the past is an interactive process between two observable and, in principle, measurable dimensions of experience, one of which exists as a document" (1982, p. 145). Content analysis of the mass media has been closely linked to social psychological studies of public opinion, attitudes and attitude change. One problem with early content analysis was that it appeared to infer how readers interpreted texts. Bereleson countered this criticism with the suggestion that the method was most useful for comparative studies of media, and continued the drive toward quantification (see Bernard Berelson, *Content Analysis in Communications Research,* New York: Free Press, 1952; Ithiel de Sola Pool and Wilbur Schramm, eds., *Handbook of*

Communications Research, Chicago: Rand McNally, 1973). Studies of stereotyping in the media—images of blacks or women, for example—or studies of media violence or pornography often use the method of content analysis. (See chapter 9 for a discussion of some of these studies and their limitations.)

For much of this century, content analysis has been distanced from literary analysis of texts not only in the objective scientific aspirations, but in that different kinds of texts were studied: letters to the editor or comic strips and cartoons—popular culture without aesthetic claims. We have seen in the text how this distance is now being bridged by some people in cultural studies. The positivist thrust within content analysis has been carried on by the culture indicators approach, which attempts to measure quantitatively ideas and values in a culture. George Gerbner's work on television violence was important in launching this approach (see his "Toward Cultural Indicators: The Analysis of Mass Mediated Message Systems," in *The Analysis of Communication Content,* New York, NY: John Wiley, 1969; also "Political Functions of Television Viewing: A Cultivation Analysis" in *Cultural Indicators: An International Symposium,* eds., G. Melischek, K.E. Rosengren and J. Stappers (Vienna: Verlag der Osterreichischen Akademie der Wissenschaften). J. Zvi Namenwirth and Robert Weber (*Dynamics of Culture,* Winchester, MA: Allen and Unwin, 1987) examine relationships between cultural indicators and political and economic change. They use content analysis on speeches from political authorities with the "relative attention paradigm" to examine how much attention societies devote to various themes over time (see also Robert Weber, *Basic Content Analysis,* second ed., Beverly Hills CA: Sage, 1990). Another, slightly different, extension of a cultural indicators approach to a cross-national comparison is R. Inglehart's *Culture Shift in Advanced Industrial Society* (Princeton, Princeton University Press, 1990).

Recently the study of texts alone has seen a resurgence. An interesting experiment in this regard is Thelma McCormack's 1982 response to atheoretical quantification: She asked social scientists with five different theoretical perspectives to interpret Martin Luther King's "I have a dream..." speech in order to show how coding and interpretation in content analysis could be informed by various sorts of perspectives. The analysis of various kinds of "texts" is central to the postmodern challenge (see chapter 11). For an example of a sociologist exploring social theory through the expressions of the postmodern self in Hollywood films see Norman Denzin, *Images of Postmodern Society,* (Newbury Park: Sage, 1991).

CONVERSATION ANALYSIS

Although there is a tendency to see conversation analysis as isolated from other currents in sociology, some of those using the method see conversation analysis as providing unique opportunities for the study of culture. For a review of some of the possibilities see Deidre Boden, "People Are Talking: Conversation Analysis and Symbolic Interaction" in Becker and McCall, eds., *Symbolic Interaction and Cultural Studies* (Chicago: University of Chicago Press, 1990). Boden describes talk as language-in-action; she sees talk as the heart of social interaction. Conversation analysis provides a method for describing and analyzing language-in-action using recordings of talk from natural settings. Boden's own work illustrates the potential of conversation analysis for the sociology of culture: The phone calls between John F. Kennedy and Governor Barnet of Mississippi during the "Mississippi Crisis" following the registration of George Meredith to integrate the university (discussed in the article in Becker and McCall), and her studies of story telling among the elderly, "The Past as a Resource: A Conversation Analysis of Elderly Talk" (with Denise Bielby), *Human Development* 26 (1983):308–319. The emphasis on revealing the ways that talk is ordered have great potential for showing us the structure of culture operating in daily interaction processes. For another example, see Don Zimmeman and Candace West, "Sex Roles, Interruptions and Silences in Conversations," pp.105–129 in Barrie Thorne and Nancy Henley, eds. *Language and Sex: Difference and Dominance* (Rowley, MA: Newbury House, 1975).

DEMOGRAPHIC ANALYSIS

Stanley Lieberson has recently argued for the application of demography for certain kinds of cultural analysis. In "A Brief Introduction to the Demographic Analysis of Culture," *Newsletter of the Sociology of Culture* 6 (1992), No. 4:21–2, Lieberson suggests that the concepts of life cycle, age cohorts, and period effects are "powerful tools that are applicable for the analysis of cultural change" (21). Sorting out age, cohort, and period effects is essential to understanding certain patterns of cultural change as well as the impact of certain events. Researchers with various perspectives can benefit from being more self-conscious regarding the issues Lieberson is raising.

BIBLIOGRAPHIC ESSAY

By Pamela J. Forman, John R. Hall, and Mary Jo Neitz, with the assistance of Rebecca Anne Allahyari, Molly Cate, Susan Neese, and Tony Waters

Ongoing dialogues among sociologists and other researchers are continually reshaping cultural studies in ways that cannot be captured by any single text. This bibliographic essay introduces some additional interesting and informative pathways into this perpetual conversation beyond those directly cited in the text. Needless to say, the books and articles noted are, at best, suggestive of a much broader range of studies. Other bibliographies should be consulted for more comprehensive listings; particularly useful in this regard is the ongoing bibliographic series compiled by Richard A. Peterson in *Culture,* the newsletter of the Culture Section of the American Sociological Association, 1722 N Street NW, Washington, DC, 20036. In addition, certain journals are of particular interest for their attention to cultural analysis. *Theory, Culture and Society* looks especially at modernity, postmodernity and consumer culture. *Media, Culture and Society* and *State, Culture and Society* also offer strong foci on cultural analysis. Most sociology journals—including both of the principal U.S. journals, the *American Journal of Sociology* and the *American Sociological Review*—have articles concerning the sociology of culture, and the interdisciplinary *Theory and Society* will have important critical assessments. On popular culture, there is the *Journal of Popular Culture,* while *American*

Studies, American Studies International and the *Journal of American Studies* can be consulted for articles specifically on American culture. Articles in *Signs, Feminist Studies,* and *Differences: A Journal of Feminist Cultural Studies* often examine cultural studies and feminism, while *Discourse: Journal for Theoretical Studies in Media and Culture* explores cultural studies, the media and literature, and the politics of sexuality.

The citations in the present essay are organized by chapter. However, all subjects covered in a given chapter are not necessarily represented in this bibliography. Moreover, the subjects of much good research are relevant to more than one chapter in the present book; it therefore may be useful to browse freely. Authors mentioned in the essay with only the year given as a citation are discussed elsewhere in the book, and their cited works may be found in the main bibliography.

CHAPTER 1: SOCIOLOGY AND CULTURE

Approaches to the sociology of culture are varied; the range—from interpretive and functionalist approaches to semiotic and poststructuralist ones—is captured in a selection of classical and contemporary readings edited, with introductory essays, by Jeffrey Alexander and Steven Seidman entitled *Culture and Society: Contemporary Debates* (New York: Cambridge University Press, 1990). Classical sources of the sociology of culture not contained in Alexander and Seidman's reader include Karl Mannheim and Georg Simmel. Among other works, Mannheim's *Essays on the Sociology of Culture* (London: Routledge and Kegan Paul, 1956), include classic analyses of worldviews. Because Simmel (1950) distinguished form from cultural content, his sociology has an unusual theoretical relationship to the sociology of culture. A survey of his work, as well as that of Max Weber, is provided by Lawrence A. Scaff in his 1988 essay, "Weber, Simmel and the Sociology of Culture" (*Sociological Review* 36: 1–30).

Beyond the classics, the renaissance of sociological interest in culture beginning in the 1960s can be traced in a number of works. The Centre for Contemporary Cultural Studies at the University of Birmingham in England was influential, along with Raymond Williams, in constructing a Marxist approach to culture. The work of Clifford Geertz was similarly important for recasting the interpretive approach to cultural analysis in anthropology. The interpretive anthropological approach has been challenged by the controversial theories of sociobiologists such as E. O. Wilson, whose approach to culture has been considered by Garrett Hardin, "Sociobiology—Aesop with Teeth," in *Social Theory and Practice* 4 (1977): 303–13. But interpretive anthropology of the Geertzian sort has been far more influential in sociology. For example, Janet Wolff's early work, *Hermeneutic Philosophy and the Sociology of Art* (London: Routledge and Kegan Paul, 1975) called for incorporation of hermeneutics into sociological analysis of culture. The book of Robert Wuthnow and his associates, *Cultural Analysis*, undertakes a more extended and more eclectic effort at founding the sociology of culture in the work of Peter L. Berger, Mary Douglas, Michel Foucault, and Jürgen Habermas. Other explorations of the legacies of major classical and contemporary theorists in sociology and anthropology are contained in Diane J. Austin-Broos's edited book, *Creating Culture: Profiles in the Study of Culture* (London: Unwin Hyman, 1988).

In the U.S., the increased interest in the sociology of culture beginning in the 1960s has origins in the study of popular culture, in previously formulated sociologies of (typically high) art and music, in the interpretive and interactionist traditions, in the Marxist turn toward semiotics and poststructuralist thought, and in the efforts to found a post-Parsonian neofunctionalism. Sociological analysts of popular culture took the lead early on in defining the sociology of culture. A series of authors have followed the path of Gary Alan Fine, Richard A. Peterson and Paul Hirsch, grappling with issues of defining the sociology of culture, its central concepts and domain as a field in relation to popular culture. Writing for the *Journal of Popular Culture* audience in 1977, Fine (11: 381–84), Peterson (11: 385–400) and Hirsch (11: 401–13) each argued for bringing sociological perspectives to the serious consideration of popular culture. In this line, Lawrence Mintz wrote for an American Studies audience about the growth in studies of popular culture during the 1970s; in "'Recent Trends in the Study of Popular Culture': since 1971," (*American Studies International* 21 [1983]: 88–103) Mintz gave particular notice to social histories that were moving beyond nostalgic and pop description to analysis of processes and their relation to social groups and strata. Chandra Mukerji and Michael Schudson published their piece "Popular Culture" (*Annual Review of Sociology* 12 (1986): 47–66) which similarly emphasized the increasing importance given by scholars to popular culture; by citing the work of a broad range of serious scholars, dealing both with contemporary and historical issues, Mukerji and Schudson showed that the study of popular culture amounted to more than a "pop" sociology.

Other reflections showed the field to encompass more than popular culture. In an interesting mapping of the field for the 1988 *Annual Review of Sociology*, Robert Wuthnow and Martha Witten describe the growth within the sociology of culture in terms of both theoretical methods and substantive areas of research. Craig Calhoun's "Social Issues in the Study of Culture," in *Comparative Social Research* 11 (1989): 1–29, places the growth of the sociology of culture in the context of parallel trends in anthropology, history, literary criticism and media studies. Michele Lamont and Robert Wuthnow pursue the project of charting a distinctive problematic of the sociology of culture by suggesting that recent developments in Europe and the U.S. point toward a focus of analysis that connects power and the codes of social life; see their "Betwixt and Between," pp. 287–315 in George Ritzer, ed., *Frontiers of Social Theory* (New York: Columbia University Press, 1990).

The interdisciplinary arena of cultural studies continues to develop and influence both theoretical and methodological foundations, as well as substantive efforts of sociohistorical inquiry. The interchanges run both ways between the established disciplines and cultural studies. Contributors to the volume edited by Howard S. Becker and Michal McCall, *Symbolic Interaction and Cultural Studies* (University of Chicago Press, 1990) point to the broadly interactionist contributions to opening up subjects ranging from cultural history, science and religion, to music and the body. Chandra Mukerji and Michael Schudson more directly link their sociological interests with the interdisciplinary projects by offering an edited book, *Rethinking Popular Culture: Contemporary Perspectives in Cultural Studies* (University of California Press, 1991). The book actually titled *Cultural Studies,* edited by Lawrence Grossberg and his colleagues (1992), demonstrates the diversity of work travelling under the banner, and comparison of it with more purely sociological approaches will help to underscore both the mutual contributions and the distinctive agendas of sociology and cultural studies.

It should also be noted that the sociology of culture has affinities with a variety of other already established substantive fields of sociology, including the sociologies of art, music, religion, knowledge and science. It is beyond our scope to trace all these affinities here; indeed, it is reasonable to suggest that certain subfields, such as art and music, are now generally understood within the framework of the sociology of culture. Other areas—the sociologies of sport and of emotions, for example—have their own distinctive problematics, but nevertheless warrant attention for their application of cultural analysis; reviews are offered by Howard Elterman in a 1986 article, "Theorizing on the Sociology of Sport" in *Arena Review* 10: 1–12, and Peggy A. Thoits, 1989. "The Sociology of Emotions," *Annual Review of Sociology* 15 (1989): 317–42.

For all the interest in culture and its diverse affinities with other sociological issues, efforts at new theorizations remain small in number, perhaps because of the postmodern critique of totalizing theories of any kind, and because previously existing theories have found new life in cultural analysis. Interpretive and hermeneutic approaches to theorizing culture have never been prone to formalization, but there have been efforts on other fronts. The most programmatic attempts have been those of Wuthnow (1987), and of Margaret Archer (1988), who have sought to offer a new account that displaces the opposition between culture and structure. That any such effort faces profound problems of reconciling inner meaning and external culture can be seen from reading the critique by Eric Rambo and Elaine Chan, "Text, Structure and Action in Cultural Sociology: a Commentary on 'Positive Objectivity' in Wuthnow and Archer," published in *Theory and Society* 19 (1990): 635–44. For Rambo and Chan, the works of Pierre Bourdieu and Ann Swidler offer less objectivist ways of theorizing culture. Similarly, Nader Saiedi draws from Bourdieu to develop his critique in "Agency and Freedom in Neofunctionalist Action Theory:

A Critique," in *Social Research* 55 (1988): 775–806. In turn, Bourdieu's theorization is subjected to a Weberian critique in John R. Hall, "The Capital(s) of Culture," in Michele Lamont and Marcel Fournier's edited volume, *Cultivating Differences* (University of Chicago Press, 1992).

CHAPTER 2: CULTURE AS MORAL DISCOURSE

Recent debates about culture and moral order have raised a set of questions about the nature of the self and the relations between the individual and community and the individual and society. These questions have been addressed in different ways by writers located in different intellectual traditions. Intense debates have also centered on specific institutions, especially religion, education, and the family, focusing on how the institutions do (or should) maintain and reproduce the moral culture of the nation.

Debates about individualism and American culture are long-standing. One of the best known studies of the changes in national character is *The Lonely Crowd; A Study of the Changing American Character* by David Riesman. A now classic study of suburban life in the 1950s is William H. Whyte's *The Organization Man* (New York: Simon and Schuster, 1956). A current study, *Culture Wars: The Struggle to Define America* by James D. Hunter (New York: Basic Books, 1991), looks at arenas where moral conflict is particularly polarized. An ethnographic approach to these issues is Harve Varenne's appreciative study of life in one small town, *Americans Together: Structured Diversity in a Midwestern Town* (New York: Teachers College Press, 1977).

An important philosophical treatment of identity and morality in modern society is Charles Taylor's *The Sources of the Self: The Making of Modern Identity* (Cambridge, MA: Harvard University Press, 1989). Taylor's work touches many of the topics raised in this chapter. He asks whether we pay a price in human wholeness for the fulfillment of our moral duties, and suggests ways that individuals in modern society can construct plural narratives: stories that will form the basis for future aspirations. A further source on narrative as a form of reasoning and interpretation is D.E. Polkinhorne, *Narrative Knowing and the Human Sciences* (Albany, NY: State University of New York, 1988).

Arguments about the moral order are often situated with reference to institutions. Tocqueville saw institutions as a mediating presence warding off the possibilities of excess individualism in modern society. In *The Good Society* (sequel to *Habits of the Heart*) Bellah, Madsen, Sullivan, Swidler and Tipton focus on institutions in American society (New York: Knopf, 1991); they argue that solutions to problems of the social and cultural order can be found through taking responsibility for our social institutions. Other writers have focused on particular institutions. Bellah has a long-standing concern with religion and moral culture. Some of his early essays on this topic are collected in *Beyond Belief; Essays on Religion in a Post-traditional World* (New York: Harper and Row, 1970).

Although religion was disestablished relatively early in the United States, certain religious forms, notably congregationalism and revivalism, have had a lasting influence on American life. William G. McLoughlin argues that revivalism has been a vehicle for cultural debates and social reform from the first great awakening in the 1740s to the present. His book *Revivals, Awakenings and Social Reform: An Essay on Religion and Social Change in America* (Chicago: University of Chicago Press, 1978) asserts that the major "awakenings" are revitalization movements that succeed in articulating personal and cultural levels of experience with changing social structures. Yet in order to do this he must broaden the definition of revivalism beyond its usual scope to continue to apply the concept when formal religious institutions declined in influence in American culture. Many authors have addressed various aspects of this decline. For Ann Douglas in *The Feminization of American Culture* the decline in power of Protestant ministers was part of a feminization of American culture. Will Herberg looks at the history of American religion in terms of its increasing inclusivity. In *Protestant, Catholic, Jew: An Essay in American Religious Sociology* (Garden City, NY: Doubleday, 1955), Herberg describes a convergence among American religious traditions toward generalized religiosity based in a common understanding of "the American way of life." By the 1980s, the old Protestant mainline felt battered by both secularists and the newly vocal evangelicals and fundamentalists. Wade Clark Roof and William McKinney use the General Social Survey to document the growth of an even more inclusive but less influential "mainline" in *American Mainline Religion: Its Changing Shape and Future* (New Brunswick, NJ: Rutgers University Press, 1987). Theologian Richard Neuhaus argues for the need for religious institutions to be a part of public moral debate in *The Naked Public Square: Religion and Democracy in America* (Grand Rapids, MI: W.B. Eerdmans Publishing Company, 1984). Frances Fitzgerald offers a different interpretation of the influence of religious institutions in American culture by focusing on outsiders rather than elites. In *Cities on a Hill: A Journey through Contemporary American Cultures* (New York: Simon and Schuster, 1986) Fitzgerald shows how sectarian forms have been adopted by groups that form communities separated in varying degrees from the dominant society. Her case studies include gay male culture in the Castro district of San Francisco, retirees, as well as two religiously based communities, Jerry Falwell's Liberty Baptist Church, and the Bhagwan's Rajneeshpurim in Oregon.

In recent years, debates about religion have often been closely allied with arguments about the family. Popular religious leaders and some politicians have seized changes in family structures as symbolic of the decay of moral culture. In *The War over the Family* (Garden City, NY: Anchor/Doubleday, 1983) Peter and Brigitte Berger offer a sociologically informed account of what they see as a decline in the family occurring with modernization in society. David Popenoe also sees a decline in the family which he describes from a functionalist perspective in *Disturbing the Nest: Family Change and Decline in Modern Societies* (New York: Aldine de Gruyter, 1988). He compares Sweden, as the society where he sees the decline as most advanced, with the United States, New Zealand, and Switzerland. Leftists and feminists have tended to see the changes in the family in a different light, however. One collection that sees benefits for women and children in some of the changes is *Rethinking the Family: Some Feminist Questions* by Barrie Thorne and Marilyn Yalom (New York: Longman, 1982). A recent ethnography that examines the meaning of changes in the institution of the family for working-class families in Silicon Valley is *Brave New Families* (New York, Basic, 1990) by Judith Stacey.

A third institution which has been at the center of recent debates about the moral culture is education, especially the public schools. Some of these debates have had an explicitly religious content, as in the debates over teaching evolution and creationism, described by Dorothy Nelkin in *The Creation Controversy* (Boston: Seabury Press, 1982). More recent is a broader debate about the centrality of the tradition of western thought within education today. Defending the "canon" of traditional works are Allan Bloom in *The Closing of the American Mind* (New York: Simon and Schuster, 1987) and Dinesh D'Souza in *Illiberal Education: The Politics of Race and Sex on Campus* (New York: Free Press, 1991). Catharine Stimpson has argued the other side. For a short but cogent defense of the efforts to build a more inclusive curriculum see her article "New 'Politically Correct' Metaphors Insult History and Our Campuses" *Chronicle of Higher Education,* May 29, 1991, p. A40. Cornell West and Bell Hooks offer a more extended and provocative dialogue in *Breaking Bread: Insurgent Black Intellectual Life* (Boston, South End Press, 1991).

The alternative moral discourse begun by Carol Gilligan with *In a Different Voice* has encouraged much interest in the ideas of self-in-relation and an ethic of care. In addition to the ongoing work of Gilligan and her associates, who continue to explore issues raised in the original studies, writers in many other fields are considering the implications of models of separate or connected selves for institutions and moral culture. Political theorists have considered what an ethic of care would mean for our conceptualizations of rights and justice; a number of pieces featured in *Feminism and Political Theory* (Chicago, University of Chicago Press, 1990), edited by Cass R. Sunstein, show Gilligan's influence. Paula England has used the model of the connected self to critique the assumptions of the rational choice perspective in the social sciences in "A Feminist Critique of Rational Choice Theories," *The American Sociologist* 20 (1989): 14–28.

There are a number of other feminist writers that are working on developing models of the connected self. Of particular interest is the work of theologian Catherine Keller in *From a Broken Web: Separation, Sexism, and Self* (Boston: Beacon Press, 1986). Keller traces notions of males as separate and autonomous back to the works of the Greeks and early Christians. In contrast, theologians Katie Cannon and Delores Williams see models of connected selves in the writings of African-American women. For examples of their work see "Resources for a Constructive Ethic in the Life and Work of Zora Neale Hurston," *Journal of Feminist Studies in Religion* 1 (1985): 37–51 by Katie Cannon, and "Women's Oppression and Lifeline Politics in Women's Religious Narratives" in *Journal of Feminist Studies in Religion* 1 (1985): 59–72, by Delores Williams. Most recently legal scholars have also begun to question the consequences of the model of the separated self for our ideas about rights, contracts, and justice. Two examples of this work are Martha Minnow's *Making all the Difference: Inclusion, Exclusion and American Law* (Ithaca, NY: Cornell University Press, 1991) and Patricia Williams's *The Alchemy of Race and Rights* (Cambridge, MA: Harvard University Press, 1991).

CHAPTER 3: FOLK CULTURE

Chapter 3 examines the development of the concept of culture by 19th- and 20th-century writers in the social sciences in terms of a dichotomy between traditional and modern culture. Images of folk cultures became mirrors of the writers' societies. In depictions of traditional societies, religion and religious ritual were seen as undergirding an integrating culture, lost in modern society. Recent work is providing grounds for reconceptualizing ritual and tradition.

The work of Peter Berger offers an explication of the process through which culture became internalized in the subjective consciousness of individuals through the religious symbols permeating daily life experiences in traditional societies. In *The Homeless Mind* Berger, Berger and Kellner contrast legitimation through shared religious symbols with the difficulty in modern society of making the institutional arrangements of the society plausible to those within it. This is also the theme, with particular reference to the problems of religion in modern society, of *The Heretical Imperative* by Peter Berger (Garden City, NY: Anchor Doubleday, 1979). Berger was influenced by Arnold Gehlen's writings about the effects of pluralism in modern society on institutions. He formulated the problem of legitimation as a matter of the "deinstitutionalization" of modern society; see Gehlen's *Man in the Age of Technology* (New York: Columbia University Press, 1980). An analysis that uses Berger's theoretical perspective with survey research to study modern evangelicals in a pluralist society is James D. Hunter's *American Evangelicalism* (New Brunswick, NJ: Rutgers University Press, 1983). For an ethnographic study of modern fundamentalists, also using Berger's perspective, see Nancy Ammerman, *Bible Believers* (New Brunswick, NJ: Rutgers University Press, 1988). For a social history of the impact of religious pluralism on a particular community see David Hackett's study of Dutch Calvinism in Albany, NY, *The Rude Hand of Innovation: Religion and Social Order in Albany, NY,*

1652–1836 (New York: Oxford University Press, 1991). An important element of the dichotomy between traditional and modern societies in Berger's work, as well as other approaches to secularization, is the separation between the sacred and the profane. In the works of the founding fathers of sociology, men in traditional societies were viewed as having access to the sacred, but not women. For the implications of this for the founding fathers' understanding of secularization and its continuing impact on current work in the sociology of religion see Victoria Erickson's *Speaking in the Dark and Hearing the Voices: Towards a Feminist Social Theory of Religion,* (Philadelphia: Fortress Press, 1992).

Despite the tendency to reduce ritual to habit, a number of writers have described the rituals—religious and otherwise—of groups and individuals in modern societies. Llyod W. Warner devoted the last volume of his "Yankee City" books to the study of symbolic life. His book, *The Living and the Dead* (New Haven, CT: Yale University Press, 1959) is well worth reading today for its images of how the community symbolized itself in mid-century America. Robert Bellah's concept of civil religion has inspired much investigation into religious and quasi-religious symbols, beliefs and rituals. For a review of this literature see James A. Mathisen, "Twenty Years After Bellah: Whatever Happened to American Civil Religion?" *Sociological Analysis* 50 (1989): 129–50. Like Bellah, Randall Collins has been inspired by Durkheim's analysis of religion and society. His essay, "The Sociology of God," pp. 30–59 in his *Sociological Insight* (New York: Oxford, 1982), describes the theory of how rituals integrate the social order. For an extension of the Durkheimian analysis to a situation of conflict see Eric Rothenbuhler's article "The Liminal Fight: Mass Strikes as Ritual and Interpretation," pp. 66–90 in Jeffery Alexander, ed., *Durkheimian Sociology: Cultural Studies.* In *Ritual, Politics and Power,* (New Haven, CT: Yale University Press, 1988), a book that ranges across countries, as well as intellectual disciplines, David Kretzer turns to political life to show how rituals and symbols are used to create legitimacy and enhance solidarity, as well as to incite and diffuse conflict.

This chapter argues that the notion of folk culture was largely a construction of intellectuals. A related topic is the construction of tradition. The essays in Eric Hobsbawm and Terence Ranger, *The Invention of Tradition* (Cambridge: Cambridge University Press, 1983) describe the invention of traditions in Europe, India and Africa. Rather than seeing traditions as specific sets of practices or things, Gary Allan Fine suggests we consider "tradition" as a form of rhetoric relating the past to the present. In "The Process of Tradition: Cultural Models of Change and Content," *Comparative Social Research* 11 (1989): 263–78 Fine draws on symbolic interaction and folklore traditions to make his argument. In their essay "G.H. Mead's Theory of the Past" *American Sociological Review* 48 (1983): 161–73, David Maines, Noreen Sugrue, and Michael Katovich explore Mead's discussion of the ways that the past is incorporated into the present, and often used to legitimate it. While there is a tendency to associate tradition with conservativism at some level, a number of writers show how that may not be the case. Donald Levine's essay, "The Flexibility of Traditional Cultures," pp. 44–54 in his *The Flight from Ambiguity* (Chicago: University of Chicago Press, 1985), documents innovation and diversity within a traditional culture, the Amhara of Ethiopia. Craig Calhoun points to cases where traditional communities will join radical movements in defense of their traditions in "The Radicalism of Tradition: Community Strength or Venerable Disguise and Borrowed Language," *American Journal of Sociology* 88 (1983): 886–914.

Folklorists contributed to the construction of folk societies through their work of collecting expressions and artifacts of the "vanishing folk cultures" within their own European societies. Folklorists today collect and analyze cultural forms and expressions, usually those outside of industrial mass production. Allan Dundes provides an introduction to the contemporary study of folklore in *Interpreting Folklore* (Bloomington: Indiana University Press, 1980). European folklorists have developed the concept of *folklorismus* to conceptualize ways that folklore is manipulated in modern societies, as when it is produced for mass consumption or used to sell mass produced items. Examples of this type of analysis can be found in *Folklore in the Modern World* (The Hague: Mouton, 1978), edited by R.M. Dorson.

One source of the deconstruction of the concept of folk culture comes from anthropologists re-examining their own tradition, in particular the ways that conventions of writing projected "objective" observations consistent with views of positive science but inconsistent with actual practice. In addition to *Writing Culture*, edited By James Clifford and George Marcus, other sources for exploring this work include *Works and Lives: The Anthropologist as Author* (Stanford: Stanford University Press, 1988) by Clifford Geertz, one of the most important figures in the interpretive turn in anthropology. See also the collection of essays edited by George Stocking, *Colonial Situations: Essays on the Contextualization of Ethnographic Knowledge* (Madison: University of Wisconsin Press).

CHAPTER 4: PRE-INDUSTRIAL SOURCES OF CONTEMPORARY CULTURE

The dominant features of cultural change in the early modern era may be traced to rationalization and routinization, the consolidation of the modern world economy, the growth of towns and cities, the emergence of new social strata, and the emergence of new forms of patronage, cultural production, and entertainment. These developments, of course, were intertwined, and recent efforts at cultural history have been increasingly focused on the connections.

The theoretical themes raised in the chapter have received extensive treatment. *The Rise of Western Rationalism: Max Weber's Developmental History* (Berkeley: University of California Press, 1981), by Wolfgang Schluchter, offers a synthesis and extension of Weber's overall argument. On the issue of rationalization, Guenther Roth holds that Weber viewed the process operating in multiple arenas, sometimes with divergent implications, rather than as an overarching social force; see Roth's essay, "Rationalization in Max Weber's Developmental History," pp. 75–91 in Scott Lash and Sam Whimster, eds., *Max Weber, Rationality and Modernity* (London: Allen and Unwin, 1987). The debate over rationalization has its richest line of research in the consideration of Weber's controversial thesis about the Protestant ethic. A useful sorting through the issues has been provided by Gordon Marshall's *In Search of the Spirit of Capitalism* (London: Hutchinson, 1982). There are also studies more generally concerned with relations between culture and economy. Alan MacFarlane's *The Culture of Capitalism* (London: Basil Blackwell, 1987) is a collection of essays about continuities between medieval and early modern England that predated and encouraged capitalist development. *An Embarrassment of Riches* (Berkeley: University of California Press, 1988) is a rich account by Simon Schama of how seventeenth-century Dutch culture reflected the contradictions of economic abundance reckoned against moral and civic issues.

Rationalization, of course, can be studied in other venues than economics and religious ethics. Physical production of material objects is worth examining because of the potential for linking issues of technology, rationalization, and social change. The classic study of technology's significance prior to the Reformation is Lynn White, Jr.'s *Medieval Technology and Social Change* (Oxford: Oxford University Press, 1962). In a more encompassing project, Brian Cotterell and Johan Kammings have written *Mechanics of Pre-Industrial Technology* (New York: Cambridge University Press, 1990); the book traces basic technologies of the production of material culture up to the industrial age. An even longer view is offered by Stephen Bayley, who documents the transformation of art to design as dependent upon the development of technologies of mass reproduction; see *The Transformation of Cultural Production and Distribution In Commerce and Culture* (London: Fourth Estate, 1989). As a case study, Robert Darnton's 1971 essay, "Reading, Writing, and Publishing in Eighteenth-century France" (*Daedalus* 100: 214–56) opens up from intellectual history to publishing and its connection to the political, social, economic and cultural circumstances that reveal a world of smut, slander and political intrigue.

Analysis of cultural transformation often is less concerned with relations between technology and social change than with the significance of cultural developments proper. Studies in this vein include Peter Burke's *The Italian Renaissance: Culture and Society in Italy* (Cambridge: Polity Press, 1986) as well as Peter Borsay's *The English Urban Renaissance* (Oxford: Clarendon Press, 1989). In the latter book, Borsay compares the English urban renaissance with the Italian renaissance, tracing cultural revivals, urban phenomena associated with high culture, and absorption and propagation of classical art and thought.

Some works trace the emergence of specific cultural genres. There is, for example, Michael McKeon's *The Origins of the English Novel: 1600–1740* (Baltimore: John Hopkins University Press, 1987), and a more wide-ranging discussion, Thomas Doherty's book, *On Modern Authority: The Theory and Condition of Writing, 1500 to the Present* (New York: St. Martin's Press, 1987). Other studies pursue a particular social realm and its relation to culture. For example, Phillippe Aries, Georges Duby and Roger Chartier, editors of the five-volume project, *A History of Private Life* (Cambridge: Harvard University Press, 1987–1997), have brought together a wealth of material. A parallel, but more sociological and comparative, work is Barrington Moore's *Privacy: Studies in Social and Cultural History* (New York: Pantheon Books, 1984). Studies on women also have yielded results that bear on an understanding of culture. Caroline Bynum's 1987 study: *Holy Feast and Holy Fast* (Berkeley: University of California Press) examines the connection between religion, the control of food, and potential bases of power for women in medieval society. *Not of Woman Born* (Ithaca: Cornell University Press, 1990), by Renate Blumenfeld-Kosinski, discusses midwives who presided over a tangle of ideological, political and legal issues which surrounded Caesarean births in medieval and Renaissance Europe.

Beyond such studies of culture per se, a number of comparative analyses trace various connections between culture, state-building, and economy. For example, a series of works make arguments about culture in relation to English—later, British—nationalism. Michael Hechter's well-known *Internal Colonialism* (Berkeley: University of California Press, 1975) effectively links a world-economy analysis of colonialism with the formation of ethnic identities in the British Isles; here, culture offers a basis of solidarity which has both economic and political implications. *The Rise of English Nationalism* (New York: St. Martin's Press, 1987), by Gerald Newman, discusses nationalism as a cultural phenomenon which made industrialization possible in England beginning in the eighteenth century, while Phillip Corrigan and Derek Sayer's *The Great Arch: English State Formation as Cultural Revolution* (New York: Basil Blackwell, 1985), considers the political implications of cultural and class changes.

Some studies have more directly addressed the relation between public cultural events and the struggles of various social strata. One is Michael Mullett's overview, *Popular Culture and Popular Protest in Late Medieval and Early Modern Europe* (New York: Croom Helm, 1987). More specific investigations include those of several authors who have analyzed the coalescence of religious and political symbols in popular festivals. The best known is Emmanuel Le Roy Ladurie's 1980 case study of a village in France, *Carnival in Romans* (New York: George Braziller). In a related vein, the book *Carnival and Theater* (New York: Methuen, 1985), by Michael D. Bristol, undertakes a critical analysis of Carnival and Lent as events of popular culture that challenged the political hegemony of the state in renaissance England, yet with only limited effectiveness. These studies raise questions that reflect a rich potential for further research on the relations of performance and power in the early modern era.

Studies of the audiences, patronage and genres for early modern cultural production by various social strata also represent a well established line of research within the histories of art, music and literature. A few examples will give a sense of the possibilities. In *Courtly Culture* (Berkeley: University of California Press, 1991), Joachim Bumke deconstructs the ideals of courtly society in the middle ages through an examination of literature. Romain Goldron's *Minstrels and Masters* (New York: H.S. Stuttman, 1968) examines the rise of secular music and minstrel schools at the end of the thirteenth century; he depicts this shift as a response to the emergence of increasingly monied classes whose members purchased musicians' services for ritual events such as weddings. Another study, David C. Price's *Patrons and Musicians of the English Renaissance* (Cambridge: Cambridge University Press, 1981), delineates how the courts, the Church and private patronage limited musicians in their professional advancement during a period of unemployment and creative restriction. Finally, for a comparable analysis of patronage, but for a later time period, there is Tia DeNora's article on the emergence of a serious music ideology in the late eighteenth century, "Musical Patronage and Social Change in Beethoven's Vienna" in the *American Journal of Sociology* 97 (1991): 310–46.

Given the long time span and the diverse kinds of questions about culture that have been pursued, the citations here only suggest that careful bibliographic research is likely to yield scholarship on a variety of questions about culture in the early modern era. Because of the increased interest in cultural history, searches for similar historical investigations concerned with other times and places than the European early modern era are likely to prove increasingly fruitful.

CHAPTER 5: INDUSTRIALISM AND MASS CULTURE

Chapter 5 is concerned with cultural ramifications of the Industrial Revolution, in particular the "consumption revolution" that accompanied the production of goods. Changes in the culture of consumption involved a movement from looking at consumption as necessary but exercised with restraint, to considering consumption as a way to promote the economy and express the self. The chapter considers changes in how goods were distributed; in addition it describes the consumption revolution as accompanied by changes in the culture of the workplace as well as changes in leisure activities.

A number of historians have turned their attention to changes in the culture of consumption. The essays by economic historians in the volume, *European Peasants and Their Markets* (Princeton: Princeton University Press, 1975), edited by William Parker and Eric Jones, provide a baseline for looking at the changes in the market. Colin Campbell, in *The Romantic Ethic and the Spirit of Modern Consumerism* (Oxford: Basil Blackwell, 1987) discusses the growth of consumption in 18th and 19th-century England.

A valuable source for approaching this literature as it concerns the United States in the late 19th and early 20th centuries is Daniel Horowitz, *The Morality of Spending: Attitudes toward the Consumer Society in America, 1875–1940* (Baltimore: Johns Hopkins University Press, 1985). See also the articles in Simon Bronner, ed., *Consuming Visions: Accumulation and the Display of Goods in America, 1810–1920* (New York: Norton, 1989), and Susan Strasser, *Satisfaction Guaranteed: The Making of the American Mass Market* (New York, Pantheon, 1989).

There is a vast amount of literature on the changes in the nature of work that accompanied industrialism. An introduction to that literature from a range of theoretical perspectives can be found in the following works: a classic Weberian study is Reinhard Bendix's *Work and Authority in Industry: Ideologies of Management in the Course of Industrialization* (New York: John Wiley and Sons, 1956); a Marxist study of changes occurring in the 20th century is Richard Edward's *Contested Terrain: The Transformation of the Workplace in the Twentieth Century* (New York: Basic Books, 1979); a broad survey of the history of American business since the 17th century is Alfred Chandler's *The Visible Hand: The Managerial Revolution in American Culture* (Cambridge, MA: Harvard University Press, 1977).

With industrialism and mass consumption people related to their environment in different ways. Richard Sennett has explored these changes in a number of his books. He contends that changing patterns of consumption and the desire for things resulted in a privatization of family life. In *Families Against the City* (Cambridge, MA: Harvard University Press, 1970) Sennett finds middle class families in the city of Chicago in the decades after the civil war increasingly withdrawing from urban life and seeking a refuge in their homes. In *The Uses of Disorder* (New York: Knopf, 1970) Sennett carries these same themes to an analysis of American cities in the latter half of the 20th century. Warren Sussman's essays collected in *Culture as History* (New York: Pantheon, 1984) are especially good on U.S. culture in the first part of the 20th century; his essays on the twenties and thirties portray an increasingly shared culture of consumption.

Mike Featherstone suggests ways that the use of the body as a vehicle for symbolic expression changed with the advent of mass consumption in "The Body in Consumer Culture," *Theory, Culture and Society* 1 (1982): 18–33. In addition to providing signals about social class, consumption also mediates the expression of sexuality, perhaps more so for women than for men. A comprehensive history of American sexuality, *Intimate Matters: A History of Sexuality in America* by John D'Emilo and Estell Freeman (New York: Harper and Row, 1988), shows how, at the same time as the link between sexuality and reproduction diminished, sexuality was being withdrawn from the family and relocated in the marketplace by capitalist economy. A speculative investigation of topics relating consumption and sexuality in the late 20th century is Jerry Jacobs' book, *The Search for Acceptance: Consumerism, Sexuality and the Self Among American Women* (Bristol, IN: Wyndham Hall, 1988). A study that brings together theories about the personal meaning of consumption with the growth of the department store is Elaine S. Akelson's social history of shoplifting, *When Ladies Go A-Thieving: Middle Class Shoplifters in the Victorian Department Store* (New York: Oxford University Press, 1989). Women were not simply passive objects reflecting cultural and social changes, but they also learned to use cultural resources for furthering their own interests. *Dining in America* (Amherst: University of Massachusetts Press, 1987), edited by Kathryn Grover, demonstrates women making increasingly conscious choices in the work they do in the private sphere to improve their status in the public sphere.

Advertising intrigues scholars as it does the public, and studies of advertising take many forms across many disciplines. Roland Marchand's detailed history, is a standard source. Some works focus on particular products, (often with reference to appeals to specific populations) such as perfumes, i.e. Robert Goldman's "Marketing Fragrance: Advertising and the Production of Commodity Signs," *Theory Culture and Society* 4 (1987) 691–725; cigarettes, i.e. David Altman et al., "How an Unhealthy Product is Sold: Cigarette Advertising in Magazines, 1960–1985," *Journal of Communications* 37 (1987): 95–106; and over-the-counter drugs, i.e., A. Vener and C. Khiplea, "Over-the-Counter Drug Advertising in Gender Oriented Popular Magazines," *Journal of Drug Education* 16 (1986): 367–81. Another approach is to focus on a particular medium such as MTV. Analysis here suggests the blurring of boundaries between the "programming" and the "advertisement": compare, for example, Virginia Fry and Donald Fry, "MTV: the 24 Hour Commercial," *Journal of Communication* 10 (1986): 29–33 with Robert Dunn, "Television, Consumption and the Commodity Form," in *Theory, Culture and Society* 3 (1986): 49–64.

For other citations to more general criticisms of mass society by contemporary interpreters of critical theory see sources listed for Chapter 7.

CHAPTER 6: SOCIAL STRATIFICATION AND CULTURE IN THE AGE OF MASS PRODUCTION

The intersection of culture and stratification is conventionally mapped by both sociologists and people in general along dimensions such as class, status, gender, race and ethnicity. The issues raised by Weber, Gans and Bourdieu are of special interest, and they have been addressed by a wide range of research. Beyond the theoretical issues, there are a variety of substantive analyses of connections between culture and stratification.

For all the ferment in social theory, class remains a central axis of interest. A number of empirical analyses provide substance by which to consider the theoretical arguments. In an historical analysis, Janet Wolff has written *The Culture of Capital: Art, Power and the Nineteenth Century Middle Class* (Manchester: Manchester University, 1988). Three other studies explore a much more recent phenomenon—the fate of the shrinking middle class in the United States, and the cultural tensions that have emerged with the shift in prospects. Benjamin DeMott is concerned in part with the middle class's changing role in setting societal standards. His book, *The Imperial Middle: Why Americans Can't Think Straight about Class* (New York: Morrow, 1990), thus bears comparison to the empirical analysis of Michele Lamont. In a related vein, Barbara Ehrenreich depicts the middle class's anxiety over losing cultural authority in *Fear of Falling: The Inner Life of the Middle Class* (New York: Pantheon, 1989). Finally, there is the book *Falling From Grace: The Experience of Downward Mobility in the American Middle Class* (New York: Free Press, 1988). In it, Katherine Newman explores the social consequences of losing one's job within a meritocratic culture that correlates self-worth with occupational status.

Other intriguing studies similarly consider the status positionings of class-based groups in relation to complex and shifting economic and cultural categories. A good deal of survey research suggests that blue-collar workers tend to characterize themselves as belonging to the middle class, despite their contradictory occupational status. In *Cultures of Solidarity: Consciousness, Action and Contemporary American Workers* (Berkeley: University of California Press, 1988), Rick Fantasia critiques such research through three case studies dealing with strike mobilization, union representation and working class power. The work of Halle (1984) suggests that the ambiguities between multiple identities are quite strong among blue collar workers. Another study, *The Southern Redneck* (New York: Praeger, 1982), by Julian V. Roebuck and Mark Hickson, explores the interaction of regional status-group labels and social class.

Notwithstanding the profound changes in culture and class formation among the working and middle classes, the strongest sociological debate about class in the 1970s has concerned the changes in social strata connected with emergence of the so-called postindustrial society, and the rise of various "new" classes connected with expansions within developed societies in knowledge and service industries. Alain Touraine's *The Post-Industrial Society* (New York: Random House, 1971) and Daniel Bell (1973) offer contrasting assessments. In Alvin Gouldner's *The Future of Intellectuals and the Rise of the New Class* (New York: Seabury Press, 1979), the origins go much deeper: industrialization itself spawned an intellectual and technocratic intelligentsia, dubbed the "new class."

One class—the poor—certainly is not "new," but the debates about the cultures of poor people, their sources, and their relations to mass media remain controversial, partly because of the implications for governmental social policy. Two studies beyond those cited in the chapter should be consulted concerning the culture of poverty thesis. One is Stephen Steinberg's chapter, "The Culture of Poverty Reconsidered," pp. 106–27 in his book *The Ethnic Myth: Race, Ethnicity and Class in America* (New York: Atheneum, 1981). The other book, *The Cultural Facade* (Urbana: University of Illinois Press, 1988) by Susan Rigdon, explores the life and times of one of the principals of the debate, Oscar Lewis.

Most generally, the debate about culture and stratification recently has been focused on the work of Bourdieu and his concept of cultural capital. For a good introduction, see the collection edited by Richard Harker, Cheleen Mahar and Chris Wilkes, *An Introduction to the Work of Pierre Bourdieu* (New York: St. Martin's Press, 1990). Two worthwhile critiques are: Richard Jenkins's "Pierre Bourdieu and the Reproduction of Determinism." *Sociology* 16 (1982): 270–81; and "The Fragmented World of Symbolic Forms: Reflections on Pierre Bourdieu's Sociology of Culture," *Theory, Culture and Society* 3 (1986): 55–66, by Axel Honneth and T. Talbot. A more constructive critique is offered by Michele Lamont and Annette Lareau, who assess Bourdieu's approach and identify an emergent research agenda; see "Cultural Capital: Allusions, Gaps and Glissandos in Recent Theoretical Development," *Sociological Theory* 6 (1988): 153–68. Other work fulfills a substantive research agenda of the sort that Lamont and Lareau sketch. The work of Paul DiMaggio and his collaborators bridges subareas in the sociology of culture, but some works are specifically concerned with stratification. For example, see Dimaggio's article with co-author John Mohr, "Cultural Capital, Educational Attainment, and Marital Selection," in the *American Journal of Sociology* 90 (1985): 1231–61. Lamont's (1992) own book offers an important comparative and empirical assessment of Bourdieu's ideas. In addition, there is the book that Lamont and Marcel Fournier have edited, *Cultivating Differences: Symbolic Boundaries and the Making of Inequality* (Chicago: University of Chicago Press, 1992); the variety of contributions in the edited book shows the potential of the earlier research agenda, not only for the study of stratification, but also for issues of power and production of culture. Another sign of the importance of the topic is the review symposium, organized by Vera Zolberg, on various recent studies by Bourdieu and his colleagues; see *Contemporary Sociology* 21 #2 (1992): 151–61, which includes a review of a book of special relevance here, Pierre Bourdieu et al., *Photography: a Middle-Brow Art* (Cambridge, England: Polity, 1990). Overall, the controversy demonstrates the power of the cultural-capital metaphor for catalyzing a theoretically informed agenda of research on a central sociological issue—stratification—by use of cultural sociological analysis.

Good work on stratification does not necessarily depend on the cultural capital model, however. Feminist theory has been an important alternative source of inspiration. In a set of essays firmly positioned within cultural studies, *Feminine Sentences: Essays on Women and Culture* (Berkeley: University of

California Press, 1990), Janet Wolff deals with men and women, public and private, and their relation to art, among other topics. Some research in effect controls for cross-class differences by concentrating on particular strata. Thus, Susan Ostrander's *Women of the Upper Class* (Philadelphia: Temple University Press, 1984) discusses how upper-class women's subordinate position is reproduced by class structures. A comparable study is that of Helen Gouldner and Mary Symons Strong: *Speaking of Friendship: Middle Class Women and their Friends* (New York: Greenwood Press, 1987). Their argument explores how similarities among the social standings of women give rise to friendship circles.

Like much of the feminist research, the debate about class and ethnicity also has had a quasi-autonomous existence. Much of the controversy concerns the importance of race in explaining the disproportionate representation of minorities in the lower classes. The early work of William Julius Wilson has served as the touchstone of the debate, and he has followed it with a later book, *The Truly Disadvantaged* (Chicago: University of Chicago Press, 1987), in which he argues that race-specific policies help only advantaged minorities. Other studies have examined the relation between the occupational structure and the cultural division of labor. In "Ethnicity and Social Change: The Interaction of Structural, Cultural and Personality Factors," *Ethnic and Racial Studies* 6 (1983): 395–409, J. Milton Yinger offers a look at institutional racism within the historical framework of a decline in low-skill job opportunities in the United States. But it would seem that the boundaries do not necessarily operate in the same way for various ethnic groups. A study of a high school shows that African Americans tend to segregate amongst social class lines, while whites and Chicanos split into subgroups more upon cultural differences; see Mark Gottdiener and Donna Malone's study, "Group Differentiation in a Metropolitan High School: The Influence of Race, Class, Gender and Culture," *Qualitative Sociology* 8 (1985): 29–41.

Another study brings us to the problem of stratification and public— rather than purely group—culture, while remaining on the terrain of ethnicity; see the article by Paul DiMaggio and Francis Ostrower, "Participation in the Arts by Black and White Americans," *Social Forces* 68 (1990): 753–78. Judith Blau, Peter Blau and Reid M. Golden have raised a related question more generally. In "Social Inequality and the Arts," *American Journal of Sociology* 91 (1985): 308–31, they correlate artistic activities with measures of social inequality, finding that the arts become concentrated in areas of greater wealth. Another approach has a more structuralist tilt: it examines the stratification of cultural objects themselves. One example is Lawrence W. Levine's *Highbrow/Lowbrow: The Emergence of Cultural Hierarchy in America* (Cambridge: Harvard University Press, 1988).

Finally, a recent genre of work contests the role of cultural capital within urban environments and transnational cultures. *Landscapes of Power: From Detroit to Disneyland* (Berkeley: University of California Press, 1991), by Sharon Zukin, analyzes new cultural forms in case studies such as an analysis of corporate suburbs, specifically Westchester, NY, which, she argues, reflect the "creative destruction" of the economy. Another essay in this book, on theme parks such as Disneyland, treats the movement of financial capital through cultural circuits.

CHAPTER 7: POWER AND CULTURE

Consideration of issues about power and culture can be taken in three different directions—theoretical, topical, or analytical investigation of particular genres or media. The theoretical literatures—for example, on functionalism, critical theory, Gramsci, and Foucault—are extensive, and they move beyond cultural studies per se. The best strategies for pursuing these literatures are to (1) consult one or more encyclopedia articles in the *International Encyclopedia of the Social Sciences* or the *Social Science Encyclopedia,* and (2) explore the work of key theorists themselves and the secondary literature on them and various theoretical schools. Here, we will touch on some key theoretical sources and intriguing appraisals, and then turn to the politics of public and mass culture, media ownership and control, government subsidy of culture, and studies of various cultural venues such as news, television entertainment, and music. (The related literature on postmodernism is considered under chapter 11.)

A number of recent studies review critical theory. They include: a book edited by Russell Berman, *Modern Culture and Critical Theory* (Madison: University of Wisconsin Press, 1989); Douglas Kellner's "Critical Theory and the Crisis of Social Theory," *Sociological Perspectives* 33 (1990): 11–33; and the reader edited by Stephen E. Bronner and Douglas M. Kellner, *Critical Theory and Society* (New York: Routledge, 1989). A particularly cogent assessment that takes account of recent research is David Zaret's "Critical Theory and the Sociology of Culture," *Current Perspectives in Social Theory* 11 (1992): 1–28. In the context of critical theory, it would also be important to look at predecessors like Georg Lukacs and Walter Benjamin. On the former, see Peter U. Hohendahl, "Art Work and Modernity: the Legacy of Georg Lukacs," *New German Critique* 42 (1987): 33–49; and on the latter, see Terry Eagleton's *Walter Benjamin* (London: Verso, 1981).

Countering the arguments of critical theorists, Alan Swingewood, *The Myth of Mass Culture* (London: Macmillan, 1977), suggests that capitalism has produced a diverse and resilient culture and promoted institutions of civil society, such that the state does not succeed at cultural domination. For a less dismissive response to left/cultural Marxism see Kenneth Thompson's *Beliefs and Ideology* (Chicester, England: Horwood and Tavistock, 1986).

Antonio Gramsci has received less widespread attention than the critical theorists, but his ideas have served as a touchstone for much good empirical research such as Todd Gitlin's. For the uses of Gramsci's theory in empirical analysis, see T. Jackson Lears, "The Concept of Cultural Hegemony: Problems and Possibilities," *American Historical Review* 90 (1985): 567–93. Perhaps the strongest formulation with roots in a specifically cultural Gramscian argument is *The Dominant Ideology Thesis* (Boston: G. Allen & Unwin, 1980), by Nicholas Abercrombie, Stephen Hill, and Bryan S. Turner. The work of Michel Foucault also has generated an extensive secondary literature, for example, a collection of essays edited by Jonathan Arac, *After Foucault* (New Brunswick, NJ: Rutgers University Press, 1988).

Theories about culture as domination become more salient when they are aligned with empirical studies that examine the meaningful content of dominant culture. Such studies face methodological controversies (discussed in chapter 9), but empirical research still produces interesting results that help advance the debate. A number of studies address historical issues. For example, in *Imperialism and Popular Culture* (Manchester: Manchester University Press, 1986), John M. Mackenzie discusses how the English working class was sold on the idea of empire through the domination of mass culture by institutions such as the movie industry, theater, juvenile fiction, the BBC, and the monarchy. On the other side of the Atlantic, Sarah Blackstone's *Buckskins, Bullets and Business* (Westport, CT: Greenwood Press, 1986), shows how the "wild west" has been portrayed in the eastern United States and Europe. These capitalistic genres of hegemonic culture bear comparison to the Soviet revolutionary cultural experiment beginning immediately after the October 1917 revolution; see Lynn Mally's *Culture of the Future: The Protelkult Movement in Revolutionary Russia* (Berkeley: University of California Press, 1990). However, in capitalism, the important cultural movements often are not carried ideologically, but commercially; instructive in this regard is a book by Stan Luxenberg, *Roadside Empires: How the Chains Franchised America* (New York: Viking, 1985).

Studies of the dominant U.S. culture (considered in chapter 2) are legion, but one book merits attention for the linkages it establishes between culture and political economy: Herbert Gans's *Middle American Individualism: The Future of Liberal Democracy* (New York: Free Press, 1988). Other studies concentrate not on a generalized culture, but on the sociology of unequally distributed knowledge. The issue is the subject of a postmodern analysis by Mark Poster in *The Mode of Information* (Cambridge: Polity Press, 1990). Elliot Freidson's *Professional Powers* (Chicago: University of Chicago Press, 1986) discusses the nature of professional knowledge, and how it maintains class-based political and legal institutions.

The most visible cultural institutions of domination are, of course, the mass media. Aside from the issue of corporate concentration discussed in the chapter, a major issue concerns the interests served by the governmental regulatory environment established by agencies such as the Federal Communications Commission and the Federal Trade Commission. *Journalism Quarterly,* the *Journal of Communication,* the *Columbia Journalism Review,* and the *Wash-*

ington Journalism Review follow issues such as concentration and regulation. Such studies within the mass communication disciplines are paralleled by sociological studies such as Elizabeth Long's "The Cultural Meaning of Concentration in Publishing," *Book Research* 5 (1986): 269–96. The implications of the expanding global communications conglomerates are addressed by Anthony Smith in *The Geopolitics of Information* (New York: Oxford University Press, 1980); by John Tomlinson's *Cultural Imperialism* (Baltimore: John Hopkins University, 1991); and in two books by Peter J. S. Dunnett: *The World Newspaper Industry* (New York: Croom Helm/Methuen, 1988), and *The World Television Industry* (New York: Routledge, 1990).

The advertising aspect of mass media also has been considered as an avenue of domination, and for its political economy. (General works on advertising are cited with the sources for chapter 5.) Some authors have concentrated on how advertising works in ways that raise issues of reception (see chapter 9), but bear mentioning here for their implications for the debate about the domination of culture: see, for example, Giancarlo Buzzi, *Advertising: Its Cultural and Political Effects* (Minneapolis: University of Minnesota Press, 1968); and Robert L. Root, Jr., *Rhetorics of Popular Culture* (Westport, CT: Greenwood Press, 1987). Advertising, of course, is not the only economic aspect of mass culture, for the culture itself often gets sold. A variety of linkages are explored by Richard Butsch in *For Fun and Profit: The Transformation of Leisure and Consumption* (Philadelphia: Temple University Press, 1990), and in Donald Lazere's edited collection, *American Media and Mass Culture* (Berkeley: University of California Press, 1988), which contains essays by forty Marxist, feminist and leftist critics. John A. Walker's *Art in the Age of Mass Media* (London: Pluto Press, 1983) considers the role of politically committed artists.

The relation of cultural expression to changing venues of cultural patronage and performance also has been explored for specific cultural forms and media. For a study of classical music, see Rose Subotnik's *Developing Variations: Style and Ideology in Western Music* (Minneapolis: University of Minnesota, 1991). Rock music has been the subject of a large, albeit uneven, literature (see also chapter 10). An important interpretive account by George Lipsitz situates rock and roll's relationship with the working and middle classes; see his article, "'Against the Wind': Class Composition of Rock and Roll Music," *Knowledge and Society: Studies in the Sociology of Culture Past and Present* 5 (1984): 269–96. Among authors who discuss the relationship between economics, technology, marketing and mass culture is Robert G. Pielke, in his *You Say You Want a Revolution: Rock Music in American Culture* (Chicago: Nelson Hall, 1986). Don J. Hibbard and Carol Kaleialoha's *The Role of Rock* (Englewood Cliffs, NJ: Prentice Hall, 1983) examines how rock and roll made music into big business. The account of Simon Frith, *Music for Pleasure* (New York: Routledge, 1988), is important for how it traces the transformation of rock from a vehicle for defining a subculture to a vehicle for conservative corporate advertisers to market middle-class consumption. Part of that transformation, of course, is bound up with the emergence of music television; see R. Serge Denisoff, *Inside MTV* (New Brunswick, NJ: Transaction, 1988).

If rock and roll represents a largely coopted genre, television is often regarded as the coopting force par excellence. Television in the U.S. rightly has received much analysis, but it is also worth noting some transnational studies. In *Prime Time Society: An Anthropological Analysis of Television and Culture* (Belmont, CA: Wadsworth, 1990), Conrad Phillip Kottak compares American and Brazilian television culture. *New Media in Europe* (New York: McGraw Hill, 1986), by John Tydeman, gives special attention to the cultural role of the state-owned television stations.

For the United States, a number of studies address the significance of television entertainment programs for shaping cultural values. For example, in *The Soap Opera Evolution* (Berkeley: University of California Press, 1988), Marilyn J. Matelski uses content analysis of radio and television soap operas to describe how the social ideals (if not reality) of America shifted between 1940 and 1980. Similarly, Ella Taylor describes the power television has had in shaping discourse about changes in the American family; see her book, *Prime-Time Families: Television Culture in Postwar America* (Berkeley: University of California Press, 1989).

Presumably, if fictional entertainment programs shape our discourse, news media must do so as well. The production of news, considered in chapter 8, can be examined for its political implications, as some contributors do in Robert Manoff and Michael Schudson's (1986) edited book. A discussion specifically addressing power and journalism is that of J. Herbert Altschull, *Agents of Power: The Role of News Media in Human Affairs* (New York: Longman, 1984). Studies that permit cross-national comparisons can be particularly informative, as *News as Hegemonic Reality* (New York: Praeger, 1988) demonstrates; in it, Alan Rachlin compares Canada and the U.S. Finally, the emergence of CNN has changed not only the economics of television news; it has shifted the character of news events themselves. For an initial survey, see Hank Whittemore, *CNN: The Inside Story* (Boston: Little Brown, 1990).

CHAPTER 8: THE PRODUCTION OF CULTURE

The production of culture perspective uses perspectives taken from the sociology of work and organizations to examine culture as a "product" that is produced in a collective process. Both mass culture produced by "culture industries" and individual works of art have been examined in these terms.

The number of studies using this perspective is very large. For a recent overview of the literature see Diana Crane's book *The Production of Culture*

(Newbury Park, CA: Sage Publications, 1992). Another way to illustrate the kinds of work being done here is to look at substantive topics. Howard Becker, Michal McCall, Lori Morris and Paul Meshejian have applied the production of culture perspective to the theater in their article, "Theaters and Communities: Three Scenes," *Social Forces* 36 (1989): 93–98. Dona Schwartz has studied the attempt of fine art photographers to distinguish their use of the medium from that of all other photographers, professional and amateur, in her article "Camera Clubs and Fine Arts Photography: The Social Construction of an Elite Code," *Urban Life* 15 (1986): 165–95. Another study which examines the distribution aspects of the production of high and popular culture through gallery gatekeepers is Heather FitzGibbon's "From Prints to Posters: The Production of Artistic Value in a Popular Art World," *Symbolic Interaction* 10 (1987): 111–28. An interesting use of Becker's approach to art worlds can be found in Ruth Finnigan's study, *The Hidden Musicians: Music Making in an English Town* (Cambridge: Cambridge University Press, 1989). Using ethnographic methods Finnigan studies the music making of local professional and amateur musicians in a small city (100,000 people). She describes the various "music worlds" and shows how they develop from and are related to music making in homes and schools, giving new insights into the practice of music in everyday routines. Liah Greenfeld has explored the production of paintings in several different contexts: French impressionists and Russian critical realists in the 1870s in "The Social Context of Artistic Style: Impressionism in France and Critical Realism in Russia" in *Knowledge and Society: Studies in the Sociology of Culture Past and Present* 3 (1981): 217–55; see also her study of the Israeli art world in *Different Worlds: A Sociological Study of Taste, Choice and Success in Art* (Cambridge: Cambridge University Press, 1989). Ramonde Moulin's work on the French art market offers another comparison; see *The French Art Market: A Sociological View,* (New Brunswick, NJ: Transaction, 1987). While sociologists dominate this perspective some literary critics and art historians also find it useful. Among the latter is Svetlana Alpers's study of Rembrandt in terms of his production process, *Rembrandt's Enterprise: The Studio and the Market* (Chicago: University of Chicago Press, 1988).

Some examples of applications of this perspective to popular culture forms include work on various aspects of the motion picture industry and popular music. Robert Faulkner has studied studio musicians in the motion picture industry. His work includes *Music on Demand: Composers and Careers in the Hollywood Film Industry* (New Brunswick, NJ: Transaction, 1983). More recently, with Wayne Baker, he has examined how the rise of the blockbuster has effected the allocation of roles in Hollywood production in "Roles as a Resource in the Hollywood Film Industry," *American Journal of Sociology* 97 (1991): 279–309. Sociologists have looked at popular musical traditions showing how the music itself is shaped by the context in which it is produced. In addition to the work of Richard Peterson on country music, studies include

Stith Bennett on rock music in *On Becoming a Rock Musician* (Amherst: University of Massachusetts Press, 1980) and Charles Keil's *Urban Blues* (Chicago: University of Chicago Press, 1966). More recent is Deena Weinstein's *Heavy Metal: A Cultural Sociology* (New York: Lexington/Free Press, 1991). Two studies focusing on transformations in African-American music traditions are Mark Newman's *Entrepreneurs of Profit and Pride: From Black Appeal to Radio Soul* (New York: Praeger, 1988) and Nelson George's *The Death of Rhythm and Blues* (New York: Pantheon, 1988).

Television, especially the news production, offers another substantive area for examining how production processes shape the content of the cultural form. In addition to Herbert Gans' *Deciding What's News,* other well known studies include Gaye Tuchman's *Making News,* (New York: Free Press, 1978), and David Altheide's work, including *Creating Reality: How TV News Distorts Events,* (Beverly Hills, CA: Sage Publications, 1976). Michael Schudson reviews recent literature on news production in his article, "The Sociology of News Production," *Media, Culture and Society* 11 (1989): 263–82. Many articles focus on the production of news, dealing with coverage of specific topics or stories; for example, environmental issues: Kandice L. Salomore, Michael Grenber, Peter Sandman, and David Sackman, "A Question of Quality: How Journalists and News Sources Evaluate Coverage of Environmental Risk," *Journal of Communications* 40 (1990): 117–30; nuclear power: William Gamson and Andre Modiglian, "Media Discourse and Public Opinion on Nuclear Power: A Constructionist Approach," *American Journal of Sociology* 95 1989): 1–37; the economy: David Harrington, "Economic News on Television: the Determinants of Coverage," *Public Opinion Quarterly* 53 (1989): 17–40; art in the mainstream press: John Ryan and Deborah Sim, "When Art Becomes News: Portrayals of Art and Artists on Network Television News," *Social Forces* 68 (1990): 869–89; and women's sports: Nancy Theberg and Alan Cronk, "Work Routines in Newspaper Sports Departments and the coverage of Women's Sports," *Sociology of Sport Journal* 3 (1986): 195–203. Three Canadians, Richard V. Erickson, Patricia M. Baranek, and Janet B.L. Chan, are producing a major study of the ways journalists and sources negotiate news reporting. The first volume *Visualizing Deviance: A Study of News Organization* (Toronto: University of Toronto Press 1987) focuses on the journalist's reliance on selected sources, and the second volume, *Negotiating Control: A Study of News Sources* (Toronto: University of Toronto Press, 1989) focuses on interactions between the sources and the journalists that produce "news." Looking at religious broadcasting from a production of culture perspective offers an interesting opportunity to show the profitable side of popular religion production. Razelle Frankl, *Televangelism: The Marketing of Popular Religion,* (Carbondale, IL: Southern Illinois University Press, 1987) examines religious broadcasting as a business.

The production of culture perspective can be applied to other forms of cultural production as well. Gary Alan Fine has recently applied the perspective to the work of restaurant chefs in "The Culture of Production: Aesthetic Choices and Constraints in Culinary Work," *American Journal of Sociology* 97 (1992): 1268–94. It is also possible to apply the perspective to the production of fads and fashions, to the "work" that people do on their bodies, for example, as does Barry Glassner in "Fit for Postmodern Selfhood," pp. 215—43 in Howard Becker and Michal McCall, eds., *Symbolic Interaction and Cultural Studies* (Chicago: University of Chicago Press, 1988). Looking at a much broader time period Hillel Schwartz has produced an analysis of dieting, *Never Satisfied: A Cultural History of Diets, Fantasies and Fat* (New York: The Free Press, 1986).

There is also a growing literature within this perspective on state support for the arts. For information about state funding for the arts across developed nations see Milton Cummings and Richard Katz, eds., *The Patron State: Government and the Arts in Europe, North America, and Japan* (New York: Oxford University Press, 1987). For a study of the detailed workings of the relations between congress and the National Endowment for the Arts in the United States see *Congress and the Arts: A Precarious Alliance?* edited by Margaret Wyszinmiriski and Pat Clubb (New York: American Council for the Arts, 1989). A volume edited by David Pankratz and Valerie Morris, *The Future of the Arts: Public Policy and Arts Research,* (New York: Praeger, 1990) reviews arts policies of both public and private institutions, as well as provides excellent sources for further reading. The general circumstances of subsidized cultural production are considered in *Non-Profit Enterprises in the Arts: Studies in Mission and Constraint* (Cambridge: Oxford University Press, 1987) edited by Paul DiMaggio. A volume edited by Martin Feldstein, *The Economics of Art Museums* (Chicago: University of Chicago Press, 1991) addresses financial issues facing art museums today, with essays by economists and art world participants.

Sue Curry Jansen conceptualizes censorship broadly in her book, *Censorship: The Knot that Binds Power and Knowledge* (New York: Oxford University Press, 1991). Jansen discards the usual definition of censorship as the conscious suppression of offensive materials by the state, and argues that censorship is the shaping of knowledge by the powerful. Her analysis of specific instances ranges from practices in ancient Greece and Rome to contemporary United States. A study that looks at indirect challenges to the freedom of expression in popular music is "Ban(ned) in the USA: Popular Music and Censorship," *Journal of Communication Inquiry,* 15 (1991): 73–87, by Steve Jones. Studies of specific forms of censorship under very different political regimes include Mabel Berezin's "Culture, State and Theater in Fascist Italy," *American Sociological Review* 56 (1991): 639–51, and Jeffry Goldfarb's *The Persistence of Freedom: The Sociological Implications of Polish Student Theater* (Boulder, CO: Westview Press, 1980). Steven Dubin's essays in his book *Arresting Images: Impolitic Art and Uncivil Actions* (New York: Routledge, 1992) analyzes recent censorship cases.

CHAPTER 9: CULTURAL OBJECT, AUDIENCE, AND MEANING

The relation of culture to its audiences—too often reduced to the "effects" debate—can be pursued in terms of three broad and overlapping issues: first, the meaning(s) that producer(s) mean to convey through cultural objects; second, the "objective" meaning of distributed culture inhering in the objects themselves (whatever the producers' intentions); and third, the responses of audiences to cultural objects. At the most general level, the meaning of individual cultural objects may depend on a larger context of meaning, an issue considered by Eugene Rochberg-Halton in *Meaning and Modernity* (Chicago: University of Chicago Press, 1986).

Beyond the question of the context of meaning, a number of authors have employed broadly hermeneutic, semiotic, and poststructuralist approaches to interpret cultural objects. For general discussions of the theoretical issues, Terry Eagleton (1983) and Wuthnow et al. (1984) are especially useful. For hermeneutic, phenomenological and other interpretive approaches, there is the book edited by Gary Shapiro and Alan Sica, *Hermeneutics: Questions and Prospects* (Amherst: University of Massachusetts Press, 1984), and a later one edited by Paul Rabinow and William M. Sullivan, *Interpretive Social Science: A Second Look* (Berkeley: University of California Press, 1989). The approach of Victor Turner is distinctive, and its potential has been explored in a series of essays edited by Kathleen M. Ashley, *Victor Turner and the Construction of Cultural Criticism* (Bloomington: Indiana University Press, 1990). A book of essays that bridge various traditions is *Hermeneutics & Deconstruction* (Albany: State University of New York Press, 1985),edited by Hugh J. Silverman and Don Ihde. The issues at stake are revealed through cases in an intriguing way by John Tagg's book, *The Burden of Representation: Essays on Photographies and Histories* (Amherst: University of Massachusetts Press, 1988).

With the postmodern blurring of theoretical traditions, it is no longer so useful to neatly divide hermeneutic and structuralist interpretations of cultural objects. In a variety of ways, critical analyses of texts now connect texts with contexts, which range from producers and their circumstances to aesthetics, ideologies and historical moment. Against the new criticism, Richard Wollheim's book, *Painting as an Art* (Princeton, NJ: Princeton University Press, 1988), asserts aesthetics as the primary basis for art criticism. One study helps show the range of cultural studies being undertaken. Jeffrey Muller's *Rubens, the Artist as Collector* (Princeton, NJ: Princeton University Press, 1989) explores the art collection of the seventeenth-century Dutch artist Rubens as a way of asking why Rubens developed his own art in the way he did. Other studies have looked at the longer term social interplay involved in the emergence of cultural icons. One of the best known is *Brooklyn Bridge, Fact and Symbol* (Chicago: University of Chicago Press, 1979), by Alan Trachtenberg.

The study of literature has proved a fruitful context for asserting a variety of continuities between cultural texts, social texts and contexts. Morroe Berger's *Real and Imagined Worlds: the Novel and Social Science* (Cambridge, MA: Harvard University Press, 1977) offers one formulation, and Oliver MacDonagh explores the historical world of historical novels in *Jane Austen: Real and Imagined Worlds* (New Haven, CT: Yale University Press, 1991). A collection of essays circumscribing the sociology of literature helps to display the theoretical and empirical issues for cultural studies; see Philippe Desan, Priscilla Ferguson and Wendy Griswold, eds., *Literature and Social Practice* (Chicago: University of Chicago Press, 1989).

Other studies have directly explored the resonance between the meaningful content of cultural objects and deeper cultural logics at work. Two general surveys display the possibilities. In *Mass-Mediated Culture* (Englewood Cliffs, NJ: Prentice Hall, 1977), Michael Real analyzes the symbolic processes embedded in cultural objects such as Disneyland and the Super Bowl. By now, critical analysis has explored virtually every genre of culture. For example, to take a movie genre, see Jane P. Tompkins's book, *West of Everything: the Inner Life of Westerns* (New York: Oxford University Press, 1992). Sometimes a historical moment yields a thematic basis for critical analysis, as with Andrew Bergman's *We're In the Money: Depression America and Its Films* (New York: Harper and Row, 1972). In other studies, a theoretical issue structures analysis of a genre. Patriarchy at work in the modern romance novel is a case in point, explored by Radway (1984), in Jan Cohn's *Romance and the Erotics of Property: Mass Market Fiction for Women* (Durham, NC: Duke University Press, 1988), and in Ann Snitow's "Mass Market Romance: Pornography for Women is Different," published in Ann Snitow, Christine Stansell and Sharon Thompson, eds., *Powers of Desire: The Politics of Sexuality* (New York: Monthly Review Press, 1983). Broadening the focus to a medium, there is Helen Baehr and Gillian Dyer's *Boxed In: Women and Television* (London: Pandora Press, 1987), and a book by Janice Winship, *Inside Women's Magazines* (London: Pandora Press, 1987). For a survey that follows the same thematic issue, see Martha Banta's *Imaging American Women: Ideas and Ideals in Cultural History* (New York: Columbia University Press, 1987).

Discussions of audiences are relatively distinct from interpretive work on cultural objects themselves, and there are relatively autonomous subliteratures. The classic literature of the "effects" debate is effectively reviewed by both Gans (1974) and Meyrowitz (1985), but research continues. Even early formulations recognized the reflexive character of media-audience relations. Jacques Ellul's book *Propaganda* (New York: Vintage Books, 1965) is a classic argument about a complex interaction between what producers want the audience to believe and what the mass modern audience wants to believe. A more recent formulation along similar lines is Antoine Hennion and Cecile Meadel's "The Artisans of Desire: the Mediation of Advertising Between Product and Consumer," *Sociological Theory* 7 (1989): 191–209.

Much of the research has centered on television news and entertainment. For essays offering an international perspective see the volume edited by Phillip Drummond and Richard Paterson, *Television and its Audience* (London: BFI Publishers, 1986). Some research suggests that distinctive worldviews emerge from watching the box. Thus, Shanto Iyengar and Donald Kinder found differences in opinions when they showed alternative versions of the evening news which emphasized different stories to comparable audiences; see their book *News that Matters: Television and American Opinion* (Chicago: University of Chicago Press, 1988). Fred Bales finds that consequences of television watching itself are different for blacks and whites; see his article, "Television Use and Confidence in Television by Blacks and Whites in Four Selected Years," *Journal of Black Studies* 16 (1986): 283–91. Given the public concern about stereotypes, cultural producers are not necessarily insensitive to the implications of their image selections, but Robert Entman suggests that there are important paradoxes to be considered; see his analysis, "Modern Racism and the Images of Blacks in Local Television News," *Critical Studies in Mass Communication* 7 (1990): 332–45.

Public debates have inspired studies of particular kinds of culture, such as pornography and depictions of violence. For a debate on violence, see two pieces: James N. Baron and Peter C. Reiss, "Same Time Next Year: Aggregate Analyses of the Mass Media and Violent Behavior," *American Sociological Review* 50 (1985): 347–63, and David P. Phillips and Kenneth A. Bollen, "Same Time, Last Year: Selective Data Dredging for Negative Findings," *American Sociological Review* 50 (1985): 364–71. Some studies focus on particular audiences thought to be especially vulnerable. Thus, children are the focus of Tannis Macbeth Williams's edited volume, *The Impact of Television: A Natural Experiment in Three Communities* (Orlando, FL: Academic Press, 1986). A quite different tack questions whether the media produce imitation or the fear of what is portrayed; see, for example, Barrie Gunter, *Television and the Fear of Crime* (London: Libbey, 1987).

Beyond the literature concerned with measuring the direct influence of culture, a range of more sociological studies have been concerned with understanding the kinds of relationships audiences establish with cultural objects. To supplement the range of approaches discussed by Holub (1984) and Maclean (1988), there is a useful work on theater by Herbert Blau, *The Audience* (Baltimore: John Hopkins University, 1990), and Jane P. Tompkins has edited a set of critical essays within structuralism, phenomenology and poststructuralism; see *Reader-Response Criticism: From Formalism to Post-Structuralism* (Baltimore: Johns Hopkins University Press, 1980).

In conclusion, several important studies in turn trace repercussions of audience response for cultural production. A case study by Joseph Horowitz, *Understanding Toscanini* (New York: Knopf, 1987), examines the interaction between cultural producer, audience, and formats of performance. And Wesley Shrum has written "Critics and Publics: Cultural Mediation in

High-brow and Popular Performing Arts," *American Journal of Sociology* 97 (1991): 347–75.

CHAPTER 10: CULTURE, ACTION, AND CHANGE

This chapter is concerned with the consequences of conceptualizing culture in terms of expressive symbols. We examine how people use culture in various contexts, with special concern for subcultures apart from and sometimes in opposition to the dominant culture. These subcultures are variously constituted including residential communities, ethnic and age groups, but also including groups of people who share tastes. We also consider the use of culture in situations of conflict, and cultural and social change.

Questions about the meaning of ethnic identification for Americans of European origin have inspired recent studies. The articles collected in Peter Kivisto's *The Ethnic Enigma: The Salience of Ethnicity for European Origin Groups* (Philadelphia: The Balch Institute Press, 1989) address this question, as does Richard Alba in his report on Albany, New York, *Ethnic Identity: The Transformation of White America* (New Haven: Yale University Press, 1990). Alba's survey methodology shows declining identification with ethnicity; the case studies reported in Kivisto's book finds more varied responses among self-conscious ethnic subcultures, yet even here ethnicity is "sublimated" and, therefore, ethnic identity is "enigmatic." Case studies of relatively segregated ethnic and religious groups reveal more self-conscious communities and subcultures. Elijah Anderson's study of Chicago's south side, *Streetwise: Race, Class and Change in an Urban Community*, (Chicago: University of Chicago Press, 1990) carries on the tradition of ethnographic studies of urban black communities. Ronald Takaki has taken on a less studied group of people in his book *Strangers From A Different Shore: A History of Asian Americans* (Boston: Little Brown, 1989). Using oral histories as well as documents, Takaki compares the experiences of Chinese and Japanese people in California and Hawaii. Sectarian religious groups such as the Amish and the Mennonites offer a chance to look at groups that are both ethnically and religiously separate from the dominant culture. Johns Hopkins Press in Baltimore has published a series of studies on the Anabaptist societies in North America, beginning with John Hostetler's *Hutterite Society* (1974), and including the more recent book *Mennonite Society* (1989) by Calvin Redekop, who argues for the centrality of religious ideology in Mennonite life, as well as Donald Kraybill's *The Riddle of Amish Culture* (1989). The latter focuses on one Amish Community in Lancaster County, Pennsylvania and explores how it maintains its cultural distinctness in the context of suburban sprawl through various sorts of compromises, acceptances, and resistances in relation to modern society.

Current studies of gangs include *People and Folks: Gangs, Crime and the Underclass in a Rustbelt City* (Chicago: Lake View Press, 1988) by John

Hagedorn. This study of black gangs in Milwaukee shows the origins of gangs in ordinary adolescent activities, but at the same time argues that the persistence of gangs is linked to the development of an underclass in declining rustbelt cities. James Vigil's study of Chicano gangs in LA, *Barrio Gangs; Street Life and Identity in Southern California* (Austin: University of Texas Press, 1988), illustrates both variation in the degree to which individuals are involved in gang activities and the fact that gang members spend most of their time in conventional activities.

A different kind of subcultural identification is found among feminists and lesbians. A number of works look at the intersection of personal identity and political ideologies in various sorts of "women's communities." Susan Kreiger in *The Mirror Dance* (Philadelphia: Temple University Press, 1983) studied a lesbian community in a midwestern college town. She explored the ways that the recognition of common lesbian identities both facilitated the building of community and constrained it. Iris Young explores similar issues in looking at "the ideal of community" outside of geographical locales with face-to-face interaction in her essay "The Ideal of Community and the Politics of Difference," *Social Theory and Practice* 12 (1986): 1–26. Sandra Morgen has studied a feminist health clinic and its organizational practices based in feminist ideology in "Contradictions in Feminist Practice: Individualism and Collectivism in a Feminist Health Center," *Comparative Social Research* (Supplement 1, 1990): 9–60. Cultural differences between two groups of women are the subject of Susan Tucker's oral history, *Telling Memories Among Southern Women: Domestic Workers and Their Employers in the Segregated South* (Baton Rouge: Louisiana State University Press, 1988).

The classic text on collective memory is Maurice Halbwachs' book, *The Collective Memory* (New York: Harper and Row, 1980). A number of recent authors have looked at the creation and evolution of George Washington as a symbol of republican virtues; see Barry Schwartz's *George Washington: The Making of an American Symbol* (New York: The Free Press, 1987), *The Invention of George Washington* (Berkeley: The University of California Press, 1988) by Paul K. Longmore, and *George Washington Slept Here: Colonial Revivals and American Culture, 1876–1986* (Cambridge: Harvard University Press, 1988) by Karal Ann Marling. The book by Gladys Engle Lang and Kurt Lang, *Etched in Memory: The Building and Survival of Artistic Reputation* (Chapel Hill: University of North Carolina Press, 1990), studies the survival of artists' reputations in the collective memory of a society. Maren Strange examines a different aspect of collective memory in *Symbols of the Ideal Life: Social Documentary Photography in America, 1890–1950,* (Cambridge: Cambridge University Press, 1989); her book shows how particular agencies and institutions have used documentary photography to raise political issues as well as to influence esthetics.

We have seen how graffiti or rap music or torn clothing can express a subculture's distance from the dominant culture, and also how these cultural expressions can be absorbed by the dominant culture. A special issue of *The Canadian Journal of Political and Social Theory* 11 (winter–spring 1987) focused on the use of the body as a means of expression in postmodern society, and the cooptation of oppositional expressions by advertising and the fashion industry. The essays in the book edited by Clinton Sanders, *Marginal Conventions: Popular Culture, Mass Media and Social Deviance* (Bowling Green, OH: Bowling Green University Popular Press, 1990) explore the possibilities for expressing non-conformity and for commercial exploitation of that expression in a number of cultural forms.

Music offers a form that is both intimately connected to cultural expression and available for cooptation by the dominant culture. Celmess Sandresky and Catherine Harris use Swidler's concepts of settled and unsettled cultures to examine the relationship between music and social change in the twentieth century; in their "Changes in Musical Languages in Unsettled Cultures," *International Journal of Contemporary Sociology* 27 (1990): 155–63 music is analyzed as a tool in the cultural tool kit. Many studies focus on issues related to music and contemporary youth culture: see for example, Anthony Pearson's "The Grateful Dead Phenomena: An Ethnomethodological Approach," *Youth and Society* 18 (1987): 418–22, and George M. Plashetes, "Rock on Reel: The Rise and Fall of Rock Culture in America Reflected in a Decade of Rockumentaries'," *Qualitative Sociology* 12 (1989): 55–71. A study by Loraine Prinsky and Jill Rosenbaum, "Leer-ics or Lyrics: Teenage Impressions of Rock and Roll," *Youth and Society* 18 (1987): 384–97, compares differences in the ways that teenagers and parents interpret the lyrics of rock music.

In other cases it is not merely non-conformity, but a more active attempt at social change that is being expressed. Studies of social movements have shown how dissident groups use symbols both to mobilize others to their cause and to give expression to their grievances. Several of the essays in Jeffery Alexander, ed., *Durkheimian Sociology: Cultural Studies,* (Cambridge: Cambridge University Press, 1988) show this process, in particular Lynn Hunt's analysis of the French revolution, "The Sacred and the French Revolution," pp. 25–43, which analyzes the manipulation of symbols in the revolution of 1789, and Edward Tiryakian, "From Durkheim to Managua: Revolutions and Religious Revivals," pp. 44–63.

Another approach is to examine movements for cultural change. One attempt to think about how cultural movements differ from social movements is Joseph Gusfield's essay, "Social Movements and Social Change: Perspectives of Linearity and Fluidity," *Social Movements, Conflict and Change,* 4 (1981): 317–39. Anthony Oberschall offers a historical analysis of the witchcraft trials in his provocative paper "Culture Change and Social Movements," presented at the meetings of the American Sociological Association, San Francisco, CA in 1989. A study by Carlos Munoz, *Youth, Identity, Power: The Chicano Movement* (London: Verso, 1989) combines the study of social and cultural change. Munoz portrays the Chicano movement as offering an ideological innovation: a distinctive cultural identity based in part in Mexican Americans's indigenous Native American roots, and in part in their working class experience. Munoz traces the evolution of that identity in the context of a student movement and its struggle to maintain ties to the Chicano community. In *The Past in Another Country: Representation, Historical Consciousness and Resistance in the Blue Ridge* (Berkeley: University of California Press, 1988) Stephen Foster shows how the struggle changed the local culture. This study of rural Appalachians documents how participation in a movement of resistance (mobilization against the building of a hydroelectric power system) in order to save their traditional way of life altered the discoursive strategies of individuals and communities.

CHAPTER 11: THE FUTURE OF POSTMODERNISM

The problem of defining postmodernism is compounded by the diverse writers travelling under its banner. There is no way of determining whether the cottage industry in publishing titles with the word "postmodern" has yet run its course, but output is so great that even specialists cannot possibly have time to read it all. Perhaps this is itself an emblem of the postmodern, and the upshot, again very postmodern, is that no list of citations can capture the terrain.

The more general literature on culture and social change is long established and extensive, but a few works should be noted. Karl Mannheim's most famous study, *Ideology and Utopia* (New York: Harcourt, Brace and World, 1936), explores how social knowledge in general is located within value-based frameworks, and it still stands as a classic on the role of ideas in social change. Donald Lowe deals with related issues of cognition in his *History of Bourgeois Perception* (Chicago: University of Chicago Press, 1982). An interesting effort to apply the model of evolutionary change to culture while avoiding the potential pitfalls of such an approach was offered in a series of essays in Marshall Sahlins and Elmer Service, eds., *Evolution and Culture* (Ann Arbor: University of Michigan, 1960). A more structuralist approach to the same problem is consolidated in Kubler (1962). In contrast both to his own earlier work and to Kubler's emphasis on material culture, in the 1970s Marshall Sahlins emphasized the significance of cultural symbols in *Culture and Practical Reason* (Chicago: University of Chicago Press, 1976). A symbolic approach is also explored by Bruce Lincoln, *Discourse and the Construction of Society* (New York: Oxford University Press, 1989); and Bernice Martin has considered the role of popular culture in *A Sociology of Contemporary Cultural Change* (Oxford: Basil Blackwell, 1981). A useful and more social theoretical exploration of the issues compares Marxian structural and Weberian approaches; see Alex Callinicos, *Making History: Agency, Structure and Change in Social Theory* (Cambridge, England: Polity Press, 1987). The most concerted empirical effort at measuring cultural change over time on a broad scale is the work of J. Zvi Namenwirth and Robert P. Weber, *Dynamics of Culture* (Boston: Allen and Unwin, 1987). And in the book *Social Change and Cultural Crisis* New York: Columbia University Press, 1984), Richard Lowenthal argues for a reasoned approach to change under crisis.

Much of the debate about postmodernism depends, in the first instance, on accounts of modernity, modernism and modernization. (See also discussions of tradition in sources in chapter 3.) For a study that looks at the accounts by modern intellectuals see David Frisby, *Fragments of Modernity: Theories of Modernity in the Work of Simmel, Kracauer and Benjamin* (Cambridge, MA: MIT Press, 1986). Frank Lechner explores globalization of culture as an aspect of modernization; see his article, "Parsons' Action Theory and the Common Culture Thesis," *Theory, Culture and Society* 2 (1984): 71–83. See as well the diverse set of essays in Mike Featherstone, ed., *Global Culture: Nationalism, Globalization and Modernity* (London: Sage, 1990). Yet many observers, even advocates of modernist outlooks, cannot help but see a crisis; assessments are offered in Gunter H. Lenz and Kurl L. Shell, eds., *The Crisis of Modernity: Recent Critical Theories of Culture and Society in the United States and West Germany* (Boulder: Westview Press, 1986).

The sense of modernity's crisis has both fueled and been fueled by discussions of the postmodern. An overview is offered by Bryan S. Turner, *Theories of Modernity and Postmodernity* (Newbury Park, CA: Sage, 1990). Gianni Vattimo, an Italian philosopher, addresses the consequences of postmodernism for the arts and sciences in *The End of Modernity: Nihilism and Hermeneutics in Post-Modern Culture* (Cambridge, England: Polity Press, 1988). A number of other good books survey the relations between the two. Among the best are Ingeborg Hoesterev, *Zeitgeist in Babel* (Bloomington: Indiana University Press, 1991), Roy Boyne and Ali Rattansi, eds., *Postmodernism and Society* (New York: St. Martin's Press, 1990), and Philip Cooke, *Back to the Future: Modernity, Postmodernity and Locality* (London: Unwin Hyman, 1990). These discursive treatments are complimented by works that themselves exemplify the postmodern. A generative source for the postmodernist account of representation is Guy Debord, *Society of the Spectacle* (Detroit: Black and Red, 1967).

Much of the dynamism of the postmodern turn has come from specifically cultural movements and from popular culture itself. Architecture has been considered: by Howard Harris and Alan Lipman, "A Culture of Despair: Reflections on 'Post-modern' Architecture," *Sociological Review* 34 (1986): 837–54; in a book by Margaret Rose that in part is concerned with Christopher Jencks's ideas, *The Post-Modern and the Post-Industrial* (Cambridge: Cambridge University Press, 1991); and in an essay by Ross Miller, "Putting on the Glitz: Architecture After Postmodernism," *Dissent* 37 (1989): 27–35. Similarly, the arts have been a continual focus of discourse, some of it concerned with the difficult issue of the avant-garde and the postmodern. The discussion of the avant-garde by Harold Rosenberg, in *The Tradition of the New* (New York: Horizon Press, 1959), anticipates the postmodern in its exploration of the juxtaposition of the primitive and the contemporary in art and poetry. For an anthology of the avant-garde movement, see Charles Russell, ed., *The Avant-Garde Today* (Urbana: University of Illinois Press, 1981). Also concerned with the avant-garde is Robert Dunn's article on populist sentiments that drive postmodernism, "Postmodernism: Populism, Mass Culture, and Avant-garde." *Theory, Culture and Society* 8 (1991): 111–35. Two edited volumes trace postmodern developments in a variety of cultural forms—in dance, photography, music, and so on, and also offer useful bibliographies for further research; see Stanley Trachtenberg, ed., *The Postmodern Moment* (Westport, CT: Greenwood Press, 1985), and Hugh J. Silverman, ed., *Postmodernism—Philosophy and the Arts* (New York: Routledge, 1990).

Tourism is a topic of study independent of postmodernist issues, but it also has proved a fertile terrain for postmodern cultural studies. Two general studies are Dean MacCannell, *The Tourist: A New Theory of the Leisure Class* (New York: Schocken, 1976), and John Jakle, *The Tourist* (Lincoln: University of Nebraska Press, 1985). Donald Horne's provocative study of tourism in Europe, *The Great Museum: The Re-Presentation of History* (London: Pluto Press, 1984), suggests that contemporary travellers are modern pilgrims; sociologist John Urry uses a different metaphor in *The Tourist Gaze: Leisure and Travel in Contemporary Societies* (Beverley Hills, CA: Sage, 1990).

Other writings broaden into the postmodern as a general culture. Selfconsciously postmodernist postures of hypermediated logorrhea are served up by Charles Newman, *The Postmodern Aura* (Evanston, IL: Northwestern University Press, 1985), and Arthur Kroker and David Cook, *The Postmodern Scene* (New York: St. Martin's Press, 1986). Perspectives on popular culture are offered by Jim Collins, *Uncommon Cultures: Popular Culture and Postmodernism* (New York: Routledge, 1989), and Iain Chambers, *Border Dialogues: Journeys in Postmodernism* (New York: Routledge, 1990). Questions of popular culture rightly raise issues of commodification. The former question is addressed: through an examination of the physical design of cultural objects by Adrian Forty, *Objects of Desire* (New York: Pantheon, 1986); by Dick Hebdige's case-study of the Italian motor scooter in his essay collection, *Hiding in the Light: On Images and Things* (London: Routledge, 1988); and in a sociological discussion by Mike Featherstone, *Consumer Culture and Postmodernism* (Beverley Hills, CA: Sage, 1991). Related issues of personal identity find treatment in Scott Lash, *Sociology of Postmodernism* (New York: Routledge, 1990).

Different, but still postmodern, concerns are addressed in works that consider the intellectual implications of intellectual ferment, some of it selfconsciously postmodern. Three important assessments are: Brook Thomas, *The New Historicism and Other Old-Fashioned Topics* (Princeton, NJ: Princeton University Press, 1991); Julian Pefanis, *Heterology and the Postmodern: Bataille, Baudrillard, and Lyotard* (Durham, NC: Duke University Press, 1991); and Jonathan Arac and Barbara Johnson, eds., *Consequences of Theory* (Baltimore, MD: Johns Hopkins University Press, 1991).

The consequences of the new intellectual situation for sociological analysis are debated in a series of essays in Steven Seidman and David G. Wagner, eds., *Postmodernism and Social Theory* (Cambridge: Blackwell, 1992), and a particularly useful guide for the would-be postmodern intellectual is offered by Pauline Marie Rosenau, *Post-Modernism and the Social Sciences* (Princeton, NJ: Princeton University Press, 1992). Another attempt to capture the situation is David Harvey, *The Condition of Postmodernity* (Cambridge, MA: Basil Blackwell, 1989). Douglas Kellner examines one of the luminaries of postmodern thought in *Postmodernism / Jameson / Critique* (Washington, DC: Maisonneuve Press, 1989). And questions of authenticity and discourse are considered by Gary Madison, *The Hermeneutics of Postmodernity* (Bloomington: Indiana University Press, 1988).

Politico-cultural issues are the subtexts of most discussions of the postmodern, especially those where the comparison to modernism is central. The discussions are particularly concerned with intellectuals, women, political groups and citizenship. Andrew Ross is notable for his engaging analysis of intellectuals and cultural politics in the United States since the 1930s; see *No Respect: Intellectuals and Popular Culture* (London: Routledge, 1989). The alienation of intellectuals is considered by Paul Hollander, *The Survival of the Adversary Culture: Social Criticism and Political Escapism in American Society* (New Brunswick, NJ: Transaction, 1988). Zygmunt Bauman identifies a changing role of intellectuals in *Legislators and Interpreters* (Ithaca: Cornell University Press, 1987). Pirkkoliisa Ahponen argues that intellectuals in postmodernity must strive to retain critical subjectivity; see his article, "Signifying the Signs—Simulating Cultural Political Subjectivity in Postmodernity," *Acta Sociologica* 33 (1990): 341–57. *After the Great Divide: Modernism, Mass Culture, Postmodernism* (Bloomington: University of Indiana Press, 1986), by Andreas Huyssen, tackles a number of substantive topics with a similar concern about the modern–postmodern impasse. Views of the political issues are offered from various perspectives in Ann Kaplan, ed., *Postmodernism and its Discontents* (London: Verso, 1988).

BIBLIOGRAPHY

Addleson, Katheryn Payne. 1990. "Why philosophers should become sociologists (and vice versa)." Pp. 119–47 in Howard Becker and Michal McCall eds., *Symbolic Interaction and Cultural Studies*. Chicago: University of Chicago Press.

Adler, Judith E. 1979. *Artists in Offices: An Ethnography of an Academic Art Scene*. New Brunswick, NJ: Transaction Books.

Adorno, Theodore. 1945. "A social critique of radio music." *Kenyon Review* 7: 208–17.

Agnew, Jean-Christophe. 1986. *Worlds Apart: The Market and the Theatre in Anglo-American Thought, 1550–1750*. New York: Cambridge University Press.

Aldrich, Nelson W., Jr. 1988. *Old Money: The Mythology of America's Upper Class*. New York: Random House.

Alexander, Jeffery. 1982. *Antinomies of Classical Thought: Marx and Durkheim*. Berkeley: University of California Press.

———. ed. 1988. *Durkheimian Sociology: Cultural Studies*. New York: Cambridge University Press.

———, and Paul Colomy, eds. 1990. *Differentiation Theory*. New York: Columbia University Press.

Alpert, Harry. 1939. *Emile Durkheim and His Sociology*. New York: Columbia University Press.

Angus, Ian, and Sut Jhally, eds. 1989. *Cultural Politics in Contemporary America*. New York: Routledge.

Archer, Margaret. 1988. *Culture and Agency.* New York: Cambridge University Press.

Bagdikian, Ben H. 1987. *The Media Monopoly,* 2nd ed. Boston: Beacon.

Bakhtin, Mikhail. 1968. *Rabelais and His World.* Cambridge: MIT Press.

Ball-Rokeach, Sandra J., Milton Rokeach, and Joel W. Grube. 1984. *The Great American Values Test: Influencing Behavior and Belief Through Television.* New York: Free Press.

Banner, Lois W. 1983. *American Beauty.* Chicago: University of Chicago Press.

Barrett, Michelle, et al., eds. 1980. *Ideology and Cultural Production.* New York: St. Martin's Press.

Barth, Fredrick. 1970. *Ethnic Groups and Boundaries: The Social Organization of Culture Differences.* Bergen, Norway: Universitets Forlaget.

Baudrillard, Jean. 1988a. *America.* New York: Verso.

———. 1988b. *Selected Writings.* Stanford, CA: Stanford University Press.

Baxandall, Michael. 1985. *Patterns of Intention: On the Historical Explanation of Pictures.* New Haven, CT: Yale University Press.

Becker, Howard S. 1960. "Notes on the concept of commitment." *American Journal of Sociology* 66: 32–40.

———. 1963. *Outsiders: Studies in the Sociology of Deviance.* New York: Free Press.

———. 1982. *Art Worlds.* Berkeley: University of California Press.

Becker, Howard S., Blanche Geer, Everett C. Hughes, and Anselm L. Strauss. 1961. *Boys in White: Student Culture in Medical School.* Chicago: University of Chicago Press.

Beckford, James. 1989. *Religion and Advanced Industrial Society.* London; Boston: Unwin Hyman.

Belasco, Warren J. 1979. *Americans on the Road: From Autocamp to Motel, 1910–1945.* Cambridge: MIT Press.

Bell, Daniel. 1973. *The Coming of Post-Industrial Society.* New York: Basic.

———. 1976. *The Cultural Contradictions of Capitalism.* New York: Basic.

Bellah, Robert. 1970. *Beyond Belief: Essays on Religion in a Post-Traditional World.* New York: Harper and Row.

Bellah, Robert, Richard Madsen, William Sullivan, Ann Swidler, and Steven Tipton. 1985. *Habits of the Heart: Individualism and Commitment in American Life.* Berkeley: University of California Press.

Bendix, Reinhard. 1974. "Inequality and social structure: A comparison of Marx and Weber." *American Sociological Review* 39: 149–61.

Benjamin, Walter. 1969. *Illuminations.* New York: Schocken.

Bennett, Tony, et al. 1981. *Culture, Ideology and Social Process.* London: Open University Press.

Benson, Susan Porter. 1986. *Counter Cultures: Saleswomen, Managers, and Customers in American Department Stores. 1890–1940.* Urbana: University of Illinois Press.

Bentley, G. Carter. 1987. "Ethnicity and practice." *Comparative Studies in Society and History* 29: 24–55.

Berger, Bennett. 1981. *The Survival of a Counterculture: Ideological Work and Everyday Life among Rural Communards.* Berkeley: University of California Press.

———. 1991. "Structure and choice in the sociology of culture." *Theory and Society* 10: 1–19.

Berger, John. (1972) 1977. *Ways of Seeing.* New York: Penguin Books.

Berger, Peter L., Brigitte Berger and Hansfried Kellner. 1973. *The Homeless Mind: Modernization and Consciousness.* New York: Random House.

Berger, Peter L., and Thomas Luckmann. 1966. *The Social Construction of Reality.* Garden City, NY: Doubleday.

Berlin, Edward A. 1980. *Ragtime: a Musical and Cultural History.* Berkeley: University of California Press.

Bernstein, Basil. 1975. *Class, Codes and Control: Theoretical Studies Towards a Sociology of Language.* New York: Schocken.

Best, Steven, and Douglas Kellner. 1991. *Postmodern Theory: Critical Interrogations.* New York: Guilford Press.

Biggart, Nicole Woolsey. 1989. *Charismatic Capitalism: Direct Selling Organizations in America.* Chicago: University of Chicago Press.

Biskind, Peter. 1983. *Seeing is Believing: How Hollywood Taught Us to Stop Worrying and Love the Fifties.* New York: Pantheon.

Black, Jack. (1926) 1988. *You Can't Win,* foreword by William S. Burroughs. New York: Amok Press.

Blau, Judith. 1989. *The Shape of Culture.* New York: Cambridge University Press.

Blau, Peter. 1955. *The Dynamics of Bureaucracy: A Study of Interpersonal Relations in Two Government Agencies.* Chicago: University of Chicago Press.

Bogard, William. 1990. "Closing down the social: Baudrillard's challenge to contemporary sociology." *Sociological Theory* 8: 1–15.

Bonacich, Edna. 1972. "A theory of ethnic group antagonism: The split labor market." *American Sociological Review* 37: 547–59.

Boorstin, Daniel J. 1962. *The Image, or What Happened to the American Dream.* New York: Atheneum.

———. 1973. *The Americans: The Democratic Experience.* New York: Random House.

Boucher, Sandy. 1988. *Turning the Wheel.* San Francisco: Harper.

Bourdieu, Pierre. 1974. "Fractions of the dominant class and the modes of appropriation of works of art." *Social Science Information* 13: 7–31.

———. 1976. "Anatomie de gout." *Actes de la Recherche en Sciences Sociales* 2: 5–81.

———. (1972) 1977. *Outline of a Theory of Practice.* New York: Cambridge University Press.

———. 1980. "L'Identité juive." *Actes de la Recherche en Sciences Sociales* 35: 3–19.

———. 1982. "La Sainte Famille: L'episcopat Francais dans le Champ du Pouvoir." *Actes de la Recherche en Sciences Sociales* 44–45: 2–53.

———. (1979) 1984. *Distinction: A Social Critique of the Judgment of Taste.* Cambridge: Harvard University Press.

Bower, Robert T. 1985. *The Changing Television Audience in America.* New York: Columbia University Press.

Brantlinger, Patrick. 1983. *Bread and Circuses: Theories of Mass Culture as Social Decay.* Ithaca, NY: Cornell University Press.

Bromley, David G. 1991. "Satanism: The new cult scare." Pp. 49–72 in James Richardson, Joel Best, and David Bromley, eds., *The Satanism Scare.* Hawthorne, NY: Aldine de Gruyter.

Brown, Patricia Leigh. 1991. "Living for folk art, and in it too." *The New York Times,* January 3: B1,4.

Brown, Richard Harvey. 1990. "Rhetoric, textuality, and the postmodern turn in sociological theory." *Sociological Theory* 8: 188–97.

Brunvand, Jan. 1981. *The Vanishing Hitchhiker: American Urban Legends and their Meanings.* New York: Norton.

Bürger, Peter. (1974) 1984. *Theory of the Avant-Garde.* Minneapolis: University of Minnesota Press.

Burke, Kenneth. 1950. *A Rhetoric of Motives.* Berkeley: University of California Press.

Burke, Peter. 1978. *Popular Culture in Early Modern Europe.* New York: New York University Press.

Burns, Elizabeth. 1972. *Theatricality: A Study of Convention in the Theater and in Social Life.* New York: Harper and Row.

Callinicos, Alex. 1990. *Against Postmodernism: A Marxist Critique.* New York: St. Martin's Press.

Cantor, Muriel G., and Joel M. Cantor. 1986. "Audience composition and television content: The mass audience revisited." Pp. 214–25 in Sandra J. Ball-Rokeach and Muriel G. Cantor, eds., *Media, Audience, and Social Structure.* Beverly Hills, CA: Sage.

Cantor, Norman F. 1988. *Twentieth-Century Culture: Modernism to Deconstruction.* New York: Peter Lang.

Carlson, James M. 1985. *Prime-Time Law Enforcement: Crime Show Viewing and Attitudes Toward the Criminal Justice System.* New York: Praeger.

Centre for Contemporary Cultural Studies. 1980. *Culture, Media, Language.* London: Hutchinson.

Chodorow, Nancy. 1978. *The Reproduction of Mothering: Psychoanalysis and the Reproduction of Gender.* Berkeley: University of California Press.

Clifford, James, and George E. Marcus. 1986. *Writing Culture: The Poetics and Politics of Ethnography.* Berkeley: University of California Press.

Cohen, Albert. 1955. *Delinquent Boys.* Glencoe, IL: The Free Press.

Cohen, Bernard. 1983. "Nuclear journalism: Lies, damned lies, and news reports." *Policy Review* 26: 70–74.

Collins, Randall. 1979. *The Credential Society.* New York: Academic Press.

———. 1986. *Weberian Sociological Theory.* New York: Cambridge University Press.

———. 1989. "Sociology: Proscience or antiscience?" *American Sociological Review* 54: 124–39.

Conner, Steven. 1989. *Postmodernist Culture: An Introduction to Theories of the Contemporary*. New York: Basil Blackwell.

Coser, Lewis. 1971. *Masters of Sociological Thought: Ideas in Historical and Social Context*. New York: Harcourt Brace Jovanovich, Inc.

Coser, Lewis A., Charles Kadushin, and Walter Powell. 1982. *Books: The Culture and Commerce of Book Publishing*. New York: Basic.

Cowan, Ruth. 1976. "The 'industrial revolution' in the home: Household technology and social change in the 20th century." *Technology and Culture* 26: 1–23.

Cox, Meg. 1991. "So, you think that you can write a children's book." *The Wall Street Journal*, November 21: 1.

Crane, Diana. 1976. "The reward system in art, science, and religion." Pp. 57–72 in Richard Peterson, ed., *The Production of Culture*. Beverly Hills: Sage Publications.

———. 1987. *The Transformation of the Avant-Garde: The New York Art World, 1940–1950*. Chicago: University of Chicago Press.

Csikszentmihalyi, Mihalyi, and Eugene Rochberg-Halton. 1981. *The Meaning of Things*. New York: Cambridge University Press.

Dannen, Fredric. 1990. *Hit Men*. New York: Random House.

Darnton, Robert. 1984. *The Great Cat Massacre and Other Episodes in French Cultural History*. New York: Basic.

Davidman, Lynn. 1991. *Tradition in a Rootless World*. Berkeley: University of California Press.

Davis, Mike. 1990. *City of Quartz: Excavating the Future in Los Angeles*. New York: Verso.

Davis, Natalie Zemon. 1983. *The Return of Martin Guerre*. Cambridge, MA: Harvard University Press.

———. 1988. "On the Lame." *American Historical Review* 93: 572–603.

Dayan, Daniel, and Elihu Katz. 1988. "Articulating consensus: The ritual and rhetoric of media events." Pp. 161–86 in Jeffrey C. Alexander, ed., *Durkheimian Sociology: Cultural Studies*. New York: Cambridge University Press.

de Grazia, Edward. 1991. *Girls Lean Back Everywhere: The Law of Obscenity and the Assault on Genius*. New York: Random House.

Denison, Daniel. 1990. *Corporate Culture and Organizational Effectiveness*. New York: Wiley.

DeVault, Marjorie. 1990. "Novel readings: The social organization of interpretation." *American Journal of Sociology* 95: 887–921.

DiMaggio, Paul. 1987a. "Classification in art." *American Sociological Review* 52: 440–45.

———. 1987b. "Nonprofit organizations in the production and distribution of culture." Pp. 195–220 in Walter Powell, ed., *The Nonprofit Sector*. New Haven: Yale University Press.

DiMaggio, Paul, and Michael Useem. 1978. "Social class and arts consumption." *Theory and Society* 5: 141–61.

Doane, Janice, and Devon Hodges. 1987. *Nostalgia and Sexual Difference: The Resistance to Contemporary Feminism*. New York: Methuen.

Dollard, John. (1937) 1957. *Caste and Class in a Southern Town*. New York: Doubleday.

Douglas, Ann. 1977. *The Feminization of American Culture*. New York: A.A. Knopf.

Douglas, Mary Tew. 1966. *Purity and Danger*. London: Routledge and Kegan Paul.

———. 1973. *Natural Symbols: Explorations in Cosmology*. New York: Vintage Books.

———, ed. 1982. *Essays in the Sociology of Perception*. Boston: Routledge and Kegan Paul.

Douglas, Mary, and Baron Isherwood. 1979. *The World of Goods*. New York: Basic.

Dubin, Steven C. 1987. *Bureaucratizing the Muse: Public Funds and the Cultural Worker*. Chicago: University of Chicago Press.

Duby, Georges. (1962) 1968. *Rural Economy and Country Life in the Medieval West*. Columbia, SC: University of South Carolina Press.

Duncan, Hugh Dalziel. 1968. *Symbols in Society*. New York: Oxford University Press.

Durkheim, Emile. (1897) 1951. *Suicide, a Study in Sociology*. John A. Spaulding and George Simpson, translators. Glencoe, IL: Free Press.

———. (1893) 1964. *The Division of Labor in Society*. New York: Free Press.

———. (1915) 1965. *The Elementary Forms of Religious Life*. New York: Free Press.

———. (1925) 1989. *Readings from Emile Durkheim*. Edited by Kenneth Thompson. New York: Routledge.

Eagleton, Terry. 1983. *Literary Theory*. New York: Basil Blackwell.

Ehrenreich Barbara, and Diedre English. 1978. *For Her Own Good: 150 Years of the Experts' Advice to Women*. Garden City, NY: Anchor Books.

Eisenstein, Elizabeth. 1979. *The Printing Press as an Agent of Change: Communications and Cultural Transformations in Early-Modern Europe*, 2 vols. New York: Cambridge University Press.

Elias, Norbert. 1982. *The Civilizing Process*, vol. 1. New York: Pantheon.

Entrikin, J. Nicholas. 1991. *The Betweenness of Place*. Baltimore, MD: Johns Hopkins University Press.

Ewen, Stuart. 1976. *Captains of Consciousness: Advertising and the Social Roots of the Consumer Culture*. New York: McGraw-Hill.

Faith, Nicholas. 1987. *Sold: The Revolution in the Art Market*. London: Hodder and Stoughton.

Fialka, John J. 1992. *The Hotel Warriors: Covering the Gulf*. Washington, DC: The Media Studies Project/Woodrow Wilson Center.

Filer, Randall K. 1986. The "starving artist"—myth or reality? Earnings of artists in the United States. *Journal of Political Economy* 94: 56–75.

Fine, Gary Alan. 1979. "Small groups and culture creation." *American Sociological Review* 44: 733–45.

———. 1987. *With the Boys: Little League Baseball and Preadolescent Culture*. Chicago: University of Chicago Press.

Fine, Gary Alan, and Sherryl Kleinman. 1979. "Rethinking subculture: An interactionist analysis." *American Journal of Sociology* 85: 1–20.

Finlay, Robert. 1988. "The refashioning of Martin Guerre." *American Historical Review* 93: 553–71.

Flax, Jane. 1989. *Thinking Fragments: Psychoanalysis, Feminism, and Postmodernism in the Contemporary West*. Berkeley, CA: University of California Press.

Foucault, Michel. 1965. *Madness and Civilization: A History of Insanity in the Age of Reason*. New York: Pantheon.

———. 1975. *The Birth of the Clinic: An Archeology of Medical Perception*. New York: Vintage.

———. (1975) 1979. *Discipline and Punish: The Birth of the Prison*. New York: Vintage.

———. 1980. *The History of Sexuality*, Vol. I: An Introduction. New York: Vintage.

Fox, Richard Wightman, and Jackson Lears. 1983. *The Culture of Consumption: Critical Essays in American History, 1880–1980*. New York: Pantheon Books.

Freud, Sigmund. (1920) 1950. *Beyond the Pleasure Principle*. New York: Liveright.

———. (1930) 1962. *Civilization and its Discontents*. New York: W. W. Norton. 1st American Edition.

———. 1990. *Freud on Women: A Reader*. Edited by Elisabeth Young-Bruehl. New York: W. W. Norton.

Fritz, Noah J., and David L. Altheide. 1987. "The mass media and the social construction of the missing children problem." *Sociological Quarterly* 28: 473–92.

Gans, Herbert. 1962. *The Urban Villagers: Group and Class in the Life of Italian-Americans*. New York: Free Press.

———. 1967. *The Levittowners: Ways of Life and Politics in a New Suburban Community*. New York: Random House.

———. 1974. *Popular Culture and High Culture*. New York: Basic.

———. 1979. *Deciding What's News: A Study of CBS Evening News, NBC Nightly News, Newsweek, and Time*. New York: Random House.

Gardner, Helen. 1959. *Art Through the Ages*, 4th ed. New York: Harcourt Brace.

Geertz, Clifford. 1973. *The Interpretation of Cultures*. New York: Basic.

Gerbner, George, Larry Gross, Michael Morgan, and Nancy Signorielli. 1980. "The 'mainstreaming' of America, violence profile No. 11." *Journal of Communication* 30: 10–29.

Gilligan, Carol. 1982. *In a Different Voice: Psychological Theory and Women's Development*. Cambridge, MA: Harvard University Press.

Gilmore, Samuel. 1987. "Coordination and convention: The organization of the concert world." *Symbolic Interaction* 10: 209–28.

———. 1990. "Art worlds: Developing the interactionist approach to social organization." Pp. 148–78 in Howard Becker and Michal McCall, eds., *Symbolic Interaction and Cultural Studies*. Chicago: University of Chicago Press.

Ginsberg, Benjamin. 1986. *The Captive Public: How Mass Opinion Promotes State Power*. New York: Basic.

Ginsberg, Faye. 1990. *Contested Lives*. Berkeley: University of California Press.

Gitlin, Todd. 1980. *The Whole World is Watching: Mass Media and the Making and Unmaking of the New Left*. Berkeley: University of California Press.

———. 1986. *Watching Television*. New York: Pantheon.

———. 1988. "Hip deep in post-modernism." *New York Times Book Review,* November 6: 1, 35–36.

Glassner, Barry. 1990. "Fit for postmodern selfhood." Pp. 215–43 in Howard Becker and Michal McCall, eds., *Symbolic Interaction and Cultural Studies.* Chicago: University of Chicago Press.

Glueck, Grace. 1989. "Border skirmish: Art and politics." *The New York Times:* Art and Leisure, November 19: 1, 25.

Goffman, Erving. 1951. "Symbols of class status." *British Journal of Sociology* 2: 294–304.

———. 1959. *The Presentation of Self in Everyday Life.* Garden City, NY: Doubleday.

———. 1961. *Asylums.* Garden City, NY: Anchor.

———. 1968. *Interaction Ritual: Essays on Face-to-Face Behavior.* Garden City, NY: Anchor Books.

———. 1971. *Relations in Public.* New York: Basic.

———. 1979. *Gender Advertisements.* New York: Harper and Row.

Goldberg, Edward L. 1983. *Patterns in Late Medici Art Patronage.* Princeton, NJ: Princeton University Press.

Goldfarb, Jeffery. 1991. *The Cynical Society.* Chicago: University of Chicago Press.

Goldman, Robert. 1984 "Legitimation ads, part I." *Knowledge and Society: Studies in the Sociology of Culture Past and Present* 5: 243–67.

Goody, Jack. 1977. *The Domestication of the Savage Mind.* New York: Cambridge University Press.

Gottdiener, Mark. 1985. "Hegemony and mass culture: A semiotic approach." *American Journal of Sociology* 90: 979–1001.

Graber, Doris A. 1984. *Processing the News: How People Tame the Information Tide.* New York: Longman.

Grahn, Judy. 1984. *Another Mother Tongue.* Boston: Beacon Press.

Gramsci, Antonio. 1971. *Prison Notebooks.* New York: International Publishers.

Granovetter, Mark S. 1974. *Getting a Job: A Study of Contacts and Careers.* Cambridge, MA: Harvard University Press.

Graburn, Nelson H. H. 1967. "The Eskimo and commercial art." *Transaction* 4: 28–33.

———. 1976. *Ethnic and Tourist Arts: Culture Expressions From the Fourth World.* Berkeley: University of California Press.

Gresham, Jewell Handy, and Margaret B. Wilkerson, eds. 1989. *Scapegoating the Black Family: Myths, Realities, A Program for Action,* special issue. *The Nation* 249 (4) (July 24–31).

Griswold, Wendy. 1981. "American character and the American novel: An expansion of reflection theory in the sociology of literature." *American Journal of Sociology* 86: 740–65.

———. 1986. *Renaissance Revivals: City Comedy and Revenge Tragedy in the London Theater, 1576–1980.* Chicago: University of Chicago Press.

———. 1987a. "A methodological framework for the study of culture." *Sociological Methodology* 17: 1–35.

———. 1987b. "The fabrication of meaning: Literary interpretation in the United States, Great Britain, and the West Indies." *American Journal of Sociology* 92 (1987): 1077–1118.

Grossberg, Lawrence, Cary Nelson, and Paula Treichler, eds. 1992. *Cultural Studies*. New York: Routledge.

Habermas, Jürgen. 1987. *The Theory of Communicative Action, Vol. II: Lifeworld and System: A Critique of Functionalist Reason*. Boston: Beacon Press.

Hacker, Andrew, ed. 1965. *The Corporation Take-over*. Garden City, NY: Anchor.

Hagaman, Dianne. 1993. "How I learned not to be a photojournalist." Forthcoming in Douglas Harper, ed., *Studies in Visual Sociology*. Philadelphia: Temple University Press.

Hall, John R. 1978. *The Ways Out: Utopian Communal Groups in an Age of Babylon*. Boston: Routledge and Kegan Paul.

———. 1987. *Gone From the Promised Land: Jonestown in American Cultural History*. New Brunswick, NJ: Transaction.

———. 1988. "Social organization and pathways of commitment: Types of communal groups, rational choice theory, and the Kanter thesis." *American Sociological Review* 53: 679–92.

Hall, Peter, and Dee Spencer Hall. 1982. "The social conditions of the negotiated order." *Urban Life* 11: 328–49.

Hall, Stuart. 1977. "Culture, media and the ideological effect." Pp. 315–48 in Curran, Gurevitch and Woolacott, eds., *Mass Communication and Society*. London: Edward Arnold

Halle, David. 1984. *America's Working Man: Work, Home and Politics among Blue-Collar Property Owners*. Chicago: University of Chicago Press.

———. 1989. "Class and culture in modern America: The vision of the landscape in the residences of contemporary Americans." *Prospects* 14: 373–406.

Harper, Douglas. 1987. *Working Knowledge: Skill and Community in a Small Shop*. Chicago: University of Chicago Press.

Harrington, Michael. 1962. *The Other America*. New York: Macmillan.

Harris, Marvin. 1979. *Cultural Materialism*. New York: Random House.

Hartsock, Nancy. 1983. *Money, Sex and Power: Toward a Feminist Historical Materialism*. New York: Longman.

Hatfield, Elaine, and Susan Sprecher. 1986. *Mirror, Mirror: The Importance of Looks in Everyday Life*. Albany: State University of New York Press.

Hauser, Arnold. (1974) 1982. *The Sociology of Art*. Chicago: University of Chicago Press.

Hebdige, Dick. 1979. *Subculture*. London: Methuen.

Hechter, Michael. 1978. "Group formation and the cultural division of labor." *American Journal of Sociology* 84: 293–318.

Heilman, Samuel. 1981. "Constructing orthodoxy." Pp. 141–57 in Thomas Robbins and Dick Anthony, eds., *In Gods We Trust: New Patterns of Religious Pluralism in America*. New Brunswick, NJ: Transaction Books.

Herman, Edward S., and Noam Chomsky. 1988. *Manufacturing Consent*. New York: Pantheon.

Hewitt, John P. 1989. *Dilemmas of the American Self*. Philadelphia: Temple University Press.

Hirsch, Paul. 1972. "Processing fads and fashions: An organization-set analysis of the cultural industry." *American Journal of Sociology* 77: 639–59.

Hochschild, Arlie Russell. 1983. *The Managed Heart: Commercialization of Human Feeling*. Berkeley: University of California Press.

Hodge, Robert, and David Tripp. 1986. *Children and Television: A Semiotic Approach*. Cambridge: Polity Press.

Holub, Robert C. 1984. *Reception Theory: A Critical Introduction*. New York: Methuen.

Horkheimer, Max, and Theodor W. Adorno. (1974) 1982. *Dialectic of Enlightenment*. New York: Continuum.

Horney, Karen. 1967. *Feminine Psychology*. New York: W. W. Norton.

Hunt, Lynn. 1984. *Politics, Culture, and Class in the French Revolution*. Berkeley: University of California Press.

Hunter, James Davison. 1991. *Culture Wars*. New York: Basic.

Huyyssen, Andreas. 1986. *After the Great Divide: Modernism, Mass Culture, Postmodernism*. Bloomington: Indiana University Press.

Jacobs, Jerry. 1984. *The Mall: An Attempted Escape from Everyday Life*. Prospect Heights, IL: Waveland.

Jameson, Fredric. 1991. *Postmodernism or, the Cultural Logic of Late Capitalism*. Durham, NC: Duke University Press.

Jay, Martin. 1973. *The Dialectical Imagination: A History of the Frankfurt School and the Institute of Social Research, 1923–1958*. Boston: Little Brown.

Jencks, Charles A. 1981. *The Language of Post-Modern Architecture*, 3rd ed. London: Academy Editions.

Jenkins, J. Craig, and Craig M. Eckert. 1986. "Channeling Black insurgency: Elite patronage and professional social movement organizations in the development of the Black movement." *American Sociological Review* 51: 812–29.

Johnson, Richard. 1986–87. "What is cultural studies anyway?" *Social Text* 16 (winter): 38–80.

Jones, Mark, with Paul Craddock and Nicolas Barker, eds. 1990. *Fake?: The Art of Deception*. Berkeley: University of California Press.

Kaplan, E. Ann. 1987. *Rocking around the Clock*. New York: Methuen.

Kariel, Henry S. 1989. *The Desperate Politics of Postmodernism*. Amherst: University of Massachusetts Press.

Kirby , E. T. 1975. *Ur-Drama: The Origins of Theater*. New York: New York University Press.

Klein, Melanie. 1984. *The Writings of Melanie Klein*. New York: Free Press.

Kohlberg, Lawrence. 1981. *The Philosophy of Moral Development*. San Francisco: Harper and Row.

Kornhauser, William. 1959. *The Politics of Mass Society*. New York: Free Press.

Kroeber, Alfred, and Talcott Parsons. 1958. "The concepts of culture and of social system." *American Sociological Review* 23: 582–83.

Kubler, George. 1962. *The Shape of Time: Remarks on the History of Things.* New Haven: Yale University Press.

Kumar, Krishan. 1978. *Prophecy and Progress: The Sociology of Industrial and Post-Industrial Society.* New York: Penguin.

Kuper, Adam. 1988. *The Invention of Primitive Society: Transformations of an Illusion.* London; New York: Routledge.

Kuritz, Paul. 1988. *The Making of Theater History.* Englewood Cliffs, NJ: Prentice Hall.

Lachman, Richard. 1988. "Graffiti as career and ideology." *American Journal of Sociology* 94: 229–50.

Laing, R. D. 1967. *The Politics of Experience.* New York: Pantheon.

Lamont, Michele. 1989. "The power-culture link in a comparative perspective." *Comparative Social Research* 11: 131–50.

———. 1992. *Money, Morals and Manners: The Culture of the French and the American Upper-Middle Class.* Chicago: University of Chicago Press.

Lang, Gladys Engle and Kurt Lang. 1988. "Recognition and reknown: The survival of artistic reputation." *American Journal of Sociology* 98: 79–109.

Lasch, Christopher. 1978. *The Culture of Narcissism: American Life in an Age of Diminishing Expectations.* New York: Norton.

———. 1984. *The Minimal Self: Psychic Survival in Troubled Times.* New York: W. W. Norton.

Leacock, Eleanor B., ed. 1971. *The Culture of Poverty: A Critique.* New York: Simon and Schuster.

Lears, T. J. Jackson. 1983. "From salvation to self-realization: Advertising and the therapeutic roots of the consumer culture, 1889–1930." Pp. 2–38 in Richard Wightman Fox and Jackson Lears, eds., *The Culture of Consumption.* New York: Pantheon.

Lechner, Frank. 1990. "Fundamentalism revisited." Pp. 77–97 in Thomas Robbins and Dick Anthony, eds., *In Gods We Trust,* 2nd ed. New Brunswick, NJ: Transaction Books.

Leiss, William, Stephen Kline, and Sut Jhally. 1988. *Social Communication in Advertising.* New York: Routledge.

Lévi-Strauss, Claude. (1962) 1966. *The Savage Mind.* Chicago: University of Chicago Press.

Lewis, Oscar. 1959. *Five Families: Mexican Case Studies in the Culture of Poverty.* New York: Basic.

Liebert, Robert M., and Joyce Sprafkin. 1988. *The Early Window: Effects of Television on Children and Youth,* 3rd ed. New York: Permagon Press.

Leibow, Elliot. 1967. *Tally's Corner.* Boston: Little, Brown.

Lincoln, C. Eric, and Lawrence H. Mamiya. 1990. *The Black Church in the Afro-American Experience.* Durham, NC: Duke University Press.

Long, Elizabeth. 1985. *The American Dream and the Popular Novel.* Boston: Routledge and Kegan Paul.

Luhmann, Niklas. 1982. *The Differentiation of Society*. New York: Columbia University Press.

Lurie, Alison. 1981. *The Language of Clothes*. New York: Random House.

Lynd, Robert S., and Helen Lynd. 1929. *Middletown*. New York: Harcourt, Brace and Company.

Lyotard, Jean-Francois. (1974) 1984. *The Postmodern Condition: A Report on Knowledge*. Minneapolis: University of Minnesota Press.

MacDonald, Dwight. 1962. "Masscult & midcult." Pp. 3–75 in Dwight MacDonald ed., *Against the Grain*. New York: Random House.

MacIntyre, Alasdair. 1984. *After Virtue: A Study in Moral Theory*, revised edition. Notre Dame, IN: University of Notre Dame Press.

Maclean, Marie. 1988. *Narrative as Performance: The Baudelairean Experiment*. New York: Routledge.

Mahoney, Eileen. 1989. "American empire and global communication." Pp. 37–50 in Angus and Jhally, eds., 1989. *Cultural Politics in Contemporary America*. New York: Routledge.

Mann, Michael. 1973. *Consciousness and Action among the Western Working Class*. London: Macmillan.

Manoff, Robert K., and Michael Schudson, eds., 1986. *Reading the News*. New York: Pantheon.

Marcus, George. 1986. "Contemporary problems of ethnography in the modern world system." Pp. 165–92 in James Clifford and George Marcus, eds., *Writing Culture*. Berkeley: University of California Press.

Marcuse, Herbert. (1955) 1962. *Eros and Civilization: A Philosophical Inquiry into Freud*. New York: Vintage.

Martorella, Rosanne. 1990. *Corporate Art*. New Brunswick, NJ: Rutgers University Press.

Marx, Karl. 1978 [1843]. "On the Jewish question." Pp. 26–52 in Robert C. Tucker, ed., *The Marx-Engels Reader*, 2nd ed. New York: Norton.

Mascialees, Frances, Patricia Sharpe, and Colleen Ballerino Cohen. 1989. "The postmodern turn in anthropology: Cautions from a feminist perspective." *Signs* 15: 7–33.

Matza, David. 1964. *Delinquency and Drift*. New York: John Wiley and Sons.

———. 1969. *Becoming Deviant*. Englewood Cliffs, NJ: Prentice Hall.

McClelland, David Clarence. 1961. *The Achieving Society*. Princeton, NJ: Van Nostrand.

McCracken, Grant. 1988. *Culture and Consumption: New Approaches to the Symbolic Character of Consumer Goods and Activities*. Bloomington: Indiana University Press.

McKendrick, Neil. 1982. "Home demand and economic growth: A new view of the role of women and children in the industrial revolution." Pp. 152–210 in Neil McKendrick, *Historical Perspectives: Studies in English Thought and Society*. London: Europa Publications.

McLuhan, Marshall. 1964. *Understanding Media*. New York: McGraw-Hill.

McMurtry, John. 1978. *The Structure of Marx's Worldview*. Princeton, NJ: Princeton University Press.

McNamara, Patrick. 1985. "Conservative christian families and their moral world: Some reflections for sociologists." *Sociological Analysis* 48: 93–100.

Meiselas, Susan. 1976. *Carnival Strippers*. New York: Farrar, Straus and Giroux.

Melucci, Alberto. 1985. "The symbolic challenge of contemporary social movements." *Social Research* 52: 789–816.

Merton, Robert. 1957. *Social Theory and Social Structure*. New York: Free Press.

Meyer, John W., and W. Richard Scott. 1992. *Organizational Environments: Ritual and Rationality*. Beverly Hills: Sage.

Meyrowitz, Joshua. 1985. *No Sense of Place: The Impact of Electronic Media on Social Behavior*. New York: Oxford University Press.

Miller, Mark Crispin. 1988. *Boxed In: The Culture of TV*. Evanston, IL: Northwestern University Press.

———, ed. 1990. *Seeing through Movies*. New York: Pantheon.

Miller, Michael B. 1981. *The Bon Marche*. Princeton: University Press.

Miller, Walter. 1958. "Lower-class culture as a generating milieu of gang delinquency." *Journal of Social Issues* 14: 5–19.

Mills, C. Wright. 1959. *The Sociological Imagination*. New York: Oxford University Press.

Molotch, Harvey, and Marilyn Lester. 1974. "News as purposive behavior." *American Sociological Review* 39: 101–13.

———. 1975. "Accidental news: The great oil spill." *American Journal of Sociology* 81: 235–60.

Morgan, David. 1982. "Cultural work and friendship work: The case of Bloomsbury." *Media, Culture and Society* 4: 19–32.

Mukerji, Chandra. 1983. *From Graven Images: Patterns of Modern Materialism*. New York: Columbia University Press.

Mullaney, Steven. 1988. *The Place of the Stage: License, Play, and Power in Renaissance England*. Chicago: University of Chicago Press.

Myerhoff, Barbara G. 1978. *Number Our Days*. New York: Dutton.

Neitz, Mary Jo. 1987. *Charisma and Community: A Study of Religious Commitment Within the Charismatic Renewal*. New Brunswick, NJ: Transaction Press.

———. 1990. "Studying religion in the eighties." Pp. 90–118 in Howard Becker and Michal McCall, eds., *Symbolic Interaction and Cultural Studies*. Chicago: University of Chicago Press.

Nelson, Cary, and Lawrence Grossberg, eds. 1988. *Marxism and the Interpretation of Culture*. Urbana: University of Illinois Press.

Norris, Christopher. 1990. "Lost in the funhouse: Baudrillard and the politics of postmodernism." Pp. 119–53 in Roy Boyne and Ali Rattansi, *Postmodernism and Society*. Basingstoke, England: Macmillan.

O'Brien, Mary. 1981. *The Politics of Reproduction*. Boston: Routledge and Kegan Paul.

Offe, Claus. 1985. "New social movements: Challenging the boundaries of institutional politics," *Social Research* 52: 817–68.

Ortega y Gasset, Jose. 1932. *The Revolt of the Masses*. New York: W. W. Norton and Company.

Orwell, George. 1933. *Down and Out in Paris and London.* New York: Harper and Brothers.

Padgett, John. 1992. "The alchemist of contingency theory." *American Journal of Sociology* 97: 1462–70.

Parenti, Michael. 1986. *Inventing Reality: The Politics of the Mass Media.* New York: St. Martin's Press.

Pareto, Vilfredo. 1966. *Sociological Writings.* New York: Praeger.

Parsons, Talcott. 1951. *The Social System.* New York: Free Press.

Peiss, Kathy. 1986. *Cheap Amusements: Working Women and Leisure in Turn-of-the-Century New York.* Philadelphia: Temple University Press.

Peterson, Richard. 1978. "The production of cultural change: The case of country music." *Social Research* 45: 292–314.

———. 1986. "From impresario to arts administrator." Pp. 161–83 in Paul DiMaggio, ed., *Nonprofit Enterprise in the Arts.* New York: Oxford University Press.

Phillips, David P., and Kenneth A. Bollen. 1985. "Same time, last year: Selective data dredging for negative findings." *American Sociological Review* 50: 364–71.

Pillsbury, Edmund P. 1971. *Florence and the Arts: Five Centuries of Patronage.* Cleveland: Cleveland Museum of Art.

Polatnick, M. Rivka. 1983. "Why men don't rear children: A power analysis." Pp. 21–40 in Joyce Trebilcot, ed., *Mothering: Essays in Feminist Theory,* Totowa, NJ: Rowman and Allanheld.

Popkin, Samuel. 1979. *The Rational Peasant: The Political Economy of Rural Society in Vietnam.* Berkeley: University of California Press.

Pritchard, David. 1986. "Homicide and bargained justice: The agenda-setting effect of crime news on prosecutors." *Public Opinion Quarterly* 50: 143–59.

Protess, David L., Donna R. Leff, Stephen C. Brooks, and Margaret T. Cordon. 1985. "Uncovering rape: The watchdog press and the limits of agenda setting." *Public Opinion Quarterly* 49: 19–37.

Radway, Janice. 1984. *Reading the Romance: Women, Patriarchy, and Popular Literature.* Chapel Hill: University of North Carolina Press.

Randolph, Vance. 1976. *Pissing in the Snow, and Other Ozark Folktales.* Urbana: University of Illinois Press.

Redfield, Robert. 1956. *Peasant Society and Culture.* Chicago: University of Chicago Press.

———. 1940. "The folk society and culture," *American Journal of Sociology* 45: 731–42.

Reich, Wilhelm. 1960. *Selected Writings.* New York: Farrar, Straus and Giroux.

Reitman, Ben L. (circa 1930) 1988. *Boxcar Bertha: an Autobiography,* as told to Dr. Ben L. Reitman. New York: Amok Press.

Rieff, Philip. 1991. *The Feeling Intellect.* Chicago: University of Chicago Press.

———. 1966. *The Triumph of the Therapeutic.* New York: Harper and Row.

Riesman, David, Nathan Glazer, and Reuel Denney. 1950. *The Lonely Crowd: A Study of the Changing American Character.* New York: Doubleday.

Rose, Susan. 1987. "Woman warriors: The negotiation of gender in a charismatic community." *Sociological Analysis* 48: 245–58.

Rosen, Ruth. 1986. "Search for yesterday." Pp. 42–67 in Todd Gitlin, ed., *Watching Television*. New York: Pantheon.

Rosenblum, Barbara. 1978a. *Photographers at Work: A Sociology of Photographic Styles*. New York: Holmes and Meier.

———. 1978b. "Style as social process." *American Sociological Review* 43: 422–38.

Rostow, Walt W. 1960. *The Stages of Economic Growth: A Non-Communist Manifesto*. New York: Cambridge University Press.

Roth, Guenther. 1976. "History and sociology in the work of Max Weber." *British Journal of Sociology* 27: 306–18.

———. 1987. "Rationalization in Max Weber's developmental history." Pp. 75–91 in Scott Lash and Sam Whimster, eds., *Max Weber, Rationality, and Modernity*. London: Allen & Unwin.

Rubenstein, Richard L. 1978. *The Cunning of History: The Holocaust and the American Future*. New York: Harper.

Ruddick, Sara. 1989. *Maternal Thinking: Toward a Politics of Peace*. Boston: Beacon Press.

Rudofsky, Bernard. 1964. *Architecture Without Architects: A Short Introduction to Non-Pedigreed Architecture*. Garden City, NY: Doubleday.

Rushing, Andrea Benton. 1988. "Hair-raising." *Feminist Studies* 14: 325–36.

Sahlins, Marshall D. 1976. *Culture and Practical Reason*. Chicago: University of Chicago Press.

———. 1985. *Islands of History*. Chicago: University of Chicago Press.

Sanders, Clinton. 1988. "Marks of mischief: Becoming and being tattooed." *Journal of Contemporary Ethnography* 16: 395–432.

Sapir, Edward. 1956. *Culture, Language and Personality*. Berkeley: University of California Press.

Scheff, Thomas. 1966. *Being Mentally Ill: A Social Theory*. Chicago: Aldine.

Scheler, Max. (1915) 1961. *Ressentiment*. New York: Free Press.

Schieffelin, Edward, and Robert Crittenden. 1991. *Like People You See in a Dream: First Contact in Six Papuan Societies*. Stanford, CA: Stanford University Press.

Schluchter, Wolfgang. 1989. *Rationalism, Religion, and Domination*. Berkeley: University of California Press.

Schneider, Jane. 1978. "Peacocks and penguins: The political economy of European cloth and colors." *American Ethnologist* 5: 413–47.

Schudson, Michael. 1978. *Discovering the News: A Social History of American Newspapers*. New York: Basic.

———. 1984. *Advertising, the Uneasy Persuasion: Its Dubious Impact on American Society*. New York: Basic.

Schutz, Alfred. 1970. *Reflections on the Problem of Relevance*. New Haven, CT: Yale University Press.

Seay, Albert. 1965. *Music in the Medieval World*. Englewood Cliffs, NJ: Prentice Hall.

Shepard, John. 1987. "Music and male hegemony." Pp. 151–72 in Richard Leppert and Susan McClary, eds., *Music and Society*. Cambridge; New York: Cambridge University Press.

Shils, Edward. 1967. "Mass society and its culture." Pp. 1–27 in Norman Jacobs, ed., *Culture for the Millions?* Boston: Beacon.

Simmel, Georg. 1950. *The Sociology of Georg Simmel*. New York: Free Press.

———. (1911) 1984. "Female culture." Pp. 65–101 in *Georg Simmel: On Women, Sexuality, and Love*. Edited by Guy Oakes. New Haven, CT: Yale University Press.

Singal, David Joseph. 1987. "Toward a definition of American modernism." *American Quarterly* 39: 7–26.

Sklar, Kathryn Kish. 1973. *Catharine Beecher: A Study in American Domesticity*. New Haven, CT: Yale University Press.

Skocpol, Theda. 1979. *States and Social Revolutions*. New York: Cambridge University Press.

Smith, Anthony. 1991. *The Age of Behemoths: The Globalization of Mass Media Firms*. New York: Priority Press.

Smith-Rosenberg, Carroll. 1975. "The female world of love and ritual: Relations between women in nineteenth-century America." *Signs* 1: 1–29.

Stack, Steven. 1987. "Celebrities and suicide: A taxonomy and analysis." *American Sociological Review* 52: 401–12.

Stauth, Georg, and Bryan S. Turner. 1988. "Nostalgia, postmodernism and the critique of mass culture." *Theory, Culture & Society* 5: 509–26.

Stevenson, Robert L., and Donald L. Shaw, eds. 1984. *Foreign News and the New World Information Order*. Ames: Iowa State University Press.

Strasser, Susan. 1982. *Never Done: A History of American Housework*. New York: Pantheon Books.

Strauss, Anselm. 1978. "A social world perspective." *Studies in Symbolic Interaction* 1: 119–28.

Swidler, Ann. 1980. "Love and adulthood in American culture." Pp. 120–47 in Neil Smelser and Erik H. Erikson, eds., *Themes of Work and Love in Adulthood*. Cambridge, MA: Harvard University Press.

———. 1986. "Culture in action: Symbols and strategies." *American Sociological Review* 51: 273–86.

Szasz, Thomas. 1987. *Insanity: The Idea and Its Consequences*. New York: Wiley.

Taub, Richard P. 1969. *Bureaucrats under Stress: Administrators and Administration in an Indian State*. Berkeley: University of California Press.

Thompson, James. 1967. *Organizations in Action*. New York: McGraw-Hill.

Thompson, Robert F. 1959. *Safari of One* (sound recording). New York: Spanish Music Center.

Thrisk, Joan. 1978. *Economic Policy and Projects: The Development of a Consumer Society in Early Modern England*. Oxford: Clarendon Press.

Tocqueville, Alexis de. (1840) 1945. *Democracy in America*. Edited by Phillips Bradley. New York: Vintage Books.

Toennies, Ferdinand. (1887) 1957. *Community and Society*. Charles P. Loomis ed., and trans. East Lansing Michigan. Michigan State University Press.

Touraine, Alain. 1981. *The Voice and the Eye*. New York: Cambridge University Press.

————. 1985. "An introduction to the study of social movements," *Social Research* 52: 749–87.

Trevor-Roper, Hugh. 1976. *Princes and Artists: Patronage and Ideology at Four Hapsburg Courts, 1517–1633*. New York: Harper and Row.

Tronto, Joan. 1987. "Beyond gender difference to a theory of care." *Signs* 12: 644–63.

Tuchman, Gaye. 1974. *The TV Establishment: Programming for Power and Profit*. Englewood Cliffs, NJ: Prentice Hall.

————. 1989. *Edging Women Out: Victorian Novelists, Publishers and Social Change*. New Haven, CT: Yale University Press.

Turner, Victor Witter. 1967. *The Forest of Symbols; Aspects of Ndembu Ritual*. Ithaca, NY: Cornell University Press.

Tydeman, William. 1978. *The Theater in the Middle Ages: Western European Stage Conditions, c. 800–1576*. New York: Cambridge University Press.

Tyler, E. B. 1871. *Primitive Society*. London: John Murray.

U.S. Census Bureau. 1975. *Historical Statistics of the United States, Colonial Times to 1970*. Washington, DC: U.S. Government Printing Office.

————. 1983. *1980 U.S. Census, Vol. a, Chapter C: General Social and Economic Characteristics of the Population*. Washington, DC: U.S. Government Printing Office.

Veblen, Thorstein. (1899) 1965. *The Theory of the Leisure Class*. New York: A.M. Kelley.

Venturi, Robert, Denise Scott Brown, and Steven Izenour. 1977. *Learning from Las Vegas*. Cambridge, MA: MIT Press.

Wagner-Pacifici, Robin, and Barry Schwartz. 1991. "The Vietnam veterans memorial: Commemorating a difficult past." *American Journal of Sociology* 97: 376–420.

Wallerstein, Immanuel. 1974. *The Modern World-System: Capitalist Agriculture and the Origins of the European World-Economy in the Sixteenth Century*. New York, San Francisco, London: Academic Press.

Warner, R. Stephen. 1988a. *New Wine in old Wineskins: Evangelicals and Liberals in a Small-town Church*. Berkeley: University of California Press.

————. 1988b. "The new pluralism in American religion and its sociology." Unpublished paper.

Weber, Max. 1946. *From Max Weber: Essays in Sociology*. New York: Oxford University Press.

————. (1905) 1958a. *The Protestant Ethic and the Spirit of Capitalism*. New York: Scribner's.

————. 1958b. *The Rational and Social Foundations of Music*. Carbondale: Southern Illinois University Press.

————. (1922) 1978. *Economy and Society: An Outline of Interpretive Sociology*. Edited by Guenther Roth and Claus Wittich. Berkeley: University of California Press.

————. (1923) 1981. *General Economic History*. New Brunswick, NJ: Transaction.

Webster, Murry, Jr., and James E. Driskell, Jr. 1983. "Beauty as status." *American Journal of Sociology* 89: 140–65.

Weinbaum, Batya, and Amy Bridges. 1978. "The other side of the paycheck." Pp. 190–205 in Zillah R. Eisenstein, ed., *Capitalist Patriarchy and the Case for Socialist Feminism*. New York: Monthly Review Press.

Weiss, Gerald. 1973. "Shamanism and priesthood in light of the Campa Ayahuasca ceremony." Pp. 40–47 in Michael J. Harner, *Hallucinogens and Shamanism*. New York: Oxford University Press.

Werckmeister, O. K. 1991. *Citadel Culture*. Chicago: University of Chicago Press.

Whorf, Benjamin. 1956. *Language, Thought and Reality*. Cambridge, MA: Technology Press of MIT.

Williams, Christine L. 1989. *Gender Differences at Work: Women and Men in Nontraditional Occupations*. Berkeley: University of California Press.

Williams, Linda. 1988. "Feminist film theory: Mildred Pierce and the Second World War." Pp. 12–30 in E. Deidre Pribram, ed., *Female Spectators: Looking at Film and Television*. New York: Verso.

Williams, Raymond. 1977. *Marxism and Literature*. New York: Oxford University Press.

———. 1982. *The Sociology of Culture*. New York: Schocken.

Williams, Rosalind. 1982. *Dream Worlds: Consumption in Late 19th Century France*. Berkeley: University of California Press.

Willis, Paul. 1977. *Learning to Labor*. New York: Columbia University Press.

———. 1990. *Common Culture*. Boulder, CO: Westview Press.

Wilson, William J. 1980. *The Declining Significance of Race: Blacks and Changing American Institutions*. Chicago: University of Chicago Press.

Winter, James P., and Chaim H. Eyal. 1981. "Agenda setting for the civil rights issue." *Public Opinion Quarterly* 45: 376–83.

Woletz, Robert. 1992. "Technology gives the charts a fresh spin." *New York Times,* Arts and Leisure, January 26: 26, 32.

Wolfe, Eric. 1982. *Europe and the People without History*. Berkeley: University of California Press.

Wolfe, Tom. 1968. *The Pump House Gang*. New York: Farrar, Straus and Giroux.

Wolff, Janet. 1981. *The Social Production of Art*. New York: New York University Press.

———. 1983. *Aesthetics and the Sociology of Art*. London: George Allen and Unwin.

———. 1987. "The ideology of autonomous art." Pp. 1–12 in Richard Leppert and Susan McClary, eds., *Music and Society: The Politics of Composition, Performance and Reception*. Cambridge; New York: Cambridge University Press.

———. 1989. "The invisible flaneuse: Women and the literature of modernity." Pp. 141–57 in Andrew Benjamin, ed., *The Problems of Modernity*. London: Routledge.

Woodard, Michael D. 1988. "Class, regionality, and leisure among urban Black Americans." *Journal of Leisure Research* 20: 87–105.

Wright, Talmadge. 1985. "The deliberate design of nondescript architecture." Pp. 83–90 in David G. Saile, ed., *Architecture in Cultural Change*. Lawrence, KS: School of Architecture and Urban Design, University of Kansas.

Wuthnow, Robert. 1987. *Meaning and Moral Order: Explorations in Cultural Analysis*. Berkeley: University of California Press.

————. 1989. *Communities of Discourse: Ideology and Social Structure in the Reformation, the Enlightenment, and European Socialism*. Cambridge, MA: Harvard University Press.

————. 1991. *Acts of compassion*. Princeton, NJ: Princeton University Press.

Wuthnow, Robert, James Davison Hunter, Albert Bergesen, and Edith Kurzweil. 1984. *Cultural Analysis: the Work of Peter L. Berger, Mary Douglas, Michel Foucault, and Jurgen Habermas*. Boston: Routledge and Kegan Paul.

Z., Mickey. 1992. "Do-it-yourself mags: Some of the news that doesn't fit." *In These Times*, February 19–25: 18–19.

Zelizer, Viviana. 1989. "The social meaning of money: Special monies." *American Journal of Sociology* 95: 342–77.

Zerubavel, Eviatar. 1991. *The Fine Line: Making Distinctions in Everyday Life*. New York: Free Press.

Zolberg, Vera. 1990. *Constructing a Sociology of the Arts*. Cambridge, NY: Cambridge University Press.

INDEX

NAME INDEX

SUBJECT INDEX